STUDIES IN ART,
ARCHITECTURE AND DESIGN
VOLUME ONE

STUDIES IN

NIKOLAUS PEVSNER

ART, ARCHITECTURE AND DESIGN

VOLUME ONE

FROM MANNERISM TO ROMANTICISM

With 267 black-and-white illustrations

THAMES AND HUDSON · LONDON

SECOND PRINTING 1969
500 2309 19
THIS COLLECTED EDITION FIRST PUBLISHED BY THAMES AND HUDSON, 1968
TEXT SET BY FILMTYPE SERVICES, SCARBOROUGH
PRINTED IN GREAT BRITAIN BY JARROLD AND SONS LTD, NORWICH

Contents

Preface

As an inveterate reader of the book reviews in the *Times Literary Supplement, The Listener* and now and then the *New York Review of Books* I know that books of essays collected years after they have been written get almost without exception a bad press. The reasons are not far to seek. Try as hard as he may, the author cannot perfectly blend into a whole what had been written over a period of many years and for a variety of purposes.

Yet it is my conviction that he should try and that books of essays should be published. For what had come out only in a learned journal, or in an ephemeral paper, and perhaps only in a foreign language, often fails to make its impact. And even if it had made an impact at the time when it was new, the record of the development of research tends to get blurred, if the research itself is no longer available.

I thought I ought to say this; for the papers represented in these two volumes stretch over a period of nearly forty years. To prepare them for re-publication allowed me, or forced me, to endeavour an objective assessment of their contents and also their significance for me and perhaps for others. They started in Germany and end in England; they started with lusty generalizations and end with humble specific facts; they started with scholarship and end in what strikes me often as superficiality. The substance, to put it in another way, tends to get thinner.

If readers agree with me in this I can plead mitigating circumstances. They will, I hope, appear convincing, if I try to show what fields I tilled in these forty years. My doctoral thesis dealt with German Baroque architecture and was complete by 1924. Between 1925 and 1935 I wrote only one book, and the papers here reprinted as Part One are a by-product of that book. They try to demonstrate that Mannerism is *the* style of the sixteenth century in Italy, in what ways it differs from the Baroque and in what way the Baroque ought to be divided into three phases. About 1930 I began to concentrate on nineteenth-century architecture, but all the notes I had made, including the preparation of a lecture course at Göttingen, were burnt in the war. Between 1935 and 1945 I brought out three books. The most scholarly of them was about the history of the artist's training *(Academies of Art, past and present)*, sign of a change in interest to social problems of art history. The change to nineteenth century architecture was to a certain extent a reflection of this as well. The other two books were *Pioneers of the Modern Movement* and *An Outline of European Architecture*. The former is an attempt at distilling the history of one trend in the later nineteenth and the early twentieth century, the latter a summary, successful in the country where it was published, because the treatment of architecture primarily as space, a familiar treatment in Germany, was new for England.

These two books were an indication of a turn from writing for scholars to writing for laymen. The difference is not necessarily one of level, it can also be one of presentation. Positively speaking it may mean a shedding of abracadabra. Negatively I need not speak; for the dangers are patent. Readers who have the patience to go through the present two volumes must judge for themselves. To turn to papers, instead of books, was necessary as soon as I joined *The Architectural Review*. The influence of this event and especially the influence of the *spiritus rector* of the *Review*, H. de Cronin Hastings went deep, just as deep as in the German years and in the efforts to analyse Mannerism and Baroque the influence of Wilhelm Pinder had gone. *The Architectural Review,* in subject matter of research, directed me towards the history of the Picturesque and of visual planning and of course towards topical problems of architecture and design.

After 1945 finally my working life changed completely, owing to the willingness of Penguin Books, that is of that great patron Sir Allen Lane, to publish *The Buildings of England*. I had always felt the necessity of such an enterprise, i.e. of providing for England what Dehio had done in 1905–12 for Germany, but of providing it in much greater detail. That, and the editing of the *Pelican History of Art* and, alas, more and more committees and councils, cut down the possibilities of preparing and writing papers. Whether I was right in committing myself to *The Buildings of England* at the expense of all else is a moot point. There are pros and cons. The pro is that the layman and the scholar need such a comprehensive compilation, the con is that it is a compilation and that, in the absence of first-hand research and under the pressure of time, it is a faulty compilation.

The papers published in these two volumes then fall into three parts: Mannerism and Baroque; the Picturesque and the problems of Neo-Classicism; the Victorian Age and after.

There now remains only one more question. If essays qualify for re-publishing, how should they be re-published? Should they be left untouched, or should they be brought up to date? My rule has been this. Views must be kept. If my views had changed, i.e. if I thought no longer valid what I had written, I would have refrained from reprinting. But a foreword to a paper is occasionally provided to refer to more recent views contrary to mine. Factual errors on the other hand have been corrected and facts left out or only recently discovered by others or myself are incorporated. The paramount example of the unchanged view is the paper on Mannerism, the paramount examples of added facts are the two papers done in conjunction with Dr S. Lang (and added to by her as by myself) on the Doric and the Egyptian Revivals. Only one paper has been largely re-written, that on Voysey.

That the late Walter Neurath and Thames and Hudson should have wished to publish so bulky a collection of essays leaves me amazed and profoundly grateful. To his name I wish to add in gratitude those of Ian Sutton and Emily Lane who from inside Thames and Hudson helped in every possible way.

N.P.

References to notes, which will be found at the back of the book, are given by asterisks in the text and numbers preceded by 'n.' in the corresponding margin. References to illustrations are given by italic numbers in the margin.

Part One
Mannerism and Baroque

1 ROSSO FIORENTINO *Moses defending the Daughters of Jethro*

Repertorium für Kunstwissenschaft, XLVI, 1925

I
The Counter-Reformation
and Mannerism

THE FOLLOWING PAPER takes it for granted that Mannerism is *the* style of Italian painting between *c.* 1520 and *c.* 1590–1625, 1590 marking the beginning of the Baroque, 1625 the end of Mannerism in its last great representatives such as Greco. Apropos Greco Max Dvořák had first formulated the conception of Mannerism as a positive and comprehensive style. His lecture was given in 1918 and published in 1924. This is when I first heard about it. But I had attended Wilhelm Pinder's lectures in 1922–24, and I used the first part of my volume of Burger and Brinckmann's *Handbuch der Kunstwissenschaft* to provide chapter and verse in terms of Italian painting. The paper here reprinted tried to do the same in terms of *Geistesgeschichte*. Since then attempts have been made to extend the use of the terms to Italian sculpture (an easy case) and Italian architecture (not so easy) and to other countries. A whole literature has grown up around Mannerism, and an excellent annotated bibliography up to 1962 has been compiled by Lisa Becherucci in the *Encyclopaedia of World Art*, Vol. IX, 1964 *(Enciclopedia Universale dell' Arte* in Italy). The most recent books are G. Briganti: *La Maniera Italiana*, Rome 1961 (in English *Italian Mannerism*, London 1962), F. Würtenberger: *Der Manierismus*, Vienna 1962 (in English *Mannerism*, London 1963), A. Hauser: *Der Manierismus*, 1964, M. Tafuri: *L'Architettura del Manierismo*, 1967 and John Shearman: *Mannerism*, Harmondsworth 1967.

INTRODUCTION 1968

Literature on Mannerism as a style has on the whole been German or Italian. Anglo-Saxon pragmatism never takes kindly to attempts at generalities, and opposition against the whole of my conception of Mannerism has indeed recently been formulated by scholars in England and the United States. They argue that Mannerism comes from *maniera,* a term which Italian aesthetic theory used in the sixteenth century and that Mannerism should be confined to *maniera.* M. Treves in *Marsyas* I 1941 had dealt with the term without proceeding to conclusions, Roberto Longhi in *L'Approdo*, II, 1953 ('Ricordo dei Manieristi') had suggested that the original use of *maniera* should be restored, a Congress of the Accademia dei Lincei in 1960 (published 1962) had dealt exclusively with the *concetti e termini* of Mannerism, Baroque and Rococo, and then, at the twentieth International Congress of the History of Art (published as *Studies in Western Art,* Princeton 1963), Craig Hugh Smith from America (his paper overloaded with notes came out as an elegant-looking book in 1963) and John Shearman from England finally formulated the point of view which is opposed to mine. In his new book of 1967 Shearman presents it brilliantly. He analyses at the start what the Italians originally meant by *maniera,* arrives at such categories as variety, virtuosity, artificiality, and then demonstrates these qualities in terms of works of art and architecture of the sixteenth century and in terms of superbly well chosen passages from sixteenth-century art theory, literature in general and music. His result has an overwhelming coherence, but what is displayed is not—and here I take issue with him—*the* style of the sixteenth century in Italy and some other countries but one of the two dominant trends. The other is totally neglected, and yet John Shearman would not deny its existence nor its importance. What he does is to say in so many words that, since *maniera* in the sixteenth-century sense applies only to his trend, Mannerism is only that trend, and the book being called *Mannerism* cannot take in anything else. So out go the best of Rosso and Pontormo, out goes Tintoretto, out goes Greco. But that, in my opinion, won't do. I find my answer easy, and hence cannot say that I am disturbed. If someone comes along and suggests that the term Gothic should be confined to the art of the Goths, he is welcome, as far as I am concerned, but another term must then be found to denote what has so far been meant by the Gothic style, namely a style with common characteristics ruling in Europe at a particular time. It is the same with Mannerism, except that I am ready for the moment—in the absence of sufficient regional and national testing—to confine the term to the style of Italy between *c.*1520 and *c.*1590–1625. I have in fact in a paper too recent to be included tried to show how limited is the applicability of Mannerism to England.*   n.1

To sum up then. If Mannerism is reduced to *maniera*, then a new term will be necessary to re-establish the fact that Pontormo, Federigo Zuccari, Barocci and Tintoretto all have essential features in common and that they are features expressing the spiritual state of Italy during the same period. The paper which I wrote in German in 1924–5, and which is here reprinted in English, tries to establish just this. Dr Shearman will note that my technique of arguing is similar to his, even if he—wholly admirably—operates with first-hand sources, whereas I confined myself to (then) recent authorities. But we both use history and literature as supporting evidence, he for his, I for my Mannerism. I hope that to reprint my old paper will help to prove that Mannerism has its spiritual as well as its courtly aspects.

Finally, one postscript to this Introduction. Since it was written, it has found backing in Sir Kenneth Clark's H. R. Bickley Memorial Lecture (Clarendon Press, 1967). As he is a convinced humanist, he calls it *A Failure of Nerve,* but he agrees with me in considering the moment of Pontormo, Rosso and Bronzino not in terms of ingenious artificiality in art but of such adjectives as ghostly, remote, disquiet, melancholy, unreal, irrational, strained, macabre, ambiguous. Once again then, whether Sir Kenneth calls the sum of these features Mannerism or not is less relevant than the recognition of qualities so different from those equally rightly invoked by Dr Shearman.

I

THIS PAPER has been written in order to put forward certain criticisms which I feel ought to be made of Werner Weisbach's book *Der Barock als Kunst der Gegenreformation,* published in 1921. Basically Weisbach's method seems to me a fruitful one, and his book is an example of a welcome tendency among modern art historians not to be satisfied with purely formal analysis, but to treat art-history as essentially part of the history of thought. He sets out to demonstrate the parallelism between the art of a period and its thought, and in doing so he takes as his point of departure the unexceptionable statement that:

'One of the mysterious processes of history is that by which a development in form and a development in the evolution of thought takes place side by side and merges one in the other, so that in the last resort the form appears as the appropriate expression of the intellectual development.'

However, to agree with this is to come face to face with the great objection to Weisbach's approach in this book: the title itself makes it clear that in his view there exists a parallel between the Baroque and the Counter-Reformation, both concepts being considered as covering roughly the period between 1520 and 1750. Now, as far as the Counter-Reformation is concerned, this is inaccurate. Historians normally use the term only to refer to the late sixteenth and early seventeenth centuries. Thus, Gothein is able to entitle his study of sixteenth-century intellectual development *Ignatius von Loyola und die Gegenreformation* ('Ignatius of Loyola and the Counter-Reformation'), and define his terms as follows: 'We refer to the second half of the sixteenth century and the first decades of the seventeenth as the age of the Counter-Reformation.'* Ranke also, in his *History of the Popes,* ends his seventh book in 1630, with the final victory of political over religious priorities and the close of an era, that of the Counter-Reformation.

    This historical problem lies at the centre of my argument; it is from this point of view that the refutation of Weisbach's theses can have the most fruitful consequences. Once it has been successfully proved that the age of the Counter-Reformation as I understand the term, which liberally interpreted means the period between 1520 and 1620, in itself constitutes a distinct and homogeneous historical whole, then and only then the conclusions drawn by Weisbach fall to the ground, and the validity of his interpretation of the artistic and cultural history of the period can be called in question.

    'Baroque', like 'Counter-Reformation', is a historical concept which Weisbach tries to apply far outside its proper chronological limits. The question of its applicability to the second third of the eighteenth century does not arise in the present context, and indeed has little relevance to Weisbach's book. Of crucial importance, however, is the question whether the period of the true Counter-Reformation, as I am trying to define it, can be subsumed under the heading of the Baroque. I am convinced that it cannot, and that it produced a style of its own which stands in the sharpest contrast to the styles of other periods, and in particular to that of the Baroque, and which requires a name of its own.

    If I am right in this, the only question which remains is how far the name 'Mannerism' is an appropriate one to describe this style. Weisbach does not discountenance the use of the term; but he uses it in a sense which is different from mine. Such divergences of interpretation are of course quite normal, though regrettable, in the case of so new a critical concept. Weisbach uses it in the sense in which it is used by early writers, to refer to the Central Italian painters of the time of Bronzino and Zuccaro, to the school of Parma, and also to El Greco.* Dvořák, on the other hand, understands by Mannerism the intellectual and artistic currents between about 1560 and the beginning of the seventeenth century, and disregards the art of Pontormo, Bronzino and Gaudenzio Ferrari.* In my interpretation of the term it applies to the common elements in the entire artistic activity of the years from 1520 to 1590 (or, in some cases, 1620), the characteristics which unite even men as disparate as Bronzino and El Greco.

    My task, then, is primarily a historical one. By reviewing the cultural and political history of the Counter-Reformation period in Italy in terms of successive generations, I shall try to demonstrate the essential unity of the period. In keeping with this objective I have marshalled the facts in such a way that as far as possible each one evokes its parallel with contemporaneous developments in art. Today more than ever, art historians tend to neglect the basic historical framework in favour of the study of formal development, and this easily leads to misconceptions as to the conditions under which works of art have been produced, and consequently to errors of interpretation. This is why I think it necessary to establish a historical framework for the study of the development of Italian Mannerism. To protect myself from the objection that I have forced historical facts into a parallelism with facts in art, I shall make a point of quoting verbally, as often as possible, the standard historical studies of the Counter-Reformation. Without exception, these reveal that the facts are agreed, and that only my conclusions are new.

n.2

n.3

n.4

2   PONTORMO *Christ before Pilate*

The concept of the Renaissance, both as it applies to art and as it applies to cultural history in general, has been fully discussed and defined by historians and art-historians, and so it can serve as a point of departure for this study.* Burckhardt and Wölfflin, in particular, have singled out as its central characteristics an anthropocentric world-view, a belief in the manifestation of the sacred through perfect humanity, and a related belief in the harmony between nature and spirit, between the world and God.   n.5

The first symptoms of an intensification of Christian religious feeling appeared in the 1520s. There had come into being in Rome a society of leading churchmen called the Sodality of Divine Love, which included men such as Sadolet, Contarini, Giberti, Thiene, and Caraffa, whom I intend to discuss in-dividually in due course. The change of heart was precipitated by the sack of Rome by the armies of the Emperor Charles V in 1527. Pope Clement VII, during whose pontificate this disaster took place, was it is true very much a man of the Renaissance, and his action in enlisting, through his alliance with Francis I of France in 1533, the political support of the German Protestants, can be ex-plained only from the viewpoint of a Renaissance indifference to religious issues.

The change affected the Papacy only with the election of the Farnese Pope Paul III (1534–49), who, in the words of the great historian Ludwig von Pastor,   12
presided over the 'transition from the period of the Renaissance to the Catholic Reformation and Restoration'. 'Old and new were ceaselessly at war within him'; for while the worldly cunning of his diplomacy, which was reflected in his features, stood in blatant defiance of the ethical precepts of Christianity, it was he who finally convened the Council of Trent. His intentions in doing so were no doubt far from straightforward; but the fact was that an assembly now existed in Europe which concerned itself with spiritual objectives. Paul III, for all his love of Renaissance amusements such as clowns, gaming, the hunt and the pleasures of the table, was by no means lacking in a genuine desire for reform. This is proved by his elevation to the College of Cardinals of dedicated reformers such as Contarini (1535), Caraffa, Pole and Sadolet (1536), Cortese and Morone (1542). The same ambivalence is apparent in his attitude to the ideals of humanism. In the decree appointing Manetti to the post of Papal Commissioner for Antiquities,* he manifested genuine disapproval of the neglect of ancient   n.6
monuments; and yet in 1540 he gave permission to the Fabbrica di San Pietro to dig up ancient works of art anywhere for use as raw materials in the building of the new St Peter's.

The humanists themselves, in the same years, manifest a very similar blend of Renaissance and Counter-Reformation ideas and habits of mind. Reference to a few of the leading figures will help to show what I mean. Sadolet (1477–1547), as his extensive correspondence shows, was still primarily a man of the Renaissance. He openly sympathized with Erasmus, and among the Reformers abhorred only Luther, whom he despised as an unlettered man. Nevertheless, he belonged to the Sodality of Divine Love, and his oration at the opening session of the Pontifical Reform Commission in July 1536 shows him to have been profoundly concerned with religious problems. Cortese presents a very similar pattern. His life's work, the reform of the Benedictine order, was a pious deed with a humanistic purpose, that of creating a community of scholars. Likewise, the deeply learned and immensely attractive Contarini (1483–1542) believed all his life that a peaceful reunion with the Protestants was possible, given good will on both sides. He was enough of a humanist to detest all coercion in matters of conscience, and above all that of the Inquisition; but he too belonged to the Sodality, set an example of reform by renouncing his privilege of exemption from taxation, and went far beyond the ideas of the Sodality by calling for the replacement of antique models of literary style in the schools by Christian ones.

The new-found emphasis on religious preoccupations in preference to humanistic ones was still more marked in the literary circle surrounding Vittoria

3   PONTORMO *Virgin and Child with St John the Baptist*

4 PONTORMO *Joseph in Egypt*

Colonna (1490–1547). The idea of such a salon was a product of humanism, as was the style of the conversation, which, as Gothein emphasizes, was conducted at a high level of stylistic perfection. As he says: 'Forms which are denuded of their original content . . . are always susceptible of intensification to the highest pitch of virtuosity.' The form had indeed lost its content; the nature and purpose of these gatherings had radically changed. The form was humanist, the content Christian.

Exactly the same transition was visible in painting. The externals—classical costume, nudity, Renaissance types—were preserved, but the essence, as reflected in the construction of the picture and the significance of the figure within it, was the opposite of what it had been in the Renaissance. In Florence the late Sarto (born 1487), Rosso (born 1494) and Pontormo (1494), in Siena Beccafumi (1486), in Rome Peruzzi (1481) and Giulio Romano (1492), and in North Italy Parmigianino (1503) offer a new, complex and even confused pictorial form combined with an exaggeration of the details of the preceding style. Everywhere there was a reaction against the anthropocentric and harmonious ideal of the Renaissance. Even when they still felt none of the new intensification of religious feeling, painters found no satisfaction in the repose and clarity of the Renaissance.

This first generation of post-Renaissance civilization, which was contemporary with the first generation of Mannerism in painting, was followed by a closely related phase of transition which led to the Counter-Reformation proper. A number of humanists who were born only a little later than those I have just discussed illustrate this new change very clearly.

Matteo Giberti (1495–1544), Bishop of Verona, was foremost among them. The first bishop to reform his diocese in keeping with the ideas of the new age (before 1542), he was a believer in the doctrine that it was a bishop's duty to reside in his own diocese, and was an outstanding administrator, filled with deep concern for the moral and social welfare of his flock. Yet he too was still so close to the ideas of humanism that he kept around him a circle of learned friends, and set up a printing press to publish editions of the Greek fathers; at the end of his life he was called to answer for his liberal opinions before the Inquisition.

Reginald Pole (1500–58) was much more deeply and painfully affected by his encounter with the spirit of the new age. Intellectually entirely a product of humanism, he was firm enough in his religious convictions to suffer exile from England and the ruin of his family, to stand at the side of the chiefs of the restoration in Rome, and even, hardest of all for a man of his liberal temper, to return as Papal Legate and counsellor to Queen Mary Tudor. And yet tolerance was so deeply implanted in his nature that he, who had suffered so much for his piety, incurred the deadly hatred of Roman fanatics such as Caraffa, and escaped the prisons of the Inquisition only by his death.

Giovanni Morone (1509–80) did not escape. The ablest diplomat in the Curia, he was imprisoned in 1557 on the grounds that he had been lax in suppressing heresy as Bishop of Modena; only the death of his enemy Paul IV removed the danger of execution.

All these humanists were basically in the same position. They sought to save a lost cause which they still regarded in many ways as their own; and they ran the danger, as so often in similar circumstances, of being misjudged and condemned unheard. By the end of the 1550s there could be no doubt of the victory of the radical Counter-Reformation.

5   GIULIO ROMANO *Decoration of the Sala dei Giganti in the Palazzo del Te, Mantua*

6 BECCAFUMI
Fall of the
Rebel Angels

In its origins this tendency went back to the 1520s, the years of transition. Its most conspicuous early manifestation was the institution of a whole series of new religious orders, accompanied by the reform of many old ones; a manifestation of piety which in every way conflicted with the essence of Renaissance culture. In 1552 the Camaldolese broke away from Monte Corona, in 1524 Caraffa and St Cajetan of Thiene founded an order of secular priests, the Theatines, whose central principles were poverty and free preaching. In 1525 the Capuchins broke away from the Franciscans; the fraternity of Barnabites was formed in 1530, and the charitable community of the Somaschi in 1532. Above all, in 1534 the first Jesuits took their oath on Montmartre. The creation of this order and the character of its founder seem to me to represent more clearly than anything else the last phase, before the Counter-Reformation reached its climax.

St Ignatius of Loyola (1493–1556) was a soldier, forced by an injury to give up his military career. In the course of a long convalescence, while he passed the time by reading romances of chivalry and the lives of the saints, the idea came to him that he could still win fame by living as a saint himself. His piety was a product of his national background and his character; the immediate cause of his decision was wholly in the Renaissance spirit, the desire for personal fame. But his stern and uncompromising dedication to his new objective goes far beyond both. He consecrated himself to the service of the Virgin Mary and withdrew to the monastery of Manresa, there to live wholly for his faith. He was released from self-doubt and misery, from visions and from nightly self-scourging by the sudden consciousness of a mission which only he could carry out. From that moment on he had no further need of self-mortification, and regarded his visions (though they continued all his life) as harmful. Self-mastery was the prerequisite for active sanctity. Without money, he went on pilgrimage to Jerusalem, and then decided to give himself a formal academic education. He studied first at Alcalá, where his close ties with the mystical conventicles always characteristic of Spanish piety brought him several times into conflict with the Inquisition. On one occasion he spent six weeks in chains.

The decisive step in his intellectual evolution was the decision to move to the Sorbonne. There, with the sharp insight of genius, he sought out companions for his future work. He won over to his ideas men such as Faber, Francis Xavier, Lainez and Salmeron. What he had to offer them was primarily one enthralling idea, the *exercitia spiritualia,* Spiritual Exercises, a system of self-sanctification. The community was not initially based on the principle of obedience but on that of *caritas,* brotherly love, the ruling idea of so many religious fraternities. Not until later did the Society of Jesus gradually evolve, in keeping with the trend of the age, in the direction of authoritarianism; many years later the oldest of the Jesuit seminaries, such as those of Cologne and Louvain, were still protesting against the new primacy of the virtue of obedience.

As the Society developed, then, strict military obedience to orders became its central principle. Its nominal dedication to fighting God's battles was purely theoretical as far as the individual member was concerned; just as the order owed strict obedience to the Pope, each member stood in a relationship of blind subordination to his superiors, and through them to the General. Ignatius stresses again and again, as if intoxicated with the idea, that to each man his superior must be Christ. It would be impossible to find a plainer expression of the idea that every doubt, every motion of individual will must be forcibly repressed. Freedom of action belongs only to the General, and he himself must live only for the idea of service; the attitude of every subordinate is one of total passivity. The correctness of this interpretation of the Jesuit ethic is confirmed by its use by the first opponents of the Jesuits in the sixteenth century. Thus, Melchior Cano, the Spanish schoolman, says in his polemic against the Society that it is destructive of the traditional courage of the Spaniard; it turns knights into chickens. This idea of the renunciation of will, the suppression of human personality, reflects the prevalent tendency of the age towards mysticism; the Jesuit order is thus deeply bound up with the *Zeitgeist* of the Counter-Reformation in its strictest form.

7   PARMIGIANINO *Virgin and Child with SS. Stephen and John the Baptist*

8 Parmigianino *Madonna with the Rose*

Here again the parallel with the arts is obvious. Dvořák showed that the suppression of the individual significance of the human being lies at the heart of the last phase of Michelangelo's work. The mature art of Tintoretto (born 1528) and Barocci (born 1526) subordinates the human figure to an abstract linear schema; and in the work of Vasari (born 1511), Salviati (born 1510), Zuccaro (born 1529) and his school, the Bolognese and the Milanese, the individual form loses its significance in favour of unmanageably crowded or decoratively-ordered pictorial elements. This negation of the individual significance of the human being, this constraint which submerges it in a welter of forms, stretches it out of its natural shape, or immobilizes it in heavy draperies, constitutes the deepest and most important link between the art of Mannerism and the dominant ideas of the age of the Counter-Reformation.

In keeping with the Jesuits' declared aim of fighting in defence of God and the true religion, the propaganda activities of the Society were from the outset on an unprecedented scale. Processions and plays were used as means to influence

9,10,2
18
11,12

9 MICHELANGELO *Crucifixion of St Peter. Cappella Paolina, Rome*

10 TINTORETTO *Moses Striking the Rock. Scuola di S. Rocco, Venice*

the public at large, and this side of the Society's activity, so central to its role in the ensuing Baroque period, constitutes a direct link between Counter-Reformation and the Baroque, although as yet ostentation was rare and the means seldom became an end in themselves.

The same applies to the Jesuit attitude to human weakness and sin. Tolerance was the rule, especially where powerful people were concerned. Rather forgive too much than give a soul up for lost. Only in cases of genuine heresy, i.e. wilful obstinacy, was rigour considered essential. Here too is the germ of a Baroque characteristic: moral relativism. However, one thing must not be forgotten: members of the Society, who were expected to set an example to other men, were punished for the least transgression by instant and irrevocable expulsion. Even the brother of Lainez himself suffered this fate. There was no question of a relaxation of moral standards within the Jesuit camp itself: the overriding principle of obedience was a sure protection.

The establishment of the Society of Jesus in its final form brings us to the full flowering of the Counter-Reformation. This was associated in Rome with one man, Giovanni Pietro Caraffa (1476–1559) who became Pope as Paul IV. As early as 1504, when he was consecrated Bishop of Chieti, he was close to reformist elements. Later he was a member of the Sodality of Divine Love, and helped to found the Theatines. His 'Manifesto from Venice' can in some ways be called the first formulation of the Counter-Reformation programme. It was in accordance with his proposals that in 1542 a Papal Bull ordained the re-establishment of the Inquisition, followed a year later by the restoration of censorship.

Like the new religious orders, these two measures are symptoms of a 'Renaissance of the Middle Ages', to use Gothein's term.* It is necessary to read   n.7
the grisly details of interrogation and torture (in Soldan's *History of Witchcraft*) before one can picture, as an art historian must, the true nature of the age. It was at this moment, in the 1540s, that the persecution of the humanists began. 'A reign of terror' (Pastor's phrase) prevailed in Rome. There was, as Gothein says, 'hardly a circle of educated men or women in Italy on whom there did not fall some suspicion of heresy'. Suspects were driven to flee into the Calvinist camp (1542 Ochino, 1549 Vergerio). Men who certainly exercised no more freedom of thought than Morone or Pole went to the stake (Carnesecchi, 1567). Perhaps most remarkable of all, it was decreed in Milan (1565) and later in Rome (1566) that doctors must refuse treatment after three days to any patient who had not confessed.

The progress of the Counter-Reformation towards its climax is clearly visible in the personalities of the successive Popes. The process began in 1555 with the twenty-two days of the pontificate of Marcellus II,* of whom Cardinal   n.8
Farnese said that his nature was 'like that of a saint' ('*come d'un santo*').* No one   n.9
would have referred to Paul IV (1555–9), with his burning hatred of Spain and his blind faith in his nephews, in similar terms. But in spiritual matters, as Pastor tells us, Paul paid no heed even to his nephews. As he grew older his piety manifested itself in obsessive suspicions which led him almost to the point of starting proceedings against Ghislieri the Grand Inquisitor himself, though he was the most orthodox of the orthodox. To Navagero, the Venetian ambassador, he said that he would gather the wood to burn his own father if he were a heretic.*   n.10

At his death there was a spontaneous popular reaction against his brand of implacable severity, and his successor, Pius IV (1559–65), was mild and worldly by nature (as his favourite building, the Casino, illustrates).* But, as the Venetian   n.11
ambassador, Soranzo, reported in 1563:

'Although it is known that the rigour with which the Inquisitors carry out their task is repugnant to him, and he lets it be understood that it would be more to his taste if they played the parts of cultivated gentlemen rather than implacable monks, he never dares to set himself up against their judgments.'

The cause of this caution on his part was probably the decisive political and personal influence of his nephew St Charles Borromeo. Michele Ghislieri remained Grand Inquisitor, and on Pius' death became his successor as Pius V (1565–72). It was in his pontificate that the Counter-Reformation reached its height. The conclave very nearly passed him over as being too harsh, and its final decision was taken 'as if through the Holy Ghost'. The greatest religious fanatic of the age had come to power. 'Rarely has there been a Pope in whom the monarch was so entirely subordinated to the priest', writes Pastor. He adds: 'All considerations of temporal policy were alien to him; he was concerned only

11 VASARI *Immaculate Conception*

12 VASARI *Paul III receiving the Homage of Foreign Nations*

with the saving of souls.' Pius V presents an extraordinary mixture of simplicity, nobility and kindness on the one hand and hatred, obduracy and mercilessness on the other. His life was a model of asceticism. At the Papal board, silence or prayer was the rule. At midday, he would take bread soup, two eggs and half a glass of wine; in the evening vegetable soup, salad, shellfish and boiled fruit. Meat was eaten only twice a week.

What sort of an age must it have been to make such a regimen possible at the Pope's table? This astonishing state of affairs was not the product of the austerity of one individual. The whole city seems to have experienced a crisis of introspection. This is proved not only by Michelangelo's last style as a sculptor, exactly contemporary with the pontificate of Pius V, or by the fact that he offered to build the Jesuit church in Rome free of charge,* but the failure of the Roman people as a whole to react in any way against the prevailing austerity. In 1576 the

n.12

Venetian ambassador Tiepolo reported that Rome was 'perhaps not far from that perfection of which human imperfection is susceptible' ('*forse non molto lontano da quella perfezione, che puo ricever l'imperfezione humana*'). Even the time-honoured civic merrymaking of the Carnival suffered; successive Ferrarese ambassadors reported that it had passed 'rather lifelessly' ('*assai freddamente*', Zibramonte 1573), and that it was 'extremely lifeless' ('*freddissimo*', Capilupi 1574) and 'extremely lean' ('*magrissimo*', Odescalchi 1577–8). In 1580, 1583 and 1584 masquerades were forbidden altogether.

A return to the medieval universality of faith made it possible for new saints and miracle-workers to make an appearance; such things had been unthinkable for men of the Renaissance. The strange mixture of mysticism and realism in the personality of St Ignatius of Loyola is symptomatic. His *Spiritual Exercises* make it clear what I mean. Their objectives are purely metaphysical, but their methods are full of worldly wisdom and are worked out in pedantic detail. The Superior is to determine by the clock exactly how long the miracle of the Mass should last; statistical entires govern the process of atoning for one's errors.*   n.13

The mixture of metaphysical ideas and realistic methods leads us to another of the basic features of Mannerist art. In spite of its abstract composition, its decorative structural schemas, even in spite of a diminishing interest in study from life, the part played by observation in painting was demonstrably on the increase. The preference for faithfully-rendered costumes and striking foreground still-lifes was apparent everywhere, and not only in Venice.* Nowhere,   n.14 however, even in Northern Europe, did it become an end in itself as it was to be in the Baroque: in Mannerism observation was always subordinated to abstract pictorial laws.

This remarkable combination of realistic detail and abstract lines of composition is analogous not only with the rule of St Ignatius, but also with the thought of other saints of the period. It is customary to regard St Teresa of Avila (1515–82) primarily as an ecstatic visionary, and to concentrate on the elements of eternal Spanish mysticism in her personality. But it would be wrong to forget that she was also a talented organizer who succeeded in reforming an order and founding sixteen convents. Gothein emphasizes her combination of 'powerful realism and ecstatic imagination'. The most popular public figure in Rome during the period, St Philip Neri (1515–94) combined the same characteristics in different proportions. Ranke's superb description of his character reveals the dominance of down-to-earth realism and cheerfulness in his nature,* but also   n.15 his celebrated miracles, his dialogues with the devil and his influence on the leading princes of the Church. A man whose prayers to receive infinite divine love are answered by a miraculous distension of his rib cage which was still clearly visible at his death is something more than an outspoken realist and social commentator.

The most important of all contemporary religious figures was probably St Charles Borromeo (1538–84), a participant in St Ignatius' Exercises. He was as famous among the people for his miracles, his mortifications* and his works of   n.16 mercy as he was among churchmen for his reorganization of the diocese of Milan. His diocesan decrees were read all over the world; immediately on publication there were orders for ten copies for Toledo and a hundred for Lyons. Naturally there was opposition to his reforms; but Manzoni's masterpiece reveals how deep the roots of piety and faith in miracles went in Milan even at the beginning of the seventeenth century.

Miracles were extremely important. St Ignatius performed none; but the next General but one, Francesco Borgia (1510–72), a much more austere figure in every way, performed several. Even Venice, most tolerant of Italian cities, where artists still maintained closer ties with the Renaissance than anywhere else, did not escape the tide of religious fervour.* In Italy 'these were the days   n.17 when Charles Borromeo was given a free hand' (Gothein). And Florence, which in Bronzino's lifetime had been so lacking in piety that between 1531 and 1548 no Sacraments were received in the cathedral at all, now had an extreme orthodox faction that referred to a work of the school of Michelangelo as 'a filthiness by the master of all filth, Michelangelo' (*'una porcheria del maestro di tutte le porcherie, Michel-Angelo'*).

Even the overseas missions of the Jesuits now developed an attitude of austerity that was quite out of keeping with the subtle wisdom of their founder St Francis Xavier. In India, under Gomez, there were forcible mass baptisms, and Barzaeus set up a Catholic police-state in Ormuzd where he launched pogroms against Jews and Moslems.

After the death of Pius V the same quasi-medieval religiosity prevailed unchecked throughout the pontificate of Gregory XIII (1572–85). This was a time of banditry and gang warfare in Rome, but also of the processions of flagellants described by Montaigne and of the sinister workings of the Inquisition. The mood held until the last year of the pontificate of Sixtus V (1585–90), a man famous for his harsh, avaricious, unbending nature and his dislike of the 'ugliness' of the Antique.

These stern Counter-Reformation Popes could not be expected to have any taste for works of painting and sculpture. To them the translation of the sacred into human terms by way of art was suspect from the outset. Accordingly, it was only in architecture that Rome produced genuine religious art; in painting and sculpture the sole aims were decorative ones. Riegl has recognized this.[18] The formal artistic consequences of this mentality are evident, but in Rome the dominance of religious modes of thought was so absolute that there remained no possibility of a direct expression in art such as took place in tolerant Venice, out-of-the-way Urbino or distant Toledo.

Barocci (d. 1612), El Greco (d. 1614), and the late Mannerists of Venice, Bologna and Milan bring us into the second decade of the new century, a moment when the leaders of the younger generation had already accomplished the transition to the Baroque which is associated with the names of Caravaggio (b. 1573) and the Carracci (b. 1555, 1557, 1560). The new art established itself finally only with Rubens (b. 1577) and Bernini (b. 1598). From the 1620s onwards the Baroque dominated European art. The thirty years since 1590 had been a period of transition in which Mannerist masters worked alongside those of the Baroque. This sequence of artistic events too corresponds to developments in religious and political history; and it will be the purpose of the next paper to prove this.*

III

Only now, in conclusion, is it possible to turn to the question whether the spirit of the Counter-Reformation as I have outlined it corresponds to the criteria established by Weisbach. In this necessarily destructive part of this study I shall be content to show that the accuracy of Weisbach's own detailed observations carries with it the refutation of his central thesis of the existence of a parallel between Counter-Reformation and Baroque.*

His first overriding concept is that of the heroic. That this has little enough to do with the Counter-Reformation as I have described it is obvious from his definition of the term itself. The ideal of the hero, and particularly that of the antique hero, can only be rooted in an affirmation of humanity, its will and its powers. This is the absolute antithesis of the dominant ideas of the Counter-Reformation, but fits perfectly into the Renaissance conception of self-assured human beauty and into the Baroque ideal of expansive strength. Weisbach's idea of the martyr as the 'hero' of the Counter-Reformation is a superficial one. There is little that is 'heroic' in a hero whose virtue resides mainly in the renunciation of will and in passive endurance of suffering. The artistic link is with Mannerism rather than the Baroque. Weisbach himself seems aware that the heroic is absent from Mannerist art, and thus spares me the trouble of a detailed refutation; for his illustrations for the section on the heroic are chosen with two

n.18

18,19,

n.19

n.20

13 PERUZZI *Augustus and the Sibyl*

14 BRONZINO *Venus, Cupid, Folly and Time*

exceptions either from the seventeenth century or the Renaissance. As for the two exceptions, Weisbach speaks of the 'Manneristic dilution' of the heroic ideal in Peruzzi's *Sibyl,* and a work by Macchietti is included purely on account of its use of antique costume. As Weisbach himself emphasizes more than once, armour in itself does not make a hero; in fact he comes to the conclusion that Central Italian Mannerist painting as a whole is 'heroic only in externals' (p. 49). When he thereupon embarks on a discussion of the seventeenth century, everything he says is accurate and valuable, but one is forced to wonder how the statement that Rubens' art 'within the iconographic limits of Christian art represents the ultimate in worldly and sensual interpretation of the sacred', (p. 66) can be fitted into the Counter-Reformation context. The objection is always the same: there would be no cause for criticism, if Weisbach restricted himself to the parallels between the civilization and the art of the seventeenth century. But the concept of the heroic has no place in a discussion of the mentality of the Counter-Reformation.

Weisbach's second category, that of ideal nudity, presents a rather more difficult problem. It is true that the Counter-Reformation officially condemned it and yet almost always tolerated it in paintings. But it is also certain that the straightforward 'antique' approach to the nude died with the Renaissance, and that throughout the late sixteenth century there is no such manifestation of frank sensual pleasures as there is later in the Baroque of Rubens and some of his Italian contemporaries. Weisbach points out that Urban VIII's decrees against nudity in art were already dead letters, and that by the Late Baroque not only palaces but churches were filled with nudes. But the straightforward sensual delight in the human body which typifies both Renaissance and Baroque is entirely absent in the Counter-Reformation period proper. Its place is taken either by a decorative but far from sensual pattern of bodies in motion, or by the draped figures that were officially imposed on artists under pain of severe penalties,* or, more significantly, by an appeal to the third of Weisbach's important categories, eroticism.

There has always been erotic art; the possibility of using art to appeal to the senses has always been exploited. But between Renaissance and Counter-Reformation the approach changed. The beautiful human bodies of the Venetian school and the cheerful obscenities of the contemporary minor arts are based on an unselfconscious acceptance of the physical. But things are very different with

13

n.21

15 BRONZINO *Harrowing of Hell*

Bronzino and Parmigianimo. Their *fin-de-siècle* figures, with their lithe slimness, the femininity of the youths and the boyishness of the girls, do not look naturally naked but questionably and indecently undressed—a concept entirely foreign to the High Renaissance.* Wherever nakedness or partial nakedness in Mannerist art is erotic in its effect, this springs from a kind of erotic preoccupation which, more than one might at first suspect, has its roots in the religious spirit of the times. It is only when the body and its sexual functions are thought of as inherently sinful that natural erotic feeling takes refuge in suggestiveness; only an age preoccupied with metaphysical objectives could have witnessed the introduction of lasciviousness into the major arts.* It would be wrong, however, to allow the erotic preoccupations of some sixteenth-century painters* to obscure the total absence of eroticism in the most important Mannerists, Tintoretto, Bassano, El Greco, Barocci, Cerano, Zuccaro and Calvaert.

With the coming of the Baroque the character of eroticism changed once more. In the work of Rubens and most of his Baroque contemporaries erotic references have the same unselfconscious naturalness as in the Renaissance. Other Baroque artists, while not entirely repudiating the suggestiveness of the Mannerists, placed more emphasis on physiological detail; this again illustrates the point that in eroticism and in the use of the nude, as in the emphasis on the heroic, the Counter-Reformation period lacks the straightforward affirmation which is characteristic both of the Renaissance and the Baroque,* and that these concepts cannot be employed as touchstones for the definition of the spirit of the Counter-Reformation period in art.

7, 8,
14, 15

n. 22

n. 23

n. 24

n. 25

16 BASSANO *Adoration of the Shepherds*

17 CERANO *Mass of St Gregory*

    The category which Weisbach emphasizes most, apart from the heroic, as characteristic of Counter-Reformation art, is that of mysticism. I agree with him that this is one of the central themes of Counter-Reformation civilization and of Mannerist art, and that mysticism can be present even alongside realistic observation. The examples he gives from the work of Barocci and El Greco provide conclusive evidence of this. I part company from him, however, when he extends this to the seventeenth century, the age of the true Baroque. Of course, a mystical tendency, like the tendency to suggestive eroticism, is one of the potentialities of Baroque culture; much more so than the heroic is part of Mannerism. But as an identifying criterion of style the concept of mysticism can be applied only to the sixteenth century. Painting in Spain, the eternal land of ecstasies and visions, *alumbrados* (illuminates) and beatified mystics, remained mystical enough in the seventeenth century; but nevertheless, in contradistinction to the

19 EL GRECO *Resurrection*

18 BAROCCI *Madonna of the Rosary*

age of El Greco, it gradually admitted figures of increasing naturalism, stability and three-dimensionality. When Zurbarán paints people in visionary states, they remain people of flesh and blood; one can imagine how they would look in a normal state. The visionary figures of the Mannerists Tintoretto and Barocci live   20,1 only through their state of ecstasy; truth to 'nature' is irrelevant.

The fallaciousness of Weisbach's approach to this question is most clearly illustrated in regard to Bernini. According to Weisbach he was Rubens' mystical counterpart, the chief representative of mysticism in seventeenth-century art; and examples like his *St Teresa* are indeed persuasive. It seems to me, however,   21 that Weisbach's basic error is to adopt the easiest and most obvious criterion of mysticism in art—the depiction of mystical states—and neglect to cast his net wider and seek out genuinely mystical pictures rather than mystical subjects. I referred in my historical survey to a number of aspects of painting which have an inner affinity with the mysticism of the Counter-Reformation. These are the renunciation of the independence of the human figure within the picture, its subordination to something external, its extreme passivity, and formal elements such as the instability of the figure, the way in which the legs are cut by the edge of the picture, or the strange insecure shifting between the vertical of the figure and the vertical of the picture plane. All these features combine to produce a sense of floating, a disembodied quality which shows Mannerist art to have an inner affinity with mysticism.

20 TINTORETTO *Removal of the Body of St Mark*

The naturalistic representation of visionary states on the other hand, even when done with the sensual intensity of Bernini, presupposes a certain objectivity, an inner detachment from the psychic experience itself.* It is true that Bernini himself knew the Jesuit Spiritual Exercises; and the visions of St Teresa are themselves full of erotic imagery. But the age of St Ignatius and St Teresa would never have tolerated so concrete a representation of what was experienced. It would then have seemed a profanation to interpret profound spiritual experiences through the medium of their physical effect on the human organism; whereas with the rise of Baroque naturalism and secularism it was precisely the physical manifestations which made visionary states an attractive subject for art. No Mannerist figure is observed with the detached relish of Bernini's *St Teresa,* and the spiritual surrender of El Greco's mystics never resembles the sexual surrender of those of Bernini. The absence in sixteenth-century art of images of the erotic explicitness of Bernini's *St Teresa* is a reminder that in the texts of St Ignatius and St Teresa one should never lose sight of the pure and sanctified objective which underlines all their ideas. The sensual delight which Bernini offers those praying to his St Teresa would have been an impossibility in the context of the Counter-Reformation and goes far beyond the eroticism of the secular art of the school of Parma. A similar instance of Bernini's surface mysticism is his *St Longinus* in St Peter's. Weisbach rightly includes him among the heroic figures. But he also seeks to link Longinus with mysticism, although the only mystical thing about him is his heaven-turned gaze. His expansive gesture, his powerful stance, and the incisive naturalism of the treatment of his draperies are typical of the Baroque preoccupation with this world rather than the next. As for the upward gaze, even Weisbach himself clearly does not feel it to be essentially mystical wherever it appears in Baroque art. 'It was schematized', he writes, 'and often reduced to a stereotyped sign like the heroic posture.'

The same rather complex reservations are necessary in respect of Weisbach's last two categories, asceticism and cruelty. It is true that the later sixteenth century was a great age of asceticism, but in art this manifested itself above all in the artist's approach to his work, in restraint and religious intensity. The same tendency which leads a monk to asceticism leads a painter to mystical Mannerism. In the seventeenth century, on the other hand, asceticism had ceased to be a characteristic manifestation of the age.* Now that emotional distance made an objective view possible, painters began to choose to paint aged ascetics, a subject which clearly also made its appeal to an interest in naturalism and in cruelty.

As far as cruelty as such is concerned, I need hardly do more than make the same point again. The age of the Counter-Reformation was, it is true, the great age of the Inquisition, the age which saw the most horrifying witch trials and the most exquisite tortures. But however great the imaginative effort, we must try to understand the depth of the prevalent belief that it was the Christian's duty to save souls and that with this end in view there could be no question of cruelty. Genuine bloodlust, open enjoyment of cruelty, makes its appearance in visual art and in literature only in the age of Baroque. Individual exceptions such as the martyrdoms by Circignano in Santo Stefano in Rome signify little; there have always, in any age, been individuals who take pleasure in cruelty.* But martyrdom as a habitual, even a favourite subject in painting is characteristic of the seventeenth century alone. No one denies this, and Weisbach illustrates it himself (p. 163) in his comparison of Siciolante da Sermoneta and Domenichino. Here, as with asceticism and mysticism, it was only with the establishment of a certain psychic distance that artists were able to transform a profound emotional experience into the subject-matter of a work of art.

Thus a close examination of Weisbach's categories leads to the same conclusion as my preliminary historical survey: most of Weisbach's concepts apply perfectly to the art of the seventeenth century, but only a minority reflect the art of the sixteenth. As he applies all of them to Mannerism as well as to the Baroque, failing to make the necessary distinction between the two styles, and as he refers

21 BERNINI *Ecstasy of St Teresa*

n.26

21

22

n.27

n.28

all his remarks to what he calls the Counter-Reformation period, despite the fact that this period was already approaching its end at the beginning of the seventeenth century, his conclusions lose their force. In formulating this conclusion I believe I am fully aware of the objections which may be put forward. It is indeed true that there are tendencies which Mannerism and Baroque have in common; no historical process represents a break with the past on every front. From the very beginning, the Jesuits employed techniques of propaganda involving a theatrical approach to their public which is entirely characteristic of Baroque culture; although it is true that in the early days the ostentatious architecture characteristic of the 'Jesuit style' (as the term is popularly understood) had not yet come into use.* Also in the Counter-Reformation period, the characteristic Baroque form of government, absolutism, was taking shape in Italy, as is revealed in the number of small states, the growth of Papal power after the Council of Trent, and the status accorded to the Jesuit Generals. And yet no one can fail to be aware of the differences between the absolutism of a Pius V and that of a Louis XIV. Equally, it is necessary to be aware of the difficulty of fitting a personality of the stature of a Michelangelo into any account of the evolution of art.

n.29

   Undoubtedly other objections can be raised; this is only to be expected in any investigation of problems which have so recently been defined. I should not, however, have engaged in so detailed a critique if I had not been satisfied that these objections do not affect the validity of my conclusions. In the course of my historical survey I alluded to a number of stylistic criteria of Mannerist art which seem to me more apposite and more comprehensive than those of Weisbach. Their very comprehensiveness makes it impossible to formulate them in as specific and concrete a manner as Weisbach does. I shall do no more, in conclusion, than summarize them briefly. The central factor is the devaluation of the human figure, which manifests itself pictorially not only in the sacrifice of physical beauty, or in unnatural distortions of form, but above all in the subordination of the figure to abstract compositional laws. Whether the application of these laws is the result of mystical or decorative impulses, the results are the same. The second essential feature of Mannerism in my opinion is the specific combination of realism in detail with totally other-worldly preoccupations. From these two central characteristics the whole of Mannerist art may be deduced.

   Stylistic concepts of this kind acquire universal validity only if architecture is taken into account as well as the other arts, and naturally this would require a far fuller discussion than is possible here. It would be necessary to take issue with Wölfflin and Frankl, and this could only be done on a basis of extensive and detailed research. This paper has served its purpose, if it has demonstrated that the age of the Counter-Reformation is a distinct and coherent unit, possessing a unique style of painting—Mannerism—and that in consequence most of Weisbach's stylistic criteria are valid only for the Catholic art of the seventeenth century.*

n.30

22 BERNINI *St Longinus*

1 RUBENS *Adoration of the Magi*

II
Early and High Baroque

IF in the preceding paper I have succeeded in showing that the century between
1520 and about 1620 had, in Italian art, a style all its own, that of Mannerism,
and that this style draws many of its characteristics from the life and thought
of the period itself, readers may be prepared to follow me in an investigation on
the same lines concerning the ensuing period, that of the Early and High Italian
Baroque, from about 1590 to soon after 1650. Following the precedent of that
other paper, I shall as far as possible quote the comments and judgments of the
standard authorities on the various aspects of seventeenth-century history. It
will be necessary to allude to many more fields of activity than in the case of
Mannerism; for few historical periods leave such an impression of complexity
and diversity as the Baroque. Brinckmann, for example, expressly repudiates any
attempt to reduce the Baroque style to an ultimate unity, which he considers
would produce only a 'common denominator so general as to be valueless to the
n.1 scholar.'*

A wide variety of problems of cultural and artistic history must thus be re-
viewed before I can show it to be possible to grasp the inner life of the Early
and High Baroque as a single entity. It will be necessary, without reducing the
whole to a mere schema, to define categories into which Bernini, Poussin,
Rembrandt and Velazquez fit without difficulty.

The first question is a chronological one: when did the period under consideration begin? It is not a particularly complex question to answer, although it
is impossible to achieve the precision with which the transition from Renaissance
to Mannerism can be located in the years round 1520. The sixteenth and seventeenth centuries overlap and interpenetrate each other, principally through the
persistence of Mannerist ideas into the Baroque period and through the tendency
of the new age to return to the problems which in the early sixteenth century
had engaged the attention of the men of the High Renaissance and the Reformation. These links with Mannerism and the Renaissance are to be met with both
in the arts and in the sciences: I need only mention in passing the transition from
Mannerism to the Baroque in such Late Mannerist painters as Tintoretto,
Bassano, Veronese, Barocci, Callot, Morazzone, Bloemaert, or, to mention a
few lesser masters, Ligozzi, Pocetti, Passignano and Cesari. The same persistence of sixteenth-century themes and problems is apparent in the field of
ideas, particularly in Northern Europe, where the Reformation had given rise
to a situation so different from that in Italy that a separate discussion would be
necessary to do it justice. In the North a number of ideas that were to be among
the most influential of the seventeenth century made their appearance in the
course of the Late Mannerist generation. Pantheism begins with Bruno (1548–
1600), philosophical and religious scepticism with Montaigne (1533–92),

religious tolerance with Bodin (1530–97) and Coornhert (1522–90), and faith in the ethical value of work in this world with later Calvinism—all questions which were among the principal preoccupations of the Baroque.

However, in spite of these significant facts, it would be wrong to draw too close a parallel between the age in which these men lived and the seventeenth century. The sharp divide between Mannerism and Baroque is not an artificial one. As Wilhelm Diltey writes: 'Between the appearance of Bruno's principal affirmation of pantheism in 1584 and the final publication of Spinoza's *Ethics* in 1677 less than a hundred years elapsed; and yet these two thinkers are separated by one of the greatest revolutions in scientific thought that have ever taken place.'*   n.2

More significant than the links between the late sixteenth century and the seventeenth are those which run between the period 1500 to 1520 and the Baroque. In the history of art these links have always been recognized: proto-Baroque elements have been identified in Michelangelo, Raphael, Titian and Correggio. It was inevitable that the artists of the seventeenth century, in their reaction against Mannerism, should feel an affinity with certain essential aspects of the High Renaissance. Surprisingly, however, in other fields of cultural history the existence of such a thing as a 'proto-Baroque' has not, so far as I know, yet been recognized.

Culturally, the link between Renaissance and Baroque lies in a belief in the freedom of the individual human being, a rejection of compulsion in matters of dogma, and a ready acceptance of the self-sufficiency of the individual. The great astronomical advances of the seventeenth century hark back to Copernicus (1473–1543), the foundation of the natural system of philosophy harks back to Melanchthon (1497–1560). Melanchthon was a figure of supreme importance for the Baroque age, both as an early proponent of religious toleration—he made attempts to bring about a union between Catholics and Protestants—and as a believer in the purely ethical purpose of theology; as he wrote to Camerarius: *'Ego mihi ita conscius sum non aliam ob causam umquam* τε θεολογιχεναι *nisi ut vitam emendarem'*: 'I am thus conscious that I study theology for no other end than to mend my life.' Biblical criticism made its appearance even before Erasmus, with Alberti's contemporary Lorenzo Valla (*c.* 1407–1457); while Erasmus himself (1467/9–1539), whom Luther called 'a foe to all religion',* was   n.3 responsible, together with the Socinians and Arminians, for the undermining of Christian dogma. Herman Rysvick, burned in the Netherlands (1500–55), and the two Behams (1500–55 and 1502–40) denied the divinity of Christ; Sebastian Franck (1499–1543) interpreted the Bible as an allegory; Macchiavelli (1469–1527) propounded the utilitarian theory of politics; and Valla actually declared *'idem est enim natura quod deus'*—'Nature and God are one and the same'.* All   n.4 these are ideas which, as I shall show in detail later, were taken up and further elaborated by the thinkers of the Baroque. This genuine affinity between Renaissance and Baroque needs emphasizing, particularly as art historians have devoted so much energy to stressing the—obviously equally genuine—contrasts between these two stylistic epochs. The statement that the age of Renaissance and Reformation was more closely related to the Baroque than the Renaissance was to Mannerism or Mannerism to the Baroque is in no way intended to conflict with Diltey's statement that between the sixteenth and seventeenth centuries there took place one of the greatest revolutions in the history of Western thought.

The antithesis between the two centuries is most apparent in Italy, the home of Counter-Reformation and Mannerism.

The most reliable pointers to the course of the evolution of art and of thought are the bare facts of political history; and the first historical signs of the rejection of the Counter-Reformation spirit appear in the 1590s, just contemporary with the epoch-making works of Caravaggio. First there was the conversation between Sixtus V and the Venetian ambassador, Donato, as a result of which the Pope, for purely political reasons, transferred his friendship from the Most Catholic King, Philip II, to the heretic Henry IV of France. In alliance with

France against Spain and the Empire, the papal army took Ferrara in 1598. In France the liberal Catholic *tiers-parti* came into being, the Jesuits were expelled in 1594, and in 1595 there came the final reconciliation with Rome. The first conclave of 1605 elected the French candidate, Leo XI, and when a second conclave in the same year elected Paul V, the result was again a Pope acceptable to France, and thus a reverse for Spain.* It was during the first year of Paul V's pontificate that there arose the immensely significant diplomatic conflict between the Papacy and Venice in which, in the teeth of interdict and excommunication, the Republic, supported by its clergy, successfully carried the point that the Pope's jurisdiction was limited to spiritual matters and that secular power was itself divinely instituted and thus entirely independent of the Church. As a consequence of this setback for the Church, Protestant propaganda in Venice intensified to such an extent that it seemed for a few years that the city would be won for Protestantism. In every respect, the pontificate of Paul V (1605–21) represents the gradual acclimatization of the Baroque. The worst excesses of the Inquisition became rare in Rome (far less frequent than in Germany, which was dominated until the Thirty Years War by the Counter-Reformation or 'Mannerist' ethic); significantly, Paul V was the first pope to follow courtly fashion and wear his beard *à la Henri IV.*

2 ANNIBALE CARRACCI *Assumption*

With the pontificate of Urban VIII (1623–44), of the generation of Caravaggio and Annibale Carracci, the transition was accomplished. The sun of the new age stood at high noon. Ranke writes: 'Clement VIII was usually to be found reading St Bernard, Paul V reading the Blessed Justinian; on Urban VIII's desk lay the latest poetry or perhaps designs for fortifications.'* What else could be expected of a ruler of the Papal States in the period we are considering? Urban VIII, who converted the Vatican library into an armoury and set up an arsenal at Tivoli, who allied himself with Gustavus Adolphus against Ferdinand, was a man of immense energy and political ability. To satisfy his absolutist and expansionist ambitions, no way lay open except military power and territorial aggrandizement. He was the last Pope to lay claim to world-wide jurisdiction. If he could not back his pretensions with actual military power, he certainly could not rely on the exercise of the spiritual authority wielded by his Counter-Reformation predecessors. Urban could not fail to see this; and he was far too strong and self-confident a personality to take it lying down. He enjoyed life and physical vigour to the full; he ate, drank, wrote poems (Ranke most significantly quotes a paraphrase of Simeon's thanksgiving written in Sapphics), enjoyed the adulation of his Roman friends, and defied convention by erecting a statue to himself with the remark that the prohibition which had hitherto prevailed against this could not apply to 'such a Pope as he was'. But for all Urban's energy, the Papacy as a world power was a thing of the past. Its war with the Farnese over Castro was a backyard quarrel, a purely monetary dispute, which it lost in any case. Not much more significance attaches to its protests at the purely secular provisions of the Treaties of Westphalia. As a political force it was no longer taken seriously; at the Peace of the Pyrenees in 1659 it was simply not consulted.

An analogous transformation overtook the institution which had set the tone of the Counter-Reformation: the Society of Jesus. It was decided at the general congregation of 1592 that the Superiors of the society should not remain in one post for more than three years, and that every six years there should be a congregation; this marked a definite intervention on the part of external powers in the affairs of the society. A characteristic symptom is the fact that under Clement VIII the first Jesuit cardinals, Bellarmine and Toledo, were appointed and thus took on political and diplomatic duties. Ranke describes in detail the state of the Society under the generalship of Vitelleschi (1615–45): admission had become easier than ever before, the property of the members, while still transferred to the Society, remained in many cases under the control of the individual member; the use of confession as a political weapon had begun; and the notorious Jesuit morality of probabilism was taking shape (the quotations collected by its opponents as evidence of Jesuit iniquity almost all stem

from the seventeenth century).* In 1641 the Society actually went so far as to   n.8
side with Richelieu in a dispute with the Pope, to whom its Counter-Reformation statutes bound it in a relationship of unconditional obedience.*   n.9

The transition from the culture of the age of Mannerism to that of the
Baroque thus reveals itself as a consistent tendency towards secularization. This
is the sense in which Croce understands it when he writes that after the Thirty
Years War the Counter-Reformation was 'finally finished'.* Ranke formulates   n.10
this with even greater precision, when he places the historical turning-point in
the year 1630—too late, because he chooses to mark the end of the crisis instead
of its beginning—with the victory of political over religious ideas. 'The religious
element moves into the background; political considerations govern the world.'

It is hardly necessary to point out how closely this change is matched by
transformations in the arts. Between El Greco and Velazquez, between Bruegel   3, 4,
and Brouwer, there took place the same process of secularization and 'externa-   6
lization' as between Sixtus V and Urban VIII.

Leaving the field of pure political history and turning to that of ideas and
feelings, one must first take into account the most direct expression of the spirit
of any age, its view of the nature of the relationship between the human and the
divine. It would be quite wrong, on the basis of the general 'externalization' of
action and motivation and the Church's loss of power and influence, to under-

3   EL GRECO *Adoration of the Shepherds*

4   VELASQUEZ *Adoration of the Magi*

5   BRUEGEL *The Peasant Dance (detail)*   6   BROUWER *The Smokers*

estimate the depth of religious feeling in the seventeenth century. In many instances it is the form of expression rather than the intensity of feeling which
differs from that of the Mannerist period. This is especially true of Catholic
religious feeling, very different from that of the Protestant or half-Protestant
North.

    In the first half of the seventeenth century the Catholic nations of the south
lived in a state of familiarity with the living God, with the angels, the saints and
the Devil, with miracles and witchcraft. Here, as in the pomp of the churches
and the theatricality of decoration, sculpture and painting, there lies an externalization and an urgent appeal to the senses;* but this rests on a new and totally
serious religious idea, highly characteristic of seventeenth-century thought: the
wish, with the help of the Faith, and the Church, to attain infinity through the
heightening of one's own personality—in its sensual, terrestrial form.

    This new and specifically Catholic idea is not the genuinely 'modern'
element in the religious feeling of the Baroque. This must be sought in the
Protestant North and in France, where it gave rise to manifestations which have
not often been classified within the general category of the Baroque.

    The most significant religious movement of the seventeenth century within
Catholic France was Jansenism, a movement founded by Bishop Cornelis Jansen
(1585–1638) which grew steadily from the mid-1630s, until Clement IX was
forced to grant it a sort of half-recognition in 1688. In many respects the ideals
of Jansenism serve to illuminate the concept of the Baroque.* Jansenism viewed
God as a highly abstract idea of truth (Jansen quoting St Augustine III Book 5,
Chapter 3: '*lex aeterna, quam diligendo non aliud diligit nisi ipsum deum seu veritatem
et iustitiam eius incommutabelim*' ('the eternal law, in loving which one loves
nothing else but God himself, his immutable truth and justice'). It commanded
the faithful to affirm the state of grace through acts of Christian charity; even its
precept of withdrawal from the world, at first sight a link with the Mannerist
age, was intended as a temporary measure, free of monkish asceticism and not
precluding social activity.

n.11

n.12

All this belongs to a new religious ideal which can also be detected within the mainstream of seventeenth-century Catholicism, a tendency to cooler abstraction in approaching the metaphysical part of religion, which in the Mannerist age occupied a central position in all religious life, and an increased interest in social and ethical questions which Mannerism had regarded as insignificant. These tendencies are apparent in the juxtaposition of faith and reason in the ideas of Cardinal Bérulle (1575–1629) and in the humane, approachable faith of St Vincent de Paul (1576–1660) and in that of the greatest of seventeenth-century French saints, Francis de Sales (1567–1622). Vossler emphasizes this in an admirable definition of St Francis de Sales' piety, 'which inwardly belongs to Heaven, outwardly is turned to the world and its social forms. He made Catholicism not only practical—it has always been that—but sociable, amiable and able to take its place in the *salons*.'* St Francis expects the Christian to care for   n.13 the poor and the sick and to teach the young; seclusion from the world should be a gradual process. It is significant for the understanding of seventeenth-century culture in general, and of that of France in particular, that St Francis de Sales founded an order for ladies, and that around him there grew up a whole series of other feminine devotional groups.*   n.14

In the quality of sociability lies an important link between Catholic (including Jansenist) religion and the contemporary Protestant sects of Great Britain and North America, the Puritans and Quakers, who regarded religious life as essentially ethical, a part of an inner life.* And, as we shall see, the Jan-   n.15 senist reduction of a personal God to an abstract moral and logical principle is a link between them and the great philosophers of the seventeenth century.

Protestant religious thought in the seventeenth century, more markedly than that of Catholicism, represents a reduction in the fervour of faith; but widespread atheism still lay far in the future. Practically all the leading philosophers of the period up to 1640, whether Catholic or Protestant by origin, Grotius, Gassendi, Boyle, Charron and Herbert of Cherbury, still sincerely believed in Revelation. Descartes, indeed, has been described by Gustave Lanson as an influence favourable to the maintenance of belief. 'And if, after 1660, free-thought lost ground, if scandalous provocations ceased, if for half a century impiety became an underground stream which could not always be detected at all, Pascal and Bossuet deserve less credit for it than does Descartes.'*   n.16

The various tendencies within the religious life of Northern Europe can thus readily be reduced to a few basic ideas. All the tendencies are based on a common view of life which finds its freest artistic expression in two apparently antithetical manifestations of the Baroque style: Poussin's crystalline structural clarity, his coolness and total consistency, bring him close to the Cartesian and Jansenist views of God just as Rembrandt's peculiar brand of religiosity belongs to the spirit of an age whose preoccupations were ethical rather than metaphysical. The psychological penetration of his view of the Old Testament, and his profoundly human interpretation of the figure of Christ, constitute the   7 profoundest expression in Western art of the identification of the divine with the ethical.

The religious feeling of the Early and High Baroque may be considered under three main headings: the Catholic tendency to externalize and to interpret ideas in sensual terms; the Protestant tendency to interpret them in ethical terms; and the philosophical tendency to interpret them in abstract terms. But are these three tendencies not basically the same? All are manifestations of a common *Zeitgeist* which sets them apart from the most characteristic expressions of the preceding and following ages. Seen in this light, it becomes apparent that the Catholic pomp of Italy has 'externalization' in common with the salon piety of St Francis de Sales with its emphasis on loving-kindness, and that the ethical bias within religion—certainly in no way inferior in value to the idealism of the Mannerist period—represents a reduction of religious problems to a this-worldly level which belongs to the same general 'rejection of the supernatural' (*Entzauberung der Welt*) as the external manifestations of Catholic ritual.

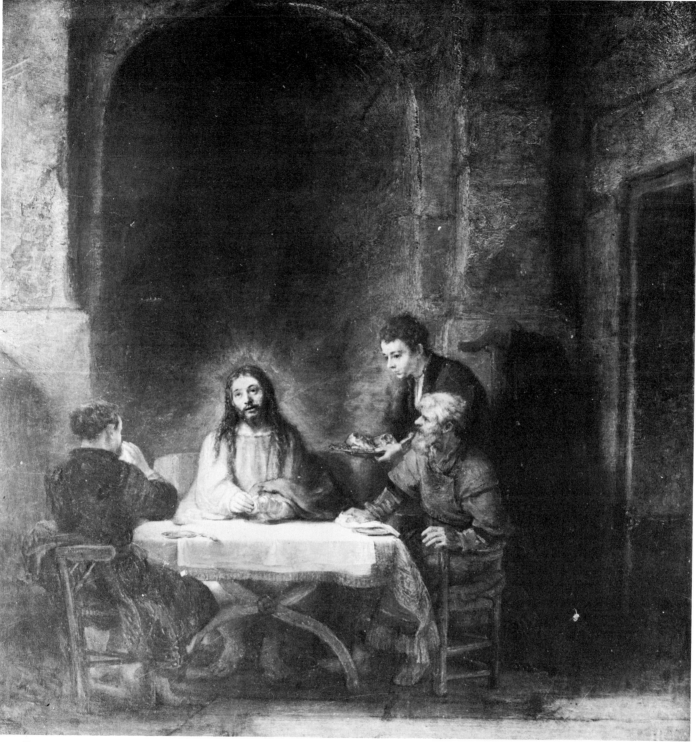

7 REMBRANDT *Supper at Emmaus*

Rembrandt's Jesus, profoundly akin to each of us in terms of the inner life, signifies the utmost in human goodness, human nobility, human compassion; the Christ of the Mannerist El Greco is a remote magical being, possessed of mysterious and incommensurable powers. Spinoza in the middle of the seventeenth century teaches tolerance and the need to love God in every object in nature; the Christian of the Counter-Reformation (and of contemporary Calvinism) had believed in a single religion by which alone he could hope to be justified, for which he would willingly take on martyrdom, and on behalf of which he waged

8 HALS *Yonker Ramp and his Sweetheart*

war against the body, which he would kill rather than allow it a sinful freedom. Even the temper of heretics changed; in 1660 the pantheist Giordano Bruno allowed himself to be burned for his faith; in 1633 Galileo, convinced that his survival was necessary for the progress of science, recanted. It is impossible to weigh El Greco against Rembrandt or the ethic of strict adherence to principle against that of compromise. But it is a fact that the Baroque world view had made up in depth of understanding what it had lost in intensity. Clearly, the seventeenth-century *Entzauberung der Welt,* with its acknowledgment of the place of human personality in religion, went hand in hand with the 'externalization' of Catholic religious art. At the same time the pomp of seventeenth-century Italian churches, another major Baroque characteristic, represents the impulse of the individual personality to flow out into an infinity never clearly imagined before this time. In its turn, this component of Catholic religious feeling cannot be understood without reference to the true centre of gravity of Western intellectual development in the 1600s, the foundation of modern science.* n.17

The overwhelming impact of the discoveries of the early seventeenth-century astronomers and physicists is hard to imagine now. Setting out from Copernicus' theory that the earth revolves about the sun—a theory that was a product of the Renaissance—their work culminated in Kepler, Galileo and Descartes. The crucial discoveries all belong to the period under discussion: Kepler's First and Second Laws to 1609, his Third Law to 1618, Galileo's Laws to 1602 and 1604, Cartesian geometry to 1637. Kepler (1571–1630), in his calculation of planetary movement, set out from a conviction that there is an overriding harmony in the universe, as indeed did Galileo (1568–1642) in the great series of discoveries which included the virtual foundation of the science of mechanics.

Behind the work of both there lay a realization of immense significance, the realization that the earth does not—as the Bible and the theologians said—stand at the centre of the universe, but forms an infinitely small part of a coherent but incommensurable universe. In the field of natural science the consequence of this was the foundation of an objective system of factual investigation; in philosophy its consequence was the new pantheism which began with Bruno and culminated in Spinoza. God could no longer, in the new cosmogonies, be thought of as extramundane: he must be active within the universe itself; and as the universe is a single coherent whole, this means that he must be active within each object. For Spinoza God is a pure state of being whose only manifestation is in the things of this world. Whoever seeks God must seek him in the universe, and in its countless phenomena.

It was inevitable that the great philosophers of the age should also be its scientists and mathematicians; for the mightiest idea of the whole Baroque age, the discovery of infinity, affects all three fields equally: philosophy, through the appearance of pantheism; science, by making possible astronomy and physics in the modern sense; and mathematics, which now became able to transcend the solid and static geometry and arithmetic of the ancients by studying number as the expression of pure relationships. The invention of differential and integral calculus belongs to the seventeenth century; and one of Oswald Spengler's most profound and fruitful insights was that which led him to place the discovery of infinity at the centre of his presentation of Western culture. He was the first to perceive the immensely illuminating parallel between these scientific discoveries, which transformed man's view of the universe, and the artistic innovations of the seventeenth century.

The 'feeling of kinship with the universe' to which Schmarsow refers in his book on the Baroque as the kernel of the '*malerisch*' or painterly style,* links the n.18 cunning deceptions of Catholic architecture with the expansive power of Rubens' or Cortona's decorative painting, and even with the profound golden 9,p. brown of Rembrandt's paintings, the artistic expression of belief in a coherent and animate universe, and with the impressionism of a Velazquez or a Frans

9   RUBENS *Apotheosis of the Duke of Buckingham (sketch for a ceiling)*

8   Hals, which like all impressionism depends on a conviction that the universe is endless movement.

The scientific discoveries of the age of Baroque were as important for the understanding of the microcosm as for that of the macrocosm. With the true realization of the infinity of the universe the idea of direct dependence on a

personal God inevitably receded from the human consciousness. And although the philosophers of the Early and High Baroque combined their new insights into the workings of nature with personal Christian orthodoxy, it remains true that the discovery of scientific independence carried within it the seeds of the atheism which Locke later bequeathed to the eighteenth century. Man felt himself to be thrown on his own resources; having cast off age-old fetters, he breathed more freely. The great thinkers of the seventeenth century were inevitably very different characters from the representatives of the Mannerist period. Diltey speaks very aptly of the 'coherent proud temper of life' which underlies the philosophy of Descartes and leads to the 'most intense consciousness of sovereignty' that any man has ever achieved.* This is what Corneille puts into the   n.19
mouth of his Augustus:

> *Je suis maître de moi comme de l'univers,*
> *Je le suis, je veux l'être.**   n.20

This self-mastery was the mark of the men who applied themselves to factual enquiry with the 'healthy senses and worldly-wise intellect'* which had formed   n.21
the ideal of the philosopher Charron (1541–1603): the *prud'homme,* a proud, manly and joyous character. A new energy and strength of will informed artists and scientists alike. Francis Bacon (1561–1616) goes so far as to assign to philosophy the purpose of achieving mastery over nature and mankind.

Natural law had taken the place of divine ordinance; the whole age was full of a passionate need to find laws, to generalize, to set up on the basis of the new autonomy of thought a natural system of science. Here, alongside the discovery of the infinite, lies the second great ruling idea of the seventeenth century: that of law.* It manifested itself during the first quarter of the century: Charron's   n.22
De la sagesse appeared in 1601, Bacon's *De Dignitate et augmentis scientiarum* in 1605, his *Novum Organon* in 1620, Herbert of Cherbury's *De Veritate* in 1624. The foundation of natural philosophy is the belief in absolute truths which are inborn in man. On the basis of certain axioms, Descartes constructed his system; Spinoza undertook to develop his theories *more geometrico,* 'in a geometrical way.' Herbert speaks of the 'mathematical certitude' of natural instinct, which only 'the insane' can dispute. It is precisely this sort of apodictically formulated thesis that affords the most illuminating insights into the nature of the self-awareness of any epoch. Inner certainty lies at the root of the ethic of the Baroque age.

In contrast to the Mannerist rejection of the corporeal as sinful, this ethic constitutes an affirmation, an acceptance of this world. The good life, for Charron, is identical with the life according to nature ('*vivere secundum naturam*'); and Diltey has pointed to the Stoic origins of the seventeenth-century ethic. Similarly, seventeenth-century political science, whose greatest exponent was Grotius (1583–1645) is based not on divine ordinance but on the given facts of human nature, which are then formulated as immutable laws. Concurrently with the principal philosophical works, there appeared the crucial works of political theory: Lipsius' *Politica* in 1612, Sarpi's *Opinione* in 1615, Grotius' *Ius belli ac pacis* in 1625. In these works generalized moral formulae yield pride of place to the criterion of the good of the state. Lipsius, for example, expressly allows the ruler as much hypocrisy and mendacity as may further the ends of the state. Charron goes so far as to formulate the general principle that one should make use of the world as one finds it, while avoiding any emotional involvement in or identification with it. Again, the unidealized view of mankind which underlies such theories as these has its roots in the scientific innovations of the Baroque age. While science gradually probed deeper into the mechanism of the human organism—Harvey discovered the circulation of the blood in 1626—the religious conviction that man was created in 'God's image' gradually lost ground to the heretical idea of man as a machine. Here lie the first seeds of the positivism of a Lamettrie, just as the pantheism of the Early Baroque reveals the origins of the atheism of the Enlightenment. But the seeds were not to germinate until much later; Descartes manages to reconcile a scientific belief in the automatic functioning of the mechanism of the human body with a religious belief in the divine substance as prime mover.

I have already made a start with the task of reducing the major religious potentialities of the Baroque period to a common denominator. Now that I have referred to the most important facts and tendencies of science and philosophy, it is time to pursue the question of religion in some greater depth. Is it possible to establish a convincing parallel between the dominant ideas of science and those of religion in the seventeenth century?

In my very generalized outline of the nature of Baroque religious feeling, Catholic and Protestant, I have tried to reduce it to three dominant tendencies. The first was 'sensualization', which finds its closest parallel in the historical victory of political over religious ideas, and which manifested itself in ecclesiastical pomp (in contrast to the asceticism of the Mannerist period), in the new-found 'sociability' of French Catholicism (in contrast to the cruelty of the Wars

n.23   of Religion),* and, most importantly, in the emphasis, within religious thought, on ethical questions. The second aspect, closely linked with a general tendency towards 'externalization', was the transformation of the highly personal God of the Counter-Reformation into an abstract concept identified with truth or goodness, eventually even with being. The third aspect was the longing to expand one's own personality into a celestial infinity.

It is easy to see that the essential philosophical innovations of the seventeenth century, as I have described them, fit comfortably into the framework of these basic concepts. Infinity I have dealt with; 'sensualization' also provides a parallel with religion. It was the recognition of the 'kingdom of this world', the human body, the human mind and all corporeal things, that made possible the beginning of natural science. Interest in metaphysics and theology waned; the idea of a coherent, self-contained universe inevitably weakened belief in the transcendental, extramundane nature of God. The men of the age saw the world not with the eyes of a saint, as they had sought to do in the Counter-Reformation period, but with those of a mathematician or physicist. Several examples have been offered of the proud, virile and affirmative stance of the leading philosophers of the Baroque period. Not to overcome nature but to 'live according to nature' is the core of the Baroque ethic: in politics the priority is to do not what is pleasing to God but what is useful to the state. Here too, as in theology, the dominant tendency is towards generalization and the formulation of laws. The foundation of natural science in the seventeenth century is based on this principle. But, in profound contradistinction to the Mannerist tendency to give

n.24   'law' the precedence over 'life',* this is not a transcendental but an immanent law: not the law of God but that of state and king. The contrast between Louis XIV's state and the Society of Jesus exactly parallels that between the Mannerist subordination of all things to divine law and the Baroque subordination of all

n.25   things to the laws of the state and of nature.*

The next step in the argument is the decisive one: the recognition that the three dominant tendencies which underlie the Baroque view of the world and of God are fundamentally aspects of one style of life which manifests itself only in this one period. Clearly, each of them is a reflection of universal types which recur in every age, and which form an important object of enquiry for students of cultural history (Diltey, Troeltsch, Max Weber, Spranger). It seems to me that from the historian's point of view, it is more important to consider how these types have manifested themselves in particular historical periods, and how within one period a single 'spirit of the age' leaves its mark on the various types. My investigation will have served its purpose if it has succeeded in extracting from the mass of phenomena this living spirit of the age.

Thus, the 'sensualization' of seventeenth-century culture is essentially different in character from parallel phenomena in other basically optimistic or positive periods such as the Renaissance or the Rococo. Immoderate and violent energy, and the production of expansive individuals, passionate in their reasoning as in their emotion, were characteristic of the age in every field of activity. This specific seventeenth-century human type is the inescapable precondition for the creation of the two greatest achievements of the Baroque age: the natural system of science and the discovery of infinity. Seventeenth-century 'natural philosophy' does not signify a passive enjoyment of the beauty of the cosmos but an active conquest of nature. The act of forcing the world into a majestic framework of abstract, *a priori* laws is not a product of the classical love of harmony but of a passionate act of reason. Giant hands were at work assembling the great blocks of the new knowledge of nature into a structure. The secularization which we have hitherto seen as a cornerstone of the culture of the seventeenth century thus shows itself to be inseparably bound up with other expressions of the Baroque temperament: the political theory of acceptance of the world as it is, the new naturalistic ethic, and the new impersonal, abstract and this-worldly concept of God.

It is equally impossible to separate from the other basic tendencies of the Baroque the second great discovery of the age, that of infinity. Like scientific method, this discovery could have come to pass only in these specific intellectual circumstances, only as the achievement of a courageous, self-reliant and expansionist generation. The overflowing energy of the age found no ultimate satisfaction in political expansion and absolutism but took up the weapons of the intellect and conquered the universe.

The same passion for conquest and aggrandizement appears in the quest for the laws of political and ethical science as in the quest for those of physics and mathematics. The all-pervading belief in a single and coherent universe in itself inevitably brought in its train the reduction of the idea of a personal deity to the pantheistic idea of a creative substance active in everything, and to the reduction of productive philosophy to the essentially personal questions of ethics and politics—in other words, a process of secularization and sensualization. It is therefore clear that no specific problem can be adequately dealt with without turning one's attention to the totality of the rich, unified and coherent historical entity which constitutes the Early and High Baroque period.

Turning from cultural history in general to the narrower field of art, I now feel justified in raising the question whether there can be said to exist a stylistic

10 REMBRANDT *Belshazzar's Feast*

11 CARAVAGGIO
*Calling of
St Matthew*

bond uniting the greatest representatives of the various artistic potentialities of the age, Caravaggio, Rubens, Hals, Velazquez, Poussin, Bernini and Rembrandt. Stylistic unity in this sense does not mean identity but an affinity of feeling and ideas which clearly sets the period apart from those which precede and follow it and which links individuals who may be totally opposed to each other in their view of the world and their chosen means of expression. I am not trying to invalidate the approach which almost all art historians have adopted hitherto and which lays its emphasis squarely on contrasts of attitude and style. My aim is merely to demonstrate the validity of another approach.

Thus the specifically Baroque element in Rembrandt (and not only the young, melodramatic, radical Rembrandt) has already been discussed, with reference to the ethical bias in his religious art, to the psychological quality of his interpretation of man, the painterly quality of his technique, and the sense of infinity in his use of light and *chiaroscuro*. Similarly, I have referred to the impressionistic technique of Velazquez, Hals or van Goyen as the artistic form appropriate to an age which recognizes and accepts the universe as a mass of infinitesimal bodies in unceasing motion.

This attitude of acceptance of the world leads to the naturalism of Caravaggio and Ribera in art, and to the materialism of Bacon and Gassendi in philosophy; it must also be one of the sources of the miraculous flowering of Dutch painting in the hands of the minor masters, admirable 'specialists' in still-life, animals, peasants, soldiers, landscapes, seascapes, townscapes or church interiors.

12 CARAVAGGIO *Basket of Fruit*

13 SAENREDAM *Interior of St Odulph's, Assendelft*

14 SALOMON VAN RUYSDAEL *Landscape with a Ferry*

15 CAREL FABRITIUS *Goldfinch*

16 HEDA *Still-life*

17 CARAVAGGIO *Amor Victorious*

18 BERNINI *Apollo and Daphne*

The other source, and the more potent of the two, must be the pantheism of the Baroque, to which every object appears equally animate, equally divine and therefore equally worthy of the artist's attention, thus challenging the primacy of religious and historical subjects in painting.*   n.26

As far as the Italian seventeenth-century is concerned *seicentismo* in literature is a wholly apposite and fully-fledged poetic manifestation of the Baroque style, and to reject Italian poetry between 1580 and 1640 *en masse* as a period of decadence, as a historian of the eminence of Carl Vossler was able to do as recently as 1927,* should be as impossible as Benedetto Croce's condemnation   n.27
of one of its components, the *concettismo*.* In fact Caravaggio and the Carracci,   n.28
the founders of Italian Baroque painting; Peri, the founder of the opera; and Marino, the founder of *seicentismo*, all belonged to the same generation (1560–75).

The most important new departure in the arts in the seventeenth century, the first flowering of the opera in Rome between 1600 and 1640, marked the acceptance of a genre in which words serve the ends of euphony alone, and in which splendour of presentation distracts attention from the intellectual content, which lies in the music. This is the most significant parallel to the much-condemned *concettismo* in poetry, and may perhaps make it easier to understand. Beautiful sound as an end in itself, and spectacular form as an end in itself, interpreted as the pleasure in make-believe—does this not apply equally well to *concettismo*, to the Baroque opera and to Baroque church decoration?*   n.29

An essential characteristic of Marinism in poetry is a tendency to lascivious   n.30
eroticism and perverse cruelty;* this too provides a striking parallel with the visual art of the same period. Marino's *Adone* appeared in 1623; Bernini's
Apollo and Daphne in 1622; Ribera's first dated painting of a martyrdom in   18
1624. Here again, it would be wrong to overlook the fundamental contrast with the sensuality of the Renaissance. Eroticism in the arts had lost its naturalness for ever in the profound crisis of the age of European Mannerism. Since then erotic art has been haunted by a malady, '*qualcosa di peccaminoso*', 'a touch of sickness', which Croce detects in Mannerism. Thus, Marino felt the need to assure his reader that 'his muse was jocund, but his life was chaste': '*Se oscena è la penna, è casto il core*'. This is as transparent a cloak as Ottonelli's and Cortona's disingenuous assumption of the licence to paint nudes commissioned by private patrons,*   n.31
and Urban VIII's witty couplet defending Bernini's *Daphne* from reproach:

> *Quisquis amans sequitur fugitiva gaudia formae,*
> *Fronde manus implet baccas seu carpit amaras.*

> The man who in love pursues the joys of fleeting beauty,
> Grasps a frond in his hand or plucks the bitter bay.*   n.32

The new dichotomy within Western man, the new subjectivism, the awakening of self-consciousness, gave a distinctive quality to the eroticism of the Baroque. Both components of *seicentismo* in literature, eroticism and the 'conceit', constitute equally important and indeed essential expressions of the spirit   17
of the age.

The most difficult problem involved in any attempt to gather the basic ideas of the Baroque style under one heading does not lie in Italy but in France. How is so-called French classicism related to the Baroque?

In my opinion it can certainly not be so completely subsumed under the heading of Late Baroque as Hans Rose maintains.* In spite of the great signifi-   n.33
cance of the start of building work at Vaux-le-Vicomte, and Bernini's visit to Paris, both of which took place in the 1660s, i.e. in the Late Baroque, I think that the most significant watershed in seventeenth-century French culture lies around 1630. Compared with the first thirty years of the century the periods 1630–60 and 1660–1700 fall into place as phases of a single style. No division into periods makes sense if it divides Poussin from classicism; and the first generation

19 ANNIBALE CARRACCI *Polyphemus, detail of ceiling in the Palazzo Farnese, Rome*

20 POUSSIN *Last Supper*

of the French classical age consisted of men born between about 1585 and 1605: Poussin (1594), François Mansart (1598), Richelieu (1585), Descartes (1596) and Corneille (1606).

If the patterns in France and Italy do not exactly coincide, if the caesuras of two parallel courses of evolution lie at different points in time, this is the result of highly interesting conflict between the universal style of the age and the constants of national temperament. In France the evolution in the direction of the Late Baroque coincided with a permanent ideal of the French mind, so that an essentially Late Baroque phenomenon, the later classicism of the age of Racine, became a major current in French civilization. A parallel development in Italian painting, in Sacchi and the late Reni, is no more than a beginning. The infrastructure of an artistic style which represents the profoundest union between national character and historical context—a 'classic moment'—must be broader than that of a relatively weak and tardy manifestation such as the Italian Late Baroque.

The existence of stylistic unity in the High Baroque depends on the question whether the first phase of French classicism belongs to it. Wölfflin seems not to think so; Poussin finds no place in the framework of his *Grundbegriffe*, and Brinckmann too (in his *Handbuch*) raised strong objections to the incorporation of French classicism in the Baroque. This question is thus the crux of my whole argument.

There can be no doubt that the greatest politician of the High Baroque age in France, and indeed in Europe, Richelieu, is a perfect reflection of the spirit of the age as I have described it. This cardinal who in the moment of danger (1629) assumed supreme military command, who, after their neutralization as a political force, treated the French Protestants with the greatest sympathy, and whose foreign allies were Protestant (Sweden, Holland, Scotland) is a perfect example of the worldliness and joy of conquest which in the Baroque view marked out a great man. It is he, and not Louis XIV, who is the representative French statesman of these years; he and not the Sun King founded French absolutism. Ranke rightly attributes to him 'the setting up of an all-embracing administration', and 'an unprecedented augmentation of royal and ministerial power'. He was the first whose preoccupations lay 'only in the ideas of unity and political power'. His biographer Andreas describes him as unscrupulous and 'full of deceit to the bottom of his soul',* and Ranke characterizes him perfectly as 'a dogmatist of power'.*   n.34
n.35

Could not exactly the same epithet be applied even to Descartes and Corneille? I have already pointed out how completely Descartes is a manifestation of the Baroque spirit, with his combination of the impulse towards mathematical infinity with the passionate urge to achieve a definitive abstract law. The parallel between Descartes and Corneille has often been drawn.* Their closest link lies   n.36
in their conscious rejection of passion in favour of will. For Descartes the passions are only 'perturbations' of the soul by the body; and Corneille writes in a letter to Saint-Evremond that: 'Love is an emotion which is too closely linked with weakness to predominate in a heroic play.' A second link is their reverence for everything that is, in Descartes' words, 'clear and distinct.' Numerous passages in Corneille glorify 'reason'; and Racine emphasized the fact in his speech welcoming Thomas Corneille to the seat in the Académie Française left vacant by his more famous brother. 'In this chaos of dramatic poetry your celebrated brother brought reason on to the stage.'

A further affinity between Descartes and Corneille is their endeavour to establish laws—philosophical and scientific in Descartes' case, political in the case of the former lawyer Corneille. He praises the independent and sacred authority of the state and he resolves the predicament of the victorious and guilty Horace with the harsh formula: 'Live to serve the state'. This attitude is not only eminently French; it is also entirely characteristic of the age in which Descartes and Corneille worked.

It is precisely this delight in law-making and this passionate reason which

21 RENI *Aurora, ceiling in the Casino Rospigliosi, Rome*

allies both Descartes and Corneille with Poussin. For it is essential to realize that, for Poussin too, passion is reason and reason is passion. Klemperer, the literary historian who has given me more insights than any other, was the very first to see this fact as central to an understanding of the period.* Those of us in the North of Europe to whom this idea remains alien and inaccessible will never really be in sympathy with the art of a Poussin, an Ingres, or a Picasso; or else we shall colour it with an Italian harmony and warmth which it does not possess. Walter Friedländer expresses it perfectly when he says in his biography of Poussin that the artist is able to 'imbue stiff, calculated forms with intense inner experience'. This experience is far more intense than that which underlies the colder and emptier rhetoric of the Lebrun period; but Poussin's antithesis, Bernini, was certainly correct in his interpretation when he called Poussin 'a painter who works from up here' (i.e. with his brain), and that '*dentro ci era il fondo e il sodo del saper*'—'there was the root and foundation of knowledge'.

n.37

This ideal of passionate reason, towards which the active* will of the so-called French classicists was directed, differs in its inflexibility and dynamism from that of classical art in Italy.* French classicism should not in fact necessarily be accepted at its face value. It is quite likely that Baroque decorative paintings were felt to be entirely in place in the classical setting of Versailles. Could it not be that the Antique formal apparatus played the same role here as in the Mannerist buildings of Palladio or the romantic classicism of 1800? Nowhere in French classicism is there the perfect unity of all the arts (i.e. of a total world view) which characterizes the High Renaissance. Perhaps, in this age of make believe, the appearance of classicism is an iron mask covering the lineaments of passion.

n.38

n.39

There is no lack of persuasive contemporary evidence to support the idea that the harmony of French classicism is more apparent than real. One testimony is offered by Vossler in his comparison between Faret's *L'homme Honneste ou l'art de plaire à la cour* (1637) and Castiglione's *Il Cortigiano*:* where the man of the Renaissance had called for 'pure and amiable simplicity', the man of the seventeenth century expects of the courtier 'self-awareness, deliberation and the considered exercise of will'. The most convincing testimony is quoted by Klemperer from *Le bon plaisir* by Regnier (1573–1613):

n.40

'And how do you think to please the king? Is it by showing him faces travailed by passion and distorted by what lies within? A great king can endure in a man only what is most noble in him; that is what his eyes must see. Let nature be at pains to seem what she ought to be . . . Sir, you shall see splendid sights, beginning with the fountains. Observe the water in the pools: drink, it would be foetid to the taste; see it start forth, and it shines and glitters . . .'

The whole passage might have been written to substantiate my argument: a strong rejection of any display of one's own feelings is accompanied by a glorification of outward show. The reference to the king is highly characteristic. Compulsion must be exercised not to the greater glory of God but to that of the king, not in the interests of an extramundane power but in those of a this-worldly one. The reference to the garden, too, is strikingly apposite. In its coercion of nature in the interests of the human desire for mathematical regularity, and in its unprecedented use of infinite perspectives, the seventeenth-century formal garden is entirely in the baroque spirit.

Returning to the narrower field of art history, it is possible to show from Poussin's work, without any reference to related disciplines, that classical harmony did not come so naturally to him as to Raphael or Titian. Early in his career, the entirely Baroque *Rape of the Sabines* stands beside the classical bas-relief composition of the *Death of Germanicus,* and Raphaelesque biblical scenes rub shoulders with Titianesque bacchanals. We know from Poussin himself that he recommended painting according to the *modi,* the 'modes of feeling', corresponding to the objects represented: soft things should be painted soft, hard things hard. So he too provides an instance, harder to see perhaps than that of Corneille or Descartes, of the element of purely apparent classicism which was so characteristic of the French and Italian culture of the age.

This typically French aspect of the Baroque is easily illustrated by examples from the wider field of cultural history. Charron recommends deception when he says that a wise man will play his part well and give no cause to others to judge the folly that is within him. Louis XIV himself writes in his memoirs: 'If one has a weak character and cannot combat one's weakness, . . . one must at least have wisdom enough to conceal it.'* Corneille's powerful line '*Il faut que l'on soit libre au milieu de ses fers,*' Malherbe's establishment of a 'rational' lyric poetry, the grammarian Vaugelas' rigid '*Remarques sur la langue française* (1647), Guez de Balzac's rejection of the Pléiade for their lack of 'order, economy, choice': all these are invitations to employ a rigid framework of law to conceal passion from view.

The whole style of the age is dramatically illustrated by Louis XIV's action during the last years of his reign, when new ideas were already on the rise, in ordering the atrocities of the *salles de réunion* and the *dragonnades.* Rarely has the ingenious cruelty of absolutism more consciously and rationally clothed its misdeeds in a specious cloak of legality.

I need only refer in passing to another relationship, that which exists between the conscious French way of 'appearing other than one is', i.e. an anti-natural behaviour raised to a moral and artistic principle, and the passion of the seventeenth century for rhetoric and a rankly proliferating form as they characterize Italian *seicentismo.* "Make-believe" as a form of human expression is called *Seicentismo',* says Klemperer, and I suggest that one might be justified in applying the same definition to French classicism.

It is true that, speaking purely formally, in Poussin, Le Vau or Perrault there is less of this cold passion, this fanatical pursuit of harmony, than in the poets and philosophers; but one must not forget that one of the greatest difficulties in interpreting the intentions of the artist in post-Renaissance art lies in the fact that, as a consequence of the profound dichotomy within Western man which was the legacy of the early sixteenth century, self-awareness and self-observation and every kind of artistic deception, have become possible. Here too, of course, appearances cannot deceive in the long run, but one must look very carefully in some instances to avoid taking for true harmony and pure classicism something which is no more than faith in their absolute value.

Seen from this point of view, the unbridgeable gulf between the Italian

22

23

n.41

22 POUSSIN *Rape of the Sabines*

High Renaissance and French classicism is patent; but the gap between the attitudes of the Early and High Baroque and those of French art in the second third of the seventeenth century narrows considerably.

These corroborative instances must suffice to suggest the wide applicability of the basic criteria of the Baroque style which have been presented here. It would of course have been possible to draw them entirely from the facts of art history or even of the evolution of form. But it seems to me that it is always useful for a complete understanding of the art of a period to search for the cultural preconceptions and potentialities which underlie it. This constitutes not only a protection against false interpretations but also the most potent resources in the endeavour to grasp historical periods as living realities.*

n.42

23 POUSSIN *Death of Germanicus*

1   GIORDANO *Triumph of Judith, ceiling of the treasury of the Certosa, Naples*

Wiener Jahrbuch für Kunstgeschichte, VIII, 1932

III
The Crisis of 1650 in
Italian Painting

ANYONE who concerns himself with Italian painting of the seventeenth and eighteenth centuries soon realizes that students of the period have, with a few exceptions, neglected a large sector of the subject, namely the second half of the seventeenth century. It is not that the recent output of monographs has been markedly lower for this period than for that which preceded it, the mature Baroque of Bernini, Poussin, Cortona and Sacchi, or that which followed, the short-lived romanticism of Magnasco, Crespi and Ricci (although a certain falling-off in the volume of research work is noticeable at this point). What has not been achieved is the recognition of the second half of the seventeenth century as a unique and individual phenomenon whose various stylistic manifestations can be gathered together under a single heading.* This paper is an attempt to establish 'Late Baroque' as a stylistic concept useful for the understanding of Italian painting in the late *Seicento*.

n.1

To do this I must concentrate on the decisive historical moment. This entails considering those major painters, in all the then productive areas of Italy, whose work, between 1650 and 1670 or even between 1650 and 1660, underwent a stylistic change which brought to the fore certain fundamentally new formal principles distinct not only from those of the High Baroque but also from those of the eighteenth century. The existence of such a stylistic turning-point—just as clear and significant as that which marked off Mannerism from the Early Baroque in the 1590s—has not hitherto been properly recognized by historians of the Italian Baroque; this is likely to be the reason for the comparative neglect of the period as such by research workers.*

n.2

The decision to restrict my study to the major painters who started work between 1650 and 1660 in those parts of Italy which were still productive removes Tuscany, Piedmont and Lombardy from consideration. The contribution of Bologna was in no way distinctive either. This leaves Naples (the most propitious territory of all for Late Baroque art), the Veneto and Liguria, and Rome, where the new style had to make its way against the opposition of native classicism. The artists whose careers began in the 1650s were members of the generation born between 1625 and 1645, with one very important exception. Giordano (b. 1632), Valerio Castello (1624), Maratti (1625), Cignani (1628), together with the slightly later Roman group of Gaulli (1629), Pozzo (1642), Antonio Gherardi (1644), Coli (1636) and Filippo Gherardi (1643) were members of the same generation; but Mattia Preti, born in 1613, was more than a decade older than the eldest of them and Francesco Maffei must have been yet ten or twelve years older. This serves as a warning that Wilhelm Pinder's emphasis on the importance of generations as units in artistic development should not be allowed to take precedence over the equally significant approach by strict chronology of works. As Pinder himself says, both are equally potent forces working to mould historical reality.

II

Nowhere in Italy are the multiplicity—and the limitations—of the possibilities of the new style as evident as in Naples. Here they were represented by Preti and Giordano, two antithetical characters with firmly parallel careers. Preti was considerably the elder; he matured late, and was solitary, retiring, gloomy, emotional and much given to religious subjects. Giordano was a youthful prodigy, brilliantly successful and influential, a showman and even something of a charlatan, cheerful and with a marked preference for mythological and erotic subjects. And yet it can be shown that in the essentials of their composition, even in the details of facial types, modelling and draperies, they match exactly, drawn by historical necessity into the same narrow, inescapable path.

An analysis of a number of particularly characteristic examples of their art will serve to bring to light what divides and what unites them. Preti,* the elder n.3 in years and in artistic outlook, draws the spectator powerfully and urgently into the action of a picture such as the *Martyrdom of St Catherine* (Valletta, Santa 2 Caterina, 1659).* The effect is restless and sombre and at the same time the n.4 composition is flowing and opulent; without individual groups being isolated, without dominant figures and without half-length figures in the foreground. The whole action is seen slightly *di sotto in sù*. All this sets up a strange, uncertain swaying motion of the kind which is familiar in Northern Italian Mannerism since Correggio. Preti in this respect is opposed to the Baroque and linked to Mannerism—Veronese's famous *Martyrdom of St George* provides a close compositional analogy—but his use of paint stems entirely from the High

2   PRETI *Martyrdom of St Catherine*

3   PRETI *Raising of Lazarus*

4 PRETI *Wedding at Cana*

Baroque, and particularly from his master Guercino. This is equally evident in the modelling of the nudes, with soft, dappled effects of shadow, and in the types represented by the heads of the saints, angels and other figures. A structure derived from Mannerism is thus infused with the passionate elan of the High Baroque, and both are informed with a new creative purpose which sets up a soft and undulating rhythm.

How Preti arrived at this style, how he developed in the years before his decisive stay in Naples (1656–60), has not in spite of the considerable volume of Preti literature been fully revealed. All we know for certain of his career before he reached Naples is that he was a pupil of Guercino and that he painted two frescoes in Rome (San Carlo ai Catinari 1642, a tentative beginner's effort, and Sant'Andrea della Valle 1651–2). The problem lies in the fact that alongside his Guercinesque, Venetian works, which can be adequately explained by the influences of his apprentice years, there is a small group of clearly earlier works by him for which there is no exact dating, and which betray the influence of Caravaggio and his principal Neapolitan follower, Battistello. These include pictures in the Brera, the Dresden Gallery, the Vienna Academy, the Palazzo Corsini and the Palazzo Doria, both in Rome, and in the Longhi Collection. On the borderline of the later group, there is the *Raising of Lazarus* in the Palazzo Rosso, Genoa.* It is hardly possible to avoid supposing that both groups coincided, or at least overlapped, chronologically: the Venetian style is already detectable beneath the dry Roman classicism of the S. Andrea frescoes of 1651–52, after which it unfolds itself in the sequence of masterpieces painted in Naples; the other, 'Caravaggesque' style in the shape of the *Raising of Lazarus* is also present in Preti's Neapolitan years, in which he had his first encounter with the work of Battistello.

As far as the problem in hand is concerned, it is enough to remember that a new manner established itself firmly as the style of the 1650s. With its undulating compositions, its fluid, rapid and uncramped execution, its preference for slanting views *di sotto in sù,* it was the style of such works of Preti's as the citygate Madonnas of Naples, the Banquets (Naples, Pinacoteca, etc.) and treatments of such great biblical themes as the Parable of the Prodigal Son.

5 PRETI *Martyrdom of St Andrew*

6   PIETRO DA CORTONA *Detail of salone ceiling, Palazzo Barberini, Rome*

7   GUERCINO *Aurora, ceiling of the Casino Ludovisi*

8 PRETI *Detail of ceiling in the Palazzo Pamfili, Valmontone*

Decorative fresco painting is another field of Italian art for which Preti represents a watershed, as is clear from a comparison between his finest and most finished work in this genre, a ceiling in the Palazzo Pamfili in Valmontone,* and the frescoes of Pietro da Cortona in the Palazzo Barberini and the Palazzo Pitti. In Preti's work stucco mouldings have lost the dominant role they have in that of Cortona; the whole surface is given over to the forms which seem to blossom at the touch of Preti's brush. Compared with the brilliant, effortless, glowing colour of this sort of painting, full of living warmth despite the chill of the fresco technique, and compared with the freedom and looseness of the construction, which distributes the formal groupings in broad, loose patches round the rim of the ceiling, Cortona's work gives an impression of solidity and even heaviness.

Here too Preti stands close to a master of the High Baroque, the Guercino of the Casino Ludovisi. This is convincingly illustrated by the obliquely moving horses and the broad, animal faces of the female figures with their snub noses and heavy cheeks. The comparison with Guercino, too, reveals that Preti introduces more light and air into his compositions, with brilliant blue, pink, off-white and blond yellow. Similarly, the composition circling round the edges of the vault contrasts with the diagonal central emphasis in Guercino or Cortona. Preti's frescoes thus show the same lightening and loosening process as his easel painting; this applies to the composition, to the attitudes of the figures, and to the execution and colouring.*

Fascinating as is Mariani's account of Preti's life and work in Malta* (where he lived almost uninterruptedly from 1661 to his death), this cannot alter the fact that from the point of view of Italian painting as a whole, his mission was accomplished by the time he moved to his distant southern island.

9 PRETI *Detail of ceiling in S. Biagio, Modena*

10 GIORDANO *Wedding at Cana*

The date 1661 coincides exactly with the time at which Preti's hated and admired rival Luca Giordano* had succeeded in establishing himself. Looking at a monochrome reproduction of a characteristic work by Giordano such as his signed *Wedding at Cana* in the Pinacoteca in Vicenza one is struck first of all by the elements which it has in common with Preti:* the unorganized structure, overflowing on all sides, deprived of stability by the way in which the figures are cut off by the bottom of the frame, and thrown wholly out of balance by the positioning of the principal figures far over to the left, also cut off by the edge of the frame. The impact of the original, on the other hand, is very different. While Preti's harmony is made up of black, sombre grey and pallid bluish and greenish tints, Giordano achieves an original and splendid combination of chestnut brown, intensified in the foreground to crimson, with background tones of white, clear grey and powerful clear blue.

These light, effortlessly applied colours are one of the principal elements of the effects achieved by Giordano. The other is the compositional scheme, already described apropos of the Vicenza picture, which he loved to apply to his most individual works, and which can be seen more clearly and completely in the *Triumph of Judith* on the ceiling of the treasury of the Certosa in Naples (1704).

Turning from this to the essence of High Baroque ceiling painting in Italy, as manifested in Cortona's *Salone* of the Palazzo Barberini, the utter contrast between the two painters and the two styles is immediately apparent. The contrast is all the more instructive because in Giordano's work the forms themselves, considered in isolation, reveal the unmistakeable influence of Cortona. The inspiration which Giordano received from Cortona in his student years in Rome (c. 1649–53) is evident even in such later works as the frescoes in Florence (Medici Gallery 1683, and the Carmini dome, 1682), in Naples, (dome of Santa Brigida); and in Spain (Cason Buenretiro and the frescoes of the staircase and church of the Escorial, 1692–1702).

In the Palazzo Barberini Cortona bases his compositional scheme on a powerful triple diagonal which sweeps across the whole surface of the ceiling; Giordano develops his action in an undulating and uninterrupted linear motion, leaving the blue sky wide open for the soaring, delicately painted angels. Similarly, Cortona's figures are wild and powerful, his colours heavy, contrasting with Giordano's soft, almost flaccid forms and his dominant shades of light blue, golden yellow and white; Cortona adopts a colossal close-up view, while Giordano paints a profusion of tiny, distant figures; Cortona is possessed by an urge to go outside the limits of the ceiling itself, while Giordano observes the limits of his frame, going beyond it only in moments of playfulness.

n.9

10

n.10

1

11

11 PIETRO DA CORTONA *Ceiling of the salone, Palazzo Barberini, Rome*

12 GIORDANO *Deposition*

The bright and festive effect of Giordano's painting is certainly a product of Venetian influence. The blond, richly coiffured ladies, the whole compositional scheme of the *Wedding at Cana* in Vicenza, irresistibly recall Veronese. Giordano's origins are thus strikingly similar to those of Preti; Venetian Late Mannerism and the High Baroque. The transformation which overtook Italian painting in the 1650s was indeed largely a product of these two artistic currents.

The fact that the style of Giordano, as I have described it, was in existence by the 1650s and early 1660s is proved by such pictures as the limpid *Madonna of the* 13 *Rosary* in the Pinacoteca in Naples (1657), the *St Nicholas* in San Niccola al Nilo (1658), the *Venus* in the Palazzo di Montecitorio in Rome (1663) or the large *Allegory* in Frankfurt (1664). However, in spite of all the sources Giordano has in common with Preti, his relationship with them is fundamentally entirely different. For Preti they are powerful youthful impressions which are fashioned into a personal style; for Giordano they are nothing of the sort. We know from De' Dominici and the early guidebook literature that Giordano deliberately set out to imitate the style of the Venetian Mannerists in order to deceive the experts and the public. Nowadays it is hard to comprehend how such pictures as the *Susanna* (Familienverein Wettin, formerly in the Dresden Gallery) or the altarpiece of the Monte della Misericordia in Naples, can have been meant to deceive anybody. But simultaneously, Giordano was quite unconcernedly 12 imitating his own master Ribera (in the *Deposition* in the Accademia in Venice, the *Madonna with Saints* in the Brera, the *St Sebastian* in Dresden, or, with a strong admixture of Cortona's influence, in his earliest dated pictures in Naples, the paintings in the choir of San Pietro ad Aram, 1654). In the case of Ribera the deception is so successful that some paintings can still not be attributed with certainty to one or the other (an example is the *Philosopher* in the Galleria Corsini in Rome). Nor is this all; there exists a number of bravura pieces by Giordano in the manner of other masters far more remote in style and background than Veronese or Ribera. These include the so-called *Peace* in the Prado, *à la* Rubens, 14 and a fascinating *Healing of the Lame Man,* painted in 1653 (formerly in the Boehler Collection, Munich), which is actually painted in the style of Dürer and even boldly signed with his monogram.

It is worth reflecting on the extraordinary attitude to art which this reveals in Giordano. The usual reason for imitation, which is the desire to follow in the footsteps of a revered master, obviously does not apply; nor does the need to link a number of absolute exemplars dating from a past golden age, as in Mannerism; nor does a motive such as Poussin's recourse to Raphael and Titian by turns, according to the 'mode' of feeling appropriate to the subject of the n.11 picture.* Giordano's motive is the pure joy of deception. He sets out to amaze, to assert his skill and his superiority. He can have cared nothing for the conception of the work of art as a process of giving form to personal spiritual experience. This indiscriminate imitativeness, and his other most conspicuous characteristic as an artist, the speed of execution which earned him the nickname of 'Fa Presto', are both products of the virtuosity of the master craftsman. No painter ever painted so much in a lifetime as he did. His opus is estimated at a total of five thousand pictures, which works out at over a hundred a year, a rate which can only have been achieved by concentrating on decorative considerations to the exclusion of anything which might be described today as artistic conscience.

It is evident that these peculiar qualities in Giordano go well with his looseness of composition and undisciplined technique. The one is a sign of an evolution from Cortona and Poussin (though it may go so fast and so far as to reverse the meaning of their art)—as is the other. But while his playing with the characteristics of others and his quickness of execution are all his, the compositional schemes, the flowing technique with its avoidance of firm formal groupings, the unstable, almost floating stance of the figures—in short the whole decorative loosening of the pictorial structure—all these characteristics appear in Preti as well as in Giordano from the 1650s onwards.

13 GIORDANO *Madonna of the Rosary*

14 GIORDANO *Healing of the Lame Man*

15 MAFFEI *Allegorical Portrait of a Podestà*   III

What Preti and Giordano did for the south of Italy, Maffei and Castello did for
the north. They were the first to set up, in opposition to the High Baroque of
Strozzi and his circle, a new style which in some respects was a continuation of
what Strozzi had tried to do, but in many more important respects was its
antithesis. This they did during the same short period, and with essentially the
same programme, as Preti and Giordano.

Francesco Maffei was born *c.* 1600 and died in 1660.* But his creative career   n.12
centres on the few decisive years around 1650, during which he painted his
great *Allegorical Portrait of a Podestà* (Vicenza Pinacoteca, *c.* 1652). Like the   15
allegorical compositions of the heyday of French academicism, it is crowded
with allegorical figures and allusions which would be comprehensible only to
someone with prior knowledge of the 'programme' on which it is based. But
Maffei's temperament, his obsession with effect, the demoniacal verve of his
brushwork and the fiery glow of his colours endow it with such life and intensity
that by comparison all the paintings in the same genre by others (Le Brun, Car-
pioni, Zanchi, Celesti) seem dim. There are only two artists in whose work
Maffei could have seen something related to the exhilarating scarlet of the two
pages on the right, the pitch black of the Inquisitor, the palpitating white, gold
and lilac grey of the female figures, the rose-pink of the flesh tints (and of the
chubby-cheeked angels): they are the Jan Liss of the last *Visions* and the late
Strozzi of the Tolentini picture or the Grimani portrait.

These two antecedents, if it is possible to talk of antecedents in the case of
Maffei, may have come to his attention when, as a young man, he was in Venice
finishing some work left unfinished in the Chiesa degli Incurabili and the Tolentini church by his own totally insignificant master Peranda. Deeply though he
was indebted both to Liss and to Strozzi, however (the case is analogous to that
of Preti and the early Guercino), he translated what he had received from them
into a new and characteristically Late-Baroque unity. Elegant, delicate gestures
and heads so small as to strain credulity take the place of the sturdy, vigorous
figures in the work of his mentors; restless highlights supplant their broad
expanses of colour; their rich, juicy technique gives way to a nervous, rapid,
sketchy, slippery application of colour which never, even in so solemn a context as this, misses a chance for a bit of *capriccio*. Broad, expansive brushstrokes
give way to brushwork of the utmost brilliance and agility, High Baroque
passion and exultant physical energy to agile, pointed suppleness.

16 MAFFEI *Nativity*

Even for these characteristics, however, marked as they were by a ravishing temperament and novel as they were, taken all together, he did not entirely lack precedents. Significantly, he sought these not among the masters of the Baroque but in Late Venetian Mannerism. From Veronese especially derive his shallow, stage-like settings, his pomp and his elegant costumes (the two pages are typical), and even his delight in humorous details like the two little lapdogs, together with the entire compositional scheme of a picture such as the *Adoration of the Magi* in the Duomo at Vicenza. From the 'second manner' of Bassano Maffei took the pose of the kneeling Virgin and the large shepherd seen from behind who appear in the little-known *Nativity* in Carpenedolo. Above all, however, Maffei took from Tintoretto the convulsive line of the subsidiary figures which melt into a light grey background, and the elongated proportions. Whole compositions, like that of the *Virgin on the steps of the Temple* in Santa Maria del Soccorso at Rovigo or that of the *Visitation* at Carpenedolo, are lifted direct from Tintoretto. It is only necessary to compare the arrangement of the group of women and the attitudes of the husbands accompanying them in the latter picture with that of Tintoretto's picture of the same subject in the Scuola di San Rocco.

17 MAFFEI *Adoration of the Magi*

18 MAFFEI *Visitation*

19 TINTORETTO *Visitation*

20 CASTELLO *Rape of Proserpina*

Both in his combination of High Baroque influences with a new appreciation of Mannerism and in his treatment of pictorial form, the Genoese painter Valerio Castello (who was born in 1624) shows a close affinity with him.*   n.13 Castello's crucial works, like those of Maffei, were all produced during the 1650s (he died in 1659). Their style is conclusively akin to that of Maffei, as can be seen from the *Rape of Proserpina* (Rome, Galleria Corsini), both in vehemence   *20* of temperament and in the rapid verve of the brushstrokes; Castello, like Giordano, is praised by contemporary biographers as a *fa presto*.

Castello preserves the strict diagonal composition of the High Baroque, but in his smaller figures, light and quick in movement and largely lacking in individuality, it begins to loosen. A clear symptom of this devaluation of the individual lies in the small-headed proportions which hark back to Mannerism and forward to the Rococo.

All in all, Castello too offers a surf of forms, splashed across the whole surface of the canvas, in place of the powerful tension of the High Baroque. The colours, glowing like those of Maffei, but combined in a way which recalls Giordano, make a considerable contribution to this pursuit of unity through essentially decorative means. Dark chestnut browns are set off by a brilliant blue sky, and in between, in Pluto's cloak, in the figures of two of Proserpina's companions on the right, and in a flying *putto*, flecks of crimson glow like tongues of flame.

A look at Castello's sources tells much the same story as a look at those of Preti, Giordano and Maffei. Just as the origins of Maffei clearly lie in Liss and Strozzi on the one hand and in Tintoretto, Bassano and Veronese on the other, Castello's links are with the Genoese High Baroque of van Dyck and Orazio De Ferraris and with the Milanese Mannerist Giulio Cesare Procaccini, who worked in Genoa for part of his career. In Castello's case, indeed, it is even possible to supplement the evidence of the pictures themselves with that of written sources: Soprani says expressly that Castello was so filled with enthusiasm for Procaccini's works that he travelled to Milan especially to see more of them.

With all this evidence, it cannot be regarded as fortuitous that the revival of interest in Mannerism came at exactly the historical moment when, with the growing tendency towards a floating, wave-like unity covering the whole surface of the picture and towards a light, lively, capricious handling of the brush, the High Baroque was turning to the Late Baroque.*   n.14

IV

In the decades following 1650 the new 'libertinism' in painting began to affect even Rome herself. The painterly freedom of the north had affected the Eternal City several times since the sixteenth century. Passignano, Ligozzi, Caravaggio, Guercino, Lanfranco, even the young Sacchi and Poussin, had turned to the north for help and inspiration. But one after the other they had succumbed to the classicism of the Roman milieu, as it is manifested in their later works, and above all in these of Poussin in whose person inborn French classicism and acquired Roman classicism grandly merged. By the 1650s a few fanatical devotees of painterly freedom were sorely needed, if Rome was not to become a prey to arid classicism of the kind which blighted the French followers of Poussin.

n.15   The pathfinders were Preti, with his frescoes at Valmontone, and the
21   Genoese painter Giovanni Battista Gaulli called Baciccia.* In 1660 Gaulli created, in his *Madonna* in San Rocco, a work of such fiery colouring and such slender, unstable figure types that its echoes of van Dyck and Castello must have been as disturbing an influence in the Rome of Cortona and Poussin as Preti's fresco itself. In 1665 Gaulli applied his new style, in all its sensual brilliance, to church decoration; this was in the spandrels of the dome of Sant' Agnese, where he does not, however, conceal inspiration from Cortona.

It was not until the 1670s that the triumph of the Late Baroque—by which I mean the triumph of the ideas of the 1650s—became complete in Rome. Its principal exponent was indubitably Antonio Gherardi. His most significant works are the paintings in the Cappella Avila in Santa Maria in Trastevere and
22,23 the ceiling of Santa Maria in Trivio, painted between about 1670 and 1675. Many of Antonio Gherardi's works are admittedly of little or no interest; but it would be wrong to judge him entirely on the basis of these, as Voss does, illustrating only an insipid *Madonna* and the Genoese, Fiasella-like *Caritas*
n.16 *romana* in the Galleria Colonna.* The frescoes in Santa Maria in Trivio reveal Antonio Gherardi as an artist of considerable historical importance. The rich warmth and radiance of his colours struck a note which Rome had heard previously only in the work of Gaulli; and yet it is impossible to find any evidence of Gaulli's direct influence. The composition of the pictures, with their intrepid illusionism, is a clear link with Veronese.

21 GAULLI *Madonna*

22, 23 A. GHERARDI *Presentation of the Virgin (left), and Assumption*

After Santa Maria in Trivio, the next event in the spread of the Late Baroque in Rome was the painting of the gallery of the Palazzo Colonna by Giovanni *24* Coli and Filippo Gherardi, two Tuscan painters who had returned to Rome from Venice in 1669 full of the festive splendour and the audacious *sotto in su* of Venetian painting. The compositional freedom of their works, and the brilliance of their colouring, which sometimes even recalls Tiepolo, are without parallel in the painting of Rome.* A general air of joyous urgency fills the interpenetrating *n.17* form; in the dome of San Niccolò in 1670, the two painters from Lucca abandoned the conventional arrangement of the figures in concentric circles, and in the vault of San Pantaleone in 1690, after Coli's death, Filippo Gherardi even anticipated the zigzag composition of the Rococo, thus forestalling both Solimena and Sebastiano Ricci, the latter by a decade and a half.

Concurrently with the work of Coli and Filippo Gherardi in the Galleria Colonna and Antonio Gherardi in Santa Maria in Trivio, Gaulli was engaged on his major work, the vault of the church of the Gesù, which was begun *c.* 1670 and finished in 1683. The whole surface of the ceiling of the nave is covered with *25* a single huge painting, framed in gilt stucco. This unifying approach, which is the legacy of Cortona's High Baroque, is carried even further by Gaulli than it ever was by Cortona in the Salone of the Barberini Palace (not to speak of Cortona's later, more tranquil and classical rooms in the Palazzo Pitti). The whole picture, which from the compositional point of view consists fundamentally of rays

24 COLI AND F. GHERARDI *Gallery of the Palazzo Colonna, Rome*

25 GAULLI *Adoration of the Name of Jesus, ceiling of the Gesù, Rome*

emanating from a focal point, consists not of colossal figures and magnificently juxtaposed groups, but of broad interpenetrating light and dark patches, extremely complex in internal structure. Uninhibited use is made of the Baroque device for drawing the onlooker into the work of art which consists in allowing figures or forms to erupt, apparently, into the real space of the room. Tangled groups of damned souls seem to hang from the ceiling like bunches of grapes; clouds balloon out over the stucco frame. This ceiling is an ultimate realization of the Baroque effort, carried out with the means supplied by the revolution of the 1650s: the glowing rust brown, gold and dark blue of the colouring and the presence of large, jostling, ill-defined shapes.

The dome of the Gesù is as significant for an understanding of the new stylistic principles of the Late Baroque as is the nave. Here the artist breaks free, as only Coli and Filippo Gherardi, in San Niccolò, had previously done, of the fixed pattern of concentric rings, and establishes a free arrangement of patches of colour.

Fifteen years after the Gesù, it was the turn of the other great Jesuit church in Rome to receive its elaborate ceiling decoration. In 1685 Andrea Pozzo began work at Sant' Ignazio with the sham dome (which now no longer exists), going on to the presbytery and finally the nave.* In spite of its late date, this work belongs within the scope of this essay, because of the slowness of stylistic change in Rome and because its creator was of the generation which is under consideration.

Like Gaulli, Pozzo strives towards the ultimate integration of the picture space with real space. While Gaulli achieved his object with the resources of his own genius alone, Pozzo enlists the aid of the device of *quadratura*, which since the time of Tassi had become progressively more ingenious.

He had first met the technique of feigned architecture as a student about 1670, when on his visits to Bologna he first saw works by Vitelli, and had prepared himself for his life's work in Sant' Ignazio by painting ceilings at Mondovi (1676–7) and Modena (*c.* 1678–80). As a trained architect and an expert in all the tricks of perspective, he continued the real space upwards in complicated structures of columns and arches, and allowed the action to take place only above these. There is one vanishing-point, so that the whole effect of the painting depends, to an unprecedented degree, on the position of the onlooker. This represents the pursuit of decorative unity carried to a pitch never achieved again in Rome. The distinction between the real and imaginary architecture, between space and apparent space, is not the only one that is deliberately blurred; the placing of the viewpoint in the dead centre of the nave obscures the distinction between the functions of decorator and architect. The painter is telling the onlooker how to look at the building, not as a longitudinal form but as a centralized one. Correspondingly, the groups must not be taken apart into their constituent figures but seen as patches of light and shade (as in Gaulli), playing round the virtually elliptical form of the sham architecture, and framing, in a way we have already recognized in the work of Giordano as typical of the late seventeenth century, the groups soaring in the Empyraean, the Trinity and the ascending saints.

Pozzo and Gaulli, as Roman representatives of the Late Baroque style of Giordano, Preti, Maffei and Castello, had to contend with the perennial Roman classicism which draws nourishment from the presence of the relics of Antiquity and the High Renaissance, and which suits the character of the Eternal City better than the painterly dynamism of the Baroque style. But nothing could be a more conclusive proof of the universality of the change which took place in the 1650s than the fact that the greatest master of contemporary Roman classicism, Carlo Maratti, constantly found himself unable to conceal his links with the 'libertinists', the champions of Baroque freedom.*

His *Virgin with Saints* (1683?) in Santa Maria del Popolo, with its clear groupings and relationships, its obviously Raphaelite Virgin with yellow disc-shaped halo and a grey *putti* on the clouds, and its decidedly Sacchiesque figure

26 MARATTI *Virgin with Saints*

27

n.18

n.19

26

27 POZZO *Triumph of St Ignatius Loyola, ceiling of the nave of S. Ignazio, Rome*

28 MARATTI *Virgin and Child with
St Philip Neri*

29 RENI *Virgin and Child with
St Philip Neri*

of a pope (on the right), is miles removed from the passionate formal conglomerations of Gaulli and Castello; but it is an exceptionally classical composition, even for Maratti. And yet it is far removed from the true classicism of the age of Sacchi and Poussin. The warmth of the painter's emotional experience, and thus of his expression, has receded; and the unified, calm diagonal stress of Sacchi or the severe relief composition of Poussin has given way to a disorganized, indecisive structure. The flow of the drapery throughout the picture is soft, slack and wave-like; the colour scheme, which reaches its peak of intensity in the salmon pink of the figure of St John and the light blue and white of the Virgin, is equally effete. A conscious desire to follow Raphael clashes here with hankering, characteristic of the new age, after the superficial, the restless and the decorative.

Industrious, reflective and cautious, Maratti clearly took his preoccupation with Raphael and the pseudoclassical Reni very seriously; witness his painstaking restoration of Raphael's Logge, and his copies after Reni, such as the *Judith* in the Galleria Capitolina. And yet, as soon as he turns from literal copying he involuntarily reverts to his own personal style, which is that of the Late Baroque.

This is shown particularly clearly in the *St Philip Neri* in the Palazzo Pitti. While it is unmistakably modelled on Reni's treatment of the same subject in Santa Maria in Vallicella, the precision and clarity, the quality of simple grandeur, which Reni succeeds in imparting to the dialogue between the Virgin and the saint, lie beyond Maratti's grasp. Maratti's profusion of forms robs Reni's single eloquent diagonal of its effect. The figures have more space below to the right and above to the left, and *putti* and other supernumeraries crowd in. The parts of the canvas deliberately left bare by Reni are filled by Maratti with figures and props; Reni's single action is replaced by a general aimless movement covering the whole surface of the picture. The treatment of the draperies is particularly indicative of this transformation. Reni uses heavy materials with few folds; Maratti indulges in a soft, fragmented, unsystematic flowing movement, linking the Virgin with the saint in unarticulated waves and subsiding in gentle ripples below.

Such pictures as this reveal how Maratti's conscious classicism succumbed to his unconscious allegiance to the Late Baroque; this naturally becomes progressively more visible as Maratti frees himself from his models and seeks to express himself independently of theoretical aesthetic reflections.

In the beautiful *Immaculate Conception* of 1671 (Siena, Sant' Agostino), for instance, it is unmistakeable that for all the intensity of the expression and the simplicity of the structure, the surface is pervaded by an overall undulatory movement like that of Giordano's painting. Maratti's colouring even corresponds to that chosen by Giordano in his most personal works: against tones of warm brown and yellowish grey there stands out a cold blue, in the figure of Philip Neri, in the terrestrial globe and the pointing angel, and a pure white in the figure of the Virgin. The same is true of Maratti's mature works in general: in the altarpieces in San Carlo al Corso, in the Oratory of Santa Zita in Palermo (1695), and in Sante Maria in Vallicella—and in the Baptisms of Christ in Santa Maria degli Angeli and in the Certosa in Naples—compositional coherence is sacrificed to a general, soft, decoratively effective wavy motion.

V

Having shown examples from Naples, Venice, Genoa and Rome of the elements which distinguish the art of the years after 1650 from the High Baroque, it only remains to attempt a general synthesis of the formal principles which characterize the Italian Late Baroque. To extend my detailed investigation, say, to Bologna with Cignani (b. 1628) or to Milan with a comparison between the work of Carlo Francesco and Giuseppe Nuvoloni would have provided confirmation but would have added nothing new to what has already been said.

The central characteristic of the new painting is its compositional schemes. Instead of the single power-laden diagonal, or the conjunction of two intersecting diagonals, of the first half of the century, there appears an unpolarized, undynamic wave-like motion which covers the entire surface of the picture; in the case of ceiling painting this actually overflows the edge of the picture and leaves the centre comparatively free. This is complemented by a technique of painting which juxtaposes the broad and uninhibited gesture with a loose dotting and sprinkling of paint. Closed formal groupings are avoided—at best the painting is a conglomeration of large, disconnected patches—and the human figure is robbed of all the self-sufficiency, strength and weight that the Baroque painters had restored to it. The figure loses its stability through oblique or *sotto in sù* viewpoints, through being partly cut off by the frame, through the influence of the softness and laxity of the whole structure, or through a return to the slender, microcephalic proportions of Mannerism. A renewal of interest in Mannerism is a feature of the Late Baroque that has recurred in the consideration of one painter after another: Castello's kinship with Procaccini, Maffei's with Tintoretto, Bassano and Veronese, and the link with Veronese in Preti, Giordano, Coli and the two Gherardis, played an essential part in the formation of their style. The preference shown for Veronese over other Mannerist painters prompts the conclusion, not entirely unexpected in view of the evidence discussed above, that the artists of the Late Baroque were attracted not by the sombre, religious and mystical elements in Mannerism but by its devaluation of figure and action in favour of the enjoyment of the pictorial organism as such, in other words its tendency towards the decorative. Hence, alongside the affinity with Veronese's festive, superficial manner, there appear echoes of the sketchy, discursive, ornamental brush technique of the late sixteenth century as a whole.

30 MARATTI *Immaculate Conception*

The desire for decorative effect in fact sums up with perfect accuracy the criteria mentioned as defining the change which overtook Italian painting in the 1650s. It supplies an explanation for the unscrupulous imitativeness of Giordano, and for the general dislike of isolated figures or unified groups (signifying finite personalities or relationships between them); it accounts, in fact, for all the features which strike one as frivolous, rhetorical, unreal, when one turns from the Early Baroque (Caravaggio, Carracci) or the High Baroque (Bernini, Poussin) to the Late Baroque.

The new style made its appearance in the course of the 1650s, even though a number of the examples cited here date from somewhat later. Preti as much as Giordano, Maffei as much as Castello, Gaulli as much as Maratti, were producing works as early as 1660 which carry an unmistakeable allegiance to the formal principles of the Late Baroque.

The defining stylistic criteria of Italian Late Baroque painting and the date of its appearance once established, an attempt must be made, however briefly, to relate the information gained to the cultural and intellectual history of the period.

n.20   The art-historian who has laid most emphasis on the watershed of 1650 hitherto is Hans Rose.* This is not the place to discuss how he throws his whole discussion out of balance by drawing his stylistic criteria only from France, or to what extent these criteria have any validity for, say, German eighteenth-century architecture, or how the exclusion of church architecture from consideration increases the imbalance, or to what extent, still on French soil, a deep division separates the phase represented by Mansart from that represented by Le Vau. In other words, this is not the place to discuss how complete the parallel between French and Italian development in this instance really is. My own opinion, as has already been indicated, is that although one phase followed another, both in Italy and in France, about 1630 and subsequently again about 1650, the relative significance of the two dates differs, largely as a result of national temperament. In France it was the 1630s that were decisive, marking the passage, not between phases but between styles; in Italy the decisive moment came in the 1650s. In spite of the links, which I have emphasized in this essay, between the masters of the Late Baroque in Italy and those who immediately preceded them—Maffei with Liss and Strozzi, Castello and Gaulli with van Dyck—I regard the new values discussed here as the dominant elements in their work. These elements in Italian art link the Late Baroque painters with Ricci, Piazzetta, Solimena and Trevisani; while their French contemporary Le Brun, and French academicism in general, hark back essentially to the world of Poussin.

This does not alter the fact that in France in the 1650s there was a transition which was in many ways akin to the phenomenon in Italian painting which I have discussed here, although much less productive and less influential. Many of the signs are the same: the tendency to the rhetorical and the decorative, the tendency to over-sweetness, the schematization and the loss of genuine emotion. These tendencies underline the painting of the age of Lebrun, but not that of Poussin.* n.21

It lies beyond the scope of this essay to speculate whether the contemporary Netherlandish style of painters such as Mieris or Netscher, or even the change which came over Rembrandt's work in the 1650s, or the cool and delicate style of Vermeer and the other Delft painters, fit into the pattern of a European stylistic phenomenon corresponding in some way to events in Italy. But a few remarks can be offered on the European political and cultural background to the change which overtook Italian painting in the 1650s. From both points of view, France was the leading power in Europe, and France will provide most of the evidence.* n.22

To put it as succinctly as possible: the central factor in the evolution of seventeenth-century France is the transition from Richelieu to Mazarin. Richelieu was a 'dogmatist of power', cold, hard, admirable both for his strength and his control; Mazarin was clever, flexible, rich and vain, an opportunist, a lover of good living and a collector of costly pictures and books.* In literature the n.23 same contrast is evident between the irresistible commands of duty in Corneille and the less inhibited passion in Racine, the masculine ideal and the feminine. In cultural history the rise of the salons as a centre of political and social life marks a similar transition. In French philosophy Descartes' work was continued by the suaver, near-Christian Malebranche (1638–1715), in English philosophy Hobbes's successor was the extrovert, more approachable Locke (1632–1704). Similarly, the pietism of Pascal gave way to that of Molinos (1640–97). However, these few facts are not meant to imply an identity between them and the appearance, in the 1650s, of the Late Baroque in painting; this is an all too common misunderstanding. The references given to aspects of the totality of seventeenth-century historical evolution are only intended to convey some idea of a single cultural process, rooted in the same basic ideas, to which Italian Late Baroque painting belongs, and to which it gives its richest and most artistic form. The qualities to which I have drawn attention in widely differing fields of human activity—the dwindling of the emphasis on personality, the subordination of individual values to decorative ones, the tendency towards superficiality the reduction in the emphasis laid on masculine strength and energy and the general tendency towards softness and submissiveness—all these apply to history, literature, philosophy as much as to Late Baroque painting in Italy.

Part Two
Romanticism and Classicism

Within the plan, the following labels appear:

A Grove of ever greens

Temple of Views

Cabinet.

Cabinet.

Fruit Garden

Flower garden

An open plain of Grass

Orangery

Aromatick Herbs as Cammomile &c

Physick garden

Flower Garden

D. Hockley Sculp.

I. Langley Delin.

B. Langley Invent.

Plate VI

1   *A garden plan combining formal and 'picturesque' elements, by Batty Langley, 1728*

The Architectural Review, XCVI, 1944

IV
The Genesis of the Picturesque

n.1   SIR WILLIAM TEMPLE (1628–1699) is chiefly known as Dorothy Osborne's   1685: SIR WILLIAM TEMPLE
suitor, and from 1655 husband, as an essayist of wide and varied interests, and a
statesman who staunchly supported an Anglo-Dutch alliance, came forward
prominently when English policy was in favour of Holland, and retired when
anti-Dutch tendencies prevailed. He lived a good deal abroad, but seems to have
been happiest on his own estate, first at Richmond, then at Moor Park, near
Farnham, gardening, fruit growing, reading and writing. It was at Moor Park
that young Jonathan Swift joined his household as an amanuesis in 1689 to belong to it until Temple died. It was also at Moor Park that Temple in 1685 wrote
his *Gardens of Epicurus*, published in 1692. They contain the following description of another Moor Park, near Rickmansworth, an estate which Temple
admired so much as to take the name of his own from it.

'The perfectest figure of a garden I ever saw, either at home or abroad, was
that of Moor Park in Hertfordshire, when I knew it about thirty years ago. It was
made by the Countess of Bedford, esteemed among the greatest wits of her time,
and celebrated by Doctor Donne; and with very great care, excellent contrivance,
and much cost; but greater sums may be thrown away without effect or honour,
if there want sense in proportion to money, or if Nature be not followed; which
I take to be the great rule in this, and perhaps in everything else, as far as the
conduct not only of our lives, but our governments . . . because I take the garden
I have named to have been in all kinds the most beautiful and perfect, at least in
the figure and disposition, that I have ever seen, I will describe it for a model to
those that meet with such a situation, and are above the regards of common
expense. It lies on the side of a hill (upon which the house stands) but not very
steep. The length of the house where the best rooms, and of most use or pleasure
are, lies upon the breadth of the garden, the great parlours open into the middle of
a terrace gravel-walk that lies even with it, and which may be, as I remember,
about three hundred paces long, and broad proportion; the border set with
standard laurels and at large distances, which have the beauty of orange trees out
of flower and fruit; from this walk are three descents by many stone steps, in the
middle and at each end, into a very large parterre. This is divided into quarters by
gravel-walks and adorned with two fountains and eight statues in the several
quarters; at the end of the terrace-walk are two summer-houses, and the sides of
the parterre are ranged with two large cloisters, open to the garden, upon
arches of stone, and ending with two other summerhouses even with the cloisters, which are paved with stone, and designed for walks of shade, there being
none other in the whole parterre. Over these two cloisters are two terraces
covered with lead, and fenced with balusters, and the passage into these airy

walks, is out of the two summer-houses at the end of the first terrace walk. The cloister facing the south is covered with vines and would have been proper for gravel-walks and adorned with two fountains and eight statues in the several an orange house and the other for myrtles or other more common greens, and had, I doubt not, been cast for that purpose, if this piece of gardening had been then in as much vogue as it is now.

'From the middle of this parterre is a descent by many steps flying on each side of a grotto that lies between them (covered with lead and flat) into the lower garden, which is all fruit trees ranged about several quarters of a wilderness which is very shady; the walks here are all green, the grotto embellished with figures of shell-rockwork, fountains and waterworks. If the hill had not ended with the lower garden, and the wall were not bounded by a common way that goes through the park, they might have added a third quarter of all greens; but this want is supplied by a garden on the other side of the house, which is all of that sort—very wild, shady and adorned with rough rockwork and fountains . . .'

So Temple's admiration, as becomes a man of Wren's, Dryden's and John Locke's generation, belonged to the formal garden. It is not quite clear from his description whether Moor Park, Herts, was of the French or Dutch kind, that is, the kind which we connect with Le Nôtre and in which embroidery parterres are combined with vast axial avenues sweeping away into seeming infinity—or the kind which we connect with Le Nôtre and in which embroidery parterres with its many walled-in compartments ('frittered enclosures' Horace Walpole called them in his *History of the Modern Taste in Gardening* of 1771) and without the concentrating power of one dominating idea.

The French garden has the grandeur of the Baroque, the bold systematizing spirit of Newton, who mastered the universe as Louis XIV mastered his country and its soil; the Dutch garden is still of the Renaissance, or rather of Mannerism, in its adding up of one clearly confined spatial unit after another.

What is curious in Sir William Temple's remarks is one short passage near the beginning and another, longer passage at the end. The first passage is that in which it is implied that Moor Park 'followed nature'. To us the formal garden, as opposed to the natural English garden, is eminently unnatural. It was not so for the age of Louis XIV. '*Imiter la nature*' is not a brand-new advice of Rousseau's century. You find it everywhere in the classic French theory of poetry. Boileau draws the same parallel of formality (that is, law and order, that is '*raison*') and 'nature'. In his *Art Poétique* (1674), where he preaches his famous '*Aimez donc la raison*' he also says:

> *Que la nature donc soit votre étude unique* (Ch. IV).

You find it again in La Fontaine:

> *Et maintenant il ne faut pas*
> *Quitter la nature d'un pas.'* (*Lettre à Mancroix*, 1664).
>
> *Ils se moquent de moi qui, plein de ma lecture,*
> *Vais partout prêchant l'art de la simple nature.*
> (*Epître à Huet*, 1687.)

And it is, needless to say, all over Molière's moralizing comedies. What it means is grand simplicity and considered virtue as against the intricacies and artificially keyed-up passions of the preceding poets and authors.

But none of the French theorists had dreamt of applying this abstract notion of nature to the actual nature which surrounds us. They had been satisfied, as Temple seems to be in the passage under discussion, with a vague equation of nature, reason and universal order. Hence the formal garden appeared to be the appropriate representation of their ideals: Nature, yes, but 'nature methodized', as Pope says in his *Essay on Criticism* Part I, or 'nature corrected and amended', as Dryden said in his English translation of Bellori's famous *Idea*.

The *Idea* was the first document of art theory to preach what the French much later called *la belle nature*. It was written in 1664. French authors of

Boileau's generation adopted its conceit with great zest, especially Dufresnoy. Dryden's Bellori is attached to his translation of Dufresnoy (1695). Here he says

'The artful painter and sculptor imitating the Divine Maker, formed to themselves as well as they are able a model of the superior beauty; and reflecting on the endeavour to correct and amend the common nature, and to represent it as it was first created, without fault . . .'

What strangely contradictory theories this system of French seventeenth century aesthetics has produced! The artist should always follow nature, simple nature, that is nature in her original, primitive state and, where man has tampered with her art, must restore her by correcting 'her individual productions.' The ideal was a 'general nature', as Reynolds much later (but still influenced by Dufresnoy) called it, and the appropriateness of the French formal garden in it may not seem quite so absurd, if it is remembered that painters and sculptors, according to these theories, could nowhere be sure of finding Nature but in the stylized formality of Greek and Roman statuary.

So the classic garden poem of Louis XIV's France, René Rapin's *Of Gardens* (1665, translated by John Evelyn, 1673) contains hardly anything about simple nature in the sense in which the English have made the world understand the term. Where he talks of woods, he sees them as 'long rows of Trees' and only on the very last pages he indulges in a Horatian vision of life 'far from all noise, all vain applause', and of happy hours 'underneath some silent shade,' or 'upon a grassy bank, For which no art but nature we must thank.'

2   *The gardens at Vaux-le-Vicomte, designed by Le Nôtre about 1660*

It was left to the English, Temple first, and Shaftesbury, Addison and Pope later, to apply the doctrine of simple nature to the garden. Nature in her original state is not regular in the Le Nôtre sense, nobody could really insist on that, once it had been pointed out, and so Sir William Temple added:

'There may be other forms wholly irregular, that may, for ought I know, have more beauty than any of the others; but they must owe it to some extraordinary dispositions of nature in the seat, or some great race of fancy or judgment in the contrivance, which may produce many disagreeing parts into some figure, which shall yet upon the whole, be very agreeable. Something of this I have seen in some places, but heard more of it from others, who have lived much among the Chinese; a people, whose way of thinking seems to lie as wide as ours in Europe, as their country does.

'Among us, the beauty of building and planting is placed chiefly in some certain proportions, symmetries, or uniformities; our walks and our trees ranged so, as to answer one another, and at exact distances. The Chinese scorn this way of planting, and say a boy that can tell an hundred, may plant walks of trees in straight lines, and over against one another, and to what length and extent he pleases. But their greatest reach of imagination, is employed in contriving figures, where the beauty shall be great, and strike the eye, but without any order or disposition of parts, that shall be commonly or easily observed. And though we have hardly any notion of this sort of beauty, yet they have a particular word to express it; and where they find it hit their eye at first sight, they say the Shara-wadgi* is fine or is admirable, or any such expression of esteem. And whoever   n.2 observes the work upon the best Indian gowns, or the painting upon their best screens or purcellans, will find their beauty is all of this kind, (that is) without order.

'But I should hardly advise any of these attempts in the figure of gardens among us; they are adventures of too hard achievement for any common hands; and though there may be more honour if they succeed well, yet there is more dis-honour if they fail, and 'tis twenty to one they will.'*   n.3

This passage is one of the most amazing in the English language. It started a line of thought and visual conceptions which were to dominate first England and then the world for two centuries. It is the first suggestion ever of a possible beauty fundamentally different from the formal, a beauty of irregularity and fancy. Temple's warning against misunderstanding of such irregularity as something that comes about without art and effort was amazingly prophetic too—prophetic of the mistakes of nineteenth century *laisser-faire* committed in the name of the Picturesque. But his words were not at once taken up. For some twenty five years they had no practical effect.

1709: ANTHONY ASHLEY COOPER, THIRD EARL OF SHAFTESBURY

Shaftesbury (1671–1713) takes us into the Vanbrugh-Hawksmoor-Archer and the Defoe-Swift generation. Like Temple, he was a convinced Whig, but he preferred the philosopher's retirement and the virtuoso's social pleasures to the bustle of politics. Only for a few years did he take an active part in the political life of England and then his sustained plea was—just as Temple's—for goodwill towards Holland. 'I who am naturally so inactive', he wrote in a letter in 1701, 'am working night and day for the common interest of Holland and this country.' This sympathy for Holland, the bourgeois republic and the country of tolerance and an unaffectedly natural art of landscape painting is very significant, as will be shown later. None of Shaftesbury's philosophical writings appeared before 1708.

The passages quoted below are from *The Moralists*, written in 1709 and pub-lished in 1711.* The book is in the form of Platonic dialogues, a form chosen by   n.4 Shaftesbury because of his own Platonic ideals and because of its easy flow, contrary to the still prevailing pedantry of school philosophy.

'Your Genius, the Genius of the Place, and the Great GENIUS have at last pre-vail'd. I shall no longer resist the passion in me for things of a natural kind;

where neither Art, nor the Conceit or Caprice of Man has spoil'd their genuine order, by breaking in upon that primitive State. Even the rude Rocks, the mossy Caverns, the irregular unwrought Grotto's, and broken Falls of Waters, with all the horrid Graces of the Wilderness itself, as representing NATURE more, will be the more engaging, and appear with the Magnificence beyond the formal Mockery of princely Gardens.'

This passage is of such far-reaching importance that it must be interpreted point for point. The first sentence receives its sense from the context of *The Moralists*— a conversation between a sceptic (whose scepticism is towards the end overcome) and a philosopher after Shaftesbury's heart, a wealthy man living in the country and spending his time in edifying conversation and solitary walks—a consciously Horatian ideal *procul negotiis*. But his communication with nature has a higher than the chiefly pastoral sense of Horace. Here are two quotations to illustrate the two approaches:

'The Verdure of the Field, the distant Prospects, the gilded Horizon, and purple Sky, form'd by the setting sun [have] . . . Charms in abundance'.

That is Horace englished, praise of native scenery, and the Genius of the Place, Vergil's *genius loci* (*Aen.* V. 95) as the genius of an English country seat. But the following is something quite different:

'Ye Fields and Woods, my Refuge from the toilsome World of Business, receive me in your quiet Sanctuarys, and favour my Retreat and thoughtful Solitude . . . O Glorious Nature! supremely fair and sovereignly Good! All-loving, and All-lovely, All-Divine! Whose looks are so becoming, and of such infinite Grace; whose Study brings such Wisdom and whose Contemplation such Delight!'

Here Shaftesbury speaks out his own soul, not ashamed of being accused of enthusiasm, on the contrary, proud of being a "new Enthusiast". Nature and the *genius loci* here are only our terrestrial help for 'obtaining at least some faint and distant view of the sovereign Genius and first beauty,' the divine principle which reveals itself in Nature. The centrepiece of Shaftesbury's philosophy is this conception of a beautiful universe, all order and all goodness. For 'Beauty and Goodness [are] . . . the same'. This emphasis on the aesthetic approach comes, of course, from Plato. It marks the beginning of modern aesthetics. Through Hutcheson it becomes a characteristic item in the system of the Picturesque. In it nature worship is the worship of visible harmony, of the 'primitive state', before the sophistication of our own age spoilt it, the state corresponding in ethics to 'simple, plain-look'd Virtue', to temperance, Shaftesbury's key virtue, and to ease, and the very opposite of that 'Folly and Perverseness' of man which, according to Shaftesbury, is 'quite out of the way of Nature'. This attitude conceals a curious contradiction. Shaftesbury's own enthusiasm may go well with rocks, cascades and wilderness—romantic scenery in fact—but Shaftesbury does not really mean what he describes, he uses his wilderness as a symbol of nature in her 'primitive state' and thus a symbol of universal order, Newton's, Hooke's and Wren's order, the all-pervading order revealed to the seventeenth century by microscope and telescope:

'that consummate Art exhibited thro' all the Works of Nature; since our weak Eyes, help'd by mechanick Art, discover . . . a hidden Scene of Wonders; Worlds within Worlds, of infinite Minuteness . . . and pregnant with more Wonders . . . than the acutest Reason, can penetrate or unfold'.

This obviously refers to the microscope. And the pages on stars, sun, planets and 'this Mansion-Globe, this Man-Container' refer to Newton's ordered universe:

'Nothing surely is more strongly imprinted on our Minds, or more closely interwoven with our Souls, than the Idea or Sense of Order and Proportion.

Hence all the Force of Numbers, and those powerful Arts founded on their Management and Use . . . What a difference . . . between the regular and uniform Pile of some noble Architect, and a Heap of Sand or Stones!'

This last sentence seems to take us back to Boileau's and Temple's equation of order and nature. In fact, it goes beyond them, away from the seventeenth and into the eighteenth century, in two significant ways: Shaftesbury's enthusiasm is new, 'Rubenisme', as it were, as against the 'Poussinisme' of Boileau. And—more important still—the application to architecture is new. It provides a first answer to one of the fundamental problems of the English eighteenth century. Shaftesbury's argument makes it possible to understand how 'regular and uniform' buildings co-exist with the 'horrid Graces of the Wilderness'. To us Palladianism seems to belong to the formal garden, 'the formal Mockery of princely Gardens'. To the Augustans it was the visible symbol of man's achievements in ordering his works according to the same eternal laws of harmony, order and proportion as Nature does in her works.

Addison and Pope a few years later further expounded this theme.

1712: THE SPECTATOR   ADDISON (1672–1719) just like Temple and Shaftesbury, was a Whig. We find him in public employment as soon as the Whigs were in power. He had been on the Grand Tour through France (where he met Boileau), Italy, Austria, Germany and Holland, from 1699 to 1703. His fame rests on the daily essay-leaflets of popular philosophy which he published with his friend Steele between 1709 and 1713, first the *Tatler*, then the *Spectator*, and then the *Guardian*, effective instruments to promote reason and virtue. Their style is unaffected, their thought limpid, their manner urbane.

'There is generally in nature something more grand and august, than what we meet with in the curiosities of art. When, therefore, we see this imitated in any measure, it gives us a nobler and more exalted kind of pleasure, than what we receive from the nicer and more accurate productions of art. On this account our English gardens are not so entertaining to the fancy as those in France and Italy, where we see a large extent of ground covered over with an agreeable mixture of garden and forest, which represents everywhere an artificial rudeness, much more charming than that neatness and elegancy which we meet with in those of our own country. It might, indeed, be of ill consequence to the public, as well as unprofitable to private persons, to alienate so much ground from pasturage and the plough, in many parts of a country that is so well peopled, and cultivated to a far greater advantage. But why may not a whole estate be thrown into a kind of garden by frequent plantations, that may turn as much to the profit as the pleasure of the owner? A marsh overgrown with willows, or a mountain shaded with oaks, are not only more beautiful but more beneficial, than when they lie bare and unadorned. Fields of corn make a pleasant prospect and, if the walks were a little taken care of that lie between them, if the natural embroidery of the meadows were helped and improved by some small additions of art, and the several rows of hedges set off by trees and flowers that the soil was capable of receiving, a man might make a pretty landskip of his own possessions . . .

'Writers who have given us an account of China, tell us the inhabitants of that country laugh at the plantations of our Europeans, which are laid out by the rule and line; because, they say, any one may place trees in equal rows and uniform figures. They choose rather to show a genius in works of this nature and therefore always conceal the art by which they direct themselves. They have a word, it seems, in their language, by which they express the particular beauty of a plantation that thus strikes the imagination at first sight without discovering what it is that has so agreeable an effect. Our British gardeners, on the contrary, instead of humouring nature, love to deviate from it as much as possible. Our trees rise in cones, globes and pyramids. We see the marks of the scissors upon every plant and bush. I do not know whether I am singular in my opinion; but, for my own part, I would rather look upon a tree in all its luxuriance and diffusion of boughs and branches, than when it is thus cut and trimmed into a mathematical figure; and cannot but fancy that an orchard in flower looks infinitely more delightful, than all the little labyrinths of the most finished parterre.'

'I have several acres about my house, which I call my garden, and which a skilful gardener would not know what to call. It is a confusion of kitchen and parterre, orchard and flower garden, which lie so mixed and interwoven with one another, that if a foreigner, who had seen nothing of our country, should be conveyed into my garden at his first landing, he would look upon it as a natural wilderness, and one of the uncultivated parts of our country . . . There is the same irregularity in my plantations, which run into as great a wilderness as their nature will permit. I take in none that do not naturally rejoice in the soil; and am pleased, when I am walking in a labyrinth of my own raising, not to know whether the next tree I shall meet with is an apple, or an oak, an elm, or a pear-tree . . . I must not omit, that there is a fountain rising in the upper part of my garden, which forms a little wandering rill, and administers to the pleasure as well as the plenty of the place. I have so conducted it, that it visits most of my plantations; and have taken particular care to let it run in the same manner as it would do in an open field, so that it generally passes through banks of violets and primroses, plats of willow, or other plants, that seem to be of its own producing.

'I think there are as many kinds of gardening as of poetry; your makers of parterres and flower gardens are epigrammatists and sonneteers in this art; contrivers of bowers and grottos, treillages and cascades, are romance writers. Wise and London are our heroic poets . . . As for myself, you will find, by the account which I have already given you, that my compositions in gardening are altogether after the Pindaric manner, and run into the beautiful wildness of nature, without affecting the nicer elegancies of art.'

I repeat the gist of these two passages before trying to interpret them. Nature is according to Addison better than Art, an artificial rudeness better than neatness, a freely spreading tree better than one trimmed in the Dutch manner into a geometrical or animal shape, and an orchard better than a parterre of 'mathematical figure'. This latter term brings up again the very contradiction which was pointed out in Shaftesbury's aesthetics; dislike of mathematics in the garden but admiration for the principles of mathematical order in the universe which Newton had firmly established, an ardent enthusiasm for 'the immensity and magnificence of nature . . . so many worlds hanging one above another, and sliding round their axles in such an amazing pomp and solemnity' (*Spectator*, No. 420).* Surely pomp and solemnity would correspond in the art of the garden to Le Nôtre and not to Addison's 'agreeable mixture of Garden and Forest.'

n.5

H. Wise and G. London, whom Addison so politely terms the heroic poets of gardening, stood entirely for the French formal style. They translated one of the most popular of classic French handbooks, de la Quintinie's (1626–c. 1700) *Parfait Jardinier*. Their translation appeared in 1699 with a second edition in 1704 and a third in 1710; but John Evelyn had already published one in 1693, and Evelyn, of course, represented the Parisian trend in later Stuart England. There is, as has already been said, also a translation of Rapin by him (1673). Another more elegant one was brought out by James Gardiner in 1709. Besides Quintinie, Dezallier d'Argenville (1680–1765) was the most widely read French gardening theorist. His *Théorie et Pratique du Jardin* appeared in 1709, with an English translation by John James the Hawksmoorian architect, as early as 1712. It is characteristic enough that James four years before had translated Perrault's *Orders*. Now all the illustrations in all these books—exactly contemporary with Addison's weeklies—represent the French style, so that it can be assumed that Addison would not have put in his compliment to Wise and London, had they not been the Royal Gardeners. For Addison is as outspoken against the formal garden as Shaftesbury. And like him he sets against it Nature.

But while Shaftesbury was at his best when he revelled in wild, uninhabited scenery, Addison's heart goes out to the humanized scenery of the English countryside. And so, while Shaftesbury never applied his nature worship to gardening, Addison did, certainly on paper if not also on his estate at Bilton in Warwickshire. His suggestions, 'Why may not a whole Estate be thrown into a kind of Garden', and again, 'a man might make a pretty Landskip of his Possessions,' are the start of English landscaping. The use of the word landscape is significant too. The word first appeared in the sixteenth or early seventeenth century to designate painted scenery and already in Milton's *Allegro* (1632) was used for real scenery of an appeal similar to that of a picture. The term Picturesque, so important during the second half of the eighteenth century, is heralded in this use.

And the character of the landscape garden of that later phase is heralded in *The Spectator* too, a type of garden as artless as Chevy Chase, the folk ballad which Addison was the first to admire, or as Roger de Coverley, Addison's favourite character in *The Spectator,* and a type of garden with plenty of individuality and variety of composition. However, this emphasis on the irregular —once more a remarkable contradiction to the rationalist's avowed faith in universal rule—is not only a national mark of freedom, but also a historical mark of the coming of a new European style in art: the Rococo—the style par excellence of variety, irregularity and the *aperçu*. So Addison unknowingly pleads for Rococo, although a Rococo in a typically English way applied to the open country and not to interior decoration.

Addison and the Rococo may seem incongruous enough a juxtaposition. What if Pope's attitude towards nature and gardening can be interpreted in the same way?

1713: THE GUARDIAN   POPE was fifteen years younger than Addison, and almost exactly the same age as Lord Burlington and William Kent. His crystal-clear classicism of form corresponds to their architectural Palladianism, too. But while they draw on Antiquity by means of the Italian Renaissance, his principal source was still the Baroque classicism of Louis XIV. *The Rape of the Lock* follows Boileau's *Lutrin,* as the *Essay on Criticism* does Boileau's *Art Poétique*. However, he did not wholly agree with Boileau. There is one difference of particular importance in our context. In Part III of the *Essay on Criticism* (1711), Pope says that

> . . . critic learning flourished most in France;
> The rules a nation, born to serve, obeys,
> And Boileau still in right of Horace sways,
> But we, brave Britons, foreign laws despise . . .

So Pope, the Tory, is at one with Shaftesbury (whose philosophy he popularized) and Addison, the Whig, in opposing English liberty to French servitude. His attitude to nature and gardening is accordingly similar to theirs. It was formulated in *The Guardian* in 1713, translated into practice in his own garden at Twickenham in 1719–25, and revised in the *Essay on Man* of 1733 and the *Epistle to the Earl of Burlington* of 1731. Pope died in 1744, four years before Kent and nine before Burlington.

'I lately took a particular friend of mine to my house in the country, not without some apprehension that it could afford little entertainment to a man of his polite taste, particularly in architecture and gardening, who had so long been conversant with all that is beautiful and great in either. But it was a pleasant surprise to me, to hear him often declare, he had found in my little retirement that beauty which he always thought wanting in the most celebrated seats of the nation . . .

'There is certainly something in the amiable simplicity of unadorned nature, that spreads over the mind a more noble sort of tranquility, and a loftier sensation of pleasure, that can be raised from the nicer scenes of art . . . This was

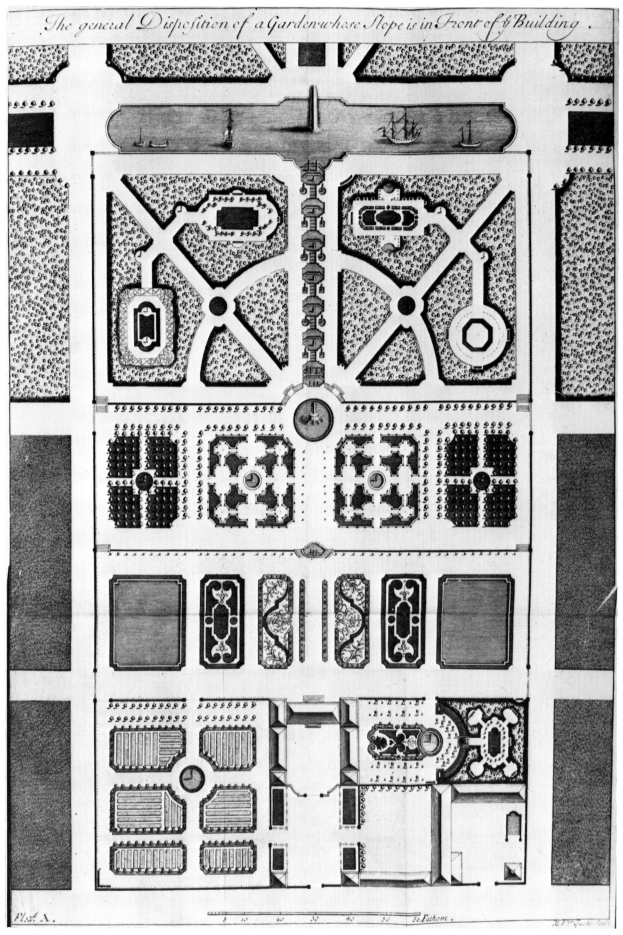

The general Disposition of a Garden whose Slope is in Front of ye Building.

3   Plan of a garden sloping away from the house, from James's translation of Dezallier d'Argenville, 1712

the taste of the ancients in their gardens, as we may discover from the descriptions extant of them. The two most celebrated wits of the world have each of them left us a particular picture of a garden; wherein those great masters, being wholly unconfirmed, and painting at pleasure, may be thought to have given a full idea of what they esteemed most excellent in this way.
These (one may observe) consist entirely of the useful part of horticulture, fruit-trees, herbs, water, etc. The pieces I am speaking of are Virgil's account of the old Corycian, and Homer's of that of Alcinous. The first of these is already known to the English reader by the excellent versions of Mr. Dryden and Mr. Addison. The other having never been attempted in our language with any elegance, and being the most beautiful plan of this sort that can be imagined, I shall here present the reader with a translation of it.'

The translation follows containing such items as 'a green enclosure all around', 'order'd vines in equal ranks', and 'beds of various herbs, for ever green, in beauteous order'—that is all features reminiscent more of the Dutch than the natural garden. However, Pope praises Alcinous's simplicity, and continues:

'How contrary to this simplicity is the modern practice of gardening? We seem to make it our study to recede from nature, not only in the various tonsure of greens into the most regular and formal shapes, but even in monstrous attempts beyond the reach of the art itself. We run into sculpture, and are yet better pleased to have our trees in the most awkward figures of men and animals, than in the most regular of their own . . . I believe it is no wrong observation that persons of genius, and those who are most capable of art, are always most fond of nature [and] . . . chiefly sensible, that all art consists in the imitation and study of nature. On the contrary, people of the common level of understanding are principally delighted with the little niceties and fantastical operations of art, and constantly think that finest which is least natural. A citizen is no sooner proprietor of a couple of yews, but he entertains thoughts of erecting them into giants, like those of Guild-hall.'

Addison had called them nine-pins. Pope, as usual more biting in his criticism than Addison, adds a whole 'catalogue of greens to be disposed of by an eminent town-gardener', containing such items as 'Adam and Eve in yew; Adam a little shattered by the fall of the tree of knowledge in the great storm; Eve and the serpent very flourishing', or 'A Queen Elizabeth in phylyraca, a little inclining to the green sickness, but of full growth.'
From the point of view of principle there is nothing new in these thoughts of Pope. There is again the Horatian conceit of blissful retirement, again the praise of unadorned nature, and again the doctrine that all good art should be based on the imitation and study of nature—a doctrine developed by Pope for the art of poetry in his *Essay on Criticism*. Here we find him preach (Part I):

> First follow Nature, and your judgment frame
> By her just standard, which is still the same . . .
> Unerring Nature . . . must to all impart,
> At once the source, and end, and test of art.
> Art from that fund each just supply provides,
> Works without show, and without pomp presides.
> Those rules of old, discover'd, not devis'd,
> Are nature still, but nature methodized.
> Nature, like liberty, is but restrain'd
> By the same laws which first herself ordained.

Twenty-two years later, in his *Epistle to Lord Burlington*, Pope applied these principles explicitly to architecture and gardening. Timon, that is the Duke of Chandos, is blamed for pompous buildings, worldly music in the chapel (the souls 'dance upon a jig to Heaven'), and formal gardens, where

No pleasing intricacies intervene,
No artful wildness to perplex the scene;
Grove nods at grove, each alley has a brother,
And half the platform just reflects the other.

Against this Baroque attitude of forcing nature into shapes of human conception, Pope sets Lord Burlington's taste—that is the new Palladian taste—and recommends, apparently as its logical counterpart, to 'consult the genius of the place in all' and evolve out of it a natural garden. 'Let nature never be forgot,' he preaches, and adds:

But treat the goddess like a modest fair,
Nor overdressed, nor leave her wholly bare.
Let not each beauty everywhere be spied,
When half the skill is decently to hide.
He gains all points, who pleasingly confounds
Surprises, varies and conceals the bounds.

Now while the principles underlying this joint recommendation of Burlingtonian architecture and landscape gardening are Shaftesbury's and Addison's, there is a new flavour in some of Pope's lines, a flavour curiously in opposition to the transparency of his style and the plainness of his thought. Intricacy, surprise and variety are qualities which amongst improvers we connect with Uvedale Price more than with the Augustans. Yet here they appear—and Pope's compliment to 'a work to wonder at—perhaps a Stowe', can remind us of the fact that at least by 1733, gardens were actually in existence which conformed to Pope's request. Lord Burlington's Chiswick Villa had one of them and it seems to have been begun as early as about 1715–20.

Pope's own garden at Twickenham was another early example—so early in fact that Pope remains the first of the garden theorists to put their principles, or at least some of them, into practice. He bought the house with five acres of ground in 1719. In a letter of February, 1719, he describes himself, as 'pursuing n.6 buildings, planting and gardening.' *

In 1720 he says that his new 'building rises'. In July, 1722, the grotto was ready for visitors. In February, 1723, Gay wrote to Swift that 'of late' Pope 'has n.7 talked only as a gardener'.* A detailed description of the whole garden is contained in a letter of Pope to Edward Blount of June, 1725. From it and the engraving in J. Serle, *A Plan of Mr. Pope's Garden,* 1745, we know that the house

4   *Pope's villa at Twickenham: the river front*

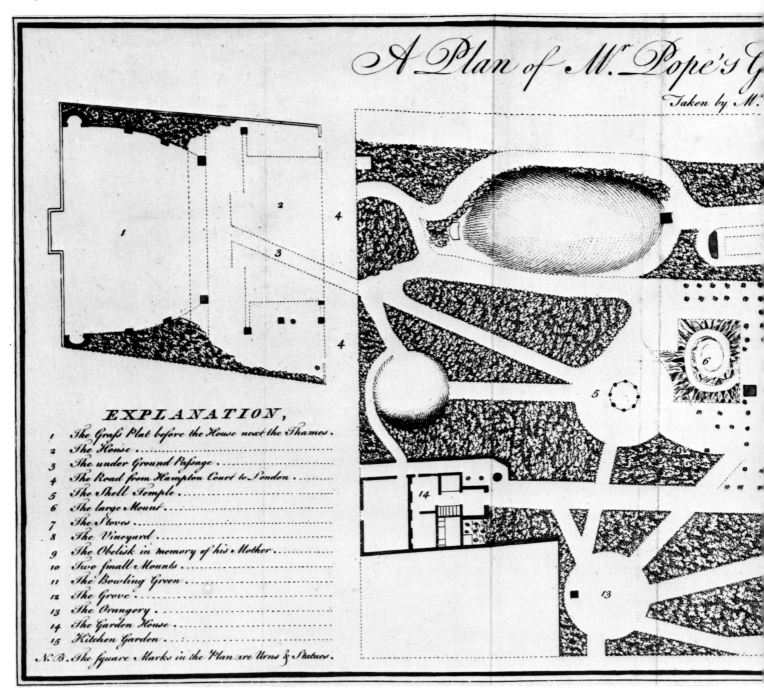

A Plan of Mr Pope's G

Taken by M.^r

EXPLANATION,

1   The Grass Plat before the House next the Thames.
2   The House ....
3   The under Ground Passage ....
4   The Road from Hampton Court to London ....
5   The Shell Temple ....
6   The large Mount ....
7   The Stoves ....
8   The Vineyard ....
9   The Obelisk in memory of his Mother ....
10 Two small Mounts ....
11 The Bowling Green ....
12 The Grove ....
13 The Orangery ....
14 The Garden House ....
15 Kitchen Garden ....

N. B. The square Marks in the Plan are Urns & Statues.

5, 6 Pope's garden at Twickenham:
Serle's plan of 1745 showing the garden's
extent from the river (far left) to
the obelisk beyond the road, and
(below right) the grotto

had a sloping lawn in front towards the river. At its back ran the road to Hampton. The garden lay on the other side of the road and to connect the two Pope had dug his grotto, and underground passages lined with bits of minerals given him by friends, and paved with pebbles. This grotto fortunately survives as part of St Catharine's High School for Girls. Where the passage emerged into the garden there was a circular shell temple and a mount of which Serle tells us that it consisted of 'various sorts of Stone, thrown promiscuously together in imitation of an old ruin.' North of temple and mount was a round-pond with straight radial paths in the French tradition. The paths further west were irregular, but the central axis of the whole composition was studiously kept. Many urns and statues were scattered about. There also existed a wilderness between garden and highway and a miniature vineyard south of the bowling green. The whole affair was so small that Pope compares his gardening efforts with those of a 'fellow who spent his life in cutting the twelve apostles in a cherry stone.'

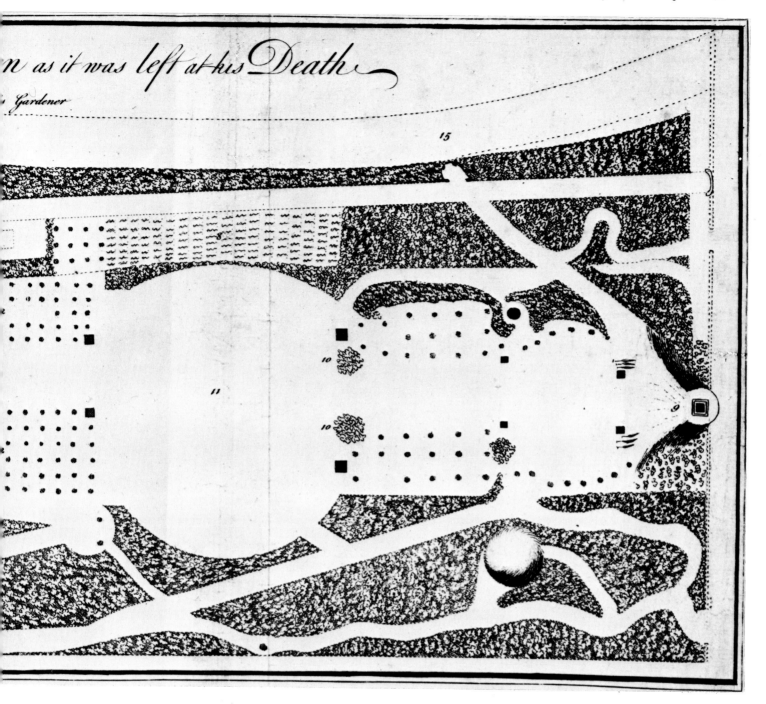

n as it was left at his Death

Gardener

The scale also prevented the garden from appearing like untouched nature in the sense in which, for instance, Capability Brown aimed at such effects thirty years later. It was a very conscious work of art, although Pope stressed emphatically 'how little it owes to art'. But then, once more, Pope's conception of nature was not Brown's nor ours. His grotto to us belongs without any doubt to the grottoes of Mannerism in the Boboli Gardens, of the Baroque in Versailles, and the Rococo, say, at the Bayreuth Eremitage. This collecting of titbits of ore is that of the sixteenth to eighteenth century *cabinets de curiosités*. Yet in his poem on the grotto Pope exclaims: 'Approach! Great nature studiously behold!'

So where are we? The garden no longer exists, but if it did, we would now probably call it Rococo more than anything else, with its wiggly paths, its minute mount, its cockle shells and minerals, and its effects of variety on a small scale.*

By 1720, then, the 'natural' style in architecture, that is, the elaborate formality of symmetrical Palladianism, and the 'natural' style in gardening, that

n.8

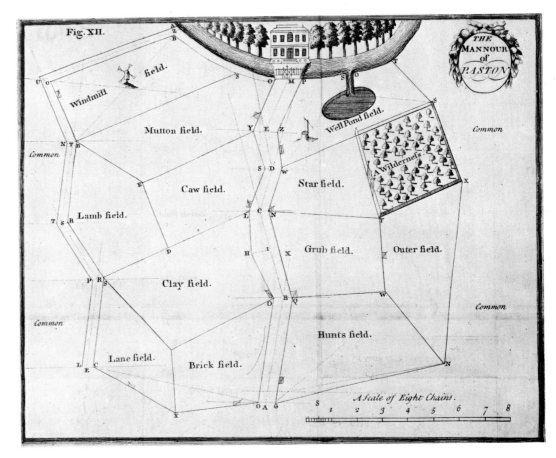

is, the elaborate formality of asymmetrical Rococo were both ready. It is well enough known how rapidly Palladian architecture spread. 'Rococo' landscape gardening conquered England with an impetus just as forceful. Pope was consulted between 1719 and 1725 on Richmond Lodge, Marble Hill, Twickenham, and Down Hall, Essex. Concurrently the most enterprising of professional gardeners got hold of the new ideas and started publicizing them.

1718: STEPHEN SWITZER STEPHEN SWITZER (1682–1745) served his apprenticeship under George London and H. Wise, the Royal Gardeners, and later worked for the Earl of Orrery, Lord Brooke and Lord Bathurst. He kept a shop in Westminster as a nurseryman and seedsman. He also edited agricultural papers. In 1715 he published *The Nobleman's Recreation, or an Introduction to Gardening, Planting, Agriculture, etc.* The book contains nothing of importance for the history of landscaping. By 1718, however, owing to the growing interest of patrons in Addison's and Pope's ideas, he brought out a second edition three times the size of the former. The title was changed to *Ichnographia Rustica*. The following quotations are taken from it.

Switzer blames English gardeners, because they 'Strain Nature beyond her due Bonds' (II,197), or 'Love to deviate from it as much as possible' (III,2). Their mistake is their 'stiff, Mathematical . . . Drafts' (III,XI) and their exclusive faith in a 'fine Sett Gardening' (III, 2). However, these gardeners—and he mentions his master, London, amongst them, because of a projected star design of straight radial avenues in the woods of Castle Howard (II, 198)—may soon be out of fashion, for a number of 'Gentlemen of very good Genius's and Dispositions . . . esteem their style, as too stiff and formal, and . . . not capable of giving so great Satisfaction to the Eye . . . as the more beautiful tho' less elaborate Works of Nature'' (III, 2).

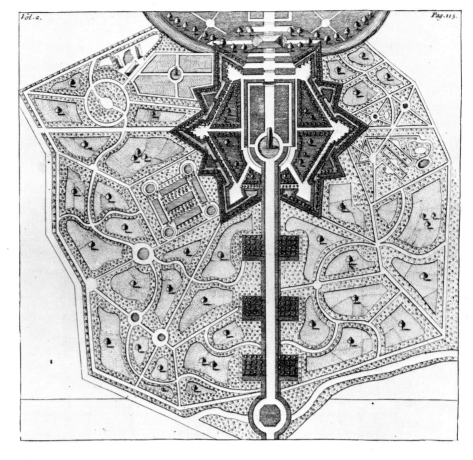

7, 8 The Manor of Paston, before (left) and after (right) the laying-out of a garden, from Switzer's 'Ichnographia' of 1718. The garden combines winding paths with a formal axis

Switzer's sympathy is obviously with these new principles. He contrasts 'the regular designer' with a 'natural gardener'. The former, he says, may be of use 'near the main Building' where 'a little regularity is allowed' (III,5) but the latter who makes 'his design submit to Nature, and not Nature to his Design' (II,200) ought to have his way for all outlying parts of an estate. 'He ought to pursue Nature . . . and by as many Twinings and Windings as the Villa will allow' (III,6) make his design 'more rural, natural, more easy and less expensive' (III,1). Whether to do that would mean creating a wilderness or a scene of pastoral peace, Switzer doesn't decide. On the one hand he pleads for 'a flourishing wilderness cut out into the utmost Variety of Walks, especially solitary Walks' (III,125) and with 'little Gardens, Caves, little natural cascades and Grottos of water' (II,201) hidden in their depths. On the other hand, he asserts that 'an even decent Walk carry'd thro' a corn field of Pasture, thro' little natural Thickets and Hedge Rows, is as pleasing as the most finish'd Parterre' (III,6).

This inconsistency we have met before: in Addison's two *Spectator* articles. And in fact Switzer mentions explicitly 'the ingenious author of the Spectator' (III,3) and takes over from him a passage such as this: 'A whole Estate may appear as one great Garden' (III,VI). Again, if he says:

'In truth the loose Tresses of a Tree . . . easily fann'd by every gentle Breeze of Air . . . are much more entertaining than the utmost exactitude of the most finisht Parterre' (III, 2–3).

we remember at once Addison's 'I for my own part—'. Switzer also knew Pope. He recommends Pope's *Windsor Forest* as one of the 'writings of the Poets on the subject . . . of Rural Scenes' with which gardeners should acquaint themselves, together with Homer, Virgil, Ovid and Milton's *Paradise* (III,6). He also incidentally recommends to gardeners that they should acquire

'a general idea of every thing that is Noble and Stately in the Productions of Art, whether in Painting or Statuary, in the great Works of Architecture, which are in their present Glory, or in the Ruins of those which flourished in former Ages' (III,6).

But he was a practical man, and he knew that a book wholly based on the new principles would not get him enough patrons. So he does not deny to 'regular Design' a raison d'être. He includes plenty of parterre patterns in his book and plenty of bosquets with straight walks. He even suggests to have in his woods figures of 'Hares, Pheasants and Sylvan Deities all cut out in wood' (II,200), and to clip hedges into the shapes of columns, pilasters and niches (II,221). His own designs of the natural kind are exactly as 'transitional' as such remarks. The straightness of the main axes is still rigorously kept, and the curves of the winding paths are tame and undetermined. The *Ichnographia* is a milestone all the same.

It shows that by 1718—that is, before Pope had bought his Twickenham estate—an enterprising gardener of thirty-six could risk to place before landowners some of the principles of landscape gardening and hope thereby to obtain their custom. His are the earliest plans of irregular gardens which have survived. But they are followed after only a few years by two engravings of real gardens which so far have not appeared in the landscaping literature.

1715 to 1722: BRITANNIA ILLUSTRATA

JAN KIP was born at Amsterdam in 1652 or 1653, went to England about 1690 and stayed there until he died in 1707. His fame rests on his bird's-eye views of English country seats, some drawn and engraved by him, the majority drawn by Leonard Knyff (1650–1721) and engraved by Kip, first in 1707 as *Britannia Illustrata*, and then again as *Nouveau Théâtre de la Grande Bretagne* in 1714 to 1716. The British Museum possesses a late edition in two volumes, again called *Britannia Illustrata,* and dated 1720 in the first and 1740 in the second volume. Gardens and grounds in the first are all formal, in the second, however, two show improvements in the new style. In the plate of Mr. Sandy's estate at Miserden a 'wandering rill' appears on the right, so artfully meandering that it must be the work of man trying to outdo nature, and behind it a serpentine lake, separated from the rill by a lock, it seems—the earliest serpentine lake I know; for the plate is signed *J. Kip del. et sculps.*, and must therefore be pre-1721. Mr Ralph Freeman's house Hammels, in Hertfordshire was designed by T. Badeslade and engraved by J. Harris. The plate in the British Museum volume is dated 1722. It shows a normal compartmented Dutch garden, except for one small area on the left, which has hedges laid out and trimmed so as to form walks more arbitrarily irregular than any of Switzer's designs.

Horace Walpole in his *History of the Modern Taste in Gardening* claims for Charles Bridgeman and the great Kent the title inventors of the new style. Of Bridgeman he says that he 'banished verdant sculpture, and . . . though he still adhered much to strait walks with high clipt hedges, they were only his great lines; the rest he diversified by wilderness . . . though still within surrounding hedges.'

Bridgeman, according to Walpole, invented the ha-ha, that is the sunk fence, but only Kent drew the most important conclusion from this disappearance of a visible division between garden and estate: he 'saw that all nature was a garden.' Of Bridgeman's work not much is known and very little survives. Kent did not return from Italy until 1719. Then, between 1720 and 1730, the movement began to spread. Twickenham must have considerably impressed a number of noblemen. Mr Sherburn in his book *The Early Career of Alexander Pope* (1937) talks of the poet's intimacy with Bridgeman and Kent, and of visits to such seats as Lord Bathurst's at Cirencester, the Hon. Robert Digby's at Sherbourn in Oxfordshire, Viscount Cobham's at Stowe, the Countess of Suffolk's (Mrs Howard) at Marble Hill, Twickenham, and the Earl of Oxford's at Down Hall in Essex. Then, in 1728, another gardening book appeared, and one apparently of wider circulation than Switzer's.

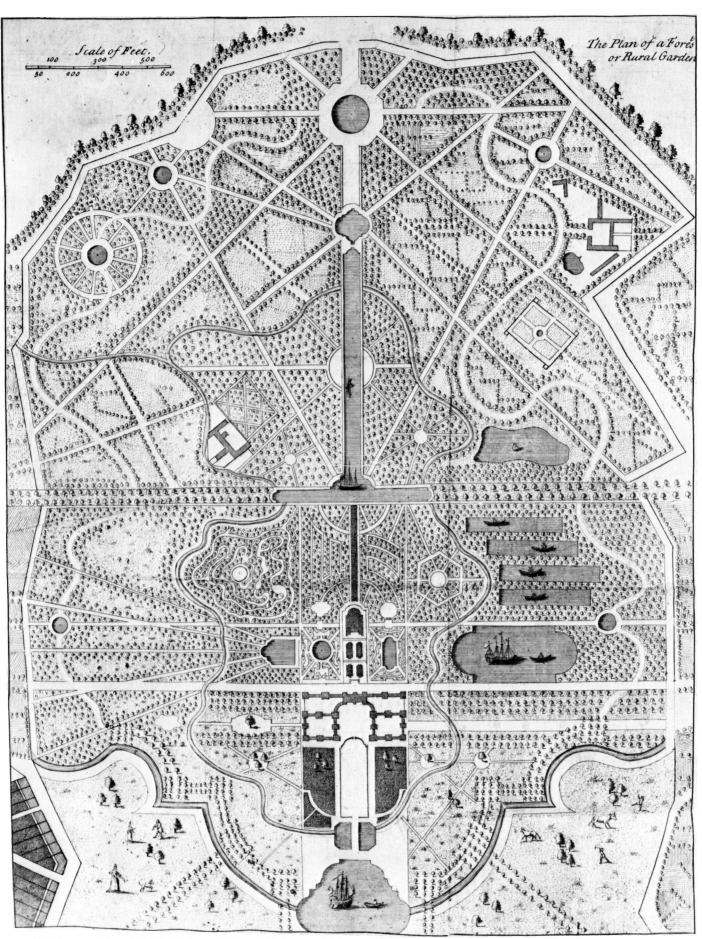

Scale of Feet.

The Plan of a Forest
or Rural Garden

9 '*A Forest or Rural Garden*', *from Switzer's* '*Ichnographia*', *1718*

10 The estate of William Sandys at Miserden, with a 'wandering rill', from Jan Kip

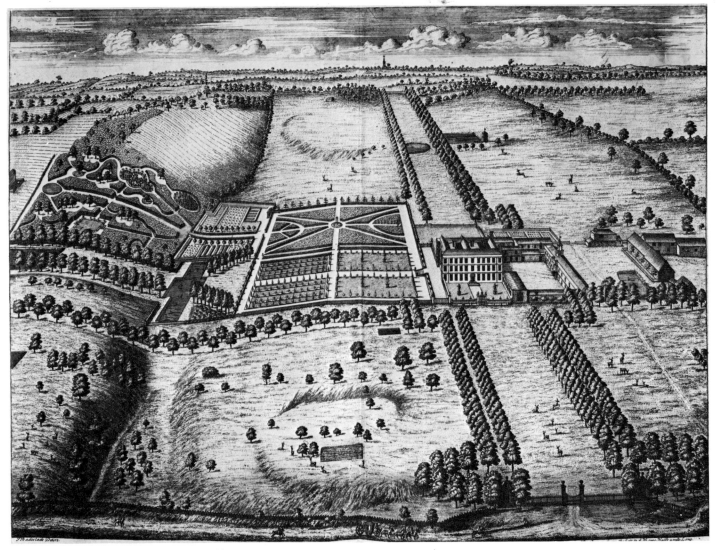

11 *Hammels in Hertfordshire, engraved by Jan Kip c. 1720*

1728: BATTY LANGLEY   LANGLEY (1696–1751) was an able architectural publicist first and foremost, something like the Loudon of his day. He was the son of a gardener, and for a time a gardener himself. In his *Principles of Gardening*, published in 1728, from which the following quotations are taken, he advertises himself on one of the first pages. His advice, he says, 'may be commanded to any part of Great Britain or Ireland for the laying out and planting of Gardens.' He does not, however, seem to have been specially successful in that line, and so started a new one, the publication of elementary handbooks for builders. He had an inexhaustible inventiveness in titles: *The Builder's Chest book, A Sure Guide to Builders, The Young Builder's Rudiments, The Builder's Compleat Assistant, The Builder's Treasury of Design, The Builder's Jewel, The Measurer's Jewel, The Builder's Director*, and *The Workman's Golden Rule*, followed each other at intervals of a few years. Just as he tried to cash in on the growing fashion for a Rococo-Gothic in the forties by placing before the public his invention of five Gothic orders, so he realized that landscape gardening would have a new and a sales value, provided it could be represented to readers as the fashionable *dernier cri*. So he calls at once, on the title page of his *Principles of Gardening*, the manner which he recommends 'a more Grand and Rural Manner than has been done before,' and states in the Introduction that 'our Gardens are much the worst of any in the world, some few excepted, that have been laid out by Gentlemen, who have a grand and elegant Taste in Designing'.

It is not surprising therefore that Langley recommends Switzer. What is less easy to understand is Langley's praise of Rapin and of John James. His sympathy may be all with the new informal taste, his business sense makes him remember in time the necessity of formal designs in such a book as this. Switzer, after all, ten years before, had not been more uncompromising. Most of Switzer's designs for parterres had been in the French style, and so are Langley's, although he warns gardeners to keep them 'Plain with grass', without too much of 'small ornaments' such as yew or holly borders, and without Wise and London's 'trifling flower Knots, Embroidery, Wildernesses of Ever-Greens,' etc.

There is the same contradiction in this attitude of Langley's as had been found in Switzer's, from whom Langley incidentally cribs freely. Switzer had paid his compliments to the 'ingenuous Gentlemen' who support the new manner. So does Langley, as quoted above. Switzer had blamed the 'Paper Engineers' for their 'stiff, Mathematical', i.e., regular plans. Langley says that nothing can be 'more ridiculous and forbidding, than a Garden which is regular,' and calls this bad fashion the 'Fault of Theoretical Engineers'. Only in one place does Langley attempt a logical argument in favour of the informal. He says:

'The Pleasure of a Garden depends on the variety of its Parts. [Hence one should make a garden] a continued series of harmonious objects [with] new and delightful scenes at every step. [This] regular gardens are incapable of doing'.

Now what recipes does Langley give to the informal gardener? The latter will find more in his text than in his drawings. He praises the

'agreeable surprizing Entertainments in the pleasant Passage thro' a Wilderness . . . especially when the whole is so happily situated as to be bless'd with small Rivulets and curling Streams of clear Water which generally admit of fine Canals, Fountains, Cascades, etc.'

'little Walks . . . in Meadows and through cornfields. Thickets . . . Groves of a regular Irregularity . . . in a Rural manner, as if they had receiv'd this Situation from Nature itself'

'Views as extensive as possible, [or, where] Views cannot be extended [the termination of walks] in Woods, Forests, misshapen rocks, strange Precipices, old Ruins, grand Buildings, etc.'

That sounds like Addison and Pope, and Langley's summing up 'when we come to copy, or imitate Nature we should trace her Steps with the greatest Accuracy that can be' seems even more evidently the outcome of Pope's nature rationalism.

12, 13 Ornamental ruins for gardens—on the left, the Arch of Constantine—proposed by Batty Langley in 1728

14 A formal garden in the French manner, from Langley's 'New Principles', 1728

However in Langley, as in the others, the Rococo could not be suppressed. Remarks such as the following do not conjure up visions of the true landscape garden. The visitor, Langley says, should be

'led through the pleasant Meanders of a shady delightful Plantation, first into an open Plain, environ'd with lofty Pines, in whose Center is a pleasant Fountain, adorn'd with Neptune and his Tritons, etc., secondly, into a Flower Garden, enrich'd with the most fragrant Flowers and beautiful Statues; and from thence through small Inclosures of Corn . . . or small Meadows, Hop Gardens, Orangeries, Mellon-grounds, Vineyards, Orchards, Nurseries, Physick-Gardens, Warrens, Paddocks of Deer, Sheep, Cows, etc., with the rural Enrichment of Hay-Stacks, Wood-Piles, etc.'

Add to this playful quickness of change Langley's suggestion of trellis obelisks, of 'private Cabinets encompass'd with a hedge of Evergreens' (so this genteel screen round the public convenience in a park has so old and respectable a pedigree), of aviaries and grottoes, and on the other hand of 'grand avenues . . . as extensive as possible' and the transitional character of Langley's book will be patent.

SUMMARY   The landscape garden was conceived in England between 1710 and 1730. It was conceived by philosophers, writers and virtuosi—not by architects and gardeners.

It was conceived in England, because it is the garden of liberalism, and England just at that moment turned liberal, that is, Whig. Thomson in *Liberty* (1736) saw this parallelism and contrasts

. . . those disgraceful piles of wood and stone;
Those parks and gardens, where, his haunts betrimmed,
And nature by presumptuous Art oppress'd,
The woodland genius mourns . . .'
                    Part V, 163–166

with Silvan Scenes, where Art alone, pretends
To dress her Mistress and disclose her charms;
Such as a Pope in miniature has shown . . .
And such as form a Richmond, Chiswick, Stowe.
                    Part V, 696–700

The free growth of the tree is obviously taken to symbolize the free growth of the individual, the serpentine path and rivulet the Englishman's freedom of

15 A symmetrical garden ending in a picturesque ruin, shown by Langley in the same plate as the design opposite, 1728

thought, creed and action, and the adherence to nature in the grounds, the adherence to nature in ethics and politics.

Whiggism is the first source of the landscape garden, the philosophy of rationalism the second. Reason is the human power to keep in harmony with the eternal order of the Universe. It is part of nature, not in opposition to nature. Only latter day perversion of man has distorted the beauty and simplicity of this primitive, rightful and natural state into the artificial pomp of Baroque and the flippancy of Rococo. The remedy was Palladianism in architecture, a style as ordered as God's (and Newton's) universe and as simple as nature. For never, philosophers asserted, had nature been so wholly understood as by the Ancients. Hence to imitate the style of the Ancients in building was to imitate nature.

But in gardening the very term imitation of nature was bound to create quite different associations. To be natural in a garden evidently was to re-create nature untouched by man.

However, this conception was at first one of thinkers, and therefore not visual. Those who evolved it never made up their minds whether it pointed to crags and precipices or to sweet fields and purling streams. This is where the amateurs came in. Christopher Hussey has told how, after the Peace of Utrecht, the Grand Tour became *de rigueur,* how the virtuoso discovered the Alps and the Italian scene, how he found them idealized and isolated in the art of Salvator Rosa, and of Poussin and Lorraine, how he brought home their paintings or engravings after them, how he encouraged the artists in England to see with the eyes of these foreign landscape painters, and how in the end he tried to convert his grounds into a sequence of Rosa and Lorraine landscapes.

For this he needed architects and gardeners. And they—brought up in the atmosphere of the early Rococo—could not help interpreting the nature of the Whig, the nature of the rationalist, the nature of the virtuosi into a nature of the Rococo, wiggly, puny and playful.

The landscape garden that tries seriously to look like Nature Unadorned, the landscape garden that has deceived us all at some stage into believing it to be England's natural scenery, belongs to the second, not the first third of the n.9 eighteenth century.*

A paper on the mid-eighteenth century with Capability Brown as the central figure was in the end never written, because I found that I had nothing new to say. So the next papers, after a much enlarged note on Sharawaggi following immediately, are on the leaders from c. 1770 onwards.

1 *Seventeenth-century European idea of an Oriental landscape*

V

A Note on Sharawaggi

WRITTEN IN COLLABORATION WITH S. LANG

THERE may be other Forms [of gardens] wholly irregular, that may, for ought I know, have more beauty than any of the others; but they must owe it to . . . some great race of fancy or judgment in the contrivance. Something of this I have seen in some places, but heard more of it from others, who have lived much among the *Chinese*; a People whose way of thinking seems to lie as wide of ours in *Europe*, as their Country does. . . . Their greatest reach of Imagination is employed in contriving Figures, where the Beauty shall be great and strike the Eye, but without any order or disposition of parts, that shall be commonly or easily observ'd. And though we have hardly any Notion of this sort of Beauty, yet they have a particular Word to express it; and where they find it hit their Eye at first sight, they say the *Sharawadgi* is fine or is admirable, or any such expression of Esteem. . . . But I should hardly advise any of these Attempts in the Figure of Gardens among us; they are Adventures of too hard achievement for any common Hands; and tho there may be more Honour if they succeed well, yet there is more Dishonour if they fail, and 'tis twenty to one they will.'

This passage from Sir William Temple's *Gardens of Epicurus* published in 1685 and quoted *in extenso* in the preceding paper, is the beginning of the Picturesque Movement in England. It may need some comments to be fully understood.

There is first of all the word Sharawadgi (or Sharawaggi, as Horace Walpole spelt it later) itself. It is certainly not a current Chinese word. The Oxford Dictionary even goes so far as to say 'of unknown origin,' but that is rather defeatist. In fact, several explanations have been attempted in the last twenty years. In 1930 the Chinese scholar Y. Z. Chang, on the suggestion of H. Woodbridge, who subsequently worked on Sir William Temple,* first tackled the philology of Sharawadgi, and came to the conclusion that the word could well correspond to the Chinese syllables Sa-lo-kwai-chi; Saro or Sa-lo signifying careless grace or unorderly grace. Kwai-chi, which was often badly pronounced as Waidgi, conveys the meaning of impressive and surprising. Both these terms are of long-standing literary association; the first occurs before A.D. 921 and the second as early as 233 B.C. Sa-ro-kwai-chi would then mean the 'quality of being impressive or surprising through careless or unorderly grace.'* One year later E. V. Gatenby suggested in *Studies in English Literature* (Tokio, October 1931, repeated in a letter to *The Times Literary Supplement* of February 15, 1934) that Sharawadgi derived from Sorowaji, not being regular, a form of the word Sorou which is used to describe an asymmetrical design. Of these two explanations the former seems more convincing. It undoubtedly corresponds to what Temple meant and seems to make sense from the philological point of view. However, it

n. 1

n. 2

offers just as Sorowaji the difficulty that it is not apparently a term occurring in Chinese dictionaries, and in fact not an actual literary term nor an expression of Chinese usage.

More recently Mr Ch'ien Chung-shu* put forward the transcription San- n.3 lan or So-lu for Shara and wai-chi for Wadgi, meaning widely scattered or disorderly composition or arrangement 'in short spaces tastefully enlivened by disorder.' Mr Ch'ien actually refutes Mr Chang's transcription which he says would mean no more than graceful (easy) and wonderful (magnificent) and is more often applied to human beings than to landscape. Also both words are adjectives not nouns.* n.4

Since none of these explanations wholly satisfies, can it be that Temple made up the word himself? This is indeed the opinion of William Cohn, who spoke of 'a literary chinoiserie wittily invented by Sir William Temple to express the joy of asymmetry.'* If we assume such a daring fantasy it would have to be ad- n.5 mitted that Temple had one of the existing dictionaries at his disposal to add the semblance of philological probability.* This is not all that unlikely, as we know n.6 for certain that Temple actually did interest himself in the Chinese language. He writes in *Of Heroic Virtue* (*Works*, 1750, Vol. II, Part II, Section III, page 247) as follows: '. . . for, by all I can gather out of so many authors as have written of China, they have no letters at all but only so many characters expressing so many words: these are said by some to be sixty, by others eighty, and by others six score thousand; and upon the whole, their writing seems to me to be like that of shorthand among us in case there were a different character invented for every word in our language. Their writing is neither from the left hand to the right like the European, nor from right to left like the Asiatic languages, but from top to bottom of a paper in one straight line and then beginning again at the top till the side be full.'

If, on the other hand, Temple did not go direct to books on the Chinese language or Chinese dictionaries, he could consult, instead of books, people who were interested in China and knew some Chinese. Such people were indeed not wholly absent. John Webb, the architect famous for his Whitehall drawings, was amongst them, and Robert Hooke, the scientist, horologist, architect, and friend of Christopher Wren.* The Royal Society seems to have been the centre of such n.7 philological entertainments. Although Temple did not himself belong to it, he was in some contact with members, as, for instance, Evelyn's entry in his diary of March 24, 1688, proves: 'After dinner we went to see Sir William Temple's . . . the most remarkable things are his orangery and gardens.'

So much for Temple's use of the word Sharawadgi. But what is in a word? More important, perhaps, than philological speculation is the question how Temple can have known what Chinese gardens were like and what principles guided their layout. That he looked round carefully for information about China is beyond doubt. Apart from the two passages already quoted, he mentioned Chinese affairs in his essay *Of Popular Discontent* (*Works,* 1750, Vol. II), and in *Of Heroic Virtue* he tells us of the published accounts of China he had used. They are 'Paulus Venetus, who about 400 years ago made a voyage from Venice (page 239) . . . Martinus Kercherus (page 255) and several other relations in Italian, Portuguese and Dutch, either by missionary friars, or persons employed by them upon trade or embassies upon that occasion (page 255).'* n.8

As for these reports of missionaries and ambassadors, many indeed came out before 1685, the year in which Temple wrote his *Gardens of Epicurus*. However, they contain little about gardens and what they say seems curiously standardized, non-committal and sometimes even embarrassed. Also they went on cribbing from each other and when no evidence was available substituted fantasy for truth. Here, as an example, is the first somewhat more detailed account of Chinese gardening. It comes from Father Ricci:* 'Dans ce jardin n.9 laissant en arriere beaucoup d'autres choses qu'on ne peut voir, ni peut-estre escrire sans plaisir, il vid un rocher artificiellement faict de divers marbres non-polis, lequel estoit proprement creusé en grotes, ou y auot des chambres, sales, degrez, viviers, arbres, et plusieurs autres, ou l'art estoit en debat avec la volupté. Ils font cela, afin d'euiter les chaleurs de l'Esté, par la fraischeur des grotes, lors qu'ils estudiet ou font des festins. La figure en forme de labyrinthe augmentoit la grace car encore qu'il noccupast pas une place des plus grandes, ceux neanmoins qui vouloient passer par tout, y estoient detenus deux ou trois heures, et en apres on sortoit par une autre porte.'

n.10   After Ricci, about the middle of the century, Semedo,* and then Father
n.11 Grueber:* 'Their Gardens are for the most part enclosed Meadows on purpose to exercise themselves with a Ball. . . . Nevertheless their Gardens are very green and delightful because of the conveniency of watering them with fresh rivers; but they have but small skill to dress and order them. All that I could take notice of in any such places was in the Kings garden, where is to be seen a great Cascade of Water, that falls from a Rock of Brass, covered all over with artificial Trees of the same substance.'

Finally, Nieuhoff, probably the most famous seventeenth century reporter
n.12 on China,* gives the following descriptions: 'In the same shire (Houchenfu) Eastward from the Metropolis, lies the famous Lake Sikin between which, and the City Walls is a fair Street, Paved with Stones, and almost a Mile long, where they divertise instead of Walks of Pleasure. The whole Lake Wall'd in comprises about five English Miles in compass, and upon the adjacent Hills, (supplied with various rivulets and Fountains) appear several Temples, Palaces, Cloysters, Colledges and the like. The Banks of the Lake, which is the foot of the Mountain are pav'd on the top with Freestone, and athwart the Lake lie several bridges, so that they may walk over it, and see the Lake in all places. The fore-mentioned Ways are all Planted with divers shading Trees, and accommodated with Benches, Arbors, and the like, for the conveniency of such as walk there, when they are weary to sit down and repose. The Chinese call it "the delightful Garden" or "Earthly Paradise." ' (Vol. II, p. 273).

'In the houses . . . [the women] have Wildernesses, Groves, and pleasant Gardens, where they delight themselves in Planting curious Flowers. . . .' (page 338).

'A rivulet call'd Yo, which hath its original in the mountain Jouven, Westward of Peking out of the Lake Si, flows through the whole Court with several winding Channels, watering the Gardens and Groves; and being so deep and broad within the Court, that laden Jonks may come up in it; so that it is not only for pleasure, but serves as a great Convenience. This River flows also by several artificial mounts made in the Court, which the Chinese with great ingenuity have raised with Rubbish and cover'd with polished Marble, wrought and interwoven with Plats of Grass; on the tops of them are trees and Flowers planted in excellent order. Lords and Persons of Quality often times spend most of their Estates in making such artificial Mounts in their Gardens and Orchards. There are some which not only have Cells very handsomely digg'd but also Sleeping Rooms, Apartments, and all manner of Closets within them, and serve the Chinese for retiring-places against the Heat in the Summer, and for Banqueting-houses to recreate themselves and their Guests in. In one of them are Mazes though not very big, yet by their strange turnings and windings of one Walk into another keep the Water two or three hours before it can get through them all and
n.13 at last comes out at another gate' (page 481).*

In addition to studying such printed descriptions of Chinese gardens, Temple may have heard talks direct from travellers or from people who had spoken to travellers. However, on the whole travellers cannot have been very helpful; for only the fewest can have seen enough, and seen with eyes wide enough open to appreciate what was the specific character of Chinese landscaping. Only Chinamen, coming to Europe and seeing how differently gardens were treated here, could have been really enlightening. But were there educated Chinamen in Europe during Temple's lifetime, and can he have met any? There was one at least in France, England and other European countries who can well have been known personally to Temple. A Belgian missionary, Father Philippe

2 Portrait of Xin-fo-Cum, the Chinese convert, painted by Kneller for James II in 1687

Couplet, S.J., brought with him, when he returned from China in 1684, one Xin-fo-Cum.* He was presented to Louis XIV* and then to the Pope. In 1687 he arrived in England, where he appeared in Oxford before September.* Earlier still, he must have been in London; for James II at Oxford referred to a Chinaman's portrait 'to the life' which was then already in his possession. At the end of 1687 and the beginning of 1688 Xin-fo-Cum again stayed in London. This emerges from some letters written by him to Dr Hyde. They are in Latin, and in one of them he apologizes for a long delay in answering, giving as his excuse that he found it difficult to hold a European pen (B.M. Sloane 853).

As regards the passage on Sharawadgi, it is, of course, tempting to connect it with Xin-fo-Cum. But Temple is supposed to have written *The Gardens of Epicurus* in 1685, and Xin-fo-Cum only arrived in 1687. However, as the book was only published in 1690, there is no reason why Temple might not have inserted the passage in question after a conversation with the Chinaman—provided he had such a conversation, which we cannot prove.

Now, supposing that for this reason Xin-fo-Cum's possible comments on gardens are discounted and the talks of missionaries and ambassadors or tales of other travellers not over-estimated, were there other sources which Temple can have had at his disposal? There is, we think, only one left: Chinese paintings of landscape. Can he have seen any—as, indeed, he saw and mentions porcelain and textiles? The answer is that he can; for Evelyn as well as Pepys had. Proof of this is to be found in their diaries. Evelyn writes, on June 22, 1664: 'One *Tomson* a *Jesuite* shewed me such a Collection of rarities, sent from the *Jesuites* of *Japan* & *China* to their order at Paris (as a present to be reserved in their *Chimelium*, but brought to Lond; with the East India ships for them) as in my life I had not seene: The chiefe things were very large *Rhinoceros's* hornes, Glorious Vests, wrought & embroidered on cloth of Gold, but with such lively colours, as for splendour and vividnesse we have nothing in Europe approches . . . *Fanns* like our Ladys use, but much larger, & with long handles curiously carved, & filled with Chineze characters: a Sort of paper very broad thin, & fine like abortive parchment, & exquisitely polished, of an amber yellow, exceeding glorious & pretty to looke on, & seeming to be like that which my L: *Verulame* describes in his *Nova Atlantis*; with severall other sorts of papers some written, others Printed: Also prints of landskips, of their Idols, Saints, Pagoods, of most ougly Serpentine, monstrous & hideous shapes to which they paie devotion: Pictures of men, & Countries, rarely painted on a sort of gumm'd *Calico* transparant as glasse: also Flowers, Trees, Beasts, birds &c: excellently wrought in a kind of selve-silk very naturall . . . Also several booke MSS. A grammar of the Language writen in *Spanish,* with innumerable other rarities.' And on July 30, 1682, he writes: '[Mr Bohune's] whole house is a Cabinet of all elegancies, especialy *Indian,* and the Contrivement of the Japan Skreenes instead of Wainscot in the Hall, . . . is very remarkable; and so are the Landskips of the Skreenes, representing the manner of living, & Country of the *Chinezes*, &c.' Pepys, on January 14, 1667–8, records the purchase from Gibson, the bookseller, of a book on China 'with rare cuts.'*

We can, on the strength of these passages, venture to sum up that Temple, with his known interest in, and understanding of China, may well have seen such landscapes or cuts and formed out of them an amazingly clear vision of the Chinese garden and its peculiar beauty, then have asked and received confirmation from those who themselves had seen less sensitively, and finally have approached scholars of the Chinese language for a term to describe what he meant, with the result that he invented an attractive term to describe a completely new vision of what variety and surprise in planning might make of the English landscape.*

n.14,
n.16

2

n.17

n.18

3, 4 Sharawaggi, in Chinese landscape (above), and in a garden at Suchow (below) which combines gnarled trees and a small bridge with highly prized water-worn rocks

1 South front of Downton Castle, built in 1774-8 for Richard Payne Knight

VI
Richard Payne Knight

This and the following two papers differ in approach. Knight is a normal scholarly paper, Price is a collection of passages put together with a view to topical application, Repton is somewhat in between.

R ICHARD PAYNE KNIGHT was the grandson of a man who had made money in the growing Shropshire iron industry, and the son of a clergyman, fifty-three years old when Richard was born in 1750.* Payne Knight, whose fame rests on his antiquarian and his aesthetic writings, was three when Hogarth's *Analysis of Beauty* came out, six when Burke published his *Origin of Our Ideas of the Sublime and the Beautiful,* twelve when Stuart and Revett's *Antiquities of Athens* began to appear, thirteen when Winckelmann completed his *History of Ancient Art,* and eighteen when the Royal Academy was founded and entrusted to Sir Joshua as its first president. He was a weak child, not sent to school till the age of fourteen and never sent to university. But he went on the grand tour to Italy about the year 1767, stayed for several years, went again in 1777, and again in 1785. His stays thus overlapped with Winckelmann's (1755–1768) and Fuseli's (1770–1778) and preceded Flaxman's (1787–1794) by a few years.

Goethe's Italian journey which stands at the beginning of the true Greek Revival in European thought, took place in 1786–1787 and is in a curious way connected with Knight's. Knight, seventeen years old, accompanied Philipp Hackaert and Charles Gore on a tour through Sicily in 1777. Hackaert, a painter from Prussia, had reached Rome in 1768, made his name as a specialist in Italian landscapes, painted much for Lord Exeter, Sir William Hamilton, and other British virtuosi, and was made painter to the King of Naples in 1786. Goethe met him at Naples and in 1811 wrote his biography. Charles Gore, twenty-one years older than Knight,* spent the years 1773–1780 in Italy, learned from Hackaert to draw and paint, had his talented daughters also taught by Hackaert, and finally settled down with them in 1791 at Weimar to be close to Goethe and his circle. He died there in 1807.

Now Knight kept a diary of his Sicilian trip, and this is, it seems, preserved only in Goethe's translation inserted into his Hackaert.* It shows Knight as a very demure young man, proud of his amateur learning, and rather dull. There is nothing in his descriptions either as observant or as human as every page of Goethe's *Travels in Italy.*

But while Knight wrote down carefully what he saw of Paestum, Stromboli, Lipari, Palermo, Monreale, Agrigento, Syracuse, Catania, Mount Etna, Taormina, and Messina, his mind must at the same time have been engaged on thoughts of his estate at home, where developments were taking place which show him in a much more interesting light.

In 1774 he had begun to build Downton Castle near Ludlow, and 1778 is the date given for the completion of the house, though it is likely that its decoration and furnishing went on a little longer after his return. It is an exceptionally

n.1

n.2

n.3

2   *Dining room in Downton Castle*

important house in three ways: in its contrast between exterior and interior, in the deliberate asymmetry of its plan, and in the sources from which Knight drew his inspiration for its appearance. On each of these three aspects of Downton Castle more or less detailed comments are needed to attain a full understanding of Knight as an amateur architect.

The first aspect need not keep us long. Downton Castle possesses an embattled, that is imitation mediaeval, exterior, but interiors in the grand Roman style, with porphyry columns imported from Italy and classic detail of the Robert Adam-Henry Holland kind. The dining room, for instance, is a miniature version of the Pantheon, round, with the typical niches, the coffered vault and the central opening of the Pantheon, but it is placed into a square sturdy tower. Knight was proud of the idea of thus combining two styles. Thirty years later still he mentions in his *Enquiry into the Principles of Taste* (p.223) his Grecian rooms and his battlements, unaware perhaps of the fact that he was not quite alone in his heresy. Robert Adam, for instance, designed Culzean Castle with battlements and a thick round tower, but a classical double staircase inside.*   n.4

So much for this if not unique, at least uncommon, feature. The second point to emphasize about Downton, its asymmetrical plan, requires far longer digressions. The fact is that an asymmetrical plan in 1775 was something extremely unusual, and that its antecedents have to my knowledge not so far been assembled in the literature on architectural history. I shall therefore have to go back for a moment to a time long before Knight was born.

II

In examining the designs of Italian, German, and Spanish (not to mention French) Baroque architects, it will, I think, be found that, however wilful the elevations, the identity of the two sides of one façade was never abandoned. Not even the most Rococo of decorators had gone beyond asymmetry in ornament. To whom is this revolution in planning then to be attributed?

The answer is, if I am not mistaken, Vanbrugh—not a surprising answer, if one thinks of it in conjunction with Vanbrugh's position in the early history of the Picturesque movement, his pleading for the preservation of the Old Manor at Blenheim, because of the 'lively and pleasing reflections' which such a memorable pile would arouse, his love of battlements and cyclopic walls, and his emphasis on wildernesses with winding paths in the grounds of Castle Howard and Charlemont.*   n.5

In architecture the decisive design is Vanbrugh Castle at Blackheath near London. Vanbrugh bought some land close to the top of Greenwich Park, probably in 1717. On December 21, 1717 he mentions 'my Country morsell'. He designed and built several other houses on his ground, but only his own villa, Vanbrugh Castle, is important in our context. As it appears now, it is obviously not in its original state.* A wing which is clearly a much later addition projects   n.6 on the right as one faces the entrance side. But even without this, there remains a building with a symmetrical centre from which some rooms extend north from the west end, and some east from the east end (see plan). There is, however,   3 something puzzling about these extensions which, I think, has not been discussed in the literature on Vanbrugh. They do not belong to the original house. Joints can be seen at the corner between entrance and east wing and also in the crucial place on the north side. So Vanbrugh's villa was originally a small symmetrical house, developed incidentally on a pattern of Elizabethan inspiration, as will be shown on p. 157. On the other hand the conversion of a symmetrical into an asymmetrical house cannot have been made after Vanbrugh's time. The vaulted corridor in the east wing and the chimney over the east end are as typical of his personal style as the excessive batter of the chimney on the west wing, and conscious imitation of Vanbrugh during the eighteenth century, to which the additions evidently belong, can probably be ruled out. So the evidence of the building itself points to an original symmetrical house enlarged

Margin references: 1,11   2   3   4

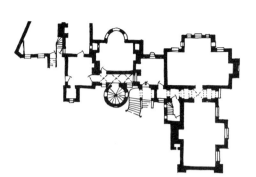

*3, 4   Plan and south front of Vanbrugh Castle,
by Sir John Vanbrugh*

by Vanbrugh himself. If he built it in 1717 or 1718, he had not much time left for his wings; for he died in 1726. What made him suddenly want so much larger a house? Sir John Summerson, with whom I examined the building,* suggests what seems to me a convincing answer: Vanbrugh married late in life, in January 1719. The Venetian window of the north wing is indeed most similar to Seaton Delaval designed between 1718 and 1720.

It is not easy to decide what made Vanbrugh design his own house in this way. As for the mediaevalizing elevations, they are certainly the outcome of his general liking for a 'Castle Air',* but what his more specific sources were cannot be proved. They may have been of three kinds: mediaeval Chester where Vanbrugh grew up and whose walls with 'a round Tower' and 'a single Cap' impressed him sufficiently for him to quote them still in a letter about Castle Howard in 1724* or alternatively France, where he had been by mistake imprisoned in the Bastille in 1692 and where such towers could be seen everywhere, or finally stage architecture by Italian or Italianizing Baroque designers with which he as an author and owner of a theatre must have been acquainted. Round towers with machicolations appeared already as an indication of a heroic mediaeval setting in Inigo Jones's stage designs.* They reappear for instance in Francesco and Ferdinando Galli Bibiena.*

Vanbrugh in the mediaevalizing lack of regularity of his own house remained apparently completely without successor for a whole generation. Mediaevalizing designs appeared here and there, but neither Hawksmoor nor Kent nor Roger Morris at Inverary Castle nor Sanderson Miller ventured to design asymmetrical mansions.

The next date of importance is 1750, the year in which Horace Walpole began to remodel his country cottage at Twickenham into a Gothic Castle.* Admittedly the alterations were for some years very modest, and the present view of Strawberry Hill, with the cloister and gallery and the Round Room and Beauclerk Tower at the end farthest away from the original cottage, is the work of only the sixties and seventies.

*5   Strawberry Hill, largely designed
by Horace Walpole*

But on February 25, 1750, Walpole had already written to Sir Horace Mann: 'I am almost as fond of the Sharawaggi or Chinese want of symmetry, in buildings, as in grounds and gardens'—where by then, needless to say, it had become a well established principle in England. Now in the completed building of Strawberry Hill part also follows part in a loose, informal sequence, apparently (and in fact) the outcome of growth rather than planning. Walpole's pattern must have been those semidemolished monastic houses as Lacock or Newstead

n.7

n.8

n.9

n.10
n.11

n.12

5

in which after the Dissolution life went on in whatever parts happened to survive. He once wrote of the 'conventual look' of one motif in one of the rooms.* n.13 However, in spite of all the exact copying which is so characteristic of the individual motifs of Walpole's interiors, no immediate sources for his façades have yet been found. And although it is no doubt true that he identified the 'gloomth' of his apartments with the scenery of the 'Castle of Otranto', his source certainly did not lie on the other side of the Alps. This fact may not seem to require emphasis. It is evidently the accepted view that the Gothic Revival with its crenellations and ogee-headed windows is wholly a matter of rediscovering a national baronial past.

Nor may Payne Knight's Downton Castle, to which we can now return, at first sight appear to contradict this view. Its round and polygonal towers and its battlements do not seem to be of a kind fundamentally different from those of Strawberry Hill. Yet Knight's source was indeed of quite another kind. The compactness of Downton Castle is perhaps the only visual hint at the buildings to which he went for inspiration. They were not buildings ever built; they were buildings drawn and painted. It has long been known and sufficiently stressed by Mr Hussey in his *The Picturesque* that Claude Lorraine, Gaspard Poussin, and Salvator Rosa are amongst the most effective inspirers of the Picturesque mood in England. The Arcadian landscapes of Lorraine and Gaspard and the savage landscapes of Salvator were the ideal of Kent and Brown and the early amateurs such as Hamilton. Payne Knight knew of many Lorraine paintings: for instance, to mention only one of special importance in our connection, *The Enchanted* 6 *Castle* which at that time belonged to Chauncey (1706–1777), a doctor, better known as an antiquary.

And as for Lorraine's drawings, Knight collected them himself, and collected them with enthusiasm, as can still be seen at the British Museum, to which he left his Lorraines. Now we need only remember what buildings in their backgrounds and what the 'Enchanted Castle' look like to recognize their forms in the design of Downton Castle. No detailed comment is necessary; the illustrations

6 *'The Enchanted Castle' by Claude Lorraine*

7, 8   Downton Castle: a lithograph by Page and an engraving after Hearne

7   are self-explanatory: an engraving of Downton by J. Smith from a drawing by
14, 8 Thomas Hearne (1744–1817), a lithograph of Downton, drawn by F. Page,* and
     The Enchanted Castle.
n.15   A full thirty years later, when Knight put his aesthetic theories on paper,*
     he wrote: 'I do not know a more melancholy object' than classical houses of
     strict symmetry in the countryside. 'Houses should be irregular where all the
n.16 accompaniments are irregular.'* 'The best style for irregular and picturesque
     houses, which can now be adopted, is that mixed style, which characterizes the
n.17 buildings of Claude and the Poussins.'*
         Two things in this passage need special stress: that Knight does not pro-
     nounce himself in favour of the imitation of mediaeval English buildings (in
     fact he speaks in another place of 'the barbarous structures of the Middle Ages
n.18 . . . rude and unskilful . . . heavy, clumsy and gloomy'*); and that he confines
     his plea for asymmetry to houses in the country, that is, houses as part of land-
     scape. In town, or rather in buildings not connected with trees, lawns, moss and
     so on, he appreciates 'neatness, freshness, lightness, symmetry, regularity,
n.19 uniformity and propriety'.*

                                III

     All this no doubt he found in his London house in Soho Square, one of those
     inimitably plain, staid, comfortable houses which the late seventeenth century
     put up everywhere on the new estates in London. Here Payne Knight kept,
     besides his drawings and paintings, a vast number of antiques, mainly bronzes,
     coins, gems, utensils, and such like, the collection which is now the pride of the
     British Museum. Marbles he never collected. Hence Horace Walpole who dis-
n.20 liked him intensely chose to call him 'Knight of the Brazen Milkpot.'*
         The truth is that Knight's interest, an uncommonly intelligent interest, and
     his knowledge, an uncommonly wide knowledge, were chiefly concerned with
     the contents of works of art, not with their aesthetic value. It will be for the next
     few pages to prove this contention.
         He had become a member of the Society of Dilettanti in 1781 (the same year
     as Charles Gore) and prepared for the Society two folio volumes of *Specimens of
     Antique Sculpture.* The first came out in 1809, the second only after his death in
     1835. The introductions to both of them are by him, but neither deals with
     ancient art as art. The first is a history of technique, although the plates contain
     the major specimens of the collection of his friend Charles Townley (then already
     at the British Museum) and some from those of Thomas Hope and the Mar-
     quess of Lansdowne, together with plenty of small works in Knight's own
     possession.
         For the second volume of the *Specimens* Knight had prepared a long dis-
     sertation on the *Symbolical Language of Ancient Art and Mythology,* which, im-
     patient with the Dilettanti's dilatoriness, he published separately in 1818. It is an

eminently interesting book, republished in America as late as 1892. The editor of this edition calls Knight 'one of the most thorough scholars of the earliest period' of the nineteenth century, a man of 'profound judgement . . . acuteness, and erudition,' and his book 'an invaluable collection of . . . curious learning . . . not superseded in any important aspect,' and 'of untold value for the unfolding of correcter views of Ancient Mythology, then have been commonly entertained.'

So Knight's competence and learning must have progressed enormously between the time when he wrote his Sicilian diary and 1818. In fact his mental development was much more rapid. Its earliest witness is a rare book, his first, published in 1786, for distribution by the Dilettanti, and soon afterwards as far as possible withdrawn. Its title is *A Discourse on the Worship of Priapus and its Connection with the Mystic Theology of the Ancients.* The British Museum possesses no copy of it, nor indeed of the American reprint which appeared in 1894, with extensive annotations and additions by Thomas Wright, the erudite antiquary.

The *Worship of Priapus* is only one of many books by Knight on antiquarian matters, but owing to its somewhat risqué plates it is less easily accessible than the others and may therefore serve to illustrate Knight's surprisingly original and in some ways modern approach to the dry subject matter of eighteenth century archaeology and philology.

His other philological books are *An Analytical Essay on the Greek Alphabet* of 1791, and the *Prolegomena* to an edition of Homer attempting to restore the original text. This was published in Latin in 1808. Knight also wrote occasionally in *Archaeologia* and other periodicals; but his 'magnum opus' is the *Symbolical Language*, and this incorporates after removal of the passages most violently attacked (even in Parliament) the essence of the *Worship of Priapus*.

Knight's approach to his subject is—I can think of no better term—psychoanalytical. He was a Whig and a hater of bigotry. His own religion seems to have been broad pantheism. He believed in what he called a 'System of emanations . . . the fundamental principle of the religions of a large majority of the human race . . . though not now acknowledged by any established sect of Christians.* n.21 The system supposes a 'universal expansion of the creative spirit' by which 'every production of earth, water, and air, participates in its essence.' Thus there is perpetual creative movement, 'emanating from and reverting back to its source.' * n.22

His pantheism made him see all creeds as one. He had no preference for the Christian over others. Christianity contains the same hoary truths as the mystery religions of the Orient and Greece, of India and America. This conception provided his starting point for the *Worship of Priapus*. Knight had received a remarkable letter in 1781 from Sir William Hamilton, British Ambassador in Naples, Knight's friend, Lady Hamilton's husband, and a famous collector of Greek vases. In this letter Hamilton told of the celebrations of St Cosmo's day at Isernia, at which male members of wax were sold to women as ex-votos. His intention in reporting this strange ritual was to show up 'the similitude of the Popish and Pagan Religion.'

Knight's tendency was different. He appears to accuse Christianity as a whole and defend paganism. The custom of Isernia seems 'monstrous and indecent', to us, but is 'a very natural symbol of a very natural system of religion, if considered according to its original use and intention':

'Antiquity humanized all natural forces and could therefore see no harm in this particular form to represent the powers of generation.'

This is a statement as bold as any in Rousseau. In Knight it can be accounted for by a mixture of the antiquarian with the Whig revolutionary, a mixture responsible for such daring statements in various books of his, as that 'Adam, in paradise, was an African black',* that the Apollo Belvedere looks strikingly n.23

like 'some Mohawk warriors'; that 'metaphysical theology is a study . . . very deservedly neglected at present'; that 'one of the greatest curses that ever afflicted the human race [is] dogmatical theology'; that the Christian religion is but 'a reformation of the Jewish'; that St Paul's doctrine of grace served only 'to emancipate the consciences of the faithful from the shackles of practical morality'; that the dove above the head of a statue of Bacchus at Hierapolis was 'the Holy Spirit, the first-begotten love'; and that the T-cross as it appears in representations of Christ Crucified was originally a male symbol.

Sexual symbolism altogether is what fascinated Knight more than anything in antiquarian lore, and if his little book, where copies exist in libraries, is now kept in the librarian's poison cupboard, it does not deserve such treatment more than Freud's writings on similar subjects. It is quite different in this respect from its immediate predecessor, Hancarville's *Veneres et Priapi,* published in 1784, and financed by Hamilton. Knight's comparisons of the shell or concha with the female parts, the serpent and the bull and the obelisk with the male member, and the Italian gesture of the thumb sticking out between second and third finger (as a safeguard against the evil eye) with the act of copulation are in fact expeditions into the subconscious, amazing for their date.

The two chief differences between the eighteenth century amateur and twentieth century nerve specialist are classical scholarship and elegance of diction. It may perhaps be advisable to illustrate this by two quotations.

The first is chosen to show Knight 'spread profuse the feast of Grecian lore' (as he rhymed about Fox):

'As fire was the primary essence of the active or male powers of creation and generation, so was water of the passive or female. Appian (De Bello Parthico) says, that the goddess worshipped at Hierapolis in Syria was called by some Venus, by others Juno, and by others held to be the cause which produced the beginnings and seeds of things from humidity. Plutarch (In Crasso), describes her neatly in the same words, and the author of the treatise attributed to Lucian n.24 (De Dea Syria), says she was Nature, the parent of things, or the creatress.'*

The second is apropos the temple prostitution at Corinth and Eryx.

'When there were such seminaries for female education . . . we need not wonder that the ladies of antiquity should be extremely well instructed in all the practical duties of their religion. The stories told of Julia and Messalina show us n.25 that the Roman ladies were no way deficient . . .'.*

These passages suffice to show the mixture of Caylus and Casanova, of scholarship and Hell-Fire Club tradition that existed in Knight's mind, the crispness of his style and his intelligent, searching approach to his subject. But, once again, with the aesthetic qualities of antique art this approach has nothing to do.

IV

Knight's aesthetic obtuseness comes out most clearly in his views on the Elgin Marbles, and it is these perhaps even more than his unusual and sometimes questionable approach to antiquarian matters that have discredited him in the eyes of literary and art critics.

Lord Elgin acquired the major portion of the Parthenon sculpture while he was British Ambassador to Turkey. It was, under manifold difficulties, transported to England and exhibited in his town house. Then, in 1815, suggestions were made for the national purchase of the marbles, and a committee collected n.26 evidence on their value, and the price that might be paid for them.*

The witnesses were Flaxman, Westmacott, Chantrey, Nollekens and Rossi amongst sculptors, Wilkins amongst architects, Sir Thomas Lawrence, West and the gentleman-dealer Alexander Day amongst painters; then there were a number of others to tell of the way in which Lord Elgin had purchased the marbles and of similar matters not related to their merit. Finally one, and only one, appeared of the influential class of the dilettanti, Payne Knight. The artists acquitted themselves handsomely. Nollekens said the marbles were 'the finest things that ever came to this country', Flaxman 'the finest works of art I have seen,' Rossi also 'the finest that I have ever seen,' Westmacott 'of the first class of art,' Chantrey 'of the highest class'; and Sir Thomas Lawrence added to this that their purchase would be 'a very essential benefit to the arts of this country.'

Some went even beyond such general statements, especially Westmacott who called the Theseus 'infinitely superior to the Apollo Belvedère', and Benjamin West P.R.A., who said:

'Had I been blessed with seeing and studying these emanations of genius at an earlier period of life the sentiment of their pre-eminence would have animated all my exertions; and more character and expression and life would have pervaded all my humble attempts in historical paintings.'

Lawrence and Rossi also preferred the Parthenon works to the Apollo. The only sculptor in fact who emphatically insisted on the superiority of Apollo—the statue which had been the idol of Winckelmann, Mengs, and their whole (slightly earlier) generation—was Flaxman, who in his art belongs indeed more to the early than the mature phase of the Classical Revival. Flaxman said that the Apollo 'partakes more of ideal beauty than the Theseus', although the latter is an original, the former a copy. He also said that the merit of the female figures was less and that the frieze had too much 'of common nature.' Similarly, Wilkins, the architect of the National Gallery and Downing College, had unqualified praise only for the architectural fragment ('in the very highest order of art'), whereas regarding the sculpture he preferred the Townley Venus, the Lansdowne Hercules, and several things in the Louvre. The frieze he called downright mediocre, and most of the other fragments 'not . . . fit models for imitation.' Thus the purchase seemed unnecessary to him, while Flaxman, in spite of his qualified praise, called it 'of the greatest importance' to the British public and the future of sculpture.

Knight had written in the first volume of the *Specimens*, that is in 1808, that the frieze and metopes of the Parthenon were 'merely architectural sculptures executed from [Phidias's] designs and under his direction probably by workmen scarcely ranked among artists and meant to be seen at the height of more than forty feet from the eye.'* So one knows what to expect now. The first statement of his evidence is that the best Elgin marbles he would 'put in the second rank . . . of art,' because in first-rate sculpture such as the Laocoön, marks of chiseling ought to be visible. The Ilissos, for instance, shows none; and Knight insisted on the validity of the argument, although he had to admit later that neither the Apollo nor the Venus de Medici shows chisel marks. **n.27**

Knight then proceeded to discredit the authorship of Phidias by quoting Plutarch—an argument justly refuted as 'uncandid' by the *Quarterly Magazine*.* **n.28**

In fact, Knight's view was that the majority of the Parthenon sculpture belonged not even to the age of Phidias, but to that of Hadrian. He left its fifth century date to the Ilissos, but expressed doubt in the case of the Theseus. He called the draperies 'complicated and stringy', the state of preservation of most of the figures too bad to form an accurate judgement, the female figures 'of little value, except from their local interests,' the metopes 'some very poor, some very fine,' and only the frieze 'of the first class.'

Maybe Knight was deliberately provocative in all this; for the chairman, Henry Bankes, was a Tory M.P. and a supporter of Pitt, whereas Knight was a friend of Fox and had published a Monody on Fox's death (1806/7). But even so, Knight's remains a painful piece of evidence, groping, fumbling, and all the time changing targets. It lacks any understanding of the creative powers of the Periclean age. Benjamin Haydon, a spokesman of later romantic theory in England, answered thus: 'Far be it from Mr. Knight to know, that in the most broken fragment the same great principle of life can be proved to exist as in the most perfect figure. Is not life just as palpable in the last joint of your forefinger as in the centre of your heart?'* **n.29**

V

Yet, in spite of his apparent aesthetic insensibility, Knight is rightly considered a pioneer of aesthetics in England. This may seem paradoxical, even after looking over at least one of his two books on matters of aesthetics: *The Landscape*, a poem which came out in 1794. It is incidentally not the only poem that Knight made public. His *Monody on the Death of the Right Honourable Charles James Fox* has been mentioned, and he also wrote a long poem in a Lucretian vein on *The Progress of Civil Society* (1796), and a verse romance *Alfred* (1823).

n.30
To avoid over-rating *The Landscape* it must be seen in its setting. The year 1794 marks the beginning of a new, the third, phase in the history of the Picturesque movement in England.* The first phase goes from Sir William Temple and Shaftesbury to Addison and Pope and on to Batty Langley and Kent; that is, from about 1699 to 1725 or 1730. The second belongs to Kent in practice, to Shenstone of The Leasowes near Birmingham and early Gilpin in theory and culminates in Capability Brown, the gardener who worked from 1750 to 1783, and the group of writers on gardening who published books between 1760 and 1775 (Lord Kames 1761, Whately 1765, Mason 1765, Walpole 1771, Chambers 1772). The second phase differs from the first in that it is not a phase of discovery but of establishment. In 1739 a fashionable magazine wrote that 'you hardly meet anybody who . . . does not inform you that he is in Mortar and moving of
n.31
Earth.'* By then the Kent elements of the landscape garden, a serpentine river or lake, clumps of trees, and a belt round the boundary had become indispensable. Capability Brown popularized and standardized them, and the number of estates remodelled by him is legion. He was the first professional gardener in England to achieve the fame of great painters and architects (Kent had been both, besides a garden designer). By then the English were told, too, that gardening is an art superior to architecture (Kames) and superior to painting (Whately), that England can claim 'a preference over every nation in Europe [in the] enchanting
n.32
art of modern gardening' (J. Warton),* and that 'the only proof of our original
n.33
talent in matters of pleasure [is] our skill in gardening' (Thomas Gray).* And by then Horace Walpole could write a *History of the Modern Taste in Gardening* (1771).

If the gardens of the first phase were characterized by a wiggly, busy, Rococo intricacy, those of the second have the gentle nostalgia of Gainsborough's beggar boys and Greuze's village maidens, and the smoothness of Reynolds's portraits and Mengs's or Benjamin West's subject paintings. Brown's is a very accomplished but not a vigorous style. The theorists regard 'softening nature's harshnesses and copying her graceful touch' as the gardener's chief task (Walpole 1771).

n.34
The third phase sets in with three publications all appearing in 1794. One of these was a masterpiece: Uvedale Price's *Essay on the Picturesque.** Price's estate, Foxley, was close to Knight's, and the two virtuoso squires must have had many conversations as their improvements went on. They were both Whigs and both friends of Fox. At a Royal Academy banquet in 1796, Farington saw
n.35
Fox sitting between the two of them.* Both had travelled widely in Italy. Price, before his *Essay* came out, had not written anything, but Knight had already shown plenty of curious antiquarian learning. But Price, it appears from a comparison of *The Landscape* with the *Essay*, had thought far more on aesthetic theory than Knight. *The Landscape* is dedicated to Price ('Do thou, O Price, the song attend/Instruct the poet and assist the friend'), not the *Essay* to Knight. And Knight went straight on from *The Landscape* to his poem on the *Progress of Civil Society* and extensive archeological work, while Price spent the next fifteen years enlarging and amending his *Essay* until it came out in its final form in three volumes in 1810. Price is a one-book author, Knight is a diffuse writer. To Price the Picturesque is the only topic that matters; if we look for a similar essential topic in Knight's life it is the symbolic meaning of religious forms, not an aesthetic subject at all.

Thus *The Landscape* is not really the outcome of much original thinking. Most of the ideas put forward are identical with Price's and probably come from Price. One or two others can be found concurrently in the third of the publications of 1794, Humphry Repton's *Sketches and Hints on Landscape Gardening.** n.36 Repton belonged to Price's and Knight's generation. He was born in 1752, and had already improved more than fifty estates when he came out with this, his first, book. He mentions the benefit which he had derived from occasional conversations with Price and Knight, and they call him the leader of his profession. Regarding similarities between the *Sketches and Hints* and *The Landscape*, Repton insists that priority is his. His book is, in fact, largely a compilation from the Red Books which he wrote and painted for each estate when he was called in. There are few similarities anyway, and many differences.

Repton regarded himself as the one legitimate pretender to Brown's throne, and carefully distinguished between Brown's art and faulty imitations by the Brownites. Knight's primary purpose in writing *The Landscape* was to attack both Brown and the Brownites (not excluding Repton).
Book I states as the poem's function:

> . . . to kill or cure that strange disease,
> Which gives deformity the pow'r to please;
> And shows poor Nature, shaven and defaced,
> To gratify the jaundiced eye of taste.*   n.37

Similarly, Book II begins:

> Oft when I've seen some lonely mansion stand,
> Fresh from th'improvers decorating hand,
> 'Midst shaven lawns, that far around it creep
> In one eternal undulating sweep.

And Book III has on its second page a crushing footnote on Brown's work at Blenheim. Knight's chief arguments against Brown are the same as Price's. Price says that 'whoever views objects with a painter's eye, looks with indifference, if not with disgust at the clump, the belts, the made water, and the eternal smoothness'* of a place freshly improved by Brown. Knight deplores 'the formal n.38 lump Which the improver plants, and calls a clump.'* He teaches that: n.39

> The wood should always from th' exterior bound
> Not as a belt, encircling the domain
> Which the tir'd eye attempts to trace in vain.*   n.40

And he works himself up into a Johnsonian rage against the modern taste which is

> Spreading o'erall its unprolific spawn
> In never-ending sheets of vapid lawn.*   n.41

The reason for Knight's disapproval is interesting. The landscape garden had originally been a protest against the formal French or Dutch garden, that is of nature against rule. Knight's protest against the landscape gardener of his time is exactly the same on a new level. He calls Hogarth's famous serpentine Line of Beauty just as arbitrary as the straight avenues of Versailles had been. He

> . . . rejects the pedant's chain;
> Which binding beauty in its waving line,
> Destroys the charm it vainly would define.*   n.42

and adds that:

> The path that moves in even serpentine,
> Is still less nat'ral than the painted line.*   n.43

Again, Price says the same in his soberer way:

'It must be remembered that strongly marked, distinct and regular curves,

9, 10 The ideal according to Brown and to Knight, engravings by Thomas Hearne from 'The Landscape'

n. 44

unbroken and undisguised are hardly less un-natural or formal, though much less grand and simple than straight lines.' *

n. 45

So Knight and Price claim for their conception of landscape a truer naturalness than Brown's. Knight demands from a master of landscape that he 'appeals from sense directly to the heart.' *

46, 47

n.48

n.49

It is impossible here to go into any discussions of the uses and misuses of the word 'nature' by aestheticians from Boileau to Wordsworth. To Brown and Shenstone nature was mild and gentle, Knight likes his nature rough and rugged. He waxes enthusiastic over 'native . . . plants in wild obscurity and rude neglect,' * 'the weeds that creep/Along the shore, or overhang the steep,' * the banks of a river 'with moss and fern o'ergrown,' * 'the thickets of high-bow'ring wood/Which hang, reflected, o'er the glassy flood,' * 'and all such motives, as they grace the foregrounds of Claude Lorraine, or humble Waterloe.'

9,10

All this again we can read in Price, presented more eloquently and more consistently. But where *The Landscape* scores over the *Essay* is in the two engravings which Knight has added to his book, engravings by Thomas Hearne of the Beau Ideal of a country house in its grounds according to Brown and to Knight. Thomas Hearne was much patronized by Knight. He had drawn Greek temples in Sicily, together with Charles Gore, when he was young. Then he specialized more and more in illustrating the antiquities and beauties of his native country. He is best known for his illustrations to Byrnes's *Antiquities* of 1777–1781, and Britton and Brayley's *Beauties of England and Wales* of 1801–1816. He also engraved three plates for Watts's *Seats of the Nobility and Gentry*. A series of water colours of the Downton estate by Hearne are at Downton Castle, and he also illustrated the house in *The Beauties of England and Wales*. His interest in the mediaeval and the picturesque made him a superb tool in Knight's hands. The two engravings in *The Landscape* have all the force of conviction which the lame rhymes lack. Shaven and defaced indeed are the grounds à la Brown with two lean and miserable bridges across a smoothly winding stream. Knight's own ideal on the other hand is—this in itself is very remarkable, as I am going to show further on*—an Elizabethan mansion set off by a foreground of moss and fern and weeds, and twisted roots and a truly rustic bridge.

n.50

It is a brilliantly successful cautionary tale, branded, however, by Repton as wildly fantastic. Repton, the man of common sense and the professional gardener, retorts that

n.51

'The painter turns with indignation from trim-mown grass, and swept gravel walk; but the gardener, who knows his duty, will remove such unsightly weeds as offend the view from a drawing-room window.' *

Yet Knight did not mean the engraving to remain a statement on paper. He set his mind on making this sort of landscape come to life. Whether he was occupied with what improvements he made to the surroundings of Downton Castle before or after *The Landscape* we do not know. The result is certainly no less rugged than the beau ideal. But then Knight was in a peculiar position. Downton lies on a steep bank above the River Teme. Down in the valley slightly to the west of the house is an old stone bridge and then the forest and rocks and whirlpools. It is a scenery as romantic as any in a Derbyshire dale. Repton knew it and appreciated it: *11*

'It is impossible, by description, to convey an idea of the natural charms (of Downton Vale), or to do justice to that taste which has displayed these charms to the greatest advantage. A narrow, wild, and natural path sometimes creeps under the beetling rock, close by the margin of a mountain stream. It sometimes ascends to an awful precipice, from whence the foaming waters are heard roaring in the dark abyss below, or seen wildly dashing against its opposite banks; while, in other places, the course of the river being impeded by natural ledges of rock, the vale presents a calm, glassy mirror, that reflects the surrounding foliage. The path, in various places, crosses the river by bridges of the most romantic and contrasted forms; and, branching in various directions, including some miles in length, is occasionally enriched by caves and cells, hovels and covered seats, or other buildings, in perfect harmony with the wild but pleasing horrors of the scene.'*   n.52

Repton's style is highly coloured; we may nowadays be too blasé to speak of precipices, dashing waters, abysses, and beetling rocks in Herefordshire. But Repton had not, as far as we know, seen more grandiose landscapes abroad. Besides, his praise of the scene and its inspirer is doubly valuable, because it comes, as we have seen and shall see again, from an adversary.

VI

I used the word romantic a few moments ago for Downton Vale, and Repton uses it too. But it is not really the exact word to apply to Knight's work and Knight himself. It is true, he seems to have done remarkably little to a romantic scenery, but he did something—see the three bridges,* the cells, covered seats,   n.53 and some other accessories of the Picturesque which Repton mentions.

Now to improve landscape is unromantic *per se*. The romantic attitude to nature is one of exploration or self-abandon. Nature is accepted as supreme; we can spend a lifetime in studying her in her smallest or her immeasurably greatest works; we can approach her with burning love or with awe—but we can never improve her. That is the faith behind Wordsworth and Constable, behind Turner and Girtin and Cotman and the great romantic scientists of the Davy caliber. The eighteenth century in contrast can say of Keswick and Derwentwater—and it is Gilpin himself who speaks:

'We often observe the craggy points and summits of mountains not well formed; and the mountain itself not exactly shapèd. With these things, however, we must rest satisfied; yet sometimes in smaller matters, a deformity may be done away. An awkward knoll on the foreground may offend, which art may remove or at least correct. It may remove also bushes and rough underwood. Further than that we dare not move—unless perhaps we wish to give the line of the lake a more pleasing sweep by paring away cautiously—very cautiously— here and there a little of the margin.'*   n.54

Knight and Price, no doubt, had more respect for nature, especially because they commanded a wider range of visual receptivity. They also—Price more than Knight—developed and analyzed several of the romantic criteria of aesthetics (contrast, surprise, variety). But the very fact that they still used them to correct nature is of the Age of Reason. We can trust Shelley's instinct in such matters; and Shelley wrote to Peacock that Knight and Price 'could not catch the hare.'*   n.55

11 Downton Castle, with the valley of the Teme beyond

Thus, as far as Knight is concerned, he emphatically belongs, in spite of the rocks and forests of Downton Vale and in spite of Hearne's engravings, to the eighteenth century and not to Wordsworth and Constable. In fact, the engravings themselves are pre-Constable, in that they display compositions à la Ruisdael, with all the stage furnishings of the Dutch landscape painters in the foreground.

And as soon as this adherence of Knight to the ideals of the eighteenth century has been seen, it will be found at once in *The Landscape* too, not only in its rhythm, but also in its long antiquarian footnotes with quotations from Pliny and passages in Greek, and in its rambling away into a hundred lines on the greatness of Greece and the history of art down to Rubens and Claude. Compared with Price's consistent and pertinent writing, Knight seems all the time to have only one eye on the immediate purpose of his book. When, for instance, he wants to illustrate the principle of unity of style, he chooses an antiquarian example and compares Greek sculpture and Greek domestic design (with a picture of a bronze jug—Walpole's brazen Milk-pot—in the author's collection). And the third of the three books of *The Landscape* is entirely on trees, their characteristics and uses, and has nothing at all to do with the Picturesque.

Also Knight is never far off applications to civil society, and the day's politics. Time and again we find him led on from 'nature's common charms' to 'social man's delight and common use';* from rooks in the morning air to 'the ills of public life' and so to the mediaeval monks' 'rankling passions,' and 'foul desires,' the vanity and 'pomp of wealth' and 'the tides of blood that flow on Gallia's shore.'*

Finally, one more example may be given to show Knight's blindness to the romantic (and incidentally also the mediaeval) mind:

'Ariosto has concluded forty-five of his forty-six cantos with the same thought differently expressed; and I have heard Italians cite this as a most extraordinary effect of a fertile and inventive genius; though they might just as reasonably extol the invention of an architect for making the capital of every column in an extensive building different.—Quanto diversus ab illo, qui nihil molitur, inepte!—Homer, as often as he has occasion to express the same thought always does it in the same words: this, plain sense naturally dictates; and plain sense and good taste are very nearly applied in everything.'*

With this quotation we can leave *The Landscape* and Downton Castle which

n.56

n.57

n.58

Knight handed over to his brother, the distinguished horticulturist, in 1809. He had anyway for a good many years spent most of his time in London, and now his interest in his estate and his improvements was probably waning. Price on the other hand went on living and planting at Foxley, and speculating on the Picturesque. How much in later years the two saw of each other we do not know. What we do know is that a public controversy, which began immediately after the publication of *The Landscape* and the first volume of the *Essay*, had alienated them considerably from each other.*   n.59

To us, so much later, there appears to be hardly any important difference between the theories of Knight and Price, and not so very much between the two of them and Repton. All the same, quarrels started directly Repton had read Knight, and Knight had read Price. Repton felt hurt by a footnote to *The Landscape* on a point of no importance.* He was also and for better reasons wounded   n.60 in his professional pride by Price's emphasis on the role of the landscape painter as against the gardener in designing improvements. So he answered Knight in the *Sketches and Hints* and also attached to the book an open letter to Price. Price answered back in the second edition of the *Essay* which came out in 1798, and Knight in the second edition of *The Landscape*.

However, the Advertisement to the second edition of *The Landscape* is also an attempt at refuting Price's main tenet: the existence of a specific aesthetic quality in objects, which, different from the Sublime and the Beautiful as analyzed by Burke, could only be covered by the term Picturesque. Knight accepts the quality but rejects the term. He is prepared to regard the difference politely as one 'rather in philosophical theory than in poetic taste.'
This is what he says:

'In morals one may found his principles in fitness and propriety, another in general sympathy, and another in immediate operation of providence, or efficient grace; at the same time that all exactly agree in what is right or wrong. So in taste, one may found his principles on a division of the sublime, picturesque and beautiful; and another, on a certain unison of sympathy and harmony of causes and effects.''

Knight then goes on referring to what he calls his 'theory of visible beauty', but as he does not expound this theory to the reader, it was easy for Price to reestablish his case, when in 1801 he put it into the form of a dialogue between Mr Hamilton (Price), Mr Howard (Knight) and Mr Seymour (a layman eager to learn). It is a very fair piece of writing exposing the difference as being indeed only one of words. Should 'freshness and decay, what is rough, broken and rudely irregular, and what has that symmetry, continuity of parts, and last finishing polish which the artist manifestly intended . . . all . . . be considered as belonging to one general class?'* Price's answer is No, and he thus insists on the neces   n.61 sity of the term Picturesque in addition to Burke's Sublime and Beautiful. Time has indeed proved its eminent usefulness, if not its necessity. Regarding the latter, which would be the logical justification of Price's system, Knight, the more analytical thinker of the two, could not be confuted, once he had gathered his objection into a more coherent form.

This he did in his *Analytical Enquiry into the Principles of Taste* which came out in 1805.* It is much more than an attack on Price, although the difference be   n.62 tween their views may have induced Knight to undertake a task not really congenial.* He is at his best when he writes on philology and folk-lore, or on the   n.63 wider aspects of politics. There is little in the *Enquiry* that reads as spontaneous as such politically founded passages against systems and system-builders as the following:

'General rules appear to me to be, in government and politics, never safe but where they are useless.'* 'Precise rules and definitions . . . are merely the play   n.64 things or tools of system-builders.'* 'Rules and systems have exactly the same   n.65 influence upon taste and manners, as dogmas have upon morals.'* 'If men once   n.66 unite to maintain systematically that there are many Gods, one God or no God . . . all the selfish, violent and atrocious passions [come out].'* 'The censor Cato,   n.67

the saint Bernard, and the reformer Calvin, were equally insensible to the bland-
ishments of love, the allurements of pleasure and the vanity of wealth; and so
n.68   likewise, were the Monsters Marat and Robespierre.'*

Now Knight did not mean that Uvedale Price was a censor, a saint, or a monster.
But he dreaded the reformer in his friend, the single-minded system-builder.
Knight's *Enquiry* is not a system, just as his treatises on mythology and mystery
are not a system. Knight's approach to aesthetics—as to all other matters—is
analytical, Price's synthetical. Without hesitation Knight can put his finger on
the weak spot of Price's system. His friend's excellent 'practical lessons of taste',
he writes, are 'grounded . . . upon false principles . . . The great fundamental
error, which prevails throughout the otherwise able and elegant *Essays on the
Picturesque,* is seeking for distinction in external objects, which only exist in the
n.69   modes and habits of viewing and considering them.'*

This argument of Knight's against Price is no more than an application of
Hume to the new case of the Picturesque. Hume, as quoted by Knight, wrote:
'Beauty is no quality in things themselves: It exists merely in the mind which
n.70   contemplates them, and each mind perceives a different beauty.'*
If then the Picturesque cannot be retained as an objective quality, what should
the word stand for? Knight takes it in its original sense of 'after the manner of
n.71   painting,' or of 'appropriate to painting,'* or more generally 'everything of
n.72   every kind, which may be or has been represented to advantage in painting.'*
So far these definitions seem superficial and by no means new. But Knight goes
on, and in this he is to the best of my knowledge wholly original: 'Painting, as it
imitates only the visible qualities of bodies, separates those qualities from all
n.73   others.'*

So what is 'appropriate to painting' or 'in the manner of painting' is what
makes us see and appreciate visual qualities in isolation.
Once this is established, Knight goes on to investigate how much or how little
of what we accept as beautiful in art and in nature really impresses us by its visual
qualities exclusively. He takes up Burke, for instance, for his equation of smooth
and beautiful. Smoothness is a quality referring to the touch, not the eye:

'[There are] things which, though smooth to the touch, cast the most harsh,
and angular reflections of light upon the eye . . . Neat new buildings [for
instance], and level lawns intersected by gravel walks marked out in exact lines,
or winding canals distinctly bounded by shaven banks, may be properly called
smooth, if we mean smoothness to the touch: but to the eye, they present nothing but harsh and discordant oppositions of colour, distinguished by crude and
n.74   abrupt lines.'*

Therefore, what Burke describes as visual values are in fact tactile values. We
have to be careful not to confuse one with the other. But common confusion
goes much further than that. It is not only that in talking of beauty we forget
about the distinctions between the various senses, we also neglect the distinctions
between what is offered us by the senses and what is added from quite different
sources. Strictly speaking the word beauty should only be used for what 'is
n.75   pleasing to the senses.'* In point of fact, we also apply it all the time to pleasure
n.76   which 'arises from our associating ideas'* with what we actually see. Let Burke
object to such an inaccurate use of the term beauty; for better or worse it is
accepted 'by idiom' to be applicable 'to everything that is pleasing, either to the
n.77   sense, imagination, or the understanding'.* Thus Knight (following, of course,
the English tradition of Locke, Berkeley, Hume, and others) divides his book
into three parts: Of Sensations, Of Associations of Ideas (subdivided into Of
Knowledge, Of Imagination, Of Judgement), and Of Passions.

Only the first part deals with strictly aesthetic perception. The second part
is twice as long and twice as original. The third is short and relatively unimport-
ant. Obviously Knight regarded it as his main job to analyze the associate
elements in the pleasures of beauty. All through his book he has plenty of
examples to clarify his intentions.

If, with Price, we accept the visual appeal of what he calls Picturesque, then the beauty of variety, texture, richness of surface, and such-like qualities should give 'a pimpled face . . . the same superiority over a smooth one as a variegated tulip [has] over a plain one, or a column of jasper or porphyry over one of common red or white marble.'*   n.78

Again Price, in order to show the picturesque beauty of irregularity, had rashly used as an example the charm of a very slight squint. Knight retorts:

'My friend, Mr. Price, indeed, admits squinting among the irregular and picturesque charms of the parson's daughter whom (to illustrate the picturesque in opposition to the beautiful) he wishes to make appear lovely and attractive though without symmetry or beauty. He has not, however, extended the details of this want of symmetry and regularity further than to the features of the face; though to make the figure consistent and complete, the same happy mixture of the irregular and picturesque must have prevailed through her limb and person; and consequently she must have hobbled as well as squinted; and had hips and shoulders as irregular as her teeth, cheeks and eyebrows. All my friend's parental fondness for his system is certainly necessary to make him think such an assemblage of picturesque circumstances either lovely or attractive; or induce him to imagine, that he should be content with such a creature, as a companion for life; and I heartily congratulate him that this fondness did not arise at an earlier period, to obstruct him in a very different choice.'*   n.79

Another example is this: a man may think he admires the heavenly form of 'a lovely bosom'. But does he really admire its form? Let him take a mould from it and 'cast a plum pudding in it (an object by no means disgusting to most men's appetites) and, I think, he will no longer be in raptures with the form.' *   n.80

Then there is the case of the carcass of an ox in a butcher's shop, a case brought up in Knight's original attack on Price. Why can we admire it in Rembrandt's paintings, but not in reality? Because, to repeat the crucial statement: 'painting, as it imitates only the visible qualities of bodies, separates these qualities from all other.'

In reality association of ideas deflects our reactions, and makes us feel delight in the nude human form, but disgust with the pimpled face, the limping, toothless woman, and the carcass of an ox. It may be perfectly true that 'rotten thatch, crumbling masses of perished brick and plaster, tattered worn-out dirty garments, a fish or a fleshmarket, all exhibit the most harmonious and brilliant combination of tints to the eye'; and that 'harmonious and brilliant combinations of tints are . . . beautiful in whatsoever they are seen',* yet the sheer visual   n.81 beauty of colour is not necessarily enough to cause pleasurable sensations, if our knowledge, imagination, judgement, or passion put up a determined resistance.

VII

To sum up, Knight's importance in the history of aesthetic thought rests on the discoveries that art isolates visual qualities, that it is possible to look at objects in this strictly aesthetic way, regardless of subject matter, but that as a rule, in spite of this faculty of the human mind, what moves us in a work of art (or of nature) is not its visual quality in isolation but a compound of aesthetic and associational matter. These discoveries paved the way for the theory of art for art's sake, as Mr Hussey has rightly observed, and they still form the foundation of most recent discussions on the legitimacy of abstract art.*   n.82

The *Analytical Enquiry* is thus a piece of brilliant criticism, the work of a logical mind, choosing to apply itself to the subject of aesthetics, because drawn into a controversy over some minor points of practical aesthetics. But it is not, as Price's *Essay* undoubtedly is, the work of a man of immediate aesthetic reactions.*   n.83

To understand Knight's character this lack of consistency in aesthetic judgement must now in conclusion be documented. To do this two topics have been chosen: Knight's views on painting and on sculpture.

On painting Knight praised on the one hand as 'some of the most interesting and affecting pictures that the art has ever produced' West's *Death of General Wolfe*, Westall's *Storm in a Harvest* and Wright's *Soldier Tent*,* on the other hand he confessed:

n.84

'[I] was never able to participate in . . . the admiration with which the works of Michelangelo have been viewed.'* 'Though not to be compared even with a third rate artist of Ancient Greece in knowledge of the structure and pathology of the human body, he appears to have known more than any of his contemporaries; and when he made his knowledge subservient to art, and not his art to his knowledge, he produced some compositions of real excellence. Such are almost all those which he designed for others to execute . . .'* 'There has always appeared to me more of real grandeur and sublimity in Raphael's small picture of the . . . Vision of Ezekiel; and in Salvator Rosa's of Saul and the Witch of Endor than in all the vast and turgid compositions of the Sistine Chapel.'*

n.85

n.86

n.87

Farington tells us that during an argument on the history of painting Knight said he preferred Carracci to all other painters and called Raphael an example of the 'infancy of Art.'* But then Knight enjoyed provocative statements. Where he is at his best is in analyses of the qualities of Rembrandt, Rubens, and the Venetians. Sir Thomas Lawrence said in 1805 that Knight's 'pleasure was derived from the luxurious displays of Rubens,'* and if Fuseli praised the 'many good observations' in the *Analytical Enquiry*ial* he can only have thought of remarks on such painters. Knight knew indeed the fascination of the sketch* and of summary treatment in paintings.* He even recommended to artists of his day as early as 1794 'to make designs at home, and put in the light and shade and colouring from nature.'* He was no doubt only happy where he could enjoy art in the picturesque way—the term used in his sense, that is, in the purely visual way, concentrating on surface, texture, and colour.

n.88

n.89
n.90
n.91
n.92

n.93

Form meant nothing to him aesthetically. 'Form', he wrote, 'considered in the abstract, is neither grand nor mean; but owes all its power of exciting sentiments . . . to the association of ideas.'*

n.94

Hence his complete failure to appreciate sculpture as such. Sculpture, he repeated in another place can only appeal 'to the imagination and the passions'* and never 'afford any . . . sensual pleasure to the eye.'* Immediate pleasure to the eye, he insists, 'can only arise from colour, or variation of light and shadow.'* Now light and shadow, at least, one would think anybody considering sculpture critically would have to admit as qualities present in the texture and modelling of works in bronze as well as stone. But that Knight, logical and analytical as he appeared in everything else, could not or would not do. Statuary—this seems the only possible answer—must have left him completely cold. Therefore, and only therefore, could he tackle it so fearlessly from a new psychological and anthropological angle. But therefore also was he forced to blunder so badly over the Elgin Marbles. So his failures and his successes, his perspicacity and his blindness appear in the end as part of one fairly consistent character.

n.95
n.96
n.97

In the preceding paper much has been said about Uvedale Price. This paper is no more than an annotated anthology from his magnum opus. *Moreover the choice of passages was largely dictated by my conviction—as firm now as it was then—that Price has a great deal to teach the planner today. Sir Uvedale Price was born in 1747, three years before Knight, and educated at Eton and Christ Church. At the death of his father in 1761 he came into a considerable fortune. With his school friend Charles James Fox he went on the Grand Tour to France and Italy in 1767. In August, 1768, the two visited Voltaire at Ferney ('He did not ask us to dine with him, but conversed a short time, walking backwards and forwards in his garden, gave us chocolate and dismissed us'—not without the present of his own books, with the remark: 'Voilà des livres dont il faut se munir'). Then Price went on alone to see Switzerland and the Rhine. Most of his life—he was knighted in 1828 and died in 1829—he spent on his family estate Foxley, west of Hereford, busy on improvements, the social amenities of the squire, and some writing. He calls himself 'an indolent writer, who can little depend on any constant and regular exertions' (III, 399), but should not therefore be pictured as weak and delicate. On the contrary, at eighty he is still described as 'all life and spirits, ranging about his woods as a setter-dog.' It is this extreme alertness that has kept his writings alive, and made them 'convert his age to his views,' as Sir Walter Scott put it. His* Essay on the Picturesque *came out in 1794, the same year as Knight's* The Landscape *and Humphry Repton's* Sketches and Hints. *Controversies arising from the contents of the three publications made Price refine his theses and add corroboration.** In the final *n.1 form they appeared as* Three Essays on the Picturesque *in 1810. It is from this edition that quotations are given in the following pages.*

VII
Uvedale Price

THE TERM PICTURESQUE was suggested by Uvedale Price to indicate certain aesthetic qualities not comprised in the then fashionable aesthetic terms Sublime and Beautiful. Burke in his *Inquiry into the Origin of our ideas of the Sublime and the Beautiful* of 1757 had been responsible for their definition and popularization. The Sublime, Burke said, is caused by terrible objects, by obscurity, solitude and vastness, while the Beautiful is connected with smoothness, gentle curves, polish and delicacy. Price accepted and praised this division, but denied that it is sufficient. There is visual delight neither caused by sombre grandeur nor by light elegance. Take a beautiful building in an advanced state of decay: Gradually, he says,

'the embellishments that belong to architecture, the polish of its columns, the highly finished execution of its capitals and mouldings, its urns and statues, are changed for what may be called the embellishments of ruins, for incrustations and weather stains, and for the various plants that spring from, or climb over the walls . . . ; and at length, perhaps, all smoothness, all symmetry, all trace of design are totally gone. But there may still remain an object which attracts notice. Has it then no character when that of beauty is departed? is it ugly? is it insipid? is it merely curious? Ask the painter, or the picturesque traveller; they never abandon a ruin to the mere antiquary, till none but an antiquary would observe it. Whatever then has strong attractions as a visible object, must have a character; and that which has strong attractions for the painter, and yet is neither grand nor beautiful, is justly called picturesque.' (II, 259–260).

Price's contrast between the antiquary and the picturesque traveller is worth noting. It is to-day the contrast between the Office of Works attitude and the John Piper attitude. Of picturesque travellers there were more in Price's time than in ours, when archaeology has robbed people of their visual innocence. The
n.2 king of the picturesque travellers was of course William Gilpin.* His eight books appeared from 1782 to 1809. Five of the eight were out before Price wrote his *Essay*. But to Gilpin picturesque is simply what is 'agreeable in a picture.' Now such a loose definition did not satisfy Price. Here are his comments:

'There are few words, whose meaning has been less accurately determined than that of the word picturesque. In general, I believe, it is applied to every object, and every kind of scenery, which has been, or might be represented with good effect in painting; just as the word beautiful (when we speak of visible nature) is applied to every object, and every kind of scenery, that in any way give pleasure to the eye. . . . Mr. Gilpin, from whose very ingenious and extensive observations on this subject I have received great pleasure and instruction, appears to have adopted this common acceptation, not merely as such, but as giving an exact and determinate idea of the word; for he defines picturesque objects to be those "which please from some quality capable of being illustrated in painting," or, as he again defines it in his Letter to Sir Joshua Reynolds "such objects as are proper subjects for painting." Both these definitions seem to me (what may perhaps appear a contradiction) at once too vague, and too confined; for though we are not to expect any definition to be so accurate and comprehensive, as both to supply the place, and stand the test of investigation, yet if it do not in some degree separate the thing defined from all others, it differs little from any general truth on the same subject. For instance, it is very true that picturesque objects do please from some quality capable of being illustrated in painting; but so also does every object that is represented in painting if it please at all, otherwise it would not have been painted: and hence we ought to conclude, what certainly is not meant, that all objects which please in pictures are therefore picturesque; for no distinction or exclusion is made. Were any other person to define picturesque objects to be those which please from some striking effect of form, colour, or light and shadow—such a definition would indeed give but a very indistinct idea of the thing defined: but it would be hardly more vague, and at the same time much less confined than the others, for it would not have an exclusive reference to a particular art. I hope to shew in the course of this work, that the picturesque has a character not less separate and distinct than either the sublime or the beautiful, nor less independent of the art of painting.' (I, 37–40).

So this is Price's promise. How then does he define the character of the Picturesque?

DEFINITIONS
OF THE
PICTURESQUE

The chief qualities of the Picturesque had already been well brought out by Sir Joshua Reynolds eight years before Price began to publish his *Essay*. In Reynold's thirteenth Discourse delivered to the students of the Royal Academy on December 11, 1786, there are some paragraphs on architecture which afford a spectacular proof of his flair for new and significant ideas.

'It may not be amiss for the architect to take advantage *sometimes* of that to which I am sure the painter ought always to have his eyes open, I mean the use of accidents; to follow where they lead, and to improve them, rather than always to trust to a regular plan. It often happens that additions have been made to houses, at various times, for use or pleasure. As such buildings depart from regularity, they now and then acquire something of scenery by this accident, which I should think might not unsuccessfully be adopted by an architect, in an original plan, if it does not too much interfere with convenience. Variety and intricacy is a beauty and excellence in every other of the arts which address the imagination; and why not in architecture?

'The forms and turnings of the streets of London, and other old towns, are produced by accident, without any original plan or design; but they are not always the less pleasant to the walker or spectator, on that account. On the contrary, if the city had been built on the regular plan of Sir Christopher Wren, the effect might have been, as we know it is in some new parts of the town, rather unpleasing; the uniformity might have produced weariness, and a slight degree of disgust.

'I can pretend to no skill in the details of architecture. I judge now of the art, merely as a painter. When I speak of Vanbrugh, I mean to speak of him in the language of our art. To speak then of Vanbrugh in the language of a painter, he had originality of invention, he understood light and shadow, and had great skill in composition. To support his principal object he produced his second and third groups or masses; he perfectly understood in his art what is the most difficult in ours, the conduct of the background, by which the design and invention is set off to the greatest advantage. What the background is in painting, in architecture is the real ground on which the building is erected; and no architect took greater care than he that his work should not appear crude and hard: that is, it did not abruptly start out of the ground without expectation or preparation.

'This is a tribute which a painter owes to an architect who composed like a painter; and was defrauded of the due reward of his merit by the wits of his time, who did not understand the principles of composition in poetry better than he; and who knew little or nothing of what he understood perfectly, the general ruling principles of architecture and painting. His fate was that of the great Perrault; both were the objects of the petulant sarcasms of factious men of letters; and both have left some of the fairest ornaments which to this day decorate their several countries; the façade of the Louvre, Blenheim and Castle Howard.'

These are remarkable words indeed, and they must have impressed Price just as much as anything he had read in Gilpin. The only thing Reynolds did not do was to connect the qualities which he praises with the term Picturesque. It was left to Price to connect Gilpin's landscape characteristics with Reynolds's remarks on architecture. Here is the result:

'The two opposite qualities of roughness and of sudden variation, joined to that of irregularity, are the most efficient causes of the picturesque.' (I, 50).

'Roughness conveys the idea of . . . irritation, but at the same time of animation, spirit and variety.' (I, 115).

'Irritation is . . . the source of our most active and lively pleasures: its nature . . . is eager and hurrying, and such are the pleasures which spring from it.' (I, 127).

In twentieth century terms Price's rough would be abrupt, and for irritation one would probably say stimulus. So Price wishes to stress the stimulating power and the piquancy of sudden contrasts. Yes—the piquancy too, for he says in another place that 'piquant is a word . . . that in many points answers very exactly to the picturesque'. (I, 73).

Now for variety: Price blames the 'modern improvers' of Capability Brown's school—against him chiefly the *Essay* was written—for neglecting

'two of the most fruitful sources of human pleasure: the first, that great and universal source of pleasure, variety—the power of which is independent of beauty, but without which even beauty itself soon ceases to please; the second intricacy—a quality which, though distinct from variety, is so connected and blended with it, that the one can hardly exist without the other. According to the idea I have formed of it, intricacy in landscape might be defined as that disposition of objects, which, by a partial and uncertain concealment, excites and nourishes curiosity—the most active principle of pleasure.' (I, 21-22 and 24).

To visual stimulus by piquant contrasts we have thus to add variety, intricacy and the raising of curiosity—in short, the unexpected, unforeseeable in all its aspects. How shrewdly Reynolds had observed that to achieve such effects of happy surprise the architect should sometimes entrust himself to accident. Price enlarges on that motif:

'Every man will allow that painters and improvers ought to study nature, and nature in contradistinction to art. Are then all parts of nature to be studied indiscriminately? No one will make such an assertion. But whence do these various combinations arise, of trees so happily grouped and connected with ground, buildings, and water; of open lawns, of closer glades, and skirtings, in planting and forming which no art has been employed? As it cannot be from design, it must be from accident. Of these lucky accidents painters have made the greatest use; wherever they meet with them they eagerly trace them in their sketch-book; these they study, arrange, and combine in a thousand different ways; these are the stores whence their greater compositions are afterwards formed. But of these accidents (if we may judge from their works) improvers have as yet made but little use. Again, wherever art interferes, the effect of these beautiful and striking accidents is generally spoiled to the painter's eye; for the prevailing taste for clearing either indiscriminately, or in distinct clumps and patches, destroys their connection, their playful variety, and intricacy. Neglect, therefore, as well as accident, is necessary to furnish these examples of nature in her most picturesque state; that is (according to the common use of the word) the state in which painters do, and improvers ought to study and imitate her; but in the latter case particularly, with such modifications as the character of the scenery may require. Accident and neglect are therefore two principal causes of those beauties (and they often deserve that name in its strictest sense) which painters, lovers of painting, and many whose natural judgment has not been vitiated by false ideas of refinement, admire: and whoever means to study nature, must principally attend to the effects of neglect and accident.' (III, 38–41).

Price's constant reference to painters is important. More of its meaning and topical applications will be said later. Here it is sufficient to recall that it was in point of fact a painter who first drew attention to the thrills of accident: Leonardo da Vinci in the famous passage of his *Treatise* in which he advises the painter to study the rough textures of walls for finding patterns in them that might suggest motifs and compositions.

Price's chief definitions of the Picturesque are contained in the foregoing paragraphs. It may, however, be helpful to supplement them by some passages on the relations between the Picturesque and the Beautiful, and the Picturesque and the Ugly.

The
Picturesque
and the
Beautiful

Price deals with gardens and grounds, not with towns and cities. Hence he is right in saying that

'Of the three characters (the sublime, the beautiful, and the picturesque), two only are in any degree subject to the improver; to *create* the sublime is above our contracted powers, though we may sometimes heighten, and at all times lower its effects by art. It is, therefore, on a proper attention to the beautiful and the picturesque, that the art of improving real landscapes must depend.' (I, 102).

In a few passages Price suggests that the two should be blended.

'The great point . . . is to mix according to circumstances, what is striking, with what is simply pleasing.' (II, 131).

More often he contrasts them—no wonder, as the differences between beauty and picturesqueness are the principal theme of his *Essays*. Just two examples out of many, the first a straightforward statement, the second a warning against exaggerations, and at the same time an excellent comparison between pleasures of the eye and the palate.

'Although smoothness be the ground-work of beauty, yet . . . roughness is its fringe and ornament, and that which preserves it from insipidity . . . One principal charm of smoothness, whether in a literal or a metaphorical sense, is, that it conveys the idea of repose; roughness, on the contrary, conveys that of irritation.' (I, 115).

'If the improver, as it usually happens attends solely to verdure, smoothness, undulation of ground and flowing lines, the whole will be insipid. If the opposite, and much rarer taste should prevail; should an improver, by way of being picturesque, make broken ground, pits, and quarries all about his place; encourage nothing but furze, briars, and thistles; heap quantities of rude stones on his banks, or, to crown all, like Mr. Kent, plant dead trees—the deformity of such a place would, I believe, be very generally allowed, though the insipidity of the other might not be so readily confessed. . . . It can hardly be doubted, that what answers to the beautiful in the sense of tasting, has smoothness and sweetness for its basis, with such a degree of stimulus, as in the most delicious fruits and liquors. Take away the stimulus they become insipid; increase it so as to overbalance those qualities, they then gain a peculiarity of flavour, are eagerly sought after by those who have acquired a relish for them, but are less adapted to the general palate. This corresponds exactly with the picturesque; but if the stimulus be increased beyond that point, none but depraved and vitiated palates will endure, what would be so justly termed deformity in objects of sight.' (I, 207–9).

Deformity in objects of sight? But Price does by no means exclude deformity from the saving grace of the Picturesque. Here is an example of time's redemption of deformity:

'The side of a smooth green hill, torn by floods, may at first very properly be called deformed; and on the same principle, though not with the same impression, as a gash on a living animal. When a rawness of such a gash in the ground is softened, and in part concealed and ornamented by the effects of time, and the progress of vegetation, deformity, by this usual process, is converted into picturesqueness; and this is the case with quarries, gravel-pits, etc., which at first are deformities, and which in their most picturesque state, are often considered as such by a levelling improver. . . . This connection between picturesqueness and deformity cannot be too much studied by improvers.' (I, 195).

The parallelism between such mellowing action of time on a hillside and on a building need hardly be pointed out. It is, of course, the chief visual explanation of the picturesque improver's delight in ruins.

So deformity can be mellowed into picturesqueness. Only what Price calls 'unmixed ugliness' cannot.

THE PICTURESQUE AND THE UGLY

'It seems to me, that mere unmixed ugliness does not arise from sharp angles, or from any sudden variation; but rather from that want of form, that unshapen lumpish appearance, which perhaps, no one word exactly expresses.' (I, 188).

Hence the ugliest buildings to Uvedale Price are

'those which have no feature, no character; those, in short, which most nearly approach to the shape, "if shape it may be called," of a clamp of brick, the ugliness of which no one will dispute.' (I, 197).

Poor Queen Anne, poor William and Mary, poor Christopher Wren. With Price and his generation the violent reaction against the quiet restraint of their well-proportioned, symmetrical, serviceable, sensible, medium-sized or small country houses begins. It did not in London prevent Bloomsbury from growing in that sober brick style just when Price wrote. But it defeated sobriety in the end, and Gothic, Tudor and Italianate palaces and villas sprouted forth all over the countryside.

With regard to colour, this is what Price condemns:

'What may be termed muddiness, is the most general and efficient cause of ugliness. A colour, for instance, may be harsh, glaring, tawdry, yet please many eyes, and by some be called beautiful: but a muddy colour, no one ever was pleased with.' (I, 200).

So tawdry colours—and perhaps also tawdry objects—may please the eye. It is one of Price's most important discoveries to have recognised the claims of the aesthetically questionable for a place in a picturesque composition. He must have felt strongly about it, or he would not have repeated the same concept three times in three different wordings.

'If I were obliged to determine between insipid congruity, and incongruity which produces grand and striking effects, I should not hesitate in preferring the latter.' (II, 231).

'Who would not prefer an absurd, but laughable farce, to a flat insipid piece of five acts?' (II, 40).

'I would rather wish that some improprieties should be risked for the sake of effect (where the mischief, if such, could be repaired) than that improvements should be confined to the present timid monotony.' (II, 157).

THE PICTURESQUE
AND THE PAINTER

But how can the improver, or the playwright, or the architect, or the artist afford the presence of absurdity? The answer is that he allots to the incongruous its proper place within a larger composition. Here is how, addressing the garden artist and the improver, Price justifies it:

'Connection is the leading principle of your art.' (III, 107). 'The greatest of all [defects], and the most opposite to the principles of painting, is want of connection, a passion for making everything distinct and separate.' (I, 238).

'Twilight does, what an improver ought to do: it connects what was before scattered; it fills up staring, meagre vacancies [and] destroys edginess.' (I, 153).

'Every person of the least observation must have remarked how broad the lights and shadows are on a fine evening in nature, or (what is almost the same thing), in a picture of Claude.' (I, 148).

A picture of Claude—another of Price's references to painters and painting, and a particularly appropriate one. Connecting objects in nature into coherent compositions is indeed the painter's job. If it is also a principle of picturesque planning —no wonder that the two words *pictor*, the painter, and *picturesque* are etymologically related. Price emphasizes the significance of this relation.

PICTURESQUE, PAINTER
AND IMPROVER

'If we suppose a person of natural sensibility and discernment, but who had never seen a picture, to have been shewn when they were first painted, the Aurora of Guido, the Nymphs and Cupids of Albano, or the Leda of Correggio, pictures in which nothing but what is youthful and lovely is exhibited, he must readily have acknowledged the whole, and every part to be beautiful; because if he were to see such objects in nature, he would call them so, and view them with delight. The same thing must have happened had he been shewn a picture of Claude, where richly ornamented temples and palaces, were accompanied by trees of elegant forms, and luxuriant foliage, the whole set off by the mild glow of a fine evening; for every thing he saw there, he would wish to see and to dwell upon in reality. But should he have been shewn a set of pictures, in which a number of the principal objects were rough, rugged and broken, with various marks of age and decay, yet without any thing of grandeur or dignity, he must certainly have thought it strange, that the artists should choose to pertpetuate on their canvas such figures, animals, trees, buildings, &c. as he should wish, if he saw them in nature, to remove from his sight. He might afterwards, however, begin to observe, that among objects which to him appeared void of every kind of attraction, the painters had decided reasons of preference; whether from their strongly marked peculiarity of character, from the variety produced by sudden and irregular deviation, from the manner in which the rugged and broken parts caught the light, and from those lights being often opposed to some deep shadow, or from the rich and mellow tints produced by various stages of decay; all of which he had passed by without noticing, or had merely thought them ugly, but now began to look at with some interest: he would find at the same time, that there were quite a sufficient number of objects, which the painter would perfectly agree with him in calling ugly, without any addition or qualification. Such observations as I have just supposed to be made by a single person, must have gradually occurred to a variety of observers during the progress of the art: many of them may have seen the artists at work, and remarked the pleasure they seemed to take in imitating by spirited strokes of the pencil, any rough and broken objects, any strongly marked peculiarity of character, or of light and shadow. They might thence be led to conclude, that a number of objects, neither grand, nor beautiful, nor ugly, are in a manner the peculiar property of the painter and his art, being by them first illustrated, and brought into notice and general observation. When such an idea had once begun to prevail, it was very natural that a word should be invented, and soon be commonly made use of, which discriminated the character of such objects, by their relation to the artist himself, or to his work.' (I, 214–219).

Price's is a good case here. The painter as the visual type, physiologically and psychologically speaking, reacts more intensely than other types to impressions of sight. Hence he is the one to tell us how a stretch of scenery, rural or urban, can be converted into a landscape, that is a piece of three-dimensional art, planned to give visual pleasure. Price indeed goes further. He tries to prove, and does it neatly, that the landscape gardener, whether he knows it or not, works like a painter. He comments on this identity of procedure in his letter of 1795, the reply to young Humphry Repton's defence of Capability Brown.

'Though your principal aim (writes Price) throughout the whole of your Letter has been to counteract my endeavours, and to weaken as much as possible the connection between painting and landscape gardening, yet your own mode of proceeding affords the strongest proof of the closeness of that connection. Consider only what your process is, when you are consulted about the improvements of a place. One of the first things you do is to make representations of the principal points, in the state in which you find them; and other representations of the state in which you hope they will be hereafter. In reality, you make the best pictures you can, with the materials you find there; and also with those fresh ones you mean to employ, and to which time must give effect.' (III, 46–47).

And as the gardener works with the painter's technique, so the improver should look to the pictures of great landscape painters for forming his taste and establishing standards. Is there

'any standard, to which in point of grouping and of general composition, works of this sort can be referred; any authority higher than that of the persons who have gained the most general and popular reputation by those works, and whose method of conducting them has had the most extensive influence on the general taste? I think there is a standard; there are authorities of an infinitely higher kind; the authorities of those great artists who have most diligently studied the beauties of nature, both in their grandest and most general effects, and in their minutest detail; who have observed every variety of form and of colour; have been able to select and combine, and then, by the magic of their art, to fix upon the canvas all those various beauties.' (I, 2–3).

Price in fact believes that by studying the achievements of landscape painters, the amateur might develop his judgment and discrimination sufficiently to do without professionals. That may have been true of him and of friends like Payne Knight or Horace Walpole. But would it still be true today? Have we still got amateurs in the Georgian sense? Who, not a painter, would see views as intensely as Price does in the following passage from the *Dialogue* of Messrs. Hamilton, Howard, and Seymour (1801)? Mr Hamilton, as we have seen, represents Price, Mr Howard, Payne Knight. It is Mr Hamilton who speaks the following words:

'You cannot imagine, what a loss there is in that group of trees, of which my old friend the clergyman was speaking. I can shew you very nearly where it stood: you see where there is a sinking in those hills to the left; from about this point where we stand, the trees just intersected that part: and as they rose a great deal above the horizon, and spread very much at top, you may imagine how well they must have divided this long continued view. You will immediately perceive too, that the noble reach of the river in the second distance, with the bridge, the town, and the hills beyond, came in to the right of the group; and being separated by it from the general view, formed quite a picture.' (III, 351–2).

Such susceptibility to visual effects the layman, in our century, has lost. And how many architects have still got it? Few: and fewer still when it comes to the pictorial approach to urban scenery. As long as it is only a matter of seeing landscape, the open-eyed may still be found in all ways of life. But the visual approach to nature in relation to buildings, to the richness of water effects, and to the garden (as against the grounds) has become rare indeed. Some comments of Price's on these topics may, in conclusion, be useful.

APPLICATIONS   Price's principles in their application to the many parts that make up the urban pattern are of the highest topical value, although proffered with a view to conditions on a country estate only. They were developed just like Knight's in opposition to Capability Brown and his followers, to the gentleness of their designs and smoothness of their effects.

'All water of which the surface is broken, and the motion abrupt and irregular . . . accords with our idea of the picturesque.' (I, 57).

'The smallest appearance of water, a mere light in the landscape, may answer a very essential purpose—that of leading the attention to those parts which are most worthy of notice.' (II, 53).

'In the pictures of Claude, the character of which is beauty and cheerfulness, detached architecture, as far as I have observed, is seldom unaccompanied with trees.' (II, 185).

'How many buildings have I seen, which, with their trees, attract and please every eye! But deprive one of them of those accompaniments, what a solitary deserted object would remain!' (II, 195).

'The accompaniments of beautiful pieces of architecture, may in some respects, be compared to the dress of beautiful women. The addition of what is no less foreign to them than trees are to architecture, varies and adorns the charms even of those who, like Phryne, might throw off every concealment, and challenge the critic eyes of all Athens assembled.' (II, 194).

'But the number of trees which an inhabitant of Holland, without fear of inconvenience, plants close to his house, is by no means necessary to picturesque composition: a very few, even a single tree, may make such a break, such a division in the general view as may answer that end.' (II, 188).

'Trees, whether single or in groups, whether young or old, are obviously of the greatest use in accompanying buildings of every kind; but there seems to be a much closer union between them and low buildings. Cottages appear to repose under their shade, to be protected, sometimes supported by them; and they, on the other hand, hang over and embrace the cottage with their branches: it seems as if they could never have been separated from each other; and there would be a sort of cruelty in dividing them. If trees thus adorn the cottage, that, in return, by the contrast of its form and colour no less enhances the peculiar beauties of vegetation, and often fixes the attention on trees which in other situations would be unnoticed. No wonder, then, if we are particularly struck with any of the beautiful exotics when so placed; with an acacia, a pine, a cedar, that shade part of a village-house; with an arbutus, or a cluster of lilacs, over-topping the wall, or the pales of its garden.' (II, 351).

'Though trees and shrubs of every kind have a peculiar and distinguished effect, in consequence of accompanying, and being accompanied by the houses of a village, there is another tribe of plants which gains still more by such a situation, and which indeed no other can shew to such advantage; I mean the various sorts of climbing plants.' (II, 352).

The truth of these sentences for housing estates today need not be specially emphasized.

With regard to the garden, that is the part of the estate most closely adjacent to the house, Price preaches the same freedom. But here he turns in a most illuminating way against the dogmas almost universally accepted by his generation. Here he founds a new school which became the leading school of the later nineteenth century, and is still ours. Brown had brought the informal pattern of the grounds right to the front of the house. Price wants a zone of formality in between, laid out with a frank display of art. He even defends the old garden art of the seventeenth century.

'It appears to me, that in the old gardens art was meant to be apparent, and to challenge admiration on its own account, not under the disguise of nature; that richness, effect, and agreement with the surrounding artificial objects, were what the planners and decorators of those gardens aimed at.' (II, 156).

'In forming a general comparison of the two styles of gardening, it seems to me that what constitutes the chief excellence of the old garden, is richness of decoration and of effect, and an agreement, with the same qualities in architecture; its defects, stiffness, and formality. The excellences of the modern garden, are verdure, undulation of ground, diversity of plants, and a more varied and natural disposition of them than had hitherto been practised: its defects, when considered as accompanying architecture—a uniformity of character too nearly approaching to common nature.' (II, 158–159).

A garden must not look like common nature. There must be something

'to mark the difference between what is close to the house, and what is at a distance from it; between the habitation of man, and that of sheep.' (II, 126).

The curious thing, and the thing that proves once more Price's originality of approach, is that for him the seventeenth century garden does not stand for stiffness as it did for nearly all the other picturesque improvers; it stands for picturesqueness. The following statement must have sounded very perverse to readers used to regarding Brown's softly undulating gardens as the acme of picturesqueness.

'In many old places, there are almost as many walled compartments without, as apartments within doors; and though there is no defending the beauty of brick walls, yet still that appearance of seclusion and safety, when it can be so contrived as not to interfere with general beauty, is a point well worth obtaining; and no man is more ready than myself to allow that the comfortable, is a principle which should never be neglected. On that account all walled gardens and compartments near a house; all warm, sheltered, sunny walks under walls planted with fruit-trees, are greatly to be wished for: and should be preserved, if possible, when once established. I, therefore, regret extremely, not only the compartment I just mentioned, but another garden immediately beyond it: and I cannot forget the sort of curiosity and surprize that was excited after a short absence, even in me, to whom it was familiar, by the simple and common circumstance of a door that led from the first compartment to the second, and the pleasure I always experienced on entering the inner, and more secluded garden. There was nothing, however, in the garden itself to excite any extraordinary sensations: the middle part was merely planted with the lesser fruits, and dwarf trees, but on the opening of the door, the lofty trees of a fine grove appeared immediately over the opposite wall; the trees are still there, they are more distinctly and openly seen, but the striking impression is gone. On the right was another raised terrace, level with the top of the wall that supported it; and over-hung with shrubs, which from age had lost their formality. A flight of steps of a plainer kind, with a mere parapet on the sides, led up to this upper terrace underneath the shrubs and exotics. All this gave me emotions in my youth, which I long imagined were merely those of early habit; but I am now convinced that was not all: they also arose from a quick succession of varied objects, of varied forms, tints, lights and shadows; they arose from the various degrees of intricacy and suspense that were produced by the no less various degrees and kinds of concealment, all exciting and nourishment curiosity, and all distinct in their character from the surrounding landscapes.' (II, 121–123).

Incidentally, Price was open to the delights and sensitive to the subtleties of all arts. So he compares gardens of the kind just described with Handel's music, as against other lighter and less formal eighteenth century music.

'The same aversion to symmetry shewed itself nearly at the same period, in other arts as well as in gardening: fugues and imitations in music began to grow out of fashion, about the time that terraces and avenues were demolished; but the improvements in modern music have a very different character from those in modern gardening, for no one can accuse Haydn or Paesiello of tameness or monotony. The passion for strict fugues in music, and for exact symmetry in gardens, had been carried to excess, and when totally undisguised and unvaried, it created in both arts a dryness and pedantry of style: but the principle on which that passion is founded should never be totally neglected. Some of the greatest masters of music in later times, among whom Handel claims the highest place, have done what improvers might well have done; they have not abandoned symmetry, but have mixed it (particularly in accompaniments) with what is more wild and irregular.' (II, 378).

However, Price is not consistent in his interpretation of the formally designed garden near the house. He was so anxious to defend it against Brown that he praised its intricacy and concealment in some passages such as that just quoted, while in others he allowed 'convenience, neatness and a dressed appearance.' (III, 168). Did he realize that neatness could be picturesque?

'Near the house picturesque beauty . . . must often be sacrificed to neatness; but that is a sacrifice, and one which should not wantonly be made.' (III, 169).

The point was that close to the house utility was evidently required just as much as display. It is doubtful if Price ever made up his mind whether utility and 'picturesque beauty' were allies or adversaries. He propounded both views.

'It is an acknowledged maxim, that what is ornamental, should, if possible, appear to answer some purpose of utility.' (II, 279).

That could be by Pugin or by a functionalist of 1930. The following passage could not:

'In all this, convenience and propriety are not the objects of consideration: not that either of them is to be neglected, but that they are objects of another kind; objects of good sense, and good judgment, rather than of that more refined and delicate sense and judgment, called taste.' (III, 49).

However, the relation of function to aesthetic appeal is only a side issue in our context. What matters is Price's apology of the terraced garden with balustrades and statuary, or the fruit garden with walled-in compartments as a source of picturesque pleasure. The application of these passages to problems of urban planning is evident.

In such passages Price is perhaps at his greatest. They show how far he had left behind the accepted dogmas and fashions of his generation. The man who could defend the compartmented 'Dutch' garden and Handel's music in 1790, without fear of being branded a reactionary, should be more to us than a representative of a style of the past. Such latitude of aesthetic sensibility raises him out of the eighteenth century to an undated position in the history of aesthetic theory.

1   *The conduit at Ashridge*

The Architectural Review, CII, 1948

VIII
Humphry Repton

HUMPHRY REPTON was born in 1752 and died in 1818. Shortly after Capability Brown's death in 1788 Repton became his recognised successor in fame and affluence. When in 1794 Uvedale Price and Richard Payne Knight published their first works as the Picturesque, they regarded Repton already as 'the most skilful and eminent' among the professional 'improvers of places' (Knight: *The Landscape*). By 1794 he had improved over fifty places, by 1803 nearly two hundred (*Observations*, p. 120), by 1816 more than four hundred (*Fragments*, p. 409).* Many Repton gardens are still preserved, although later alteration and unchecked growth of vegetation has changed their appearance. Miss Dorothy Stroud's *Humphry Repton* (London, 1962) has given us plenty of facts on his career and his *oeuvre,* but she does not treat specially of Repton as a theorist. The following passages are intended to act as a preliminary summary of Repton's theories. They were laid down in five books:

n. 1

1794 *Sketches and Hints on Landscape Gardening*
1803 *Observations on the Theory and Practice of Landscape Gardening*
1806 *An Inquiry into the Changes of Taste in Landscape Gardening* (incorporating a reprint of *Sketches and Hints*)
1808 *Designs for the Pavilion at Brighton*
1810 *Fragments on the Theory and Practice of Landscape Gardening*

They will hereinafter be quoted as *Sketches, Observations, Inquiry, Designs* and *Fragments,* with page-numbers from Loudon's one-volume edition of all of them (1840). In this handy edition the book can still be used with profit today, for Repton's is a sound, sensible way of presenting his facts and views, and the volume with Loudon's footnotes comprises a vast amount of gardening tradition and lore. Moreover, anyone not wholly allergic to history cannot fail to be impressed by the historic range of a book in which Horace Walpole is still quoted as a live critic of architecture ('In a conversation I had the satisfaction to enjoy with the late Earl of Oxford,' *Observations*, p. 218), while Ruskin's very first essays in authorship are already taken notice of (' . . . a distinguished writer, who takes the signature of Kataphusin, in the Architectural Magazine'; Loudon's note, p. 32).

Loudon's illustrations are enjoyable in a homely way, but they represent only very inadequately the exquisite illustrations in aquatint which grace Repton's own editions. This immense care for visual presentation is the first quality which shows that he still belongs to the eighteenth century tradition. After all he was over forty-five when the new century began.

Repton's interest in visual presentation did not stop at mere care for good book illustration. He invented a special technique for showing what his pro-

2 'Lord Sidmouth's in Richmond Park', as it was

posed improvements would actually look like. This technique he used in the Red Books, leather-bound volumes which he prepared for prospective and actual clients as well as in the printed books, which are mostly compiled from the Red Books. He sketched himself a number of views of house and grounds in the state in which he saw them, and then painted a proper water colour drawing with his improvements in their finished state over which a flap indicates things in their present state. Thus the client's and reader's first impression is the view as it is, their second—a skilfully calculated surprise—the view as it should be. These flaps he calls slides. They are an expensive method of illustration, but the best, I would say, to this day. If it is no longer used, the reason is that there exists only a very small public nowadays ready to pay a high price for aesthetic thrill. You need the eighteenth century virtuoso, sensitive, sensuous and leisurely, to insist on visual perfection at any price.

Many of Repton's practical suggestions, especially in his earlier books, demand the crazy visual single-mindedness of the Georgian amateur.

'The net fence, through which the water appears, is so near the windows, that, by the laws of perspective, it acts as a false standard, and by it we measure the size of the pool. It was for this reason that I desired some cattle might be driven on the banks, which, as I have elsewhere shewn, are the best standard for assisting the judgment with respect to the distance, and, of course, the dimensions of other objects.' (*Sketches*, p. 73).

'At Hurlingham, on the banks of the Thames, the lawn in front of the house was necessarily contracted by the vicinity of the river, yet being too large to be kept under the scythe and roller, and too small to be fed by a flock of sheep. I recommended the introduction of Alderney cows only; and the effect is that of giving imaginary extent.' (*Observations*, p. 135).

'I am peculiarly happy in being called upon to mark a spot for new cottages, instead of those which it is necessary to remove, because, the turnpike-road being removed, there will be no access for the inhabitants but through a part of the park, which cannot then be private. I must advise, however, that some one or more of the houses in this dell be left, and inhabited either as a keeper's house, a dairy, or a menagerie, that the occasional smoke from the chimneys may animate the scene.' (*Observations*, p. 245).

In these passages cows, sheep and pheasants are just so many spots of colour and form in pictures. There were no puritan qualms yet about the relative values of moral and aesthetic matters.

*3 Repton's proposed improvements: the
same plate, 'slide' removed*

Plenty more examples could be given of Repton's intense visual sensibility. Many of the qualities brought out most consistently by Repton appear in Price's *Essay* too, others are fresh observations of his.

'Trees of a conic shape mixed with Gothic buildings displease, from their affinity with the prevalent lines of the architecture [while with classical buildings] they have a beautiful effect, I believe chiefly from the circumstances of contrast.' (*Sketches,* 56).

'The contrasted greens of wood and lawn are not sufficient to gratify the eye; it requires other objects, and those of different colours, such as rocks, water, and cattle; but where these natural objects cannot easily be had, the variety may be obtained by artificial means, such as a building, a tent, or a road.' *(Sketches,* 80).

Repton's last book has a whole Fragment on contrasts, discussing for instance—

'The contrast betwixt aspiring and drooping plants, the contrast in texture; some plants and flowers appearing as if composed of silk; others, of cloth or velvet; some smooth as satin; others, harsh, rough and prickly, and the contrast of size; some, like the aloe, the horse-chestnut, or the tulip-tree, bearing their blossoms above the reach of man; and others, like the diminutive rock-plants, and miniatures of nature, requiring to be raised, or placed on tables, and in flower-pots or baskets.' (*Fragments,* 493–94).

The following three passages are on optical illusion, on the effects of sunlight and on views out of windows.

'A plain appears a hill, or a hill a plain, according to the point of view from whence each is seen.' (*Observations,* 151).

'Certain objects appear best with the sun behind them, and others with the sun full upon them; and it is rather singular, that to the former belong all *natural* objects, such as woods, trees, lawn, water, and distant mountains; while to the latter belong all *artificial* objects, such as houses, bridges, roads, boats, arable fields, and distant towns or villages.' *(Observations,* 155).

'A view seen from the windows of an apartment will materially differ from the same view seen in the open air. In one case, without moving the head, we see from sixty to ninety degrees; or, by a single motion of the head, without moving the body, we may see every object within one hundred and eighty degrees of vision. In the other case the portion of landscape will be much less, and must depend on the size of the window, the thickness of the walls, and the distance of the spectator from the aperture. Hence it arises, that persons are frequently disappointed, after building a house, to find that those objects which they expected would form the leading feature of their landscape are scarcely seen, except from such a situation in the room as may be inconvenient to the spectator.' (*Observations*, 150).

It is unnecessary to add after this that Repton also knew the importance of aerial besides linear perspective (*Sketches*, 75) and the importance to buildings of vegetation and colouring, especially

'those weather stains, which time alone can throw over the works of art, to blend them with the works of nature.' *(Fragments, 428).*

In all this Repton appears as radical as Uvedale Price and Payne Knight. But that impression is deceiving. They were revolutionaries; he was a man of compromise who never forgot his practice and his clients. He disliked novelty and extremes.

'True taste, in every art, consists more in adapting tried expedients to peculiar circumstances, than in that inordinate thirst after novelty.' (*Sketches*, 24).
'Fashion is neither to be directly opposed nor imperiously guided, either by the theory of authors, or the practice of professors. I have occasionally ventured to deliver my opinion freely in theory, but in my practice I have often feared to give offence, by opposing the taste of others, since it is equally dangerous to doubt a man's taste as his understanding.' (*Inquiry*, 352).

Such remarks, as we have already seen, were distasteful to both Knight and Price. Both must have met Repton in the neighbourhood of their Welsh border estates of Downton and Foxley as early as 1780, if not earlier still (*Sketches*, 95). A controversy began in the very year 1794, when Repton's *Sketches*, Knight's *The Landscape* and Price's first *Essay* came out, and it went on with attack and defence throughout Repton's published work.

It seems at first a futile controversy; for Repton is quite at one with Price and Knight on a good many points. His adversaries tried to brand him as the reincarnation of Brown, and believed (wrongly) that the 'dull, vapid, smooth and tranquil scene' (Knight, *Landscape*) which was Brown's ideal, was also Repton's. Yet Repton is just as lustily aggressive as Price and Knight against placing a house pat on the lawn (*Observations* 127), against 'tame and sleepy' serpentine rivers and lakes (*Observations* 164), against the clump (*Observations* 170) and the belt (*Inquiry* 334)—that is the whole apparatus of Brownian landscaping. And when Repton—ineffectively, for he was not a systematic writer—tried to get down to principles he took most of them straight from Price. Here for instance are what he summed up at the end of his *Sketches* as the main

'sources of pleasure in landscape gardening: I Congruity — II Utility — III Order — IV Symmetry — V Picturesque Effect — VI Intricacy — VII Simplicity — VIII Variety — IX Novelty — X Contrast — XI Continuity — XII Association — XIII Grandeur — XIV Appropriation — XV Animation — XVI The Seasons (112–114).'

Even as late as 1816 he allows us 'to extract pleasure from *variety,* from *contrast,* and even from *novelty* (*Fragments,* 550); and when we read that intricacy is 'the due medium between uniformity on the one hand, and confusion on the other' (*Observations,* 184) we might be reading Price himself. The same applies to this sentence:

'The mind requires a continuity, though not a sameness; and, while it is pleased with succession and variety, it is offended by sudden contrast, which destroys the unity of composition.' (*Observations,* 184).

Yet there were professional contrasts as well as important contrasts of principle between Repton on the one hand and Price and Knight on the other. Taking the professional first, Repton was a gardener—that was his trade and sole source of

4   *The garden of Frome House, after Repton's improvements; the cattle and the wire fence give a sense of distance*

income—Price and Knight were wealthy amateurs. Repton had in fact invented the title landscape gardener for himself to establish his status (*Sketches*, 28).

'You so earnestly recommend every gentleman to become his own landscape gardener. With equal propriety might every gentleman become his own architect, or even his own physician: in short, there is nothing that a man of abilities may not do for himself, if he will dedicate his whole attention to that subject only. But the life of man is not sufficient to excel in all things; and as 'a little knowledge is a dangerous thing, so the professors of every art, as well as that of medicine, will often find that the most difficult cases are those where the patient has begun by *quacking himself.*' (*Sketches*, 108).

'Natural taste, like natural genius, may exist to a certain degree, but . . . the professor only acquires a knowledge of effects before they are produced, and a facility in producing them by various methods, expedients, and resources, as the result of study, observation, and experience.' (*Observations*, 123).

'It is . . . absolutely necessary for the landscape gardener to have a competent knowledge of architecture.' (*Sketches*, 52).

'[He must also] possess a competent knowledge of surveying, mechanics, hydraulics, agriculture, botany, and the general principles of architecture. It can hardly be expected that a man bred, and constantly living, in the kitchen garden, should possess all these requisites; yet because the immortal Brown was originally a kitchen gardener, it is too common to find every man, who can handle a rake or spade, pretending to give his opinion on the most difficult points of improvement.' (*Sketches*, 30).

Now as for matters of principles, there are three of Price's to which Repton objects: the importance of landscape painting for all questions of landscape improvement, the importance of neglect and accident, or rather seeming neglect and accident, and the importance of the Picturesque over all other criteria.

'The spot from whence the view is taken, is in a fixed state to the painter; but the gardener surveys his scenery while in motion; and, from different windows in the same front, he sees objects in different situations; therefore, to give an accurate portrait of the gardener's improvement, would require pictures from each separate window, and even a different drawing at the most trifling change of situation, either in the approach, the walks, or the drives, about each place.' (*Sketches*, 96).

'The part which the painter calls his middle distances, is often that which the landscape gardener finds under the control of others; and the foreground of the painter can seldom be introduced into the composition of the gardener's landscape, from the whole front of a house, because the best landscapes of Claude will be found to owe their beauty to that kind of foreground, which could only be applied to one particular window of a house, and would exclude all view from that adjoining.' (*Sketches*, 98).

'The finest pictures of Claude (and here . . . I may refer to a picture at Attingham) seldom consist of more than one-fifth of that field of vision which the eye can with ease behold.' (*Observations*, 227).

'The view from an eminence down a steep hill is not to be represented in painting, although it is often one of the most pleasing circumstances of natural landscape.' (*Inquiry*, 856).

'The light which the painter may bring from any point of the compass must, in real scenery, depend on the time of day.' (*Inquiry*, 356).

And finally, one especially sound argument: the painter 'sees things as they are,' the landscape gardener 'as they will be' (*Fragments* 467).

But all the other arguments are also sound, obviously the arguments of a man who knows his job and keeps his eyes open. Equally sensible though aesthetically less attractive are Repton's digs at the Picturesque in Price's and Knight's sense.

'Since we cannot be quite reconciled to [our buildings] being in a state of ruin, which would certainly be most picturesque, we must build them in such irregular forms that trees may be introduced in various hollows and recesses to be left for this purpose: those will, indeed, very soon contribute to produce those weather stains, and harmonious tints, which are more grateful to the painter's eye than polished marble.' (*Observations*, 228).

'In our markets . . . instead of that formal trim custom of displaying poultry, fish, and fruit for sale on different stalls, why should we not rather copy the picturesque jumble of Schnyders and Rubens.' (*Observations*, 228).

'The author of the poem appears to forget that a dwellinghouse is an object of comfort and convenience, for the purpose of habitation; and not merely the frame to a landscape, or the foreground of a rural picture.' (*Sketches*, 99).

'The *quarry long neglected,* may supply a home for swallows and martens; the *mouldering abbey,* for ravens and jackdaws; the *ruined castle,* for bats and owls; and the *antiquated cot,* whose chimney is choked up with ivy, may perhaps yield a residue for squalid misery and want [but they are all] ill adapted to the residence of man.' (*Sketches*, 100).

'Extremes are . . . to be avoided; and I trust that the taste of this country will neither insipidly slide into the trammels of that smooth-shaven "*genius* of the bare and bald," which [Knight] so justly ridicules, nor enlist under the banners of that shaggy and harsh-featured *spirit,* which knows no delight but in the scenes of Salvator Rosa.' (*Sketches*, 191).

So it is the spirit of compromise that separates Repton from the amateurs. What principles on the positive side he wished to set against the Picturesque appears clearly already in the *Sketches*, and in these principles lies Repton's greatest historic if not aesthetic significance. The first of his principles is that convenience and utility must be rated higher than aesthetic values.

'I have discovered that utility must often take the lead of beauty, and convenience be preferred to picturesque effect, in the neighbourhood of man's habitation.' (*Sketches,* 99).

'Propriety and convenience are not less objects of good taste, than picturesque effect.' (*Sketches*, 104).

'In *Architecture*, there is not less beauty in the Grecian columns, than in the Gothic spires, pinnacles and turrets. In like manner, *Gardening* must include the two opposite characters of native wildness, and artificial comfort, each adapted to the genius and character of the place; yet, ever mindful, that, near the residence of man, convenience, and not picturesque effect, must have the preference, wherever they are placed in competition with each other.' (*Sketches*, 102).

'Symmetry is also allowable, and indeed necessary, at or near the front of a regular building.' (*Sketches*, 87).

'How far gravel roads are admissible across the lawns of a park? Surely very little doubt will remain on this subject, when we consider a park as a place of residence; and see the great inconvenience to which grass roads are continually liable.' (*Sketches*, 79).

The recommendation of symmetry near the house occurs in connection with a couple of remarkable paragraphs on differences between ancient and modern gardening.

'The perfection of Landscape Gardening consists in the four following requisites: First, it must display the natural beauties, and hide the natural defects of every situation. Secondly, it should give the appearance of extent and freedom, by carefully disguising or hiding the boundary. Thirdly, it must studiously conceal every interference of art, however expensive, by which the scenery is improved; making the whole appear the production of nature only; and, fourthly, all objects of mere convenience or comfort, if incapable of being made ornamental, or of becoming proper parts of the general scenery, must be removed or concealed. Each of the four objects here enumerated are directly opposite to the principles of ancient gardening, which may thus be stated. First, the natural beauties or defects of a situation had no influence, when it was the fashion to exclude, by lofty walls, every surrounding object. Secondly, these walls were never considered as defects; but, on the contrary, were ornamented with vases, expensive iron gates, and palisades, to render them more conspicuous. Thirdly, so far from making gardens appear natural, every expedient was used to display the expensive efforts of art, by which nature had been subdued.

And, lastly, with respect to objects of convenience, they were placed as near the house as possible: The stables, the barns, and the kitchen-garden, were among the ornaments of a place; while the village, the almshouse, the parish school and churchyard, were not attempted to be concealed by the walls or palisades that divided them from the embellished pleasure-ground.' (*Sketches*, 84–85).

This sounds a mere statement of facts. But Repton had actually gone further already before 1784. In the Red Books of Hasells and Cobham, first published in the *Observations* of 1803, but composed, Repton assures us, as early as 1790, he recommends action such as this:—

'The straight terrace ought not to be disturbed: although it is a remnant of geometric gardening of the last century, yet it is an object of such comfort and convenience, that it would be unpardonable to destroy it, for no other reason than because a straight walk is out of fashion.'

'The view from hence is so fine, so varied, and so interesting, that the spectator must be fastidious indeed, who could turn away disgusted, because it is over a clipt hedge, or with a broad walk in its foreground.'

'As an appendage to this ancient mansion, I would prefer the broad and stately mall along a straight line of terrace, to their too frequently repeated waving line of beauty.'

'The steep descent from the house has been cut into a number of terraces, each supported by a red brick wall and if these several walls had been of stone, or architecturally finished like the old costly hanging gardens of France and Italy,

5   *At Endsleigh on the Tamar, Repton used fencing and treillage and a formal terrace, as well as follies*

they might, perhaps, have added more magnificence to the house than any improvement which modern gardening could suggest. I therefore make a compromise between ancient and modern gardening, between art and nature, and by increasing the height, or rather the depth, from the upper terrace to the lower level of the ground, I make *that* the line of demarcation between the dressed ground and the park.' (*Observations,* 234–240).

If Repton is correct in the date given to this report—and there is no reason to doubt it—then he was by far the first to utter such heresies, and Knight must have been greatly impressed by him, when he rhymed in 1794:—

> Oft when I've seen some lonely mansion stand,
> Tir'd with th' extensive scene, so dull and bare,
> To Heav'n devoutly, I've address'd my pray'r,—
> Again the moss-grown terraces to raise,
> And spread the labyrinth's perplexing maze;
> Replace in even lines the ductile yew,
> And plant again the ancient avenue,
> Some features then, at least, we should obtain,
> To mark this flat, insipid, waving plain.

In fact Repton more than once implies that Knight, and Price also, took ideas from him without acknowledging them. And it cannot be denied that Price in the second volume of his *Essay* and Knight in his *Inquiry into the Principles of Taste*, both published after Repton's *Sketches*, are much more outspoken about the visual qualities of ancient gardening than they had been up till then. This, for example, is a passage from Price:

'Terraces, flights of steps, etc., are abrupt; but they are regular, and symmetrical; their abruptness prejudices bold and striking effects of light and shadow; less bold and varied indeed than those which arise from irregular abruptness, as from rocks and broken ground, but definitely more so than those which proceed from smoothness and flowing lines.' (*Essay* II, 132).

'However unnatural raised terraces, fountains, flights of steps, parapets, arch statues, vases, balustrades, etc., may be called . . . they are . . . not more artificial than the houses which they are intended to accompany.' (*Essay* II, 185).

However, Price kept his head clear. He described the gardens of Rome admirably in the second volume of the *Essay*, but went on to say that only the weatherstains, rifts, and other signs of decay make them as picturesque as they appear to us. He did not recommend their re-introduction into gardening. But Knight, more Italianate and less clear in his own mind what he wanted, did:

'We require, immediately adjoining the dwellings of opulence and luxury, that everything should assume its character and not only be, but appear to be dressed and cultivated.'

'[Near the house] I think the avowed character of art of the Italian gardens preferable . . . to the concealed one now in fashion.'

'[In Italian gardens] the mixture of splendour, richness, and neatness was beautiful and pleasing in the highest degree.'

'[Terraces] are indeed now rather old-fashioned; but another revolution in taste, which is probably at no great distance, will make them new again.' (*Inquiry*, pp. 158, 159, 219, 222).

Knight might well prophesy a change of taste; for in Repton's books it had already taken place. There was more genius no doubt in both Price and Knight than in Repton, but one can sympathize with Repton's annoyance.

There remains, however, a significant difference between the feelings underlying Repton's and Knight's defence of terrace, avenue and dressed garden. On the one hand we have visual delight in strong contrasts, on the other the professional gardener's anxiety to add to his client's comfort.

In this lies a more than personal contrast. It is representative of a basic change from the late eighteenth to the nineteenth century. Late eighteenth century contrasts are the outcome of visual sensibility, nineteenth century contrasts that of eclecticism. The buildings in Oxford Street, or the Strand and Fleet Street, or in Princes Street, Edinburgh, may be visually thrilling (or acutely painful), in their unmitigated contrasts of style and proportion, but they are not designed thus to impress us. They are simply so many individual units not consciously connected at all with each other. In the field of landscaping it was Repton who took the step of abandoning the broad unity of the eighteenth century in favour of a technique of adding part to part, each of a nature complete in itself and isolated—individualism or, if you will, liberalism and relativism, or indeed, as we shall see, historicism—in short the predominant qualities of the nineteenth century.

To recognize Repton's role as a pioneer of nineteenth century values, we must again start from his insistence on convenience and utility, and the way in which it showed itself in the defence of Italianate gardening. Both become stronger and more self-confident from 1794 to 1803, from 1803 to 1808, and from 1808 to 1816.

In 1803 he wrote:

'The leading feature in the good taste of modern times, is the just sense of General Utility.' (*Observations,* 125).

'It is . . . from the artificial considerations of utility, convenience, and propriety, that a place derives its real value in the eyes of a man of taste.' (*Observations,* 242).

'A house is an artificial object, and to a certain distance around the house, art may be avowed.' (*Observations,* 203).

'Flower-gardens on a small scale may, with propriety, be formal and artificial.' (*Observations,* 214).

Now a passage from 1808:

'Every residence of elegance or affluence requires its garden scenery; the beauty and propriety of which belong to art rather than to nature. In forest scenery, we trace the sketches of Salvator and of Ridinger; in park scenery, we may realize the landscape of Claude and Poussin: but, in garden scenery, we delight in the rich embellishments, the blended graces of Watteau, where nature is dressed, but not disfigured by art; and where the artificial decorations of architecture and sculpture are softened down by natural accompaniments of vegetation.' (*Inquiry,* 364).

And finally some lines published in 1816:

'I . . . suggest [the adoption of] a decided artificial character for the garden; boldly reverting to the ancient formal style, which, by some, will be condemned as departing from the imitation of nature.' (*Fragments, 481*). 'I am quite sure that the old magnificent taste for straight lines, and artificial shapes of ground, adjoining to a palace, was more consonant to true taste and greatness of character, than the sweeping lines and undulating surface of modern gardening.' (*Fragments, 540*).

The more interest Repton took in the garden as against the park the more did he feel incensed by the agricultural interests of his age. For it must not be forgotten that his is the time of Coke of Norfolk and all the other large scale amateur farmers. At the beginning of the picturesque movement, in Addison and Shenstone's writings for instance, the field and the fruit tree were still objects pleasant to the mind and therefore to the eye, nature was equally admired in the raw and as tamed by both the improvising squire and the industrious labourer. Now Repton writes of The Leasowes:

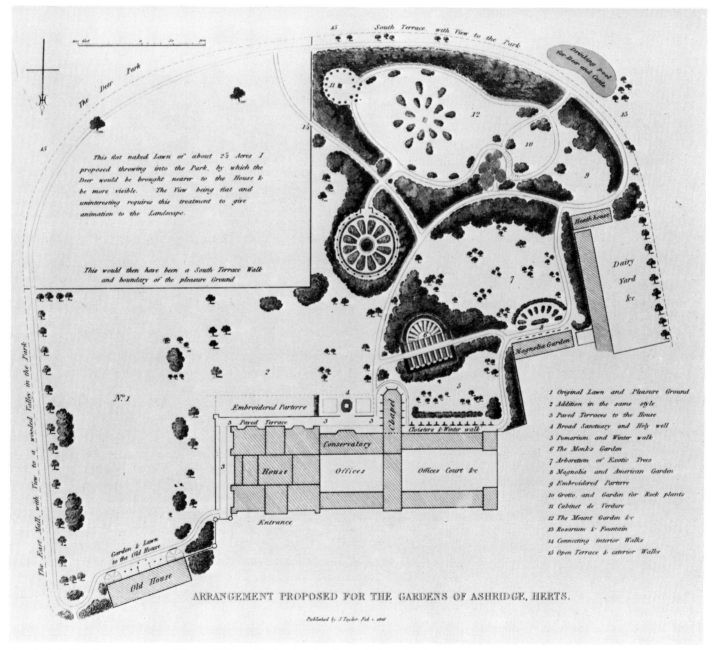

1 Original Lawn and Pleasure Ground
2 Addition in the same style
3 Paved Terraces to the House
4 Broad Sanctuary and Holy well
5 Pomarium and Winter walk
6 The Monk's Garden
7 Arboretum or Exotic Trees
8 Magnolia and American Garden
9 Embroidered Parterre
10 Grotto and Garden for Rock plants
11 Cabinet de Verdure
12 The Mount Garden &c
13 Rosarium & Fountain
14 Connecting interior Walks
15 Open Terrace & exterior Walks

ARRANGEMENT PROPOSED FOR THE GARDENS OF ASHRIDGE, HERTS.

Published by J. Taylor. Feb 1, 1816

6   *At Ashridge Repton proposed fifteen different kinds of garden, from the formal to the picturesque*

7   *The rose-garden at Ashridge*

'I have never walked through these grounds without lamenting, not only the misapplication of good taste, but that constant disappointment which the benevolent Shenstone must have experienced in attempting to unite two objects so incompatible as ornament and profit. Instead of surrounding his house with such a quantity of ornamental lawn or park only, as might be consistent with the size of the mansion, or the extent of the property, his taste, rather than his ambition, led him to ornament the whole of his estate; vainly hoping that he might retain all the advantages of a farm, blended with the scenery of a park. Thus he lived under the continual mortification of disappointed hope, and with a mind exquisitely sensible, he felt equally the sneer of the great man, at the magnificence of his attempt, and the ridicule of the farmer, at the misapplication of his paternal acres.' (*Observations*, 207).

'The *farm* . . . is for ever changing the colour of its surface in motley and discordant hues; it is subdivided by straight lines of fences. The trees can only be ranged in formal rows along the hedges; and these the farmer claims a right to cut, prune, and disfigure. Instead of cattle enlivening the scene by their peaceful attitudes, or sportive gambols, animals are bending beneath the yoke, or closely confined to fatten within narrow enclosures, objects of profit, not of beauty.' (*Observations*, 208).

In 1816 he summed up with a broad generalization:

'A rage for farming superseded the delights of a garden.' (*Fragments*, 434).

Instead of the *ferme ornée*, the smooth Brownian park and the picturesque forest-scenery à la Knight's Downton, Repton's ideal is now a garden of many parts, variety of a new kind. At Woburn Abbey we find:

'The terrace and parterre near the house, the private garden, only used by the family, the rosary, or dressed flower garden, in front of the greenhouse, the American garden, for plants of that country only, the Chinese garden, surrounding a pool in front of the great Chinese pavilion to be decorated with plants from China, the botanic garden, for scientific classing of plants, the animated garden, or menagerie, and, lastly, the English garden, or shrubbery walk, connecting the whole; sometimes commanding views into each of these distinct objects, and sometimes into the park and distant country.' (*Inquiry*, 330).

And at Ashridge a little later there were 'fifteen different kinds of garden' including for instance a rosary, an American garden and 'the monk's garden restored.' (*Fragments*, 528–30).

So here are eclecticism and historicism complete. In park furnishings, this had of course been anticipated by the earlier improvers (Gothic ruin, Chinese pagoda, miniature Pantheon, Palladian bridge, Hermit's cell and so on), but the garden itself was only now affected by it. Also what had been playful in the past now becomes more massive and pedantic. Repton defends his eclecticism like this:

'I will hope there is no more absurdity in collecting gardens of different styles, dates, characters, and dimensions, in the same inclosure, than in placing the works of a Raphael and a Teniers in the same cabinet or books sacred and profane in the same library.' (*Fragments*, 536).

This is the argument of a man to whom it is a matter of course

'that an artist must adopt either [Greek or Gothic architecture], according to the wishes of the individual by whom he is consulted.' (*Fragments*, 424).

This seems to Repton as it should be; all that must be avoided is to unite the two styles in the same building (*Observations* 129, *Designs* 385). His own sympathies are, there can be no doubt about that, with what he calls House Gothic or the Mixed Style of Queen Elizabeth's Gothic* (*Sketches*, 55, *Observations*, 288–89, *Designs*, 385, etc.) He regards it as more convenient and adaptable than any other and likes the easy way in which it can be developed asymmetrically. For in spite

n.2

of his plea for formal gardening he remains to the end picturesque in his dislike of 'the spruce affectation of symmetry.' (*Observations*, 281).

What is new in his work is, to put it in another way, that the broad, sweeping freedom of irregular composition which Price had advocated now becomes a busy irregularity of many separate parts, some of which can and indeed must be formal and regular. But, then, Price speaks of parks, Repton more and more of gardens. Indeed he blames the writers of his day for blurring the differences between forest, park and garden and feels himself as the restorer to its own rights of the garden. (*Sketches*, 78, 95, *Inquiry*, 364).

8 The flower-garden at Valleyfield, in Scotland, with a trellised bower and formal lake

In all this Repton seems to be more in sympathy with the designers of Twickenham and Chiswick, that is with Pope and Kent, than with Brown, Price and Knight. Twickenham and Chiswick were gardens, not yet parks. They were still composed in compartments, and straight axes alternated with wriggly compartments. These compartments of course were very different from Repton's, and to get the character of his style it is now necessary to hear him describe the ornamental garden with its elements.

Some of these elements, such as the American Garden with its rhododendrons and so on, the terrace close to the house and the rosary or dressed rose garden, have already been mentioned. A rockery is also suggested more than once (e.g., *Observations*, 215). It is, however, in such smaller furnishings as hoops, aviaries, treillage, covered ways and conservatories that Repton excels.

Hoops and Aviaries: 'The open trellis-fence, and the hoops on poles, over which creeping and climbing plants are gracefully spread, give a richness to garden scenery that no painting can adequately represent.' (*Fragments*, 536).

'. . . the entrance to the flower-garden to be under a covered passage of hoops, on which may be trained various sorts of creeping plants; and the farther end may be decorated by an architectural building, which I suppose to consist of a covered seat between two aviaries.' (*Observations*, 216).

Treillage: 'To conceal a house near the entrance of a flower-garden at Taplow, I covered the whole with treillage many years ago . . . I believe I may have contributed originally to the introduction [of treillage].' (*Observations*, 257).

'The corridor, or covered-way, is a sheltered communication from the house to the stables, conservatory, flower-houses, tennis-court, riding-house, chinese-dairy, game-larder, etc.' (*Fragments*, 551).

'Amongst the refinements of modern luxury may be reckoned that of attaching a greenhouse to some room in the mansion, a fashion with which I have often been required to comply.' (*Observations*, 217).

'Of all the improvements in modern luxury, whether belonging to the architect's or landscape gardener's department, none is more delightful than the connexion of living-rooms with a greenhouse, or conservatory.' (*Fragments*, 456).

Many more motifs could be singled out, the 'basket of roses' (*Fragments*, 604), the 'botanical arrangement of all the grasses' from America (*Fragments*, 552), the 'numerous tribe of geranium, ericas and other exotic plants' (*Observations*, 217) and so on. In conjunction with the illustrations, however, this selection may be sufficient for this paper.

It will be noticed that most of the quotations just given come from the book of 1816. That is characteristic. The older Repton grew, the more did he concentrate on the ornamental garden.

'I have lived to reach that period when the improvement of houses and gardens is more delightful to me than that of parks or forests, landscapes or distant prospects.' (*Fragments*, 605).

What is so remarkable in this development of Repton and of landscaping in general is that it took place at the very moment when painters turned more seriously and enthusiastically than ever to wild nature, or rather nature in her most dramatically creative mood. Repton's (younger) contemporaries are Crome and Cotman, Girtin, Turner and Constable. There is a characteristic split here much wider than that between say Richard Wilson and Capability Brown. When painting at last takes nature close to her heart, Repton converts gardening into a department of furnishing. And when the travelling urge at last brings the whole middle class close to grandiose romantic nature in the Lakeland or Switzerland, in South Devon or along the Rhine, the garden of the middle class loses its romantic breadth and becomes a fanciful appendage of the house.

And the more this evolution progresses the more importance does the smallish suburban or town garden assume. Repton was in a curious position there. Constitutionally (and perhaps for commercial reasons too) he was all for serving the aristocracy and gentry and not the middle class, all for the country mansion and all against the villa.

'In this country there will, I hope, for ever exist different orders and degrees of society, which must generally depend on the proportion of property, either inherited or acquired by different individuals.' (*Sketches,* 94).

'Rank and affluence are not crimes in England.' (*Sketches,* 95).*   n.3

'To the wealthy mechanic, or the more opulent merchant, perhaps the view of a great city may recall ideas of labour, of business, of difficulty, and dangers, which he would wish to forget in the serenity of the country; but the country gentleman, who never visits the city but to partake in its amusements, has very different sensations from the *distant* view of a place which, by its neighbourhood, increase the value and the enjoyment of his estate.' (*Observations,* 299).

'We daily see wealth, acquired by industry, or by fortunate speculations, succeeding to the hereditary estates of the most ancient families.' (*Inquiry,* 345).

'Good taste can only be acquired by leisure and observation; it is not, therefore, to be expected in men, whose time is fully employed in the more important acquirement of wealth or fame.' (*Observations,* 260).

'Amongst the most obvious effects of sudden wealth in the country, is the change of property from the hereditary lords of the soil to the more wealthy sons of successful commerce, who do not always feel the same respect for the antiquity or dignity of venerable mansions; and, although some may have sufficient taste to preserve the original character of such places, yet, in general, the display of recent expense in the *newness* of improvement is too prevalent.' (*Designs,* 361–62).

This social development seemed to Repton in his old age to be reflected in a decline of taste.

'The taste of the country has bowed to the shrine which all worship; and the riches of individuals have changed the face of the country.' (*Fragments,* 567).

'. . . prevalence of bad taste generally accompanies wealth suddenly acquired. . . .' (*Fragments,* 492).

'It is not, therefore, to be wondered at, that the art of landscape gardening should have slowly and gradually declined.' (*Fragments,* 410).

What upset Repton most, it appears, was the mushroom growth of villas around London and other cities. It sounds again and again as if this represented to him the quintessence of the bad new days.

'We have continually to regret the mutilation of the old *halls and manor houses,* where the large bay windows, the lofty open chimneys, and picturesque gables of Queen Elizabeth's time, give place to the modern sashes and flat roofs, with all the parish frippery of trellis, and canvas, and sharp-pointed pea-green Gothic porches, or porticoes of Grecian columns reduced to the size of bedposts.' (*Designs,* 862).

'I saw red houses, with all the fanciful apertures of Venetian and pseudo-Gothic windows, which disgust the traveller, who looks in vain for the picturesque shapes and harmonious tints of former times.' (*Fragments,* 440).

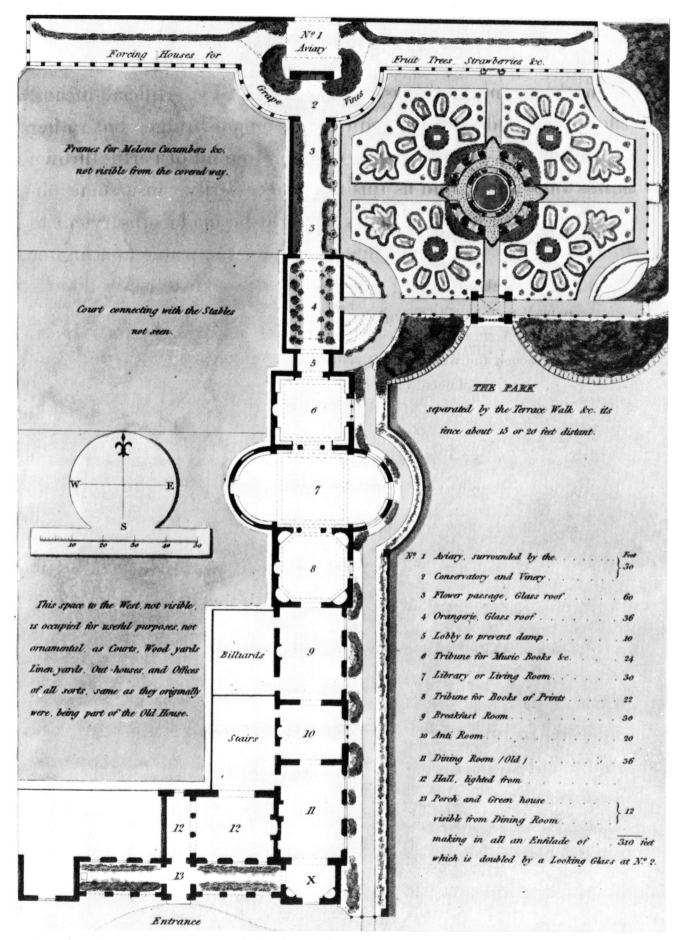

Nº 1
Aviary

Forcing Houses for

Fruit Trees, Strawberries &c.

Grape   2   Vines

Frames for Melons Cucumbers &c.
not visible from the covered way.

3

3

Court connecting with the Stables
not seen.

4

5

THE PARK

6

separated by the Terrace Walk &c. its
fence about 15 or 20 feet distant.

W   E

S

7

10   20   30   40   50

8

This space to the West, not visible,
is occupied for useful purposes, not
ornamental, as Courts, Wood yards
Linen yards, Out-houses, and Offices
of all sorts, same as they originally
were, being part of the Old House.

Billiards   9

Stairs   10

11

12   12

13

Entrance

		Feet
Nº 1	Aviary, surrounded by the	}30
2	Conservatory and Vinery	
3	Flower passage, Glass roof	60
4	Orangerie, Glass roof	36
5	Lobby to prevent damp	10
6	Tribune for Music Books &c.	24
7	Library or Living Room	30
8	Tribune for Books of Prints	22
9	Breakfast Room	30
10	Anti Room	20
11	Dining Room (Old)	36
12	Hall, lighted from	
13	Porch and Green house	}12
	visible from Dining Room	
	making in all an Enfilade of . . .	310 feet
	which is doubled by a Looking Glass at Nº 2.	

X

9 *A corridor and sequence of conservatories leading from the house to various gardens: a proposed plan which, Repton said, had been plagiarized from him*

10 Repton's own garden at Harestreet, a study in framing

'I should feel it a kind of sacrilege in taste to destroy an atom of that old, ruinous, and almost uninhabitable mansion at Rûg, if it were to be replaced by one of those gaudy scarlet houses, which we see spring up, like mushrooms, in the neighbourhood of large manufacturing towns.' (*Observations, 245*).

'Everyone who has observed the symmetrical elevations scattered round the metropolis, and the small houses with wings, in the neighbourhood of manufacturing towns, will allow that symmetry so applied is apt to degenerate into *spruceness.*' (*Observations, 302*).

In planting, what goes for Repton with these despicable villas of the tradesmen is larches, firs and Lombardy poplars (*Fragments, 431, 440, 509*), mean trees because fast-growing trees. However, larches or no larches, and brick villas or no brick villas, Repton could not help being called in more and more often after 1800 to improve suburban gardens, and as his own way of life seems to have been one of snug middle-class comfort, he could not help being attracted to what problems the smaller garden, the garden as part of the house, offers to the landscape designer.

'In the neighbourhood of every city or manufacturing town, new places, as villas, are daily springing up; and these, with a few acres, require all the conveniences, comforts, and appendages of larger and more sumptuous, if not more expensive places. And these have, of late, had the greatest claim on my attention.' (*Fragments, 469*).

'In several villas near London [my task] has been to surround with a border of shrubs and flowers, three or four areas of different dimensions, from an eighth to three-quarters of an acre of garden ground; to raise crops of fruit and vegetables, perfectly hid from the lawns and walks by the surrounding screen of flowering shrubs and evergreens; which, in some cases, will even hide dwarf walls, and pits and frames for forcing early fruits.' (*Fragments, 558*).

The villas which Repton discusses specially are one at Streatham belonging to the Earl of Coventry—it had to be an Earl to be admitted into the published book —and Repton's own at Harestreet, Romford, Essex,

'. . . the humble cottage to which, for more than thirty years, I have anxiously retreated from the pomp of palaces, the elegance of fashion, or the allurements of dissipation; it stood originally within five yards of a broad part of the high road: this area was often covered with droves of cattle, of pigs, or geese.

I obtained leave to remove the paling twenty yards further from the windows; and, by this *appropriation* of twenty-five yards of garden, I have obtained a frame to my landscape; the frame is composed of flowering shrubs and evergreens; beyond which are seen, the cheerful village, the high road, and that constant moving scene, which I would not exchange for any of the lonely parks that I have improved for others.' (*Fragments*, 601–3).

With these lines I can close. They show Repton at the end of his journey, the journey which had taken him from Georgian to Victorian mentality, from the improving of large estates according to the best picturesque principles of Brown via a more sensible acceptance of domestic comfort in park and garden to the highly finished yet varied and intricate gardening which was to rule with modifications down to 1880 and 1890.

Only one more remark must be added. About the town garden, Repton has little to say. He did landscape London squares, it is true, and in this development his role is so important that it would require an article to itself. But the picturesque square was and is only an exclave of the country in the city. It remains alien and is never properly absorbed, although the contrast between an acre of romantic landscape and the wholly urban brick terraces of Bloomsbury was no doubt appreciated by Repton and his patrons, the owners of the estate.

I find only one remark in the six hundred pages of Repton's collected works in which picturesque principles are applied to the metropolitan scene but, as the Price Florilegium on p. 126 to 137 has already revealed, the principles of the Picturesque can be applied with great profit to the planning and grouping of buildings today. The following remark of Repton's, since it corroborates this, may serve as my tailpiece:

'It is commonly observed by those who have seen both St. Peter's, at Rome, and St. Paul's, at London, that the latter appeared the largest at the first glance, till they became aware of the relative proportion of the surrounding space; and I doubt whether the dignity of St. Paul's would not suffer if the area round the building were increased, since the great west portico is in exact proportion to the distance from whence it can now be viewed . . . but if the whole church could be viewed at once, like St. Peter's, the dome would overpower the portico, as it does in a geometrical view of the west front.' (*Observations*, 149).

Lord Holford knew that, when he designed the St Paul's Precincts.

11 *Repton in his bath-chair inspecting a special raised flower-bed*

1   *Audley End: screen and staircase by Vanbrugh, about 1720*

The Architectural Review, CVII, 1950

IX
'Good King James's Gothic'

IN his admirable introduction to Sir John Vanbrugh's letters Professor Geoffrey Webb names two types of plans which the great architect used for his principal houses, the one chiefly to be found at Castle Howard and Blenheim, the other at Seaton Delaval, and the little Mince-Pie House at Blackheath. Professor Webb does not discuss their origins, and as I cannot find suggestions anywhere else either, it might be worth submitting that the Mince-Pie House and the Seaton Delaval plan,* represent the earliest instance on record of a conscious Elizabethan or Jacobean Revival or rather of an understanding of what the Elizabethan and Jacobean style was about. The drawings on this page will save me the trouble of elaborate proof. The square shape and the position of the staircase turrets are eloquent enough, and Chastleton, one of the chief Jacobean representatives of the type, is, as the crow flies, only ten miles from Blenheim.

That Vanbrugh Castle at Blackheath, Vanbrugh's own house, also depends on Elizabethan precedent is perhaps less obvious, owing to the fact that the building is not now in its original state. Vanbrugh added to it twice during the 1720's.* If a drawing of the state of 1718 is made, it becomes evident that we have here a U-front with projections in the inner corners between the long and the short arms of the U, that is a type often found in Elizabethan houses; Stanton Court, and Dorfold, Ches., are familiar examples. One chief difference between Vanbrugh's design and Stanton and Dorfold is that in such Elizabethan examples the main doorway nearly always enters the house parallel to its main wing and not at right angles as at Vanbrugh Castle, However, examination of Vanbrugh Castle proved the existence of a blocked arched door in the very place where it would be expected.

Once Vanbrugh's interest in the style of Elizabeth and James I can be regarded as established, it may not appear too daring to suggest another more spectacular instance. Vanbrugh, it is accepted, designed the staircase and the stone screen between hall and staircase at Audley End. There are as a matter of

Margin references: 4,5   n.1   2   n.2   6   3   1

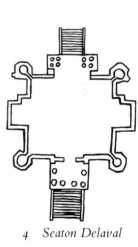

4   *Seaton Delaval*

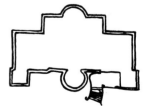

5   *Mince-Pie House*

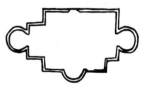

6   *Vanbrugh Castle*

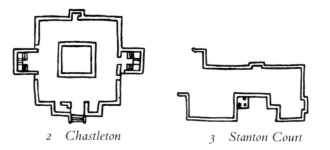

2   *Chastleton*   3   *Stanton Court*

*7   Audley End: plaster ceiling of the staircase hall,
probably by Vanbrugh, c.1720*

*8   Hampton Court: plaster ceiling above
George II's Gate, by Kent, 1732*

fact no documentary proofs of his connection with Audley End, but Messrs.
Avray Tipping and Hussey succeeded in establishing his authorship.* Now the   n.3
ceiling of the staircase hall is Jacobean in pattern, and illustrated as such by Tipping.* I have, however, never been able to reconcile these wilfully shaped stars   n.4
with what Jacobean ceiling designs I know,* and would thus tentatively submit   n.5
that we possess here a Vanbrughian paraphrase* of the Jacobean style.   n.6

II

And why should it really be so surprising to find Vanbrugh as the pioneer of
an Elizabethan Revival? In recent years he has been more and more clearly recognized as a prodigious innovator. There is no need to remind anybody of the
originality and importance of his wildernesses with their winding paths at Castle
Howard and Claremont, of his battlements at Kimbolton and Vanbrugh Castle,   *p.111,*
and of the picturesque, asymmetrical plan of Vanbrugh Castle in its final state.*   n.7
In all these respects: in picturesque planning, in landscaping and in the use of
mediaeval elements in domestic architecture, Vanbrugh preceded Kent who is
usually credited with their introduction. Kent was unquestionably the smaller
man, even if he was the more versatile and plausible man. In his hand mediaeval
forms and picturesque garden layouts turned from the Baroque into a Rococo,
too often called Strawberry Hill Gothic, as if Horace Walpole had been its inventor. But Walpole started at Strawberry Hill only after Kent's death, and
plenty of Gothick villa and country house façades are now known which were
designed in the thirties and forties—even if we forget about Wren's and Hawksmoor's retention of Gothic forms for certain specially traditional, that is ecclesiastical and collegiate, purposes.

*9   Hampton Court: George II's Gate,
remodelled by William Kent in 1732*

Now amongst Kent's surviving Gothic works there is one in which he
appears Gothic only outside but unmistakably Jacobean inside. I am referring to
George II's Gateway at Hampton Court, dated 1732 on the façade. On the first   9
floor of this part are two rooms not open to the public but kindly shown to me
by permission of the Lord Chamberlain. The photograph makes it clear that here   8
is the progeny of Vanbrugh's Audley End. And again, Jacobean or Elizabethan
interest in Kent should not come as a surprise. After all, he illustrated Spenser's

10 Sir Thomas Gresham,
by John Bushnell, 1667

11 Stowe: Temple of the British Worthies,
by William Kent, 1733

11   Faerie Queene (published in 1751), and in his Temple of the British Worthies at
Stowe introduced King Alfred, the Black Prince, Sir Thomas Gresham, Raleigh,
Drake, Milton and others in more or less historical costumes.

In the history of period as against idealized costume England is altogether
of prime importance, more so than has so far been appreciated. As early as 1667
10, n.8 Bushnell carved Sir Thomas Gresham in sixteenth century dress.* Scheemakers
did the same at St. Thomas's Hospital in 1737. And Shakespeare figures kept as a
matter of course to the dress well known from the Stratford bust and painted
portraits—see Scheemakers in Westminster Abbey and Roubiliac in Garrick's
Shakespeare Temple at Hampton. Roubiliac besides modelled a series of busts
for the library of Trinity College, Cambridge with Bacon (1751) and Raleigh
(1757) in Elizabethan and Cotton in Carolean costume. Such busts, Mrs Esdaile
n.9 has shown in an excellent paper,* were very popular at that precise moment.
Rysbrack did a good many pairs and sets of them. Vertue saw a Raleigh, a
Bacon, a Spenser in Rysbrack's studio as early as 1732, and Mrs Esdaile's paper
was devoted to a series made in 1756–58 for Sir Edward Littleton of Teddesley,
Staffs.

Why did English clients prefer the correct costume of the past to the Roman
toga or to that ideal drapery of which Reynolds, to recommend it as pertaining
to the Grand Manner, had said: 'It is drapery; it is nothing else'? The answer is,
I suggest, a typically English respect for historical precedent, combined with an
equally typical English scepticism against the new claims of classical drapery to
all-over rulership. The corollary to this scepticism and relativism is the fact that
Reynolds himself and other Georgian painters used van Dyck costume for
12   portraits of boys and handsome young men—see for instance some of Knap-
ton's Society of Dilettanti portraits at the St. James's Club (1741) or Reynolds's
Second Earl Spencer or Gainsborough's Blue Boy. Here — and also in Tiepolo's
frescoes with Rococo Venetians in Veronese costumes (paralleled characteristically by his Chinese and Peasant masquerades of the Villa Valmarana) we have
indeed the very same attitude as in the fashionable play with Gothic forms. And
if Reynolds could paint little Master Crewe in costume and attitude to make
him appear a miniature Henry VIII, why should architects and virtuosi not have
been tempted by a touch of Jacobean ornament here and there?

12 Horace Walpole in van Dyck dress,
1754

13, 14   Burton Constable: drawing room (left) and library ceilings, by Lightoller, c. 1757–60

Kent was indeed not entirely alone in the admission of occasional Jacobean motifs. In the volumes of *Country Life* one can find quite a few instances. At Burton Constable in Yorkshire, a Jacobean house, there are imitation Jacobean plaster ceilings in the Hall and the Long Gallery by Lightoller of Bath, c. 1757–60; *13,14* of the same date was the fretwork staircase balustrade at Marks Hall, Essex, no *15* doubt meant to be Jacobean, and a chimneypiece at Baggrave Hall in Leicester- *16* shire; and only a few years later, in the early 1760s, Capability Brown did two bath houses in a Jacobean style, one at Burghley, the other at Corsham.* Just *n.10* over twenty years later, at Audley End, about 1785, many of the ceilings received patterns of thin ribs and pendants, and when one passes the threshold into the nineteenth century there are the stables at Longleat by Wyatville of 1801–11 and the gatehouses to Burghley, by Legg (1801) and to Wollaton, by Wyatville (c. 1804).

Apart from the explanation of these admittedly not very frequent examples of a Jacobean Revival in eighteenth century architecture and decoration given just now, there is another, more immediate and simple. It is to be found in a passage from a letter of Horace Walpole referring to Belhouse in Essex—the seat of his friend Thomas Lennard Barrett, later Lord Dacre. Barrett had redecorated his Tudor house inside and out in a Gothick style from 1745 onwards. Walpole visited it in 1754, admired its Gothic as 'very true' and also commented on his friend's (genuine) Jacobean fireplaces in the terms which I have made the title of this essay. He calls them 'a good King James's Gothic.'*   That it is indeed *n.11* true to assume that to Walpole and his friends at that time there was no essential difference of style between 1500 and 1600 is borne out by a letter from Lord Dacre himself (of May 1756)* in which he tells of Capability Brown's intention *n.12* to preserve, while carrying out improvements at Burghley, 'the house . . . wherever it is Gothick.' As there is nothing Gothic at Burghley House this remark can only refer to the Elizabethan mansion.

Nor was Walpole's the first generation to look in this way at Elizabethan and Jacobean architecture. John Evelyn in a diary entry made July 23, 1670 calls Audley End 'a cheerefull piece of Gothic-building, or rather *antico-moderno*', and John Aubrey at about the same time implies the same, when he first quotes Bishop Gardiner's chantry at Winchester as a sign of the influx of classical architecture in England and then adds: 'In Queen Elizabeth's time Architecture made no growth but rather went backwards.'*   *n.13*

Further quotations to corroborate this placing of the Elizabethan style in a Gothic context can be provided. Thus, in 1765, the second Earl of Buckingham wrote to Lady Suffolk about a room at Blickling which it unmistakably Jacobean: 'Gothic it was, and more Gothic it will be, in spite of all the remonstrances of modern . . . lovers of Grecian architecture',* and in 1791, Thomas Heron, in *n.14* his (MS) *Antiquities of Chilham* says that the house is in the first style of Inigo n.15 Jones 'which bordered much on that bastard style then used, called King James Gothic.'*

So it must probably be accepted that Neo-Elizabethan motifs, where they are introduced in the 1730s, were meant to be Domestic Gothic in a wide enough sense. Kent at Hampton Court presumably thought he was quite correctly Tudor when he designed the ceilings illustrated. But antiquarian discrimination progressed fast in the mid-eighteenth century, and Walpole in his n.16 later years saw the difference between Perpendicular and Elizabethan clearly.* He may have received some enlightenment from a remarkable passage on the phases of the Gothic style in the second edition of Thomas Warton's *Observations on the Fairy Queen* (1762, vol. II, p. 184, etc.), where he could read: 'Most of the great buildings of Queen Elizabeth's reign have a style peculiar to themselves . . . where, though much of the old gothic is retained and great part of the new taste is adopted, yet neither predominates; while both, thus indistinctly blended, compose a fantastic species, hardly reducible to any class or name.' In any case, when Walpole some years later gave advice to James Essex, himself the most archaeologically-minded of the Goths, on the proposed *History of Gothic Architecture,* he fully realized that the Gothic style 'deceased in Henry the Eight's reign,' and added: 'In Queen Elizabeth's time there was scarce any architecture at all: I mean no pillars, or seldom, buildings thus becoming quite plain. Under n.17 James a barbarous composition succeeded.'*

That was in 1769. But there were probably not many yet during Walpole's and Essex's life-time who saw so clearly the stylistic distinctions prior to the coming of Inigo Jones. At least Repton, himself a man of no mean visual capabilities, could still in 1794 write exactly as young Walpole and young Barrett had done: 'I venture to deliver it as my opinion that there are only two characters of buildings; the one may be called perpendicular, and the other horizontal. Under the first I class all buildings erected in England before, and during the early part of Queen Elizabeth's reign, whether deemed Saracenic, Saxon, Norman, or Gothic of the thirteenth and fourteenth centuries; and even that peculiar kind called Queen Elizabeth's Gothic, in which turrets prevailed, though battlements n.18 were discarded, and Grecian columns occasionally used.'*

15 *Marks Hall: staircase, c.1760*

16 *Baggrave Hall: the drawing room, c.1760*

17 Mamhead, by Salvin, 1828

18 Loudon's 'Beau Ideal of an English villa', 1833

19 Glenarm Castle, by Richard and William Morrison, c.1825

III

So far we have been looking at a fashion or an entertainment which did not change much in the course of seventy years or so either in character or in extent. There is in this respect little to choose between Kent's and Repton's attitudes. However, obviously a good deal must have happened to Elizabethan appreciation during the first thirty years of the nineteenth century, it it was possible by 1835 that the national competition for the new Houses of Parliament could insist on designs to be done in either the Gothic or the Elizabethan style. There was indeed at that moment a movement afoot to establish Elizabethan as the national English style *par excellence* for secular architecture. It was paralleled in France by the choice of the style of François Premier for the extension of the Paris Town Hall. The date here is 1837–41. In Britain the beginning was a little earlier. Miltown in Ireland is of 1818, Borris in Ireland of shortly before 1819, Glenarm in Ireland of shortly before 1825. All three are by Richard and William Morrison, and all three are illustrated in Neale's *Seats*.* Of the next ten years are Salvin's Mamhead in Devon (1828) and the prodigious Harlaxton in Lincolnshire (1831 etc.). Moreover, T. M. Clarke's *Domestic Architecture of the Reigns of Queen Elizabeth and James I* came out in 1833, P. F. Robinson's illustrations of Hatfield, Hardwick and Castle Ashby in 1833–41, Loudon's *Encyclopaedia of Cottage, Farm and Villa Architecture* (including an Elizabethan house called 'the Beau Ideal of an English villa' and 'drawn up by a highly estimeed . . . amateur architect'*) in 1833 too, and these were followed by J. Hakewill's *Attempt to determine the exact Character of Elizabethan Architecture* (1835), C. J. Richardson's *Observations on the Architecture of England during the Reign of Queen Elizabeth and James I* (1837), Henry Shaw's *Details of Elizabethan Architecture* (1839) and Joseph Nash's ambitious *The Mansions of England: Olden Time* (1839 etc.).* When Barry in the course of three years from 1835 to 1837 designed the Houses of Parliament in Perpendicular Gothic, the Reform Club in the Cinquecento *palazzo* style and Highclere as a bigger and better Wollaton, the standing of Elizabethan as equal to Gothic and Italian was established.

The new appreciation of the Elizabethan style is no doubt connected with the general desire of the coming Victorian Age for something of bolder variety, thicker relief, a more restless play of light and shadows and altogether more robustness than could be offered in Gothic, or classical shapes. In connection with this change of style it is worth recording that occasionally even before Salvin and Shaw the Elizabethan style had appeared as more than as a variety of Gothic or a

19

n.19

17, 2

18

n.20

n.21

20 Harlaxton Hall, by Salvin, begun in 1831

21
whim. One example is Eshton Hall, Yorks., by Webster of Kendal, built in
1825–27, as 'a faithful composition from some of the finest specimens of . . .
domestic architecture prevalent . . . at the latter end of the reign of Queen
Elizabeth.'*

n.22

However, the most important sign of the approaching change of taste is
much earlier still. It is Thomas Hearne's engravings to Richard Payne Knight's
The Landscape, illustrated on p. 119. Knight, as we have seen, wanted the strongest possible contrast of the 'shaven and defac'd' lawns and the timid clumps of
Capability Brown with the dramatic rough landscaping which he himself
liked. A contrast in architecture was not called for by the text of Knight's poem;
but Hearne, probably at Knight's request, introduced it, and chose a normal
plain utilitarian Georgian house, and an Elizabethan house in the style of Hardwick. This understanding of the stout vitality of the Elizabethan style goes far
beyond anything Georgian I have recorded and is indeed the first true resumption of Vanbrugh's as against Kent's and Walpole's Jacobean—a resumption
which took place, as one should expect, at the very moment when altogether the
Palladian eclipse of Vanbrugh ceased and Reynolds, Adam and Uvedale Price
re-discovered his power and genius.

21 Eshton Hall, by Webster of Kendal,
1825–7

1   *Strassburg Cathedral in the eighteenth century*

X

Goethe and Architecture

This paper was published in 1951. Since then several German scholars have written on the subject. They are H. von Einem: 'Goethe und die bildende Kunst' in Beiträge zu Goethes Kunstauffassung, *1956 (first printed in 1950 in* Studium Generale), *H. von Einem: 'Goethe und Palladio' in the same collection of essays, J. Wirth:* Goethe-Handbuch I, Berlin *1961 (under 'Architekturtheorie'), A. Horn-Oncken: 'Über das Schickliche',* Abhandlungen der Akademie der Wissenschaften in Göttingen, Phil.-Hist. Kl., *3rd series No. 70, 1967. Dr Horn-Oncken quotes C. Weickert: 'Die Baukunst in Goethes Werk',* Vorträge *und Schriften der Deutschen Akad. der Wissenschaften, Berlin 1950, and G. Wietek:* Untersuchungen über Goethes Verhältnis zur Architektur, *Ph.D. thesis, Kiel 1950, neither of which I have seen.*

n.1 'My ATTITUDE TO ARCHITECTURE has been merely historical, theoretical and critical.'* It was with reference to the events and thoughts of only one year, 1821, that Goethe made this declaration. But it applies, as I shall try to show, to the whole of his life, with one exception.

Only once, when Goethe was twenty-one, did a building succeed in exciting him so deeply and unexpectedly that the account of his experience, written while it was still fresh in his mind, changed the values of a whole architectural epoch in Germany, if not in Europe. The building in question was Strassburg Cathedral. When Goethe arrived at Strassburg, he had already travelled a long way, mentally, from the pleasing and easy-going Rococo of his father's house. Oeser, at Leipzig, had taught him to understand the pure beauty of classical art, and had introduced him to the writings of Winckelmann, who had rediscovered the true Greek spirit of 'noble simplicity and calm grandeur'. The way this came about was remarkable but does not concern us here. Winckelmann looked at Greek statues and managed to conjure up, through them, their austere Greek prototypes; but while he could describe the character of these in words, his eyes and his taste remained fixed on the somewhat effeminate charms of the *Apollo*
n.2 *Belvedere* and the rather theatrical pathos of the *Laocoön*.* Goethe, when still a student at Leipzig, had gone to see classical statues where Winckelmann had first seen them, in the Elector's collection at Dresden; but he had been still more interested in the Flemish painters of homely scenes than in the nobility of Greek and Roman sculpture.

Strassburg, to the young Goethe, meant first and foremost Herder. And Herder, while he could awaken Goethe's enthusiasm for Shakespeare and for folk poetry (including Ossian), could not be his guide in the realm of architecture. Herder had said about poetry: 'The more primitive—that is to say, alive and freely functioning—a nation is, the more primitive—that is to say, alive, free, meaningful and lyrically active—its songs will be, if it has any. The further a nation is from an artificial, scientific way of thinking, speaking and writing, the less deadened and stultified will be its song and verses.'* But on the subject of n.3 architecture, Herder's only contribution was this: 'Architecture is for the most part a functional art; only a part of it can be considered philosophically.' Its n.4 essential qualities are 'exact regularity and noble order'.*

Strassburg Cathedral made Goethe suddenly aware that Herder's ideas about nature and creative genius could become the key to a new understanding of Gothic architecture. Until then, Gothic architecture had been reviled by the rationalists as 'abstruse and chaotic'* or considered by those with a taste for eccen- n.5 tricity as a graceful pastime, rather like *chinoiserie*. One should remember Horace Walpole's letters about Strawberry Hill, with his allusions to 'venerable bar- barism',* and his description of his staircase as 'so pretty and so small, that I am n.6 inclined to wrap it up and send it to you in my letter',* and of 'lean windows n.7 fattened with rich saints',* and then turn to Goethe's essay *Von deutscher Baukunst,* n.8 *D. M. Erwin von Steinbach.* The essay was written at Strassburg, published later at Goethe's own expense in 1772 (with the date given as 1773) and afterwards re- published by Herder in his *Von deutscher Art und Kunst,* appended to an essay by Frisi, which is a remarkable revelation of Herder's rationalist attitude to archi- tecture, in contrast to Goethe's original vision.* n.9

'When for the first time I went towards the Minster, general notions of taste filled my head. By hearsay, I honoured the harmony of the masses, the purity of the forms, was a sworn enemy of the tangled arbitrariness of Gothick ornament. Under the Gothick heading, I piled up, like the articles in a dictionary, all the synonymous misunderstandings of the confused, the unregulated, the un- natural, the patched up, the botched, the overladen, which had ever passed through my head. Foolishly, as a people which calls all the foreign world bar- baric, I named Gothick all that did not fit into my system, from the neatly- turned, gay-coloured cherub-dolls and paintings our bourgeois nobility adorn their houses with, to the solemn remnants of older German architecture, whose few fantastical frettings made me join in the universal song: 'Quite squashed with ornament'. And so, as I walked towards the Minster, I shuddered in prospect of some malformed, curly-bristled ogre.

'With what unlooked-for emotions did the sight surprise me, when I stepped before it! A sensation of wholeness, greatness, filled my soul; which, composed of a thousand harmonizing details, I could savour and enjoy, yet by no means understand or explain. So it is, men say, with the bliss of Heaven. How often have I come back to enjoy this sacredly profane bliss, to enjoy the gigantic spirit of our elder brethren in their works. How often have I come back, to be- hold, from every side, from far and near, in every differing light, its dignity and glory.'

The wholeness and grandeur that Goethe rediscovered in mediaeval archi- tecture were the last qualities that rationalism and the Rococo age would have been able to see in the multiple ornamentations of a Gothic building.

'In a small taste, says the Italian, and goes by. Childish things, babbles the Frenchman after him; and clicks open his snuff-box à la Grecque, in triumph. What have ye done that ye dare despise! Has not the Genius of the Ancients, rising from its tomb, chained thine, O Latin foreigner! Creeper in the mighty fragments to cadge proportions, cobbler of summer houses out of the holy wreckage, looking upon thyself as guardian of the mysteries of Art because thou canst account, to inch and to fraction, for gigantic buildings! Hadst thou but felt, more than measured—had the spirit of the masses thou gapest at come upon thee, then hadst thou not imitated only because they did it and it is beautiful. Then by necessity and truth hadst thou created thy designs, and living beauty might plastically have welled from them.'

This insistence on feeling, as opposed to measurements, is well known to us from Herder and Hamann. But it was Goethe who recognised visually that a Gothic façade 'rises like a most sublime wide-arching Tree of God' and that, just as a tree does not grow capriciously, so it is the special beauty of the Gothic style that 'all purposes to the whole.'

Goethe imagined Erwin von Steinbach, who is believed to have been the architect of the Strassburg façade, saying to him:

'All these masses are there of necessity, and dost thou not see them in all the older churches of my town? Only I have raised their arbitary proportions into harmony. How above the main porch, which lords over two smaller ones to either side, the wide rose windows opens, answering to the nave; and commonly but a hole for daylight, how, high above, the bell-loft asked for the smaller windows! All that was necessary; and I shaped it into beauty.'

As well as Erwin, in *Von deutscher Baukunst* Goethe glorifies another hero, who was equally disregarded in the 1770s and whose rediscovery was as significant and far-sighted an act on Goethe's part as was that of Gothic architecture. 'Manly Albrecht Dürer,' he declares, 'jest of our new hands, how dearer to me thy most wooden-carved form'. In Dürer, whose woodcuts and perhaps also whose engravings he knew, Goethe found refuge from 'the soft doctrine of modern beauty-lisping', the 'painters of rouged dummies' and women in 'stagey postures' and 'lying complexions'—that is to say, in Dürer he found relief from the tradition of French Rococo. There can be no doubt that Goethe's nationalist feelings about the German fatherland, confronted by France, played some part in his impulsive reactions at Strassburg. A whole polemical section of *Von deutscher Baukunst* is aimed at the Abbé Laugier, who had written two successful booklets on the theory of architecture in 1753 and 1765.* These books in fact contained a collection of fair and impartial judgments on the development of the Gothic style, but Goethe was unwilling to allow them or even to speak of them. Gothic had to be German. Speaking of Strassburg Cathedral, he says: 'This is German architecture, this is ours . . . quickening out of the strong, rough German soul.' Historically, he was mistaken in saying this, but no more so than Rickman when, forty years later, he invented the term Early English.

When *Von deutscher Baukunst* appeared, Goethe had left Strassburg. If we are to believe the accounts in *Dichtung und Wahrheit,* published forty years later, his enthusiasm for Gothic suddenly began to cool. During his return journey Goethe writes,* contemplating the Elector's classical statues at Mannheim: 'My faith in northern architecture was somewhat shaken'. Perhaps he did not remember very correctly; in fact, *Werther* came in 1774, and another journey to Strassburg in 1775, and his account of that visit begins thus:*

'Once again on thy tomb, blessed Erwin, I feel—thank God!—that I am as I was. You are one and living, begotten and blossoming, not patched and pieced together.'

Nevertheless, the conclusion Goethe now reached announced a new attitude:

'With every step the conviction grew that creative power in the artist is a burgeoning feeling for proportion, measure and propriety; and that only through them can an independent work of art be produced, just as other created things grow out of their individual germinating powers.'

This insistence on proportion and propriety is a slight correction of his more uncontrolled enthusiasm of two years before, and in a surprising way a close approximation to the ideas taught by the French theorists of the Enlightenment. Here for the first time is an indication of Goethe's approaching classicism, which in terms of the appreciation of architecture amounted to a retreat.

In the same year, 1775, he moved to Weimar, and Weimar, with his public life and new responsibilities, curbed his enthusiasm and clarified his thinking. In

2   Goethe in the Campagna, painted in 1787 by Tischbein

1779 the first version of *Iphigenie auf Tauris* appeared, and in 1786 Goethe was at last face to face with Italy and classical Antiquity.

Antiquity meant to him—above all else—the ruins of Rome and the Greek temples of Paestum and Sicily. And Italy meant Palladio.

Palladio, the calmest but at the same time the most academic of Italian sixteenth-century architects, had—by means of Lord Burlington's propaganda, buildings and publications—become the ideal of rationalists and classicists in England from 1715 onwards. And so, when architects and *virtuosi* on the Continent begin to reject the Rococo in favour of a pure Mediterranean style, they often found inspiration in contemporary work in England, even before going to Italy to seek the direct stimulus of Roman architecture and the Renaissance.*   n.13

This is true of Frederick the Great, of Jacques-Ange Gabriel in France, and of the theorists in Germany and elsewhere, and it is also true of Goethe. It was in the works of Palladio that he first saw classical order and harmony in architecture on Italian soil.

The immediate effect of this lesson was that ancient Roman decoration, when Goethe saw a fragment of the entablature of the Temple of Antoninus and Faustina in the Casa Farsetti at Venice, made him at once recant his previous delight in the Gothic style:

'This is, indeed, something very different from our queer saints, piled up one above the other on little brackets after the Gothic style of decoration, something different from our shafts like tobacco-pipes, our little steeple-crowned towers, and foliated terminals. From all these I am now, thank God, set free for n.14   ever!'*

But neither Palladio nor Rome was preparation enough for the masculine, severe beauty of the Greek temples. These, it is well to remember, were at that time a very recent discovery in Europe. I cannot say which of the then recent publications on the subject were known to Goethe. But he had certainly followed the writings of Winckelmann, and so must have been prepared for the austere grandeur of Paestum. However, this is how Goethe described his feelings on arriving at Paestum:

'The first impression could only arouse surprise. I found myself in an entirely alien world. For as the centuries shape themselves from the grave to the pleasing, so they shape mankind at the same time, nay create it. Now our eyes and with them our whole being are attracted and decisively determined by a slenderer architecture so that these obtuse, conical, closely set masses of columns appear irksome, even terrible. However, soon I pulled myself together, remembered the history of art, thought of the age whose spirit considered such an architectural style appropriate, presented to myself the severe style of sculpture, and in less than an hour I felt attracted, nay praised my genius for permitting me n.15   to see these well-preserved fragments.'*

Here, it seems to me, is a very important statement, which was to remain characteristic of Goethe's attitude to architecture during the remaining forty-five years of his life.

This is the same man who, fifteen years earlier, had seen without any outside assistance what elemental powers were embodied in a Gothic cathedral; the same man who knew enough about the elemental powers hidden beneath the calm surfaces of Greek art, to write about the Greeks:

> *Sie aber, sie bleiben*
> *In ewigen Festen*
> *An goldenen Tischen.*
> *Sie schreiten vom Berge*
> *Zu Bergen hinüber:*
> *Aus Schlünden der Tiefe*
> *Dampft ihnen der Atem*
> *Erstickter Titanen,*
> *Gleich Opfergerüchen*
> *Ein leichtes Gewölke.*

Yet now the author of *Von deutscher Baukunst* and of *Iphigenie* had to force himself, by means of historical reflections, to appreciate the meaning of classic Greek architecture.

He really did have to force himself, though eventually his knowledge of art history allowed him, when he revisited Paestum soon afterwards, to call it 'the last and, I might almost say, the most noble image I could take intact with me n.16   northwards.'*

But Paestum did not long remain the most noble image of classical beauty for Goethe. From the very beginning, and without any effort, he had been fascinated by Palladio. About Palladio he had written, from Italy: 'He was a n.17   profoundly great man. . . . There is truly something divine in his compositions.'*

Goethe said of Palladio's Scuola della Carità, though it was only in a fragmentary state when he saw it, that it had 'a perfection of composition and exact-n.18   ness in execution that I have never met before.'* And, speaking again of Palladio to his friend and guide in artistic matters, Heinrich Meyer, he summed up in 1795: 'The more one studies Palladio, the more incredible one finds the man's n.19   genius, mastery, richness, versatility and grace.'*

The Greek Doric temples, on the other hand, less than two years after his journey to Italy, had already become so remote from his sensibility that he could say 'that their appearance is majestic, nay, even ravishing', but add that human nature tends to progress from the massive to the graceful, as the mind seeks 'more sublimity and freedom'.* Thus at the time of *Iphigenie* and his association with   n.20
Schiller, Palladio's erudite, delicately proportioned classicism meant more to Goethe than the strong and sturdy spirit of Greece.

It will be noticed that I am using the same words—strong and sturdy—to describe Doric temples, as Goethe had used in 1772 to describe a Gothic cathedral.

In fact, it can be shown that the Doric style, when it was first met with, struck Palladian architects (men like Sir William Chambers in England) as rustic and barbarian, just as Gothic architecture had done. Chambers, in a draft (of about 1769) for a lecture to be delivered to the recently formed Royal Academy in London and quoted and commented on in another essay in this volume, protested vehemently that there had been a serious attempt to 'cheat us into a Reverence for Attic Deformity. Such attempts might bring 'even the Gothic in Vogue again.'

But while the young Goethe had, by sheer force of intuition, been able to appreciate the unity and grandeur in the apparently primitive and barbarian disorder of a Gothic façade, the mature Goethe at Paestum could no longer achieve this. By then he was looking for *das Sinnlich-Harmonische*—aesthetically harmonious art and architecture, pleasing qualities* rather than deep and dis-   n.21
turbing new experiences.*   n.22

Goethe the art critic, to put it briefly, was becoming academic. This can be seen only too clearly in the competitions held at Weimar from 1799 to 1805 and in Goethe's comments on the winning drawings. But these did not concern architecture, and we must look ahead to 1815 and later to find Goethe once again taking up a position in a controversy concerned (at least partly) with architecture.

What happened is well enough known. Tieck, Wackenroder and Schlegel had taken Goethe's youthful enthusiasm for Dürer and the Gothic style as the starting-point for a vehement and romantic theory of a *Neudeutsche, Religiös-Patriotische Kunst* (a new German, religious and patriotic art). The phrase is Heinrich Meyer's, not Goethe's, but in 1817 Goethe published an essay with this title in his *Kunst und Alterthum,* and he published it with great spirit. He wrote to his friend Knebel that the essay would 'burst like a bomb among the Nazarene artists. It is just the moment to seize their twenty-year-old monstrosity, to grasp it vigorously and to pluck it out by the roots.'*   n.23

Such violence seems rather ungenerous on the part of the author of *Von deutscher Baukunst.* But the truth of the matter is that Goethe, ever since the young Romantics had appeared on the scene, had turned against that essay as against other such outbursts of his own youth. In 1810 he wrote to Reinhart:*   n.24

'Even I used to be caught up with this sort of thing, and I indulged in a kind of idolatry of Strassburg Cathedral . . . The weirdest thing of all, as I see it, is the German patriotism which chooses to regard this obviously Saracen plant as a product of its own native soil.'*   n.25

And in the twelfth book of *Dichtung und Wahrheit,* written in 1813, he compares the literary style of *Von deutscher Baukunst* to 'a dust-cloud', and adds that it might have had some immediate effect at the time it was published 'if only I had chosen to express these views, whose value I do not want to deny, clearly and intelligibly, in an articulate style'.*   n.26

'Whose value I do not want to deny' is an interesting phrase. Goethe at this time was evidently trying to achieve an objective appreciation of Gothic architecture; it was precisely this attempt at objectivity which caused his irritation with Schlegel and his circle, and it also made him antipathetic to this group, and in the end incomprehensible to the most convinced Romantics.

Sulpiz Boisserée, who was responsible for so much of the revival of interest in primitive Flemish and German painting, is best known for his infectious enthusiasm for the completion of Cologne Cathedral according to the then recently discovered original designs. Boisserée wrote sadly in his diary, after his first meeting with Goethe in 1818, of the great man's 'anger and aversion' concerning Gothic architecture and his 'passion for Palladio, to the point of absurdity, nothing but Palladio and more Palladio.'*

n.27

Yet Goethe himself told Boisserée on the same occasion: The plan for the cathedral 'had been a revelation to me. It gave me a new vision. I thought that I now had mastered the whole mystery of architecture.'*

n.28

In all this, Goethe's efforts at impartiality are evident.

And if we read some of the principal passages in Meyer's article, written in 1817, we can also see how carefully he tried to remain neutral, and to substitute thoughtful reasoning for abuse.

'The attractive simplicity, the touching innocence of primitive painting was not consciously art—it was part of the intellectual background of the masters and the time in which they lived. So it is no longer enough just to imitate them. The fact that, later, scholars and even poets confused religious qualities with artistic has certainly been even more harmful.'

Architecture in the Gothic way, in particular, 'can no longer thrive, since the kind of craftsmanship it called for has completely disappeared'. And so, Meyer concluded, 'there are artistic reasons as well as technical, ethical and mechanical ones to explain why it is altogether impossible to recall the spirit of past ages, and to borrow the characteristics of those times.'*

n.29

However, at the end of this balanced and critical passage, Meyer does not hesitate to recommend 'concentrating wholeheartedly on ancient Greek art' in order to 'rouse pleasing impressions in ourselves.'

Goethe was of the same opinion. The romantic attitude to the world and to life was physically repellent to him.

'Classical, to me, means healthy, and romantic means sick. . . . Most of what is new is not romantic because it is new, but because it is weak and sickly and ailing. And what is old is not classical because it is old, but because it is strong, fresh, joyful and healthy'.*

n.30

And on the subject of *Faust* Part II, he told Eckermann: 'I have endeavoured to make everything clear-cut, in the classical sense, and nothing vague or indefinite.' *

n.31

'In the classical sense', not 'in classical forms', it should be noted. Among the maxims and reflections of the years 1810–5, published in Goethe's papers in the Weimar edition, is one which reads: 'Those who have to borrow their proportions (what can be measured) from the ancients, must not complain, if we want to borrow from them what cannot be measured.'

Another eulogy of the Greek Doric order, that is of Greek Doric forms, is to be found, it is true, in Goethe's last writings—in fact, in Part II of *Faust,* but its significance is limited. The passage in question occurs when Faust calls forth Helen in the Emperor's great hall:

> *Durch Wunder Kraft erscheint allhier zur Schau*
> *Massiv genug, ein alter Tempelbau.*
> *Dem Atlas gleich, der einst den Tempel trug*
> *Stehn reihenweis der Säulen hier genug ;*
> *Sie mögen wohl der Felsenlast genügen*
> *Da zweie schon ein gross Gebäude trügen.*

> 'By magic power there rises to our gaze
> A massive temple of the ancient days.
> Bearing it up, great rows of pillars soar,
> Resembling Atlas, who the heavens bore.
> This task, this granite load, for them is light,
> For two could bear a mansion with their might.'

The architect replies:

Das wär' antik! Ich wüsst'es nicht zu preisen
Es sollte plump und überlästig heissen.
Roh nennt man edel, unbehilflich gross.
Schmal-Pfeiler lieb ich, strebend, grenzenlos;
Spitzbögiger Zenith erhebt den Geist:
Solch ein Gebäu erbaut uns allermeist.

'So, that's antique! I can't say I admire it:
Top-heavy stuff, for those who may desire it,
What's crude they noble call, what's sprawling splendid;
For me the shaft that rises fine and swift,
High-pointed arch, infinity suspended,
That is the style the lofty soul to lift.'*   n.32

So it is clear after all that the Greek temple is mentioned only as a means of attacking the Gothic style.

However—and this is undoubtedly Goethe's most interesting late contribution to architectural criticism—he did not in the end become completely anti-Gothic, just because he did not like the Romantics.

The following passage is very important:

'In old German architecture, we see the flowering of a remarkable age. When one is confronted directly with such a flower, one can only marvel at it; but if one looks into the innermost secret life of the plant, to see how it uses its strength and gradually unfolds, then one sees things with quite different eyes, and with understanding of what one sees'.*   n.33

Thus Goethe's ideas about plant life, and about *Gestaltung* (morphology) and metamorphosis in general, are here applied to architecture. It was an intellectual process, just like the process by which Goethe succeeded in appreciating the ruins of Paestum.

Indeed he even confessed, and this time it was apropos of the effect on him of a Gothic rather than a Doric building (Cologne Cathedral), that at first it had caused in him 'an extraordinary malaise', that it had struck him as 'something incomplete and portentous'. 'Even the interior of the cathedral, to be frank, makes an inharmonious though meaningful impression on us. Only when we are in the choir . . . is our desire truly fulfilled.'* As at Paestum, the psychological   n.34 transition from fear to positive appreciation had been made possible by allowing historical insight to counteract the immediate effect made by the building.

A few pages before the passage referred to above, in an essay called after his youthful work, '*Von deutscher Baukunst—1823*', published in *Kunst und Alterthum*, Goethe expressed his gratitude to those who had recently published books and engravings, illustrating mediaeval architecture. He had in mind the Boisserée brothers, Georg Moller and Büsching, since their writings and propaganda 'have made us feel the value and worth [of Gothic buildings] in the right way, that is, historically.'*   n.35

Similarly, but referring more broadly to the powers and effects of genius in general, Goethe said, a few years later:

'Genius is the creative force through which decisive and influential actions came to pass. . . . The man who first invented the shapes and proportions of historic German architecture—so that in the course of the centuries it led to the building of Strassburg and Cologne Cathedral—was a genius. In fact, his ideas have kept their creative force and are still at work today.'*   n.36

Today? Can Goethe have intended this to allude to something other than the posthumous survival of Gothic principles? It is, however, a fact that—surprisingly—the second *Von deutscher Baukunst* of 1823 appeared strangely tolerant even of the neo-Gothic movement of the day. All that Goethe says apropos of these artists is that they 'have actually used this style for buildings that are to be

built and used in the present day, and have taken pleasure in the atavistic sensa-
n.37   tion inspired by being in such surroundings.'*

As we have seen, the title of this essay, *Von deutscher Baukunst,* is a conscious
repetition of the one written fifty years earlier. It is not without sympathy that
Goethe refers here to the enthusiasms of his youth, and he makes a point of de-
claring that he found no reason to be ashamed of them.

But in 1773 it was a question of instinctive delight in completeness and in a
multiplicity of forms that seemed to conform to no measure, while already by
1775 this had become 'a burgeoning feeling for measure, form and propriety',
without now having the redeeming feature of depth of feeling.

The first *Von deutscher Baukunst* had, as I have said, been written primarily
as an attack on Laugier—that is, an attack on the critical views of a French
rationalist. This time the reason for Goethe's writing was his pleasure at finding
himself in agreement with a passage on Gothic architecture, which occurred in
the main work of the most rationalist of French architectural writers. He quotes
n.38   it from the fifth book of the fifth part of François Blondel's *Cours d'architecture :**

'All the satisfaction we experience from beauty as art depends on the observation of rules and proportions. . . . Thus we feel pleasure as we look at some
of these massive Gothic buildings, whose beauty is the expression of symmetry
and harmony between the whole and its component parts, and between the
different parts themselves. And this prevents our seeing and noticing the distasteful decoration which encrusts it. But it is even more convincing to find that, if
we examine their measurements carefully, they have on the whole the same
proportions as buildings constructed in accordance with good architectural
principles, buildings whose contemplation gives us the greatest pleasure.'

Goethe's approval of this mistaken method of judging the Gothic style was the
unfortunate result of the process that I have tried to describe here.

'My attitude to architecture has been merely historical, theoretical and
insofar as buildings are concerned. He appreciated them as evidence of the
Zeitgeist as much as for their visual value; his interest was theoretical in its
insistence on the preconceived criterion of correctness; and it was critical insofar
as *Wohlbehagen,* the feeling of comfort and ease, and similar qualities were
regarded as more important characteristics than creative genius.

1   SCHINKEL *Design for a mausoleum for Queen Louise of Prussia, 1810*

Journal of the Royal Institute of British Architects, 3rd Series, LIX, 1951-2

XI
Karl Friedrich Schinkel

I T is doubtful whether the history of architecture can at any period be treated in exclusively national terms. For no period however would such treatment be less possible than for the last two hundred years. From about 1760 onwards, the history of architecture in the West develops as a Franco-Anglo-German alliance —or an Anglo-Franco-German, or a Germano-Anglo-French alliance. Any neglect of this fact would seriously impair the results of national scholarship.

2 Take one example. The younger Dance was born in 1741. He was certainly the most interesting architect of that moment in England. But if one wants to understand that particular moment fully, one has to go to France and examine the work of more than half a dozen architects who were all born between 1730 and 1740; men of varying achievements, but all of them revolutionaries of pure form, men who believed in austerity rather than elegance, and in heavyweight rather than in featherweight. They are Boullée, who was born in 1728; de Wailly and Peyre, born in 1729 and 1739, and who built the Odéon in 1779; Antoine, born 1733, who built the Mint in 1771; Ledoux, born 1736, who built the salt works at Chaux from 1773 and the toll gates of Paris from 1785; Gondoin, born in 1737, who built the School of Surgery in 1769–86; Brongniart, born 1739, who built the Capuchin Monastery in Paris in 1783; and Chalgrin, also n.1 born in 1739, the architect of the Arc de Triomphe.* The whole group represents one style, which is, broadly speaking, the Dance style.

The inspiration of these men comes from Rome, seen through the eyes of Piranesi; but it also comes from the Palladio-Burlingtonian achievement of England. If the revolution of about 1760–70 was less violent in England, it was due to the existence of this very movement—a movement towards classicism at a time when France and Germany still revelled in a delicious Rococo, sometimes frivolous, but sometimes of inspired frenzy.

If we now go on half a generation, we reach Percier and Fontaine in France, born in 1764 and 1762 respectively, the architects of the First Empire. But to find the man of the greatest genius of the Percier-Fontaine generation one has to go back to England and to Sir John Soane, who was born in 1753. However his brilliant development of conceptions which came originally from Dance cannot be fully understood without Peyre, Ledoux and Piranesi.

Soane's generation was followed in England by that of Wilkins (born 1778) and Smirke (born 1780)—the generation of Downing College and the British Museum. Wilkins was a Fellow of Caius. Smirke is described by Sir John Summerson as serious, methodical, solid, competent, dull. Neither of the two allows us to see the best of which that generation was capable; nor was there anybody very important of the same age in France.

2 DANCE *Newgate Gaol, London, begun in 1769*

To find genius, we have to go to Berlin and look at the drawings of Gilly, born in 1772, who, alas, died of consumption as early as 1800. And to find the highest sense of beauty, and of duty, the most successful attempt at a theory of architecture in neo-classical terms—of Schiller's aesthetics in terms of architecture —and the keenest interest in the Industrial Revolution in terms of the factory and the machine, of cast iron, zinc and papier maché, one must look at the works and read the diaries and letters of Schinkel.

There are two sides to Schinkel's character. On the one hand he was a painter, a stage designer, and a designer of panoramas. On the other he was *Geheimer Oberbaurat* at the age of thirty-four. He was an honorary member of the Academies of Prussia, Denmark, Rome, Bavaria, Russia, Austria and Sweden, and an honorary member of the Institut de France and of the Institute of British Architects—in fact, he was one of the very first batch of honorary members of the British Institute.

Karl Friedrich Schinkel was born in 1781.* He was the great-great-grandson n.2 of a cloth shearer, and a great-grandson, grandson and son of Prussian Lutheran pastors. At his grammar school he recommended himself 'by a staid and modest behaviour' and by 'laudable industry'.* He was taught architecture by an able n.3 civil servant, David Gilly, who came from a French family which had migrated with the Huguenots to Berlin at the end of the seventeenth century. But Schinkel owed very much more to the brilliant son of David Gilly, Friedrich Gilly. In a letter to Friedrich Gilly's father, written from Paris in 1804, Schinkel said that 'if anything at all is to develop in me and lead to some progress, I owe these ad- vantages solely to the instructive intercourse I had with him.'* n.4

Schinkel went at his own expense to Italy and Paris in 1803, at the age of twenty-two. Gilly and Paris are the chief sources of his style in architecture. As for Paris I have already emphasized that there were at that period more than half a dozen men of importance.* Boullée was the earliest and, presumably, the most n.5 influential of them, but Ledoux is the most familiar in this country owing to the folio publication he brought out in 1804.* Some remarks on three designs by n.6 Ledoux may be justifiable to get the right atmosphere for Gilly and consequently, in the end, for Schinkel.

In 1778 Ledoux designed the theatre at Besançon, with a severely antique
6 semi-circular auditorium, amphitheatrical seating and a Greek Doric colonnade
in front of the top tiers. The Greek Doric style was a recent discovery at that
n.7 time,* and the early use of this severely powerful, overpowering order, so
violently opposed to Rococo elegance, is characteristic of Ledoux. Amongst the
3 toll gates of Paris the Barrière des Bonshommes, just south of the Trocadero, by
the river, is especially telling. It was designed in 1785. A building like this cannot
be properly appreciated without knowing England. The screen of columns
with straight entablature in front of an apse is a famous Robert Adam motif,
but Ledoux uses it with squat and heavy Greek Doric columns. Also the apse is
a complete semicircle in its elevation as against the elegant, shallow arches which
Adam preferred. Three or four years after the Barrière des Bonshommes,
5 Ledoux designed a savings bank for Paris. The design consists of three completely
separate blocks with very heavy attics and no pediments to the wings. This sense
of unmitigated cubes is of importance.

Little of the Ledoux-Boullée style survives now, but at the time when Gilly
went to Paris in 1797 he could see and draw a street with arcades on the most
grotesquely heavy, square, tapered pillars, meant no doubt to look Grecian and
4 primeval. It is the Rue des Colonnes, built in 1784 by Legrand and Molinos,
both born in 1743, as part of a scheme of urban design, with the Théâtre Faydeau
n.8 as its centre.*

3 LEDOUX *Barrière des Bonshommes,
Paris, designed 1785*

4 LEGRAND AND MOLINOS *Rue des
Colonnes, Paris, 1784, drawn by Gilly*

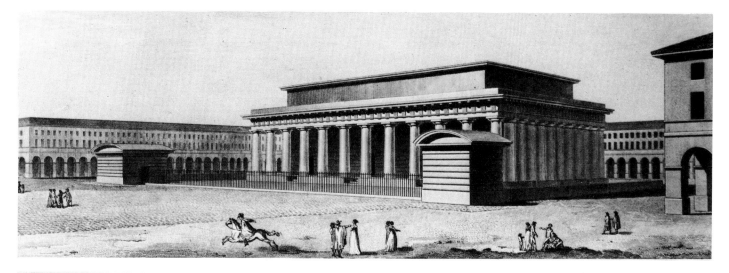

5 LEDOUX *Design for a savings bank
in Paris, c.1790*

6 LEDOUX *Auditorium of the Theatre at
Besançon, 1778*

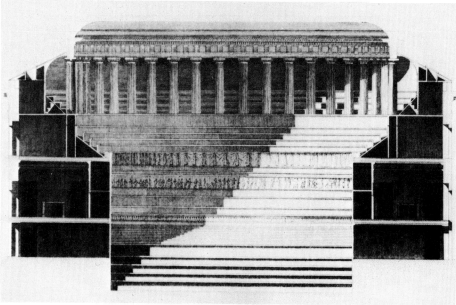

So uncompromising and unattractive a style is naturally to be found at its best in fantasies on paper rather than in executed buildings. Take for instance the gaol designed by Ledoux for Aix en Provence, presumably in 1787. It is primarily a study in basic geometry, a cube with heavy pedimented angle projections and low porticoes crowned by colossal segmental pediments. All windows are as inconspicuous as possible. Altogether, usefulness in such designs tended to go by the board. Hence Ledoux's chief work is a series of designs for an ideal town with buildings of this basic geometrical kind. As far as their function goes, they are given such vague names as Temple de Mémoire, Asile de la Félicité, Oikema, or Ecole de Morale. They may well be described as buildings for building's sake. That is characteristic of this moment. In Ledoux architecture becomes absolute in the sense of abandoning its ties with mere use, just as at the same moment art becomes absolute and cuts its ties with the patron (Blake, etc.). As regards style, the Ecole de Morâle, for instance, is a combination of cubes and cylinders, with inclined planes, a flat roof and an arched colonnade. In various ways, many features of these designs are curiously twentieth century, and that is no doubt what has led to the re-discovery of Ledoux.

Now Friedrich Gilly went to Paris in 1797. However, he must have absorbed this style fully before. How that can have happened, we do not know. It seems most likely that his case is one of independent growth from the same sources which had been available to the French architects: namely, Rome of the 1750s and 1760s, seen through the eyes of Piranesi. Gilly himself never went to Rome, but there were others, such as, for instance, the architect Johann Christian Genelli, who in 1787 sent up to Berlin from Rome a design for a national monument to Frederick the Great in the form of a small Greek Doric temple. Even so it remains mysterious how young Gilly at the age of twenty-two, that is in 1794, can have designed an interior such as the one illustrated with Doric columns, the semi-circle of the window recess, the emphatically few and low pieces of furniture and—this is Gilly's most personal contribution—that magnificent sense of axes and of the placing of simple forms in space.

In 1797 he also designed a national monument for Frederick the Great—a very much larger scheme which culminates in a Greek Doric temple, the earliest on that scale to be pretty well a replica of a fifth century Greek temple. But more interesting still are the unmitigatedly cubic base on which it is placed and the triumphal arch which leads into the precinct. The triumphal arch is entirely original in shape—an unmoulded, sheer block, pierced by two coffered vaults at right angles. The details may well remind one of contemporary French forms, but once again, the design was done before Gilly went to Paris.

7   GILLY *Interior, 1794*

8   LEDOUX *Design for a gaol for Aix-en-Provence, 1787*

9 GILLY *Triumphal arch, from the monument to Frederick the Great, 1797*

Then, in 1798, and coming back from Paris where he had studied recent theatres, Gilly designed a national theatre, also only a sketch and never built. It is amazing how here period forms have receded to a minimum. We still find cubes and semi-circles, *à la* Ledoux and a little *à la* English Palladianism, but on the whole the building is, for its date, just as independent of period precedent and as original as anything designed at that time by Soane. Gilly's auditorium was to be semi-circular and amphitheatrical, under the influence, no doubt of theatres in France and especially Ledoux's at Besançon.

10 GILLY *Design for a national theatre in Berlin, 1798*

11 GILLY *Design for a mausoleum*

12 The Marienburg in the late 18th century

But to see Gilly's imagination as its most independent and daring one must go to such less explicit designs as that for a mausoleum. The complete abandonment of mouldings in the piers and lintels gives one an impression vacillating between the twentieth century and Stonehenge. It must have struck people at Gilly's time as something shockingly elementary, not to say primeval. Now we shall see later that, when the Greek Doric style came back during the last third of the 18th century, it also impressed people as something elementary and primeval. That is how Neo-Mediaevalism and Neo-Doricism could be reconciled, and reconciled on a higher plane than simply the plane of English garden furnishings. It is interesting in this connection that Gilly, a few years before (in 1794), went to West Prussia, there to draw for publication the most glorious monument of the Gothic style in East Prussia, the Marienburg.* It is a strange accident—though of course no more than an accident—that the Marienburg is one of the very few genuine Gothic buildings on the Continent in which certain features depend, as far as one can see, essentially on England. In this the great importance is heralded which English Gothic was to have on the romantic Gothic Revival in Germany. And so, with the romantic Gothic Revival and with Gilly, we can move on to Schinkel.

Schinkel's earliest designs—done when he was twenty and twenty-one— are obviously connected with both Gilly and the French style of Ledoux. The basic cubic shapes, the semi-circles, the arcades, the colonnades, can hardly be mistaken.* Yet when in 1803 Schinkel went to Italy, he appears from his letters to have been impressed at least as much by the architecture of the Middle Ages

11

n.9,

n.10

as by Rome and the Greek temples of Sicily and Paestum. The general tenor of his letters from Italy is curiously calm and even. Schinkel uses a great deal such terms as splendid, magnificent, wonderful, excellent, but nowhere does he seem to be really carried away. He speaks with admiration of the Gothic Cathedrals of Siena and Milan, and of the Sicilian 'Saracenic' buildings. But nowhere is he very specific in his predilections. The most interesting of his letters goes to his master, David Gilly.* In it he says, for instance, of the Saracenic style that 'one could make use of it', and of the brick architecture of the fifteenth century in Ferrara and Bologna, that it contains elements 'applicable by us'. He also speaks in more general terms of the Italian Middle Ages as a style 'too little observed and appreciated'. 'When it comes to Antiquity', however, he writes to his master, 'it offers nothing new to an architect, because one is from childhood familiar with it'. And so amongst his drawings we find few of Greek and Roman antiquities, but a view from his window in Rome, drawn with great incisiveness and accuracy of observation, and one of the interior of Milan Cathedral, rather exaggerated in height, but very delicately observed in the detail.

Schinkel went back via Paris, and on his return to Berlin he found Prussia in the throes of a disastrous depression: 1806 was the year of the Battle of Jena, and the year of the peace which gave to France all Prussia west of the Elbe. There was little work for an architect, and so Schinkel developed into a successful painter. He painted landscapes, and very soon turned to panoramas. Panoramas were, of course, a craze of the moment. Their history is entertaining in itself. It begins with the theatrical designer and painter de Loutherbourg in London, whose *Eidophusikon,* as he called it, was first shown in 1781 and was a kind of panorama in which were seen such things as Niagara Falls and Satan marshalling his Troops by the Fiery Lake. The panorama in its proper sense was invented by

13 SCHINKEL: *view from the artist's window on the Pincio, 1803/4*

14 SCHINKEL *Drawing of the interior of Milan Cathedral, c.1804*

15 SCHINKEL *Evening, a drawing, 1811*

a Scotsman, Barker, in 1789. In 1799 he exhibited, for instance, the Battle of the Nile—again a rather sensational subject.* In 1800 the first panorama appeared   n.12
in Berlin, and from 1808 Schinkel did one every year; for instance of the Piazza in Venice, the Grottoes of Sorrento, the Cathedral of Milan by moonlight and torchlight. Effects of light were always very important for the panoramas, and soon Schinkel went on to the Eruption of Vesuvius. Then came the Gardens of Semiramis, the Egyptian Pyramids and, in 1813, the Fire of Moscow; 1814, the Battle of Leipzig; 1815, the Island of St Helena. After that economic conditions improved in Prussia, and he did no more, His success as an architect had begun.

Meanwhile, an example of his art is the drawing called *Evening*, done in   15
1811, which is, architecturally speaking, interesting for three reasons. First, it is a Gothic building. Secondly, it is a Gothic building in a forest glade, that is a most un-Gothic setting. Thirdly, it is entirely un-Gothic in its conceit and plan. It has Gothic detail, but it is a central church which one might well classicise with a few strokes of the pen. Also, the glade is cut by a canal, as formal as if it were the canal at Versailles. These classical elements no doubt crept in against Schinkel's intentions. The combination of landscape setting and Gothic architecture touched the romantic vein in Schinkel's heart. Similarly, in an oil painting of 1813, he placed a cathedral in lonely splendour on a rock.* Already in Italy or a   n.13
little later, he had made a large cartoon which is described as 'How Milan Cathedral ought to be placed'.* We find that it ought to be placed in complete   16
isolation on a rock by the sea. This, again, is not a Gothic building in a Gothic setting, but a Gothic building in a romantic setting. The combination of architecture and landscape is also one of the most interesting features in Schinkel's theatrical designs. His setting for *Alceste* (1817), for example, showing an altar in front of a dark cave and wild rocks behind, is what a painter like Friedrich did at the same moment in Germany and a parallel to what, at the same time, Turner and Crome sometimes did in England. Equally remarkable are the sets for *The Magic Flute* (1815), where an Egyptian Temple is placed in a cave under rocks.   17
Neo-Egyptian incidentally was at that particular moment the great fashion and a very recent fashion (see p. 213).

16 SCHINKEL *Fantasy of Milan Cathedral on a height overlooking Trieste*

17 SCHINKEL *Entrance to the Palace of the Queen of the Night, for 'The Magic Flute', 1815*

Schinkel's Panorama of Palermo (1808) was shown to the accompaniment of distinguished singers, a combination of painting and music in itself very much of the romantic movement. The combined effect caused a sensation in Berlin and was brought to the notice of the King and Queen and shown to the Royal Family; thus it started Schinkel's reputation at Court, and when in 1810 the much-beloved Queen Louise of Prussia died, Schinkel knew that a mausoleum was to be erected and could expound to the King his views in the matter. The design which he submitted is a Gothic hall, of the same exaggeratedly soaring proportions as he had given to Milan Cathedral. The piers of the mausoleum are Italian Gothic, too. Schinkel's description is interesting for the sensations which the interior was to stimulate. Piers and vault should create 'the feeling of a lovely grove of palm trees'.* The tomb-chest in the middle should be like a couch 'with many sprouting leaves, lilies and roses'; and the light to be let in should be rose-coloured.

Schinkel's memorandum on this mausoleum starts with several paragraphs of architectural philosophy.* In a typically German way he is convinced that he must start from scratch. He therefore begins by telling the King that architecture derives from physical needs. It was only with the Greeks, he says, that we find 'the command of spirit over matter'. The Romans, he went on, although the inventors of vaulting, did not develop this. They were satisfied with combining their vaults with the opposed principle of Greek architecture. The change came only when the Germans appeared, 'a true *Urvolk*'. Incidentally, this misconception of the national sources of the Gothic style was, of course, universal. It was French to the French (and rightly so), German to Goethe, and Early English to Rickman. The German mediaeval style is, quite clearly, the acme of architecture to the Schinkel of 1810. Only with the Gothic style is 'the spirit wholly in

1

n.14

n.15

18 SCHINKEL *Guard House, Berlin, 1816–18*

19 SCHINKEL *Schauspielhaus, Berlin, 1818–21*

conquest of mass and matter'. Only now the buildings make visible 'what ties us to the super-human—to God'. There is a later note added to the memorandum which is also in his writing and which confirms that 'the art of the Middle Ages is from the beginning higher in its principle than Antiquity'.

That was in 1810. Nothing came of it. The mausoleum was eventually built in a severe Greek Doric style by Gentz, another interesting architect of Berlin.

When conditions improved in Prussia after the Battle of Waterloo, Schinkel suddenly found himself the most sought-after architect of the country, the recognised leader of architecture in Prussia. No sooner had this change in his circumstances taken place than all he designed on a large scale, or nearly all, turned neo-Greek. In less than ten years now Schinkel designed what have to be regarded as his masterpieces. In 1815 he was made *Geheimer Oberbaurat*, in 1816–18 he built the new Guard House for the Royal Guards in Berlin, in 1818–21 the Theatre, and in 1823–30 the Museum. They were all severely damaged in the Second World War.

18 In the Guard House the connection with the Franco-Gilly background is clear. The building is basically a cube. Again there are parapets, and the slightly projecting angle blocks and severely Greek portico are French in origin. The Guard House is of elementary shape; when it came to a more complicated 19 building, the Schauspielhaus, the theatre which was finally executed not to Gilly's designs of twenty years earlier but to Schinkel's, we see a more complex group of forms, arranged symmetrically, on a very successful plan in which the main auditorium is balanced by a concert hall and a foyer. The style is more elegant. The order used is Ionic; pediments are introduced, but the severity which Schinkel had inherited from Gilly is yet there, in what is, perhaps, Schinkel's favourite motif and, as far as I can see, one of the most influential motifs he used. It is the arrangement of bands of very slender, tall windows, separated by completely unmoulded piers or mullions. In the Schauspielhaus the motif appears both as one band and as two superimposed tiers.

20 SCHINKEL *Old Museum, Berlin, 1823–30*

The concert hall inside is very much more ornate than anything by Gilly. *22*
Gilly would certainly never have used the restless motif of diagonal coffering
which Schinkel chose for the ceiling of the hall, and if he had, he would have
done it differently. Schinkel's other motifs tend to be restless, too. He was keenly
interested in the design of any detail of furnishing, as will be seen later, and thus
sometimes tended to overdo them. Here lies perhaps a first hint at the coming of
the new Victorian intricacy.

But Schinkel's most successful building is the Old Museum in Berlin, de- *20*
signed in 1823 and completed in 1830. Its façade reminds us at once of that of the
British Museum, built twenty years later but designed at about the same time. *21*
In fact, Smirke defended himself against the rumour that he had taken this over
from Schinkel. The differences are more interesting than the similarities;
Smirke's façade for the British Museum is still essentially Palladian in the eight-
teenth-century tradition, with its recessed centre and projecting wings.* *n.16*
Schinkel is entirely uncompromising and gives his building an absolutely
straight, smooth, sheer front, with one giant order running right through from
the square angle pier on the left to that on the right. There is no pediment whatever, the whole being crowned by the heavy architrave and cornice, and the
centre slightly raised, again with a roof appearing to be completely flat.

21 SMIRKE *British Museum, London, designed 1820s, built 1842–7*

22 SCHINKEL *Concert hall in the Schauspielhaus, 1818–21*

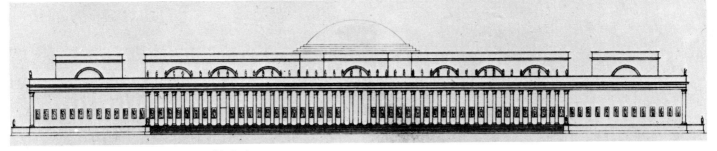

23 DURAND *Design for a museum, published 1802–9*

24 SCHINKEL *Roman Bath at Charlottenhof, 1831–3*

25 SCHINKEL *Design for a Basilica, c.1830*

The building of a public museum as such was very much in the air at that moment. It is very characteristic of the coming of an age of middle-class predominance that now the treasures accumulated by princes were by gradual transference to museums and galleries given over to everybody. Amongst the designs of younger architects, under the influence of Boullée and Ledoux, which were made for various academic purposes, one finds very often designs for museums. There was especially one of the younger members of this group, Jean-Nicholas-Louis Durand (1760–1834), who became professor at the Ecole Polytechnique which had been founded in 1804—a characteristic innovation of the nineteenth century. In the published précis of his lectures (1802–9) one finds a design for a museum, with a long completely flat colonnade in the middle, 23 crowned by a kind of Pantheon dome. This dome rises above a central rotunda, and Schinkel's museum has just such a domed rotunda in the same place.* n.17

However, there is again one motif which, I should say, would not have been used twenty years earlier. The staircase to the upper storey, it will be noticed, 26,27 leads up from the centre behind the colonnade in two arms to the left and right; it is not enclosed by walls, but on both sides open to the colonnade, resulting in an extraordinary interpenetration of space as it is now called. In this relaxing of the severe closure of room against room which had been the rule of Neo-Greek architecture there is in terms of space (as in the concert hall in terms of ornament) a hint at the more picturesque style of the future.

Having now reached the 1820s, we find that Schinkel was so much the accepted premier architect, and that he was so busy not only in Berlin but in all the provinces belonging to Prussia, in Pomerania. Silesia and everywhere, that it would be impossible in any form other than that of a whole book to do more than to pick out a few aspects of his later work.

The first of these is his ever-freer treatment of the Neo-Greek. One finds this in his vast schemes of 1834 for a palace on the Acropolis (for Prince Otto of Bavaria, the newly elected King of Greece) and for a palace for the Empress of Russia at Orianda, on the Krim, designed in 1838.* One also finds it, actually n.18 executed, though on a much smaller scale, in the various buildings connected with the Villa of Charlottenhof, at Potsdam, in the Royal Park. It can be seen to perfection in the Roman Bath of 1831–33. Here is not only a combination of 24 picturesque landscape gardening with classical architecture, but here is picturesque architecture also. The building is no longer severely symmetrical. It is grouped with a little Neo-Greek temple on the left, and leads up to the domestic part of the house with a kind of chalet roof, and then a campanile-like tower with a typically Italian roof. That mixture of classical and Italianate is, for Germany certainly, Schinkel's creation. But the style of landscape gardening at Charlottenhof is of course English. It became popular in Prussia thanks to the work of Prince Pückler-Muskau, whose park was at Muskau, and whose book called *Hints on Landscape Gardening* (1834) depends entirely on England and Repton. For the building, however, the most interesting architectural question remains for us: how far are the many semi-classical and semi-Italian villas in England* connected with Schinkel? That question would deserve further n.19 research.

A very similar problem is set by a drawing for a type of church known
25 amongst Schinkel's works as a Basilica. The obvious influence of the Early
Christian and of the mediaeval Italian style on such buildings is what matters.
One sees the use of the round arch—in Schinkel's own writing already the term
'Rundbogenstil' comes in, a term used by scholars in America today to denote
this kind of German work. In the façade the Italian element is chiefly recognizable in the combination of the round-arched windows with the little angle
turrets, as you find them in the Romanesque cathedrals of Cremona, Ferrara and
so on. Schinkel used these motifs chiefly in the 1830s—he died in 1841—and so
it is worth remembering that Klenze, his opposite number in Munich, had built
such a basilica already in 1826–37 (Allerheiligen–Hofkirche) and Friedrich
Gärtner in 1829–44 (Ludwigskirche, also Munich) and that in England basilicas
suddenly appeared after 1840: 1842 is the year of Christ Church, Streatham, by
Wild; 1844 of the parish church at Wilton, by Thomas Henry Wyatt; and 1846
of Vulliamy's All Saints, Ennismore Gardens, Kensington. It is not likely that
there was a connection between these English buildings and Berlin or Munich—
n.20 e.g. Klenze and Gärtner, or Schinkel and his successor Persius* who died young?

Having tried to trace a line which may lead from Schinkel to England,
England can certainly retaliate; for if one forgets about the *Rundbogen* and the
Italian turrets, and also incidentally the Doric portico, and looks merely at the
bare bones of the Basilica, one is obviously very close to St George's Chapel at
Windsor. Now this building Schinkel knew, because in 1826 he went on a
journey through England. He went to make studies for his Museum which was
in construction, but he was far more interested in other things, and of these more
n.21 must be said.*

26, 27 SCHINKEL *Stair of the Old Museum,
1823–30, from the colonnade (above)
and from the landing (below)*

28 SCHINKEL *Great Hall, Antonin, 1822*

In his letters from England he says surprisingly little of the English Middle Ages—but then, he never talked much about his impressions of the past. And that the English version of Gothic interested him can hardly be denied. A proof of this seems to be his designs for a cathedral as a memorial to the Napoleonic War. It was to consist of a big west tower and a nave, widening out into a completely circular chancel, with one central pier and a vault spreading out fan-wise from it.* This motif, of course, is that of English chapter houses. But Schinkel's   n.22
designs were done seven years before his journey to England, and so they may perhaps be English only via the lithographs of the Marienburg after Gilly's drawings.

Another doubtful connection with England is to be found at the big hunting lodge for Prince Radzivil, near Ostrovo, in the province of Posen. The house, called Antonin, has a huge centre chimney in the form of a column surrounded by galleries on two storeys. The appearance is strikingly similar to that of the Ranelagh in London, built in 1741 and pulled down in 1805.* But how could   n.23
Schinkel have known this? Antonin dates from 1822. Could engravings have reached him? Very much less puzzling is a design such as that for Kurnick in the Province of Posen. Here, in 1834–35, there is without any doubt an English Perpendicular or rather Neo-Perpendicular ancestry. It is in fact known that his client wanted something English. I know of no immediate parallel, but the building could easily be by any English early nineteenth century architect.

Now it is a familiar fact that early nineteenth century architects in England used Perpendicular or Classical forms seemingly at random. There is in the work of Schinkel at least one case which proves that to him also, for certain purposes, the two styles were interchangeable. The case is that of the Werdersche Kirche,*   n.24
in the centre of Berlin, for which he made designs in the Classical as well as the   *31*
Gothic style. The Classical ones have a series of domes abutted on the left and   *29*

29, 30 SCHINKEL *Designs for the interior of the Werdersche Kirche—on the right, as built—1828*

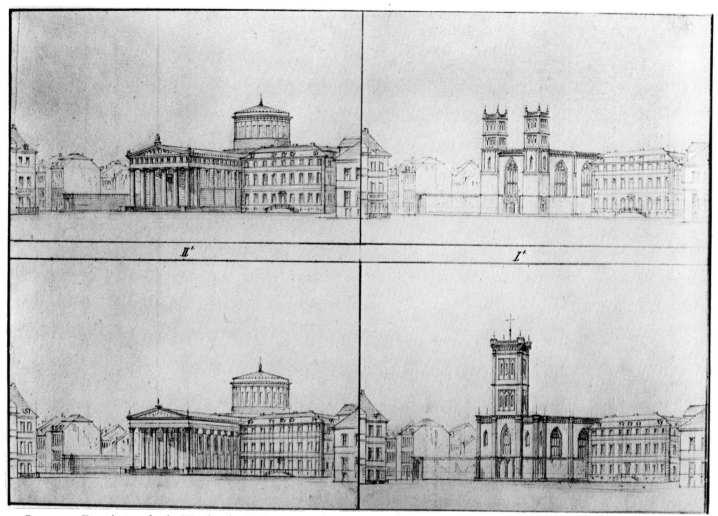

31 SCHINKEL *Four designs for the Werdersche Kirche, 1824; the version top right was chosen*

right by shallow tunnel-vaults, with narrow open galleries set into them on Ionic columns. The source is the Madeleine in Paris (which was of course not yet completed at the time). The church was in the end carried out in Gothic with rib-vaulted bays instead of domes, side abutment *à la* Albi and an open gallery with a balustrade decorated by a quatrefoil frieze and resting on Gothic piers and pointed arches. The exterior is severely plain, of brick, with geometrical tracery in the windows, but also no doubt reminiscent of such English buildings as King's College Chapel, Cambridge, the type of the Royal Chapels, with a narrow nave and angle turrets. The English precedent here may not be very evident, because Schinkel has squared up his design so rigidly. It is this squaring up of all forms which leads to Schinkel's most original contribution to architecture.

There is no contemporary parallel in other countries to such buildings as Schinkel's School of Architecture in Berlin, of 1831–35. The use of brick and the type of window, with two mullions and little segmental pediments, are clearly a reflection of what Schinkel had seen at Ferrara or Verona, but he has placed these windows in an uncompromisingly maintained grid of uprights and horizontals. The pilasters, if one may call them that, which articulate the elevation, are so elongated that they are really rather like mediaeval lesenes. The whole is more akin to Louis Sullivan than to the Italian Renaissance. The Bauakademie is an extremely original and at the same time curiously utilitarian composition for a building which, after all, was to some extent representational.

This is the moment to refer to at least one passage from Schinkel's theory of architecture which was intended ultimately to become a book. Many pages of

32, 33 SCHINKEL *The School of Architecture in Berlin, 1831–5*

preparatory notes survive. The extract of special significance in the present context is: 'Utility is the fundamental principle of all building', and by that he means utility of plan, of construction, of decoration. Utility of plan implies the highest economy of space, the highest order in the arrangement of space, and the highest convenience in the arrangement of space. Utility of construction calls for the use of the best materials, for the best treatment and assembly of the materials, and for the most clearly visible indication of the best materials and the best treatment of materials. Utility of decoration calls for the best choice of place for decoration, for the best choice of ornaments, and for the best treatment of ornaments.*   n.25

The School of Architecture is an ideal example of the application of this theory, and in looking at the detail one finds Schinkel's three principles admirably exhibited. The plan is indeed simple and straightforward, the material—local brick—is frankly exhibited, and ornament is well and sparingly used. The decoration of the doorway is incidentally very original, although perhaps   35 vaguely connected with the way in which at Bologna Jacopo della Quercia had arranged his reliefs round the portal of S. Petronio.

34 SCHINKEL *Design for a Bazaar, 1827*

The grid system was all that was needed for utilitarian buildings such as the military prison in the Lindenstrasse at Berlin (1825) and the most puzzling of all his designs, the so-called *Kaufhaus* (that is a bazaar), datable to 1827. It was   34 meant to be Unter den Linden, in the centre of Berlin, and is another example of the amazingly progressive or forward-looking style which Schinkel could use when he liked. But he did not always like to use it, and the distinction he makes here in his theory is typical of the whole nineteenth century. In the notes for his theoretical book Schinkel tells of his own experiences. He says that so many

35 SCHINKEL *Doorway of the School of Architecture in Berlin, 1831–5*

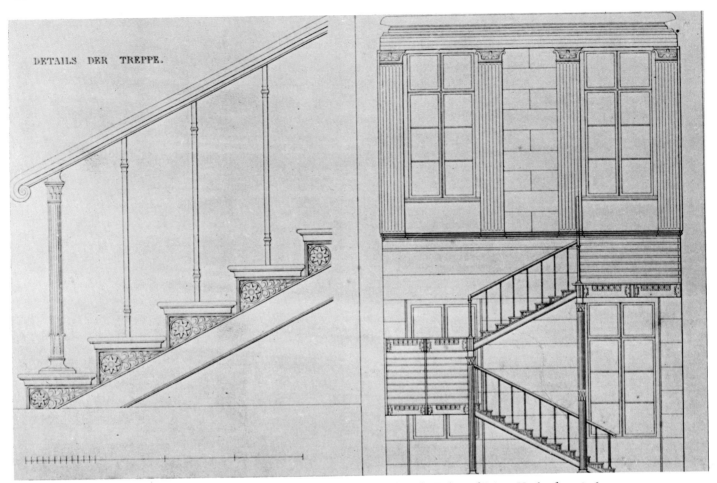

DETAILS DER TREPPE.

36 SCHINKEL *Detail and general view of the cast-iron stair with marble treads in the Palace of Prince Karl, after 1826*

people had used period forms in their buildings that he felt repelled by the way in which it was done. So he turned to the 'radical abstraction' of developing buildings entirely out of construction and function. But that results in something 'dry and rigid', as it leaves out two equally important elements: 'the historic and the poetic'. He ends by admitting that to choose rightly amongst these elements remains a matter of feeling and not of reason.* n.26

This is a memorable passage, for it contains the complete apology for the nineteenth century's acceptance of different styles for different buildings: the grid for use, the evocation of Greece for representation. In fact, one might describe Schinkel's theatre as a first synthesis of the grid and the portico. As for the grid and such designs as the Kaufhaus, Schinkel had no doubt profited from his visit to England. The Kaufhaus was designed in 1827, the English journey took place in 1826.

Schinkel was meant to study museums on the journey, but he actually looked far more interestedly at commerce and industry than at the fine art of architecture, owing perhaps to the fact that he travelled with Peter Christian Beuth, the head of what was called the Deputation of Trade, that is to say, the Board of Trade, of Prussia. In his very detailed notes Schinkel describes not only what he saw of the British Museum, which was under construction, but bridges, the Thames tunnel—he spoke to Brunel about it—and the docks. He visited breweries, potteries, ironworks, engineering shops, a papier maché factory, spinning mills, and so on; and he was, as an architect, immensely impressed by the gigantic mill landscape of Manchester. He had never seen anything like that, 37 and indeed could not have seen it anywhere else.*

37 SCHINKEL *The mills of Manchester, 1826*

In Prussia certainly there were no such factories. The only comparable n.27 enterprise was perhaps the Royal Iron-Foundry, in which Schinkel indeed took a very keen interest. Very early—even internationally speaking—the monument on the Kreuzberg in Berlin, a memorial to the Napoleonic Wars (1818–21) was a cast iron structure, 60 ft. high.*

36 After Schinkel had been in England he built two complete iron staircases for the palaces of Prince Karl and Prince Albrecht, and he also designed much on a smaller scale, bridge railings, garden seats, and so on, all done extremely taste-fully, with a great deal of understanding for the simplicity and smoothness which *38* is necessary in cast iron. But Schinkel also designed damask napkins, to be carried out by a weaver, and he designed a great deal of furniture. When he did that, he worked, of course, for craft rather than for industry, that is to say, in the eighteenth century sense rather than in the nineteenth century sense, but his *n.29* attitude was already nineteenth and not eighteenth century.'*

In 1821 the Prussian Board of Trade started a publication, not discontinued until 1837, which was called *Examples for Manufacturers and Craftsmen*. In the introduction Schinkel speaks of the necessity of 'adding perfection of form to technical perfection.' His best example, again, is English: Wedgwood. Perfec-tion of form was almost entirely seen in terms of Antiquity. But, Schinkel adds, the antique style needs adapting to modern needs, and 'it would be asking too much from the craftsman to leave the adapting to him'. The craftsman must not be 'tempted to design himself' and so the *Oberbaurat*, that is the architect-designer in the nineteenth and twentieth century sense, is doing it for him.

To Schinkel, that was one of his duties. He took altogether a very con-scientious and Prussian view of his duties. If the results we have seen are as distinguished as they are, that is due to a large extent to that particular moment in German history, in which it was Schinkel's good luck to live and work, the moment of Goethe and Schiller, of the Humboldts and Schelling, of Schlegel, Fichte, Hegel and so on. Never at any moment had there been so many men of genius in Germany.

Schinkel was not himself a man of genius. Never, as far as we know, did he make any efforts to break away from the set and accepted routine of his suc-cessfully discharged duties. Successful he was indeed, and deservedly so. And if he was not a man of genius, he was a man of the highest professional achieve-ments, the best architect of his generation in Europe, the best architect, that is to say, of that peculiarly academic moment of restraint and reflection which im-mediately preceded the onrush of the rich and muddy Victorian torrent.

38 SCHINKEL *Design for the border of a damask napkin*

1   *The Temple of Ceres, from Dumont's 'Les Ruines de Paestum', 1769*

The Architectural Review, CIV, 1948

XII
The Doric Revival
WRITTEN IN COLLABORATION WITH S. LANG

2 *Detail of Mengs's 'Parnassus', 1761*

I n March 1761, Anton Raphael Mengs completed the ceiling painting in the central saloon of Cardinal Alessandro Albani's villa outside the gates of Rome. It represents Parnassus and was hailed by Winckelmann, the Cardinal's librarian and the greatest antiquarian of his age, with enthusiasm: 'A more beautiful work has not appeared in all modern times; even Raphael would bow to it.'* High praise, indeed; for Mengs was evidently here challenging Raphael, whose *Parnassus* in the Stanza della Segnatura was familiar to everyone. Compare the two and, while Raphael appears at once the stronger and warmer, Mengs is correct in a sense which the Renaissance had not known. His Apollo is derived from the Apollo Belvedere, though what this smooth piece of later Greek statuary (the paragon of ideal beauty to the eighteenth century and right down to the days when the Elgin Marbles arrived in London) still possesses of vigour and contrast has been further smoothed out into the somewhat effeminate elegance of the 'First Classical Revival,' the period of Flaxman and of Robert Adam.

To the right of Apollo we see a Muse holding a scroll with Mengs's proud signature. Her elbow rests on a column of proportions strikingly different from those of Apollo and the dancing maidens. It is a Greek Doric column of short stature—Doric of a phase prior to the Parthenon. The presence of this column in this picture has not so far found sufficient comment, although it is of no small significance.

Few people realize that the Greek Doric column, fluted and without a base, which is to us the symbol of Greek greatness, was virtually unknown about 1750, and that by 1760, when it had become known to a few virtuosi, antiquarians and architects, it was the object of passionate controversy. This complete blindness to what could be seen on the Acropolis, in Sicily and at Paestum can only have been caused by the tendency of scholars and amateurs to trust their books rather than their eyes and by the fascination of Rome. Even so, it sounds strange now to read what James Adam writes from Paestum in the year of Mengs's *Parnassus*: 'The famous antiquitys so much talk'd of late as wonders . . . curiosity apart don't merit half the time and trouble they have cost me; they are of an early an unelegant and unenrich'd Dorick, that afford no detail and scarcely produce two good views. So much for Pesto'.* But whatever the reaction, the existence of columns without bases could not be ignored altogether. They existed in Rome, at the Marcellus Theatre (though unfluted and thus Tuscan, and not Greek Doric) and in a few other places in Italy too. So one had to come to terms with them. But they remained a source of embarrassment—as, indeed, they had already been to Vitruvius.

3 *Doric temple, from Fra Giocondo's Vitruvius, 1511*

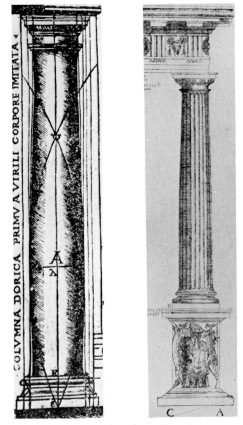

4,5 *The Doric order, from Cesariano, 1521 (left), and Shute, 1563*

A summary of this story of perplexity may not be without interest. Vitruvius (IV, 1) never says in so many words that the Doric column has no base. He describes the origin of the Doric and Ionic orders among the early Greek builders thus:

'Wishing to set up columns . . . they measured the imprint of a man's foot and compared this with his height. On finding that in a man, the foot was one sixth of the height, they applied the same principle to the column, and reared the shaft, including the capital, to a height six times its thickness at its base. Thus the Doric column, as used in buildings, began to exhibit the proportions, strength and beauty of the body of a man. Just so afterwards, when they desired to construct a temple to Diana in a new style of beauty, they translated these footprints into terms characteristic of the slenderness of women, and thus first made a column the thickness of which was only one eighth of its height, so that it might have a taller look. At the foot they substituted the base in place of a shoe; . . . Thus in the invention of the two different kinds of columns they borrowed manly beauty, naked and unadorned, for the one, and for the other the delicacy, adornment, and proportions characteristic of women. . . . posterity, having made progress in refinement and delicacy of feeling and finding pleasure in more slender proportions, has established seven diameters of the thickness as the height of the Doric column and nine as that of the Ionic.'*   n.3

Later Vitruvius returns to the Doric column (IV, 3), but only to emphasize the difficulties any architect will find in the disposition of metopes and triglyphs. Hence, he sums up, 'antiqui vitare visi sunt . . . doricae symmetriae rationem.'

The Middle Ages never forgot Vitruvius entirely. Eginhard, Charlemagne's biographer, knew him. Thomas Aquinas had read and used him.* Petrarch possessed a copy, Boccaccio asked for one to be copied for his own library. Yet when Cencio Rustici found a manuscript at St Gall in 1414, it amounted almost to a re-discovery. Alberti's *De Re aedificatoria,* written about 1450, consciously emulates Vitruvius. But on the Doric column he is not very helpful. Where he discusses it (VII, 7) he never seems to query the presence of a base. The most interesting remark of Alberti's—interesting, as will be seen, in view of future developments—is one in which he implies doubts in the trustworthiness of the Greek stories about the earliest Doric columns and puts forward his own view that they were originally used 'apud vetustissimos Aetruscos' (VII, 6).   n.4

Alberti's work remained in manuscript. It was only printed in 1485; the *editio princeps* of Vitruvius' *Ten Books* by Johannes Sulpitius was printed by G. Herrolt in Rome at an uncertain date.* The first illustrated Latin edition, by Fra Giovanni Giocondo, came out in 1511, followed by Cesariano's sumptuously illustrated Italian translation in 1521. Cesariano's Doric column is slender and unfluted and has a base.   n.5

3

4

By then the Renaissance was waning, and with the coming of Mannerism art theory and academic art teaching appeared. The first Book of Orders came out in 1537: Sebastiano Serlio's *Libro IV.* After the middle of the century it was followed by many more (H. Blum 1550, Vignola 1562, John Shute 1563, Delorme 1568, Palladio 1570); for Mannerist theory was convinced that by fixing rules for the columnation of a façade or an interior all other measurements would fall into place.   5

The reaction to the Doric column amongst these first theorists of the Five Orders is varied. Cesariano says that 'some hold that the Doric column originally had no base; but to me the contrary seems true'; Serlio in his Third Book of 1540 illustrates those Tuscan columns without bases which existed in Italy,* and in his Fourth Book discusses them—but where he shows the five orders together he shows the Doric with a base (f.VI). In the Third Book he illustrates especially the *templum pietatis,* which had earlier on been drawn by Serlio's probable master Peruzzi. Peruzzi must have thought the lack of bases very unusual and to make sure that there was no mistake he added to the drawing the statement *base non aver.**   n.6

n.7

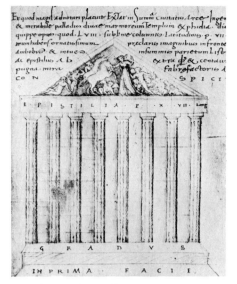

6 *Palladio's Doric order, 1570*   7 *Doric temple in Rome drawn by Palladio*   8 *The Parthenon by Ciriaco d'Ancona, from the Codex Hamiltonianus, mid-15th century*

Serlio's engravings were used as evidence by his followers, one of whom was Labacco, who in his *Libro* of 1557 reproduces a Tempio Dorico which stood near the Theatre of Marcellus. Labacco only quotes Vitruvius's statement on the triglyphs, but is silent on the problem of the base. Hans Blum (*Quinque Columnarum exacta descriptio,* Zurich 1550) also gives a base; so does Vignola. Shute tells the Vitruvian story, says nothing about base or no base in his Introduction and in his plates of Tuscan and Doric puts the bases in without remark. Delorme is no more explicit; he also has no plate of a Doric column without a base. Only Palladio, according to his greater faith in Vitruvius and Antiquity, says (ed. Ware 1738, I, Cap. 15): 'This order has no base peculiar to it, which is the reason that in a great many edifices the columns are to be seen without bases,' and consequently draws it in at least one place without one. However, even he feels it necessary to comment that the use of a base 'adds very much to its beauty,' and in any case gives his one drawing a length of eight diameters instead of Vitruvius's six or the less than six of early Greek buildings. In Palladio's own buildings there are no columns without bases.*

However all these architects ought to have known better: Ciriaco d'Ancona who had visited Athens on several occasions brought back with him to Italy an unambiguous drawing of the Parthenon, which he incidentally attributed to Phidias. Ciriaco's original sketchbook is lost, but he himself made copies of some of the drawings, and excerpts from his MSS, for various friends; there is such a copy made for Bishop Donato in the so-called Codex Hamiltonianus.* Later in the century Giuliano da Sangallo incorporated a drawing of the Parthenon into the Barberini Sketchbook.* He made several changes in this drawing: he obviously did not know how to place the metopes, and gave the capitals a composite air, yet he did follow Ciriaco in leaving off the bases of the columns. A rough copy of Sangallo's drawing exists in the Codex Destailleur, fol.28v, but the copyist apparently did not believe the visual evidence and added bases to the columns.* Then there is a copy of Ciriaco's drawing in the Codex Manzoni, fol. 73, again with bases to the columns. Huelsen suggested that this was a copy after a different drawing by Ciriaco,* but it is more likely that it was again the copyist who, wanting to do the right thing, added bases: for why should Ciriaco who was right in one drawing go wrong in another?

In the seventeenth century the French treatises are almost unanimously in favour of the 'modern' Doric, that is the one recommended by Serlio, Vignola and Palladio. This applies to Claude Perrault (*Traité,* 1664, translation John James, 1708) who speaks of the Doric column and 'its base, when it has one' and then goes on to accept the Attic base for it, as the one 'most in use', and to Blondel (*Cours,* 1675) who is more determinedly French and modern than any of the

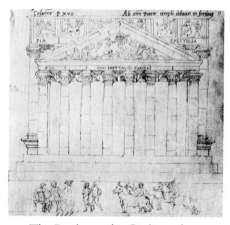

9 *The Parthenon by Giuliano da Sangallo after Ciriaco , c.1500*

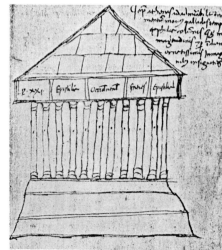

10 *The Parthenon, from the Codex Manzoni, late 15th century*

11

n.8

,n.9
9
n.10

n.11
10
n.12

others. He reports (Pt 2, Liv. I, Cap. VII, p. 35) that Vitruvius gives no base to the Doric column and adds: 'Ce que nous avons de plus beau dans cet ordre est avec la Base Attique, qu' autrement les Colonnes en paroissent estropiées. Ainsi l'usage qui a corrigé ce défaut doit . . . prevaloir.' The same attitude characterizes Daviler's *Cours* (1691) and the various discussions of the Académie Royale d'Architecture reported in their Procès-Verbaux.* The only exception is Fréart de Chambray, the champion of the *Anciens* in the architectural *Querelle des Anciens et des Modernes,* who pleaded obstinately for Vitruvius against the 'licentious', 'debauched' habits of his day (*Parallèle,* 1650, quoted from J. Evelyn's translation 1664, p. 11). But of course he also, just like Palladio, thought only of the Tuscan order of the Theatre of Marcellus and knew no Greek Doric examples.   n.13

11 Doric temple engraved by Labacco, 1557

In 1675 Spon, a French physician, and Sir George Wheler went to Athens and from then on the link between Athens and the West was never again broken.*   n.14 Spon and Wheler published an account of their journey* containing primitive   n.15 illustrations of the Parthenon and the Theseion.* Fifty years later Fischer von   12, n.Ɩ Erlach, the Viennese architect, in his curious omnium gatherum, the *Civil and Historical Architecture* (1725, English edition 1730, Lib. I, pl. 19) copied Spon and Wheler's pictures of the Parthenon. But these early illustrations were not of a kind to impress anybody or make anybody think; and so the eighteenth century in its books on architecture went on exactly as the sixteenth and seventeenth had done. A few examples will suffice. First, Batty Langley, who in 1721 (*A Sure Guide to Builders*) gives the accepted view: 'This order was originally made without a base . . . but a base adds a Grace to a Column and strengthens its standing also. . . .'; then Robert Morris in 1723 (*An Essay in Defence of Ancient Architecture*): 'As no footsteps of the Grecian Buildings now remain, we must of necessity have recourse to the Antiquities of the Romans'; then we have Flitcroft's beautiful drawings of the orders in the British Museum; and, finally, for the fifties and sixties Isaac Ware and Robert Adam. Adam, in his letter to Lord Kames dated March 31, 1763,* discusses whether the Doric column should be   n.17 fluted or not, and how much ornamentation might be permitted for its base and capital, but never queries the use of a base and the relative slenderness of the shaft—that is to say, the characteristics of his own Roman Doric and Tuscan Doric in the Admiralty Screen, say, or the Bowood Mausoleum. And Isaac Ware, in his treatise of 1756, states that 'those who would give an additional beauty to the Doric column, order it a base which is called the Attick or Attiurgick', although he quotes Palladio as having 'determined that the Doric has no proper base' (p. 155) and refers as evidence explicitly to the 'Parthenion' (p. 153).

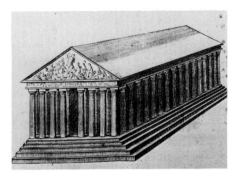

12 The Parthenon from Spon and Wheler, 1678

Now Ware's information on the Parthenon was no longer based on Spon and Wheler or Fischer von Erlach. By the time he wrote, Stuart and Revett had been sent by the Society of Dilettanti to Athens, had made measured drawings of buildings there, including the Parthenon, and returned to London in 1755. They had not published anything yet, but architects in England no doubt knew of their discoveries.

However, the discovery of the Greek Doric order in the flesh, as it were, is connected not so much with Athens as with Sicily and Paestum, more accessible—though by no means easily accessible—to the traveller, whether scholar or artist or nobleman following the Grand Tour. The documentation of this discovery can be given here in outline only.

13 Paestum, from Berkenhout, 1767

The early Doric temples of Girgenti (Agrigento) in Sicily had been visited by D'Orville as early as 1727, but were not published until Pancrazi's *Antichità Siciliane* of 1751–2. D'Orville's *Sicula* came out in 1764. By this time—or, more precisely, by some time between 1754 and 1758—the Scottish architect Robert Mylne had also been to Girgenti. He told Winckelmann of his impressions, and Winckelmann based on these his *Notes on the Architecture of the Ancient Temples at Girgenti,* which was written in 1759.*   n.18

Winckelmann knew Paestum at first hand too. But though in his *Notes on Ancient Architecture,* written in 1760,* he boasts of being the first to give news in   n.19 detail of the temples there, he was neither the first to see nor to illustrate them.

14 The order at Paestum, from Major, 1768   15 Temple of Neptune at Paestum, from Dumont, 1769

The town (but not the temples) of Paestum was mentioned for the first time by Antonini in his *La Lucania,* 1745, and subsequently by Mazzochi in his *Collectanea,* 1754. But already one year after *La Lucania* had come out, a Neapolitan architect of little merit, Mario Gioffredo, saw the temples and told several friends of them. Among these friends were Count Gazola, M. Soufflot, and the painter Natali; and with Natali, Gioffredo returned in 1750 and 1752 and measured the buildings. It may be his drawings which eventually appeared in P. A. Paoli's final publication of 1784. Soufflot, on the other hand, the future architect of the Panthéon in Paris, who travelled in Italy in 1750 as one of the companions of Mme de Pompadour's brother Marigny, the newly appointed Royal *Surintendant des Bâtiments* (the other was Cochin, the engraver and antiquarian) went to Paestum with another architect, Dumont, and also made careful measurements of the temples. What happened next, it is difficult to reconstruct. Count Gazola seems to have entrusted his plan to Soufflot (or rather his companion Cochin) to have it engraved in Paris. Then there were delays, and the next thing Gazola heard was that a publication of Paestum in Paris was imminent. He was upset and tried to stake his claim on priority of publication. Another man a little later tried to do the same.* Bruce of Kinnaird in a letter to Strange refers to his plan of publishing a book on Paestum and to the fact that for this book Strange had engraved plates in 1764. Bruce now writes in 1768: 'I hear with the utmost concern that the engraving of my prints of Paesto at Paris has produced an edition there by M. Soufflot . . . I suppose during my absence he has seen my prints and probably copied them'.* Anyway, Dumont's *Suite de plans . . .* came out in 1764,* and his engravings must be regarded as the first seriously published record of a Greek Doric temple—in spite of Spon and Fischer von Erlach, and an odd picture of Paestum in Galiani's edition of Vitruvius of 1758. Then, in the second half of the sixties a number of publications, using the same artists' drawings and even the same engravings appeared in quick succession: Filippo Morghen (drawings by Antonio Jolli) 1766, Berkenhout* in London (from Jolli-Morghen) 1767, and then the standard edition: Thomas Major in London 1768 (from Jolli-Morghen, from Soufflot-Dumont and also from Gioffredo-Natali as published in 1784).

n.20

n.21
n.22

,n.23
14

16 *Temple of Roma and Augustus in Rome,
from Stuart and Revett, 1761*

17 *The Parthenon, from Stuart and Revett, 1788*

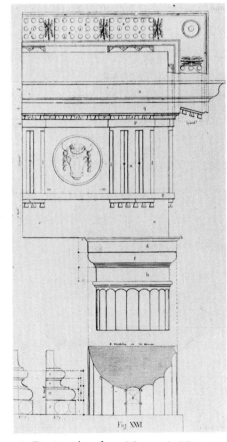

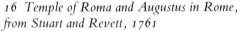

18 *Doric order, from Newton's Vitruvius,
1771*

Meanwhile Greece had at last begun to make herself felt. Stuart's and
Revett's proposal of a journey to Greece had been printed as early as 1748; R.
Dalton made drawings on a journey with Lord Charlemont in 1749 and published these as engravings in 1751 and 1752 (Theseion 1751, Parthenon 1752);
Stuart and Revett started out on their journey in 1750 and returned to England
in 1755. However, with a truly British disregard for novelty, the Society of
Dilettanti delayed the publication of the first volume of the *Antiquities of Athens*
for seven years, and when it finally came out, it contained but one late example
of Doric, the Temple of Roma and Augustus. The Acropolis appeared only in   *16,17*
1788, deplorably late, though—as we shall see—just in time for the opening of the
next act of the Doric Revival. A Frenchman had been quicker; Le Roy went to   *19*
Athens in 1754, the year before Stuart and Revett left it. He made a much less
thorough job of his recording, but managed to publish *Les Ruines des plus beaux
monuments de la Grèce* in 1758. So, by 1758, the Acropolis could be studied in
engravings, as (to recapitulate) could Girgenti by 1752 (or by 1761 when Piranesi
produced an engraving of it) and Paestum by 1758 or 1764.

But while so many concurrent publications point to some common feeling
for these temples of the sixth and fifth centuries, it is still necessary to go to
literary comment for confirmation as to whether such a common feeling really
existed. In some degree, at least, the rush to Paestum and Athens was simply part
of a much more general and much less discriminating rush to all parts of the
known world that seemed to promise archaeological discovery. The Dilettanti
in England, men like Caylus or Mariette in France and the Roman collectors such
as the very Cardinal Albani at whose Villa this Doric Tour started, were equally
interested in Roman statuary, coins and cameos, in the Late-Hellenistic temples
of Baalbek and Palmyra (published by Wood for the Dilettanti in 1753 and 1757)
and the Late Roman palace of Spalato (measured by Robert Adam in 1757 and
published in 1764). But if we look at comment on Greek Doric in the Books of
Orders and similar publications between 1750 and 1775, we find it on the whole
still as insensitive as it had been before 1750. One Italian, one French and two
English examples will suffice. The same Gioffredo, who was the first to see
Paestum, writes in his *Architettura* of 1768 that the Doric column was indeed in
the early stages without a base, but that the use of a base—as in his own illustra-
tions—shows '*maggior gusto e perfezione.*' Chambers in the 1759 edition of his
Civil Architecture blames Fréart (see above) for his 'blind attachment to the
Antique', and ends by saying that he himself in his plates has 'in imitation of
Palladio, and all the modern architects except Vignola' used an Attic base for his
Doric. Even William Newton, the assistant of Athenian Stuart, in his Vitruvius
of 1771 hesitates. He shows a Doric temple with columns without bases (pl.
14–16) and the Doric order (pl. 26) too. However, in a corner of his plate of the   *18*
Doric order he gives two bases—no doubt in case his readers might not like the

19 *The Parthenon, from Le Roy, 1758*

20 *Garden temple at Hagley by Stuart, 1758*

bareness of Doric. Finally, the younger Blondel in his *Cours* of 1771 gives measurements of Greek temples from Le Roy, but prefers explicitly the slender form of Doric with a base which the Renaissance and the following centuries had developed. His view of the matter is that the Doric column, started short and baseless, and that 'il a fallu des siecles pour parvenir à la beauté, à la regularité, et à la perfection des ordres que nous connoissons' (I, p. 195).

    If it is realized that this comment on fifth century Greece was still possible in Paris in 1771, Winckelmann's definition of the character of classic Greek art must seem all the more amazing. As is well known, it appears for the first time in his *Thoughts on the Imitation of the Works of the Greeks,* written in 1755 (and trans-

n.24 lated into English by Fuseli in 1765) before he had even seen the South.* The statuary in the possession of the Elector of Saxony was enough for him to recognize 'unity of the whole structure, a noble relation of parts, a fuller measure of richness . . . and a noble ingenuousness and calm greatness' as the essence of Greek classicity. Olympia and the Elgin Marbles and the temples of Paestum could not be described more appropriately; yet it remains a fact that in Rome Winckelmann's favourites were such late and relatively 'Baroque' or 'Rococo' works as the Apollo Belvedere, the Laocoön, and the Belvedere Torso. His enthusiastic praise for the feminine charms of Mengs's *Parnassus* has already been quoted. When it came to architecture, he called the columns of Girgenti and Paestum 'mature,' the entablatures 'great and magnificent' and the ornamentation 'great and simple', and stated that 'as elegance is added to architecture beauty declines'. But he is nowhere as emphatic on architecture as he is on the fine arts, and concentrates in his papers on Girgenti and Paestum on description and antiquarian questions.

    The case of Athenian Stuart is even more surprising. It is true—and memorable indeed—that as early as 1758 Stuart put up a prostyle Greek Doric temple

20 for Lord Lyttelton in the grounds of Hagley. This is the earliest monument of the Greek Revival anywhere in the world. Yet here, as well as at Shugborough (where *c.* 1765 he put up for Lord Anson copies of the Tower of the Winds, the

23 Lysicrates Monument, Hadrian's Arch in Athens and another Doric temple), the observant eye cannot fail to notice that of Greek feeling there is little. The setting operates against it probably more than anything. The strong, severe clarity of Athens cannot be replaced by the leafy intricacies of an English park. In a landscape garden with its variety of vistas the Greek copy becomes an ornament, a stage property of exactly the same qualities as a Gothic ruin or a Chinese bridge. Stuart's patrons no doubt wished to be in the latest fashion and to demonstrate their archaeological interest by such three-dimensional quotations from the Greek. But it was far from them—and they would probably have considered it pedantry anyway—to regard their garden ornaments as professions of faith in one aesthetic or cultural ideal as against all others.

21 Detail of one of Piranesi's Carceri showing a Doric column, c.1761

So the real story of the Greek Revival—that is of the revival of a genuine aesthetic and cultural enthusiasm for Greece—begins only after Hagley, and after the publication of Stuart and Revett's first volume. There was still a long way to go from archaeological interest to emotional understanding. The first version of Goethe's *Iphigenia* was written only in 1779 and its final version (in verse) in 1787, while he was experiencing the South for the first time. What then were the vicissitudes of the Doric column from the sixties to the eighties? The phase of discovery was followed by one of controversy. Those who had made the discoveries were proud of them and ready—with or without deeper aesthetic conviction—to fight for the superiority of what they had discovered. Their attitude could easily be justified from the purely literary worship of all things Greek which had existed for centuries without interfering much with the styles of the writers and artists who shared it. Poussin, to give only one example, wrote to Chantelou in a letter of 24 November, 1647 about 'nos braves anciens Grecs, inventeurs de toutes les belles choses'. If what was theoretically acceptable, then surely the buildings of the Greeks, whatever they looked like, must have been better than any other buildings also, and in particular better than those of the Romans, until then the unquestioned source of architectural inspiration.*   n.25

So a battle of styles began between the Greeks and the Romans, fought with remarkable violence on both sides.*   The leader of the Romans was Piranesi,   n.26 who wrote his treatise *Della Magnificenza ed Architettura de' Romani* in 1760 (publ. 1761). Its avowed purpose was to counteract Le Roy's *Les Ruines de la Grèce* by insistence on the older age and more venerable character of Etruscan—that is Italian—as against Greek civilization. Consequently to Piranesi the Tuscan, unfluted Doric, order was more ancient than the Greek Doric. That in itself was not new. Attention has been drawn to Alberti's remark on the priority of the Etruscans, and Piranesi quotes learned witnesses, especially Dempster's *Etruria* of *c.* 1620, only published in 1723–6, and Gori's *Museum Etruscum* of 1736–43.

As is not surprising in view of his bellicose attitude in *Della Magnificenza*, there is in Piranesi's own engravings of the sixties only one instance of a Greek Doric column, and that in a very special context. In pl. 16 of the second edition of the *Carceri* appears a solitary Doric column. The date is *c.* 1761—that is exactly   21 contemporary with the *Magnificenza*—and it is obviously meant as an indictment of Doric as the order of *terribilità* suitable only for the gloom of the prison.

Meanwhile the other side had found its heralds too. Mengs, one might say, is one of them, even if the Doric column in his *Parnassus* is no more than a stage property or at most a sign to the connoisseur that the painter was in the know; and Gavin Hamilton, the other leader of neo-classical taste in Rome in the same years, went only one step further when he put a whole Doric temple into the background of his *Hector's Farewell to Andromache*.*   However the picture, being   n.27 painted in Rome, is bound to have been regarded as an answer to Piranesi. But the first written and argued answer came from Le Roy himself and was conciliatory. It is contained in his *Observations sur les édifices . . .*, published in 1767. He had said, in his *Les Ruines de la Grèce* (Pt. II, Intro. p. vi), that he had gone to Greece chiefly because Vitruvius was obscure and had been inadequately interpreted by Perrault, and that architects should study all Greek and Roman monuments, and Vitruvius, and the best modern buildings, consider them 'comme autant d'éléments,' and create out of them the best order of architecture for present use. Regarding Piranesi's special grievance, Le Roy insisted on the priority of Greece over Tuscany. In a similar spirit Mariette, the French collector and scholar, had replied to Piranesi in the *Gazette littéraire* in 1764, calling the Etruscans merely Greek colonists, and praising the 'belle et noble simplicité' of Greek art. Now 1764 was the year in which Winckelmann's *History of Ancient Art* was at last published, and it has already been shown that, several years before, Winckelmann had begun to plead for the greatness and simplicity of the style of Girgenti and Paestum.

The English Romans, that is Palladians, sensed the danger to their own position in this growing appreciation of Greek architecture, and so the year 1767 brought the first violent Palladian counter-attack. James Paine, the architect of Nostell Priory, Wardour Castle and Worksop Manor, in the introduction to his *Plans, Elevations, etc., of Noblemen's and Gentlemen's Houses* (p. II, note) goes out of his way to hit at the 'most despicable ruins of ancient Greece'. This aggressive wording went beyond Piranesi and was promptly answered by a little known military engineer, Stephen Riou, who had built fortifications in Flanders about the time of the campaigns of Tristram Shandy's uncle Toby, or a little later.

n.28 Riou, in 1767 and 1768,* called the Tuscan order 'spurious', and the addition of a base to the Doric order 'a vulgar modern error' and 'a downright innovation against the most deliberate intention of the ancients'.

The centre of the opposition against the Grecians was Sir William Chambers, co-founder of the Royal Academy at just that time. In 1759, in the first edition of his *Civil Architecture*, as we have seen, he was not yet aware of any Grecian danger, and wrote of the Doric order very much as most other authors. When, however, he realized that the barbarity of columns without any bases was actually being perpetrated and advocated, he decided to speak up for academic rightness. His opportunity seemed to come when, sometime between 1768 and 1770, Thomas Sandby, the Professor of Architecture at the Academy, was prevented by illness from lecturing. Chambers prepared a lecture of which a draft
n.29 survives at the Royal Institute of British Architects.* In it he endeavoured to
n.30 establish the Egyptians as the inventors of what is called Greek architecture.* After this he goes on:

'How distant the Grecians were from perfection in Proportions in the Art of Profiling and I may venture to say in the whole Detail of the Decorative Part of Architecture will appear at first Sight to every one whether Ignorant or informed who unprejudiced compares the Columns, Capitals, Bases, Pedestals, Entablatures and Ornaments in the works of Messrs. le Roy, Rivett, Steward and other ingenious travellers with the Antiquities of Rome he may find in Palladio, Serlio, Desgodetz, Sandrart, Piranesi and many other Books in which they are accurately delineated. . . . But should any Man be diffident of his own Judgment, or trusting to the Encomiums of a few Ingenious but too partial Travellers, discredit the Testimony of his own Eyes, he cannot have a more corroborating Proof of the Imperfection of the Grecian Architecture than that it is diametrically opposite in almost every Particular to that of the Romans, whose Works have been admired, copied and imitated by all the great Architects from the fourteenth century . . . till this Day'.
And so on, to this climax:

'The memoirs of two or three or half a dozen can have but little Weight in a matter of this Nature, they might with equal Success oppose a Hottentot and a Baboon to the Apollo and the Gladiator as set up the Grecian Architecture against the Roman. . . . It hath afforded Occasion of Laughter to every intelligent Architect to see . . . what Encomiums have been lavished upon things that in Reality deserve little or no notice'.

It is not necessary to quote these infuriated pages in full, but a few of the expressions used are too remarkable to be missed. Chambers foresees that if it were seriously tried to 'cheat us into a Reverence for Attic Deformity . . . a general outcry of artists and connoisseurs would perhaps bring even the Gothic Architecture in Vogue again.' He compares the style of the Lysicrates Monument with 'the Taste of Borrommini'. The Parthenon and Theseion are 'too imperfect to deserve a serious Criticism'. 'Many of our Parish Churches are much more considerable Buildings.' The things about which he is particularly annoyed are the comparatively small size of Greek buildings, the lack of a Greek domestic architecture equal to Greek temples and the simplicity of Greek construction.

'In the Constructive Part of Architecture the Ancients were no great Proficients. . . . Many of the Deformities which we observe in Grecian Buildings must be ascribed to their Ignorance in this Particular, such as their Gouty Columns.'

The Gouty Columns bring us back to our narrower problem of the Doric Revival. How much else of this flood of abuse needs comment? One phrase in particular, I think, the one in which the Apollo stands for Rome and the Hotten-tot and Baboon for Greece. The voice of Chambers is in this case that of Lord Kames, the celebrated writer on aesthetics. In his *Elements of Criticism,* published in 1762, he raves against the Greek drama, its 'imbecility', its 'absurd terrors', its unreasonableness and impropriety, and compares the emotions felt in reading Greek plays to 'what is felt in perusing the descriptions of the Hottentots' (cap. XIV).*   n.31

It may well be that Chambers remembered this passage when he wrote his lecture of *c.* 1768. But he was neither a fool nor a pharisee. There is no denying the fact that, when the Doric of the sixth and fifth centuries was first seen, it did not appear to the eyes of men of taste as grave and severe classicity but as ugly, barbaric, primeval, sub-human. That is why Paestum and Girgenti could, for such an amazingly long period, have remained undiscovered.

On the side of the Grecians stood Thomas Blackwell whose *Enquiry into the Life and Writings of Homer* had established Homer as early as 1735 as the great Natural Genius, delighted with heroes and gods whose chief occupations are drinking, fighting, cheating and loving. Blackwell's Homer had made the greatest impression first on Edward Young of the *Original Composition*, and then on Herder and through him on Goethe. Blackwell thus helped to create the enthusiasm of the German *Sturm und Drang* for folk-art, and the art of the primi-tive stages of civilization. So once again the admiration for ancient Greece and for the Nordic Middle Ages become one.

The champions of Doric were champions of Nature versus sophistication, strength versus effeminacy. Fuseli, the painter of *Sturm and Drang,* of Homer and Shakespeare and Ossian, could at the same time translate Winckelmann and write an essay on Rousseau.* Lord Monboddo, that picturesque, air-bathing   n.32 Caledonian philosopher, called Pythagoras, the archaic sage, 'undoubtedly the greatest philosopher that ever was in Europe' and at the same time urged his fellow Britons to recognize in the Orang Outang 'the first stage of human pro-gression'.* Once you believe in the humanity of the Orang Outang, perhaps a   n.33 baboon is, after all, not so very inferior to the Apollo Belvedere.

Monboddo (whose *Of the Origin* . . . incidentally was translated into German in 1785 and prefaced by Herder) wrote this: 'Of the Greek masters, whom are we to prefer, the more antient, or the later writers? This question Horace has determined; for he has told us that the more antient are the best.' (*Of the Origin,* Vol. III, p. 375).

And indeed at the same time, Aeschylus was being re-discovered. Richard Cumberland wrote in *The Observer* (1786–90) that '*Agamemnon's* beauty would be lowered by a comparison with Sophocles and Euripides' and that Aeschylus and Shakespeare are 'nearly allied in genius', and Robert Potter published his edition of the Tragedies in 1777, prefaced by an introduction in which he says that Aeschylus left it 'to posterity to admire the force of his genius, and to doubt, whether he was ever excelled, or even equalled, till our Shakespeare arose'.

A comparison with the Gothic style could, about 1770, assume quite a different meaning from that intended by Chambers. In 1762, Bishop Hurd had stated in his *Letters on Chivalry and Romance* (all devoted to high praise of what he calls Gothic and we would call Romantic) that 'Greek antiquity very much resembles the Gothic' (p. 19). Ten years later the discoverers of Fingal's Cave, Sir Joseph Banks and the Swede von Troil, wrote of it: 'Compared with this what are the Cathedrals . . . built by man?'* To the sublimity of Fingal's   n.34 Cave, that is Nature, 'what has been added . . . by the whole Grecian school?' These natural pieces of basalt surpass even 'what time has left of Palmyra and Paestum'. Again, one year later, in 1773, Goethe's encomium of Strassburg

Cathedral appeared, and Gothic for the first time stands for 'wholeness, greatness
n.35 . . . dignity and glory', that is for Genius as against 'school and rules'.* And in
1774 an otherwise not very important traveller and writer, William Young,
published *A Journal of a Summer's Excursion to Naples, and from thence over all the
Southern Parts of Italy and Malta.* The journey was made in 1772. In the journal we
read apropos Selinus:

'The Order of all these Buildings is of a Stamp which proves them anterior
to the Refinements of the Grecian School; in the ages of polite Literature in
Greece, these Temples must have been regarded in the same Light as a truly
n.36 venerable Gothic Cathedral in present days.'*

Venerable Gothic Cathedrals, humanity of the Orang Outang—it does
seem as if, at least in the ears of a few, the insults of Chambers would have
sounded flat and ineffectual. Those few were members of a younger generation.
For older men it must, indeed, have been very hard to appreciate the nobility of
Doric architecture. Even Goethe, convinced of Greek greatness, after he had
lived through his revolutionary Gothic and Shakespearian phase and achieved
the mature classicity of his *Iphigenia,* wrote home thus from Paestum (23 March,
1787)—an eminently revealing passage already quoted in this volume (p. 169):

'The first impression could only arouse surprise. I found myself in an entirely
alien world. For as the centuries shape themselves from the grave to the pleasing,
so they shape mankind at the same time, nay create it. Now our eyes and with
them our whole being are attracted and decisively determined by a slenderer
architecture so that these obtuse, conical, closely set masses of columns appear
irksome, even terrible. However . . . in less than an hour I felt attracted, nay
praised my genius for permitting me to see these well-preserved fragments.'

n.37 That was at Paestum;* a month later, visiting the Temple of Concord at Girgenti
he found 'its slender style already approaching our idea of the beautiful and
pleasing', and in comparison with Paestum like 'a divine image to a colossus'.

It can in fact be said all round that Doric (or Tuscan) columns of a height of
less than six diameters, i.e. of a squatter shape than the Parthenon, could only be
appreciated by a conscious effort. Early Doric remained tantamount to Nature
and primitivism, and was therefore only—first intellectually and later visually—
admired by men of revolutionary tendencies, while those of a more classic cast
convinced themselves that Periclean Doric was indeed the ideal of masculine
perfection.

It now remains to find out who the leading Dorians were. The first in
theory seems to have been Francesco Milizia (1725–98). It is illuminating to
follow his attitude from the *Saggio di Architettura Civile* before 1768 (*Opere
Complete,* Vol. IX) to the *Principi di Architettura Civile* of 1781 and on to the
Dizionario of 1787. In the first book he writes (p. 27) of the Doric order:

'The proper base of this order, whenever it needs one, is that which is usually
called Tuscan, a base most beautiful and simple. For this masculine order suffers
no multiplicity of members.'

In 1781 this has become (Pt. I, cap. 8, sec. 1):

'No architect nowadays would have the courage to put up any column
without a base. . . . Architects say that . . . on no condition whatever should we
omit the base which strengthens the foot of the column and increases its stability
. . . These reasons are sound enough, but it would all the same perhaps not be a
pity if the base were suppressed in certain cases.'

Finally, in 1787, Milizia states that the Doric column 'has no need of a base' and
'the slimmer it is made, the more is it debased'.

Between these years, 1768 to 1787, the Doric column became acclimatized
in the principal countries, still as a rare plant, but as a demonstration of modernity.
The very first were Athenian Stuart and his companion, Nicholas Revett.

*22 Detail of the temple of Neptune, from
Piranesi's drawing for his 'Paestum'*

23 *Garden temple at Shugborough by Stuart, c.1768*

24 *Ayot St Lawrence church by Revett, 1778–9*

25 *Doric chimneypiece at Downton Castle,*
c.1778

Stuart as we have seen repeated his Hagley performance at Shugborough and   *23*
Revett introduced the Doric in the Delian form, i.e. with the lower third of the
shaft unfluted* in the portico of Trafalgar House near Standylynch in Wiltshire   n.38
about 1770 or a little earlier and repeated it yet more daringly in a church portico,
less than ten years later: at Ayot St Lawrence in 1778–9. In between Richard   *24*
Payne Knight, revolutionary in other ways as well, had a chimneypiece put up in
his house, Downton Castle, which has Doric columns;* the date must lie just   *25*,n.3
before 1778. Also to the seventies belongs a drawing of a temple front with nine
Doric columns by James Essex, among the materials for his projected *History of*
*Gothic Architecture.** Moreover these were precisely the years when Soane was   n.40
converted. In 1776 he won the Royal Academy Gold Medal with his design for
a Triumphal Bridge. It has Roman Doric columns such as England had used ever
since Wren and Vanbrugh and such as Peyre had used in his *Oeuvres d'Architecture*
of 1765, Soane's principal source of inspiration at that moment. In 1778 he
reached Rome. Early in 1778 he visited Paestum with his eccentric and unreliable
patron the Earl of Bristol, Bishop of Derry. In the same year he re-did his Triumphal Bridge for the Parma Academy, and now it has Doric columns.* The   *26*,n.
change may be connected as much with Piranesi as with the visit to Paestum. For
Piranesi's *Paestum* came out in 1778, the year in which the great inspirer died. The   *22*
publication of the book may be taken to prove that towards the end of his life
Piranesi had changed his views on the value of the Early Greek style. For although, when *Paestum* appeared, Piranesi was dead and his son Giovanni Battista
signed himself as responsible for it, the etchings must obviously date back to
the elder Piranesi's last year or years.* However, a glance at the text of the book   n.42
shows that even now that silence on Paestum and the Doric style could no
longer be of any avail, Piranesi still wanted to try to get advantages for his
Etrusco-Roman case out of it. What he says is this: 'The ancient town of Paestum
called by the Greeks Possidonia was in ancient times under the rulership of the
Lucanians, and then under that of the Romans'. By omitting the fact that Paestum
at the time of the temples was Greek, he can sum up their importance as a new
proof that the arts 'flourished no less in Italy than in Egypt and Greece'. Should
the only other Piranesi plate which seems a homage to the Doric style be ex-   *27*
plained in a similar way? It is a view of what Piranesi calls three propylaea in a
Thermae building, and he uses Doric columns with the utmost emphasis on their
massive, squat, four-square character. Perhaps one can assume that Piranesi had
indeed come round to an aesthetic appreciation of Doric, but felt that he could
justify it intellectually only by linking it up with Rome, the only city which
people connected with such gigantic thermae. However, the etching appears

26 Design for a Triumphal Bridge by Soane, 1778

only in Piranesi's *Collected Works* and may be by the son. Neither Giesecke nor Hind nor Focillon offers a satisfactory answer.

    The earliest French uses of the Doric order so far recorded ante-date Piranesi and Soane, though not Stuart and Revett. They must be explained from Le Roy

n.43 and especially Dumont.* They are a room on the ground floor of Ledoux's
n.44 early Hôtel Montmorency (1772),* the remodelling of the chancel of St
n.45 Nicholas-des-Champs by Antoine (before 1774)* and a design by Cherpitel for
n.46 St-Pierre-du-Gros Caillou (1775).* Belanger is known as the designer of the Folie Saint-James close to the Bois de Boulogne, and this, built and equipped in 1778–85 received a tetrastyle Doric temple front as part of a rock and water
n.47 display.* Here we have once again reached 1778, and 1778 is also the year of
77,6 the beginning of Ledoux's Theatre at Besançon, the most famous French example of the early Doric which, later on, France was to favour less than England and
n.48 Germany.*

27 Detail of architectural fantasy by Piranesi

28 Model of Warwick Gaol, by Thomas Johnson, before 1779

28   For England the mystery building is the gaol of Warwick by Thomas Johnson, architect and contractor, and for all we know, an entirely provincial personality. As it was built in 1779–82, it has attached Tuscan columns, but the model preserved in the County Museum has proper Greek Doric columns. Who was Thomas Johnson to have been ahead of Soane in this symptom of modernity? Had he seen Italy or had he just studied Major? Just as interesting is the appearance of a Doric temple during exactly the years of the Warwick gaol in the background of *The Victors at Olympia*, one of James Barry's wall-paintings in the Royal Society of Arts. Thirdly there is Richard Wilson, the landscape painter. He died in 1782, and so his landscape with a Doric temple at Bisterne Manor in Hampshire may be as early as Barry's paintings or yet earlier. The last of these *incunabula* is the rotunda built in 1780 by Charles Cameron for the Empress

n.49 Catherine II at Pavlovsk in Russia.*

29 *Great Packington church by Bonomi,*
1790

Doric in the eighties and the early nineties remained rare, in spite of the fact that in 1788 at last the second volume of Stuart & Revett's *Antiquities of Athens* had been issued with the measured drawings of the Parthenon. The highlights in Britain are the portico of All Saints, Newcastle, by David Stephenson, of 1786–96, with the columns still slender, the plans for Chester Castle of 1788, submitted by Thomas Harrison who had spent the years 1769–76 in Italy, Bonomi's splendid interior of the church of Great Packington in Warwickshire of 1790, 29 Castle Goring, in Sussex, of *c.* 1790 by Biagio Rebecca, with one side Doric and the other Gothic, young Benjamin Latrobe's Hammerwood Lodge in Sussex of *c.* 1793–4, where the columns are of the Delian variety, Francis Johnson's Townley Hall in Ireland, of 1794,* and then Soane's design for the House of n.50 Lords of 1794–6 and the design for a sepulchral church for Tyringham of 1796 and so into the nineteenth century, when with Thomas Hope's Picture Gallery in his town house in Duchess Street of *c.* 1800,* and William Wilkins and of n.51 course Soane the Doric achieved full acceptance and popularity. The death knell of the resistance against it is a passage in the third edition of Chambers's *Civil Architecture* which was published in 1791. He writes (p. 19):

'None of the few things now existing in Greece, though so pompously described, and neatly represented, in various publications of our time, seem to deserve great notice, either for dimensions, grandeur of style, rich fancy, or elegant taste of design'.

The Parthenon he calls less considerable than St Martin's in the Fields, and he ends by saying that since the Greeks were

'so deficient in architecture . . . , it follows that our knowledge ought not to be collected from them, but from some purer more abundant source . . . which can be no other than the Roman antiquity yet remaining.'

30 *Design by Gilly for a monument to*
Frederick the Great, 1797

The Doric Revival in Germany was inspired from England before it found confirmation in Italy. The earliest cases are in Central Germany: the Park Temple near the castle of Gotha, of the late seventies or later,* the Römisches 31, n. Haus, in the park of Weimar, designed by J. A. Arens in 1792 and built in 1793,* n.53 and the Temple of Venus at Wörlitz near Dessau of 1794, where however the columns have, if not a proper base, at least a kind of projecting roll at the foot. Of about the same time also, and certainly of before 1796, were the Temple of Hygeia, the Mausoleum and the Entrance to the Castle in the gardens of Machern in Saxony, and of before 1795 the well house, a semicircular niche in the gardens of an estate with the English name of Greenfield, though also in Saxony.* But n.54 already before then, in 1786, Hans Christian Genelli, architect-father of the better-known painter Bonaventura Genelli, had sent to Berlin from Rome a design for a memorial to Frederick the Great, which was a complete Doric 32 temple, and in 1788 the same Arens who was to design the Römisches Haus at Weimar had designed a country house with Doric columns,* and he also did n.55 this while in Rome.* n.56

Friedrich Gilly, the greatest German architect of the end of the eighteenth century, never saw Rome. But when, in 1796, he began work on the most

31 *Garden temple at Gotha*

32 Genelli's design for a memorial to Frederick the Great, 1786   33 Market, by Lépicié, 1779

grandiose, most moving and most severe scheme of the early Greek Revival, his design for the national monument to Frederick the Great, he must have been inspired by Genelli in crowning this vast monument with a Doric temple. He placed the temple high up on a colossal substructure and created a precinct around it with triumphal entries of sombre majesty (see p. 179). The scheme was of supreme originality, but what he did decide to use of period motifs was Doric. His own comment was: 'Not Corinthian, no rich magnificence . . . Let the only magnificence be simple beauty, the very simplest'.* He had indeed already favoured Doric columns in designs of 1794 when he was only twenty-two years of age. Tuscan columns without bases appear already in 1791, and how that came about will be explained presently. Heinrich Gentz, six years older than Gilly, gave his Mint in Berlin a portal arch with Doric columns as early as 1798 (completed 1800), and Gilly's father, David Gilly, who outlived him, gave them to the house for the Vieweg family at Brunswick in 1801–4. Friedrich Gilly had died in 1802. Five years before his death, in 1797, he had visited Paris and London, but while Ledoux, Chalgrin and the other French architects of the more revolutionary trend evidently impressed him much, they cannot have confirmed his faith in Doric Greece. For—and a few lines on this may serve to round off this article—France did not favour the Doric order. Against the odd appearances of Doric columns in Ledoux's work and that of some others stand dozens of a similarly squat and inelegant Tuscan. Tuscan, indeed, played in Paris the part played by Doric in London and Berlin—and for good reasons. Tuscan had been the choice of Piranesi in his *Magnificenza*, and Tuscan had ever since remained the characteristic order of archaic Rome, that is of republican Rome. So when political revolution began to stir amongst the young artists of the French Academy in Rome, they looked up to Roman virtue and heroism, to Roman history and the oldest Roman architecture, that is, to what was regarded as primeval Etruscan. Hence short, broad Tuscan columns appear in Ledoux, in Wailly (Krafft & Ransonette, *Plans . . . des plus belles maisons . . . à Paris,* 1802, pl. 43–44: House, built by the architect for himself, 1778), in Brogniart's Cloisters of the Capucins in Paris of 1780, and in an interesting painting of an imaginary market hall by Nicolas-Bernard Lépicié dated 1779.* The columns here have no capitals, just square abacus blocks. This motif was taken over in the painting which was for reasons of content and form to become the symbol of the revolutionary movement: Jacques-Louis David's *Oath of the Horatii,* painted in Rome and exhibited in Paris in 1784. Its severely plain background consists of nothing but two Tuscan columns and three plain arches.*

Twenty-three years lie between David's *Horatii* and Mengs's *Parnassus.* The one begins, the other ends this story. What had still been an oddity of antiquarian interest to Mengs and Gavin Hamilton had become to David, to Ledoux, to Soane, to Genelli and Gilly the manifestation of a new and fervently pursued human ideal.

30

n.57
178,8

n.58

34

n.59

34 Detail of 'The Oath of the Horatii' by David, 1784

1   *Egyptian capriccio by Hubert Robert, 1760*

XIII
The Egyptian Revival

WRITTEN IN COLLABORATION WITH S. LANG

'Piranesi will go down to posterity with deserved reputation, in spite of his Egyptian and other whimsies, and his gusto of architecture flowing out of the same cloacus as Borromini's and other hairbrained moderns.'—James Barry to Edmund Burke.

n.1   *April 8, 1769.**

2   IN 1812 Edward Bullock opened his Egyptian Hall in Piccadilly, a permanent side-show where thirty-two stuffed monkeys and eleven stuffed sea lions could be seen side by side with 'an exquisite model in rice paste of the death of Voltaire by Monsieur Oudon,' a Holy Family done in wool, Mexican curiosities and an

n.2,3   Egyptian mummy.* The architect of the façade was P. F. Robinson,* and it was one of his first buildings of consequence. The Sale Room was not by him but by

n.4   Papworth, as appears from an illustration in Ackermann's *Repository* dated 1819.*

      The Egyptian Hall, and especially Robinson's façade, set a fashion, but it also followed a fashion. The great Sir John Soane disapproved of the fashion. 'What,' he exclaimed, 'can be more puerile and unsuccessful than the paltry attempt to imitate the character and form of their (the Egyptians') works in small and confined spaces; and yet, such is the prevalence of that monster, Fashion, and such the rage for novelty, that we frequently see attempts of this kind by way of

n.5   decoration.'*

2 Egyptian Hall, Piccadilly, 1812

3   Amongst the progeny of the Egyptian Hall Foulston's Library at Devonport, of 1823, and the Egyptian House at Penzance, of *c.* 1830 are copies rather than imitations. But what did Robinson himself imitate? The familiar answer is a French vogue started by Napoleon's Egyptian campaign. The campaign took

5   place in 1798. Vivant Denon published his *Voyages dans la Basse et la Haute*

n.6   *Egypte* in 1802.* In 1807 Thomas Hope, enthusiastic follower of the Parisian

8   Empire style, illustrated Egyptian furniture and decoration in his *Household Furniture,* and Percier and Fontaine, Napoleon's favourite architects and deco-

n.7   rators, also used Egyptianisms.* That far the story is well-known and seems convincing. The echoes of the early nineteenth-century fashion of Paris and London can be heard in the English provinces and as far away as America. Egypt was associated with mystery and the cult of the dead, with 'immense grandeur' and 'magnitude,' the 'colossal,' the 'uniform and monotonous,' the 'awful and

6   majestic.' (John Martin, a painter addicted to these qualities, made use of the new fashion irrespective of historical truth.) The same terms are applied by

n.8   Soane to Egyptian architecture.* But Egypt also conjured up huge masses of stone and overpowering might, and so Masonic Lodges, cemeteries, law courts and prisons took to Egyptian borrowings. Other buildings occasionally participa-

n.9   ted too. The Egyptian Hall in Piccadilly and its offspring are an example.*

3 Library, Devonport, 1823

4   Another is the remarkable flax-spinning mill of John Marshall at Leeds. This, with its Egyptian temple façades, inspired by the Temple of Dendera, its chimney-stack in form of an obelisk, its iron columns and brick arches inside, and its original roof garden (with drainage inside the columns) belongs to the years

n.10   1838–40.*

4 Marshall's Mill, Leeds, c. 1840

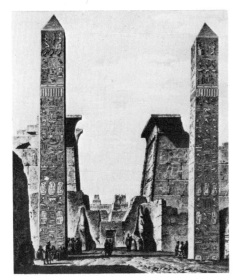

5   *Luxor, from Denon's 'Voyages', 1802*

6   *The Feast of Esther, by John Martin*

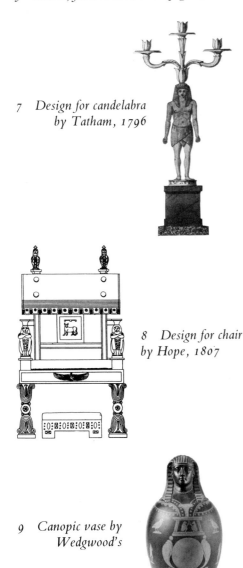

7   *Design for candelabra by Tatham, 1796*

8   *Design for chair by Hope, 1807*

9   *Canopic vase by Wedgwood's*

But the Egyptian Revival of 1800–1840 cannot be the whole story, or else how could one explain those cases of Egyptianism in England and on the Continent which can with certainty be dated before Denon? They are not frequent, but by no means exceedingly rare. Thus, for example, Thomas Hope, the celebrated patron and collector and author of *Household Furniture,* the book already mentioned, installed in his mansion in Duchess Street some time between 1799 and 1803, but very probably before 1803, an Egyptian room filled up with granite, serpentine, porphyry and basalt. Two chairs from it are now at Buscot Park, in Lord Faringdon's collection. Hope knew Egypt personally, and that may be the explanation, though, as we shall see, other explanations are as likely.*   n.11
In Buckingham Palace is a pair of candelabra which come from Carlton House   7
and are decorated with Egyptian figures.* They were designed for Henry   n.12
Holland by Charles Heathcote Tatham, an interesting architect not yet sufficiently appreciated. He was in Italy in 1796 and sent the design from there. Between 1796 and 1802 an Egyptian Cabinet was illustrated in *Ideenmagazin für
Liebhaber von Gärten* edited by J. G. Grohmann.* About 1793–4 or in 1797 at the   n.13
latest James Playfair did an Egyptian room at Cairness in Aberdeenshire and
in 1794 the younger Dance designed an Egyptian chimneypiece for Shelburne
(now Lansdowne) House.* About 1780 is the most likely date for the former   n.13a
gate at Sherborne Castle with two Egyptianizing statues in niches. It was drawn
by Thomas Hardwick and may have been designed by Chambers.* In 1778   n.14
Soane published an Egyptian temple in his *Designs in Architecture* and in 1777
John Carter, in *The Builder's Magazine,* illustrated a design for an 'Egyptian
Pyramidical Dairy'.* Also, Wedgwood's made a type of Egyptianizing vases   9, n.15
known as Canopic vases after Canope, a town in Egypt from which the Emperor
Hadrian took the name Canope for part of his villa near Tivoli—though whether
they were introduced so early or only after Denon we do not know.* A good   n.15a
deal more will have to be said further on about Hadrian's Canope.

Similarly for France a number of cases go back to well before the Napoleonic   n.16
campaign.* The most remarkable, because the earliest, of them are a painted   1
Capriccio with Egyptian motifs signed by Hubert Robert, '*Delineavit Romae   n.17
1760*,'* and a drawing of an Egyptian temple offered by its designer Cherpitel to
Marigny, Mme de Pompadour's brother whom we have met in the preceding   n.18
essay.* The date here is 1762, and 1766 is the date when Desprez's funerary
temple was premiated by the Paris Academy of Architecture. He later had it   n.19
engraved and dedicated it to Voltaire.* In 1777 Desprez went to Rome and
there he did the four memorable aquatints of tombs, very primeval and hence   45, 4
very progressive as architecture, two of them provided with Egyptian-looking
figures. As Desprez arrived in Sweden in 1784, they must be before that date. *   n.20

Other Egyptianisms worth recording are these: a pair of Egyptianizing terracotta statuettes signed by Clodion, in the possession of Mr and Mrs John Harris. These are undated, but can probably be connected with large Egyptianizing figures made in 1773 for the funerary chapel of Count Grimaud d'Orsay.* The date of a salon in a financier's house in the Place Vendôme is 1786, and 1787 that of a temple front in the park of Etupes by General Kléber.* One year later Desprez began to use Egyptian motifs in his designs for stage sets in Sweden and also in other designs.* Egyptianizing capitals appear in the Doric Botanical Institute at Uppsala by Templeman and Desprez in 1788, a pyramid with Doric porticos in a design of the same year.*

In Italy the best known examples are the decoration of the Camera dei Papiri in the Vatican Library by Anton Raphael Mengs, done about 1770, and the prominent use of two Egyptian figures to flank a doorway in the Museo Pio-Clementino in the Vatican. The two figures came from Hadrian's Canope. In addition a book published in 1787 described a part of the gardens of the Venetian senator Angelo Querini's Villa Altichiero, near Padua, in which some pieces of Egyptian sculpture were displayed. The owner had called it Canope.*

Now in most of these cases the attitude to Egypt is patently different from that of the early nineteenth century. The sense of portentous might in Egyptian masonry and details does not seem to be present. Indeed no coherent conception of a specific Egyptian character seems present at all. Forms are used for the fun of using them. The intention of the odd garden pavilion or fireplace is additional variety rather than a statement of mood. The age of Strawberry Hill and Chinoiserie allowed entry to Egyptian forms as yet another piece of exotic entertainment not different in kind from the Pagoda, the Mosque and the Alhambra in the grounds of Kew or indeed the prostyle Greek Doric temple at Hagley.*

Two questions, however, remain. Where did information come from which enabled designers to do Neo-Egyptian, and who started the Rococo fashion as against the early nineteenth century Romantic fashion? The second question must be answered first, and can be answered in full. The source of the fashion, as of many others, is Piranesi. His Caffè Inglese near the Piazza di

10,11

n.21

n.22

n.23

n.24

12

n.25

n.26

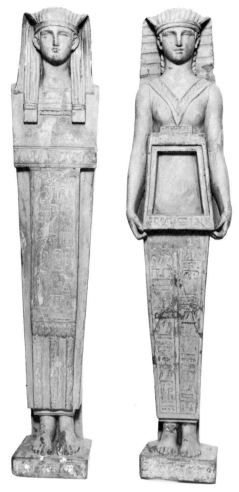

10, 11 Terracotta statuettes by Clodion, c.1773

12 Detail of decoration by Mengs in the Camera dei Papiri, c.1770

Spagna in Rome dates from about 1760, and its walls were crowded with Egyptian motifs assembled no doubt largely for the fun of it; and his *Diverse Maniere d'adornare i Cammini* came out in 1769 and includes quite a number of Egyptian specimens. Here we have indeed a primary source;* for Piranesi himself wrote a letter on 18 November 1768 to Thomas Hollis, which is now at the Society of Antiquaries attached to their copy of the *Cammini*. In this he writes:

14

n.27,1

13 Design from Piranesi's 'Cammini', 1769

'Vederete in quest' Opera usato cio che peranche in questo genere non era conosciuto. L'Architettura Egiziana, per la prima volta apparisce; la prima volta, dico, perchè in ora il mondo ha sempre creduto non esservi altro che piramidi, guglie, e giganti, escludendo non esservi parti sufficienti per adornare e sostenere questo sistema d'architettura.'

Here then is the Egyptian Revival as a *capriccio,* in the sense in which Tiepolo etched capricci and Guardi painted capricci, and in which the term went on to Goya and his famous series of the *Caprichos.* The capriccio is a Rococo form, and Piranesi's Egyptian may indeed be called a Rococo-Egyptian, if one takes a broad enough view of the possibilities of the Rococo. A style which comprises Neumann's architecture can well comprise Piranesi's *Carceri* and even the grandest of his Roman visions. That this interpretation of his Egyptian revival has nothing outré or far-fetched is borne out by two characteristic references, one caused no doubt by the *Cammini,* the other curiously anticipating them.

The younger Blondel in volume III of his *Cours d'Architecture* published in 1772 writes this—a passage of the greatest interest indeed:

'Il y a plusieurs années qu'il sembloit que notre siècle étoit celui des Rocailles; aujourd'hui sans trop savoir pourquoi, il en est autrement. Alors le goût Grec et Romain nous paroissoit froid, monotone: à présent, nous affectons la charge de la plupart des savantes productions de ces Peuples; et, sans trop y réfléchir, nous prétendons que les autres Nations s'assujetassent à faire usage de notre manière

14 Decoration by Piranesi for the Caffè Inglese, 1760, published in 1769

15 Sixteenth-century engraving of a Roman figure of Father Nile

de décorer, soit que nous imitions, dans nos appartements, la bissarrerie des ornaments de *Pekin,* soit que nous ramenions, dans l'ordonnance extérieure de nos édifices le goût pesant des premières inventions de Memphis. . . . Il ne nous reste plus qu'à introduire le goût gothique dans notre Architecture, et peut-être

n.28   n'en sommes-nous pas éloignés'.*

In 1757 Sir William Chambers in the preface to his book on *Chinese Buildings* quoted the use made of Egyptian pieces by Hadrian in his Canope as classical authority on the strength of which we also should be permitted to indulge in innovations for the sake of variety. The innovations he then recommends are Chinese motifs.

     For the moment, what is important is that China and Egypt are linked in

n.29   both these passages,* and that both passages are clearly Rococo in their way of arguing. Blondel's remark is his shocked answer to Piranesi's *Cammini* with their actual revival of Egyptian forms, Chambers's remark is no more than a suggestion of a potential revival, based on an actual revival sixteen hundred and fifty years ago.

     But what' are the links between Hadrian's and Piranesi's revival, if any exist? Evidently the pre-history of Neo-Egyptian must be traced back much further than is usually done, and that is what the rest of this essay sets out to do in a very tentative way.

     It could, of course, start in ancient Greece and with the acceptance of Isis and other Egyptian deities into the Greek Pantheon. Isis was considered the daughter of Chronos or Hermes or Prometheus and identified with Ceres or the many-breasted Diana of Ephesus or indeed more generally with Nature. Rome had an Iseum and Pompeii had one. Caracalla used Egyptian motifs in capitals in his Baths and may have built a Serapeum. Other Roman Emperors brought obelisks from Egypt and re-erected them. There were also pieces of Egyptian sculpture and copies from them. The most famous display has been mentioned already more than once: Hadrian's Canope in his villa near Tivoli. Sphinxes were known widely, and one of the best-known works of Roman sculpture, the re-

15   clining figure of Father Nile now in the Vatican Museum, rests his elbow on a sphinx. Whether such tombs as the pyramid of Cestius or the Sepulchrum

Scipionum (also known as the Meta Romuli) were designed in imitation of Egyptian pyramids cannot now be said with certainty. They are slenderer in shape and stand midway between an obelisk and a pyramid. Roman writers knew a great deal about Egypt, which is not surprising, as the principal monuments of her art and architecture lay within the boundaries of the Empire. And as the works of Pliny, of Diodorus Siculus (*temp.* Augustus) and of Ammianus Marcellinus (fourth century AD) were used in the early Middle Ages and rediscovered in the Renaissance, so knowledge of Egypt also continued and reappeared.

Amongst the Fathers of the Church Eusebius and Gregory of Nazianzus say much about Egypt, and in the seventh century Isidore of Seville in his *Etymologies,* the most popular early medieval encyclopaedia, mentions hieroglyphs and obelisks and (as a 'genus sepulcrorum') pyramids.*   n.30 But after the conquest of Egypt by the Mohametans in 642 knowledge of the country and its monuments naturally grew dimmer. However, certain works of the Egyptians remained visible in Rome—notably the obelisk now in the Piazza di S. Pietro. This stood all through the Middle Ages just east of the two round chapels which were added on the south side of Old St Peter's. So some interest in the curious nature of Egyptian culture and script must have kept alive. For otherwise how could one account for the re-use of Egyptian capitals from the Baths of Caracalla when the church of Sta Maria in Trastevere was built in the twelfth century, and for the earliest case of an Egyptian revival which has so far come to light, the completely solitary and unconnected appearance of four sphinxes carved in Central Italy in the thirteenth century? One of them is now in the museum at Viterbo and others are at Città Castellana and in the Cloister of S. Giovanni in Laterano in Rome.*   n.31 They are by Cosmati decorators, that at Viterbo being signed *Fra Pasquale*   16 *1279.*   n.32

16 Sphinx at Viterbo, by Fra Pasquale, 1279

17 Alberti's device, the winged eye, c.1450

Travellers on their way to and from the Holy Places occasionally touched Egypt, and the tales of those from France have been collected by J. M. Carré.*   n.33 They have not much to tell us. But they mention the 'sépultures des rois d' Egypte qui on nommait piramides' and the 'statue d'Isis' nearby 'qui se monstrait plus haute que les tours de Nostre Dame de Paris.'*   n.34 It seems from Carré's book that the great pyramid was entered by a traveller for the first time in 1504.*   n.35 Meanwhile in Rome a few of the many Egyptian pieces brought by the emperors for the purpose of the cult of Isis had begun to reappear prominently, for instance when the church of Sta Maria sopra Minerva was rebuilt in 1347.*   n.36 At the same time an Egyptian cynocephalus was found in Rome. But in none of these scattered pieces of evidence concerning Egypt can one discover any special interest in Egyptology. That changed with the Renaissance.*   n.37

The first fact which must be recorded is Cristoforo de Buondelmonte's discovery in 1419 of the so-called *Horapollo,* a fifth-century Greek text on hieroglyphs.*   n.38 What Buondelmonte discovered was a fourteenth-century transcript or version of the book. He found it on the island of Andros in the Aegean. The book, for better or worse, had an enormous influence on Egyptological studies in the fifteenth century and after. Ficino translated it into Italian in 1463. The translation was printed in 1471, the Greek text (by Aldus) in 1505. Scholars thought that here at last they had found the key to the mysteries of Egyptian wisdom.*   n.39 For an idea that Egypt held the secret of much magic and wisdom seems never to have disappeared completely. So it was most welcome when Poggio Bracciolini, in a German library, came across a manuscript of Ammianus Marcellinus which discussed hieroglyphics. Niccolo Niccoli copied it with his own hands. A little later Poggio translated parts of Diodorus Siculus, who also had passages on hieroglyphics and matters Egyptian.

By then, that is about 1410–15, the Anonimo Magliabecchiano had already noticed a 'Julia' on Roman soil near the Porta Salaria, and a Julia is a *guglia* or an obelisk. He also mentions an obelisk in the Circus Maximus which was still half-covered by debris. In spite of actual hieroglyphs which could be seen on those obelisks, humanists in Florence asked Ciriaco d'Ancona who set out for Egypt in 1435, probably on a trading mission, to look for inscriptions; he found near the largest of the pyramids near Gizeh an inscription which he copied and sent home to Florence.

At about the same time, Flavio Biondo in his *Roma Instaurata,* completed in 1446, also discusses obelisks, pyramids and hieroglyphics. Alberti, always in the forefront of humanist interests, mentions all of these, though only in passing in his *De Re aedificatoria.** However Alberti's, and probably also other humanists', attitude to these new finds was somewhat ambivalent. Horapollo's text, dating from a period when the true knowledge of hieroglyphics had already been lost, gave an entirely fanciful explanation of their meaning as well as a wrong description of their visual appearance. Alberti when discussing hieroglyphs, though certainly aware of Horapollo, only used Ammianus Marcellinus and Macrobius in the sample explanations he gives of hieroglyphs. What is more surprising is that neither he nor anybody else at the time seems to have checked the literary against the visual evidence. There is no report that anybody realized that the hieroglyphic inscriptions which could be seen in Rome on sphinxes, lions, and those obelisks that were visible (and not still buried), or in the copies of Ciriaco, had little or no similarity to the descriptions they could read—or at least that many of the signs described did not exist in actual inscriptions. Alberti, it seems, was the first humanist to use a motif believed by him to be a hieroglyph as a personal emblem: the winged eye with the motto *Quid tum.*

The next mention of Egyptian obelisks and hieroglyphs in Rome was by Poggio who in his *Historia de Varietate Fortunae* (ed. Paris 1723, p. 20) speaks of obelisks in the Hippodrome (i.e. the Circus Maximus) and on the Capitol, apart from the one by St Peter's. Of Pius II it is recorded that he ordered some obelisks to be unearthed.*

Another architect-theoretician, writing just after the middle of the century, goes further than Alberti. Filarete in his novel-like treatise not only describes obelisks but so fires his fictitious patron's imagination that the prince orders one to be erected in Sforzinda, the ideal city which Filarete was building on his behalf; it was to be decorated with letters in the shape of 'animals or other things, almost like the Egyptian ones'. Here there is no idea of the inscriptions having a symbolic meaning: they were to be added only to give a true Egyptian flavour to the obelisk, and their function was mainly a decorative one.* The town was never built, so neither was the obelisk, but in consequence of this growing interest Egyptian motifs were occasionally introduced by Quattrocento artists into their works. Among the earliest are the pyramid in the background of Ghiberti's Gates of Paradise, i.e. the second of his bronze doors for the Baptistery in Florence (1425–52),* and the obelisks on Pisanello's medal of John VIII Palaeologus (1438–39) and on other medals of his. After 1450 and especially after 1480 cases get more frequent. But the only two important ones still concern original Egyptian pieces re-used in Quattrocento contexts, and not Egyptian motifs re-created by Italian artists. The first refers to the foundation of the Capitoline Museum by Sixtus IV about 1475. He exhibited there two sphinxes of basalt.* The second is the re-erection at the portal of the Episcopal Palace at Tivoli of two *telamoni* which came probably from Hadrian's Canope. They are now in the Museo Pio-Clementino.* The re-erection was, it seems, due to Pius II (1458–64).* They were drawn by Giuliano da Sangallo about 1500.*

In paintings of the late Quattrocento and early Cinquecento Egyptiana appear more often than is generally realized. They take several forms. One is the use of Egyptian iconographical schemes in Renaissance guise. Pinturicchio's decoration of the Appartamenti Borgia (1493–95) is based on Nanni da Viterbo:* Nanni fabricated a family tree for the Borgias, tracing them back to Osiris, faked Egyptian texts and proceeded to excavate Egyptian sculpture on Italian soil. The intention was to link up Etruscan with Egyptian and ultimately the Pope with Osiris.* The fakes are said to be in the Museum of Viterbo, but on a visit in 1956 could not there be traced.

Other Egyptiana used by artists at that time were pseudo-hieroglyphs

18 Panel of Florence Baptistery doors, by Ghiberti, c.1435

19 Telamoni at Tivoli, drawn by Giuliano da Sangallo, late 15th century

n.40

17

n.41

n.42

18
n.43

n.44

n.45
n.46,
47

n.48

n.49

taken from the frieze of the temple of Neptune and from S. Lorenzo Verano, both in Rome. Mantegna used them—in his *Triumph of Caesar*—and so did the illustrator of the *Hypnerotomachia Poliphili,* that most exquisitely illustrated of early Venetian books. The *Hypnerotomachia* came out in 1499, and one immediate derivation from it, established by Professor Gombrich,* carries us over from the Quattrocento to the Cinquecento.

21

n. 50

Bramante, the architect who turned the Early into the High Renaissance, intended to put up on the Belvedere in the Vatican an inscription in pseudo-hieroglyphs commemorating Julius II and himself. The technique of these pseudo-hieroglyphs was clearly to be that of an inscription printed and deciphered in the *Hypnerotomachia.* Bramante also intended at one stage to turn the axis of his new church of St Peter's by ninety degrees for no other reason but to have the old obelisk in front of the new church. Fontana in the end achieved this nearly a hundred years later, by shifting not the church but the obelisk.*

n. 51

During the Cinquecento Egyptian evidence multiplied. The most conspicuous monument which had the greatest influence visually, the Tabula Bembi or Mensa Isiaca, was found early in the century, certainly before 1520. It is named after Raphael's friend the humanist Pietro Bembo, who was librarian of the Vatican and later cardinal. It is, however, not known exactly where and in what circumstances it was found. * It is a bronze tablet inlaid with gold and silver and covered with hieroglyphs, figures and all kinds of monsters half-man, half-beast. The Tabula Bembi was published by Enea Vico in 1559.

20

n. 52

20 Detail from the Tabula Bembi

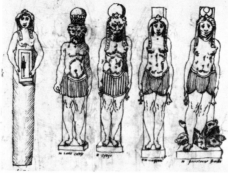

22 *Telamoni from the Codex Ursianus, mid-16th century*

21 *Woodcut from the 'Hypnerotomachia Poliphili', 1499*

23 *Sarcophagus drawn by Heemskerck in Rome, c.1532*

24 *Cynocephalus from the Codex Pighianus, mid-16th century*

25 *Drawing from the 'Peruzzi Sketchbook'*

It seems also that more pieces of Egyptian sculpture were found at the time, in addition to those already known, and the Roman obelisks were slowly brought to light; moreover the available monuments were recorded and appear again and again in archaeological compendia. A sizeable collection of drawings of Egyptiana was made by the archaeologist-architect-artist Pirro Ligorio, about the middle of the sixteenth century.* Some copies from his drawings, probably from his studio, went to Fulvio Orsini and in the seventeenth century, together with other Orsinian material, formed part of the manuscript Vat. lat. 3439, the so-called Codex Ursianus.* There we find also other recognizable copies of genuine hieroglyphic inscriptions from Roman obelisks and other monuments. The Tivoli telamoni appear together with an unidentified Egyptian figure in the so-called Peruzzi Sketchbook in Siena. This sketchbook is certainly not by Peruzzi's own hand; however, in view of Peruzzi's link with Raphael (see below) he may have been the designer of the originals, although that too has been doubted.*

Foreign artists too came to Italy to record the ancient monuments, among them Maarten van Heemskerck, who drew antiquities in Rome during his stay of 1532–35; he shows a sarcophagus resting on two sphinxes as well as other sphinxes and obelisks. More important as an archaeologist was the Dutchman Pighius from Campen, who assembled a large and important archaeological compendium known as the Codex Pighianus with drawings, by various hands, including one of the famous cynocephalus found in 1346 and several of the Tabula Bembi. The codex belongs to the mid-sixteenth century.

Yet another foreigner was the Portuguese Francisco da Hollanda in whose Escorial sketchbooks we find the Egyptian lions from the Pantheon, which had also been drawn by the author of the Codex Ursianus.*

n. 53

n. 54

25

n. 55

23

24

n. 56

All the Cinquecento Egyptiana so far mentioned are records rather than works of art in their own right. The case is different when we come to Raphael's Stanze. Here on the entrance and exit walls of the Stanza dell' Incendio (1514–17) unmistakable Egyptian telamoni appear as part of the decoration round the large pictures. Executed by Giulio Romano from Raphael's designs,* they seem uninfluenced by philological or iconographical considerations, and escaped comment for a long time. Raphael had earlier already made use of the motif of the many-breasted Diana of Ephesus who (as has been said before) was often identified with Isis, on the throne of the figure of Philosophy in the ceiling of the Stanza della Segnatura (*c.* 1509). Giulio Romano used Egyptian motifs in his *Triumph of Scipio* at the Louvre later on. The telamoni were borrowed from those at Tivoli mentioned before. In this case the task of the artist cannot have been too difficult, since the 'Egyptian' telamoni were of Roman origin and showed little of the Egyptian parentage, whereas true Egyptian sculpture went of course against all the principles and aspirations of Renaissance art, and would have presented great difficulties to any Renaissance artist who wanted to get anything of the Egyptian style over. It is not even certain that at the time these telamoni, which had no hieroglyphic inscriptions, were recognized as Egyptian.

Far more interesting and more spectacular than the telamoni from the Stanze is one page from the so-called Colonna Missal, now in the John Rylands Library at Manchester, which looks like a catalogue of Egyptiana known to the Renaissance. This page also shows the difference in attitude between the fifteenth and sixteenth centuries; whereas Pinturicchio, although illustrating an Egyptian story, used contemporary forms, the illuminator of this page, perhaps Giulio Clovio,* displays actual Egyptian features: the top row is still in the tradition of Pinturicchio, i.e. Egyptian gods are portrayed in Renaissance guise, in the centre Apis, on either side a cat, and then on one side a ram and on the other a lion. But in the rest of the page we find the 'column' echoed by an obelisk, flanking this two motifs from the Tabula Bembi, below motifs from obelisks, further down an image of the cynocephalus (found in 1346 and recorded in the Codex Pighianus) on one side, and two animal-headed gods which could be seen in the drawings of Ligorio on the other. At the bottom we find one telamone from Tivoli on one end, a motif from the Tabula Bembi on the other, and two sphinxes in between. The initial, for good measure, incorporates the Diana of Ephesus. The solution to the puzzle why all these Egyptian motifs were used, lies no doubt in the person of the patron, Cardinal Pompeo Colonna. The Colonna like the Borgia derived their ancestry from Apis and Egypt.*

Not until Piranesi's *Cammini* do we find such a multitude of Egyptiana as in the Colonna Missal. Otherwise the Cinquecento confined itself almost exclusively to the Tivoli telamoni and to sphinxes. Thus for instance the sarcophagus of Angelo Cesi, in his monument in Sta Maria della Pace, rests firmly on two frontally placed sphinxes. The date here must be *c.* 1550, and the sculptor

26
n.57

28

n.58

24

n.59

27

26 *Detail of the Stanza dell' Incendio painted by Raphael and Giulio Romano, 1514–17*

27 *Detail of the tomb of Angelo Cesi, c.1550*

28 *Page from the Colonna Missal* ▶

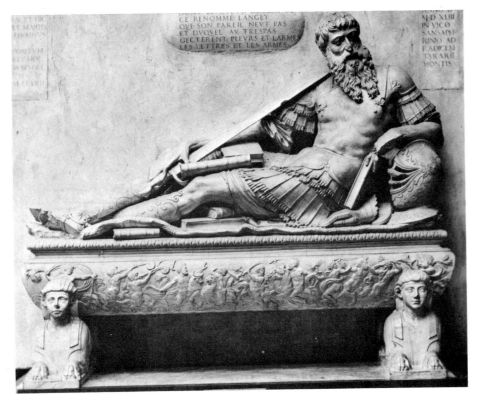

29 *Tomb of Guillaume du Bellay, 1557*

31 *Engraving after painting by Primaticcio at Fontainebleau, 1540s*

30 *Doorway at Fontainebleau, c.1540*

was Vincenzo de Rossi. The case is different with Guillaume du Bellay's tomb   29
in Le Mans Cathedral, of 1557. Both have a semireclining effigy on a sarcophagus,* and both sarcophagi are carried by sphinxes. Rossi's source is not far to   n.60
seek. He may well have known such antique sarcophagi as that drawn by Heems-   23
kerck, and the sculptor of the du Bellay monument (probably Pierre Bontemps)
may just have known Rossi's. But there is also a tenuous connection between
Guillaume du Bellay and Egypt. Du Bellay, who was the brother of the bishop
of Le Mans and the cousin of Joachim du Bellay, poet of the Pléiade (who incidentally wrote a poem on Diana), was a friend of Pierre Belon, and Belon was
sent to the East as an ambassador of François I, saw Egypt, dared to enter a
pyramid, and in 1553 published his *Observations* on what he had seen in Greece,
Asia Minor, India, Arabia and Egypt. He described pyramids and also a sphinx.

There is a second tomb in France resting on sphinxes, that of Diane de   33
Poitiers. But this tomb is the end of a story which begins with a doorway at
Fontainebleau, and we must trace it from its beginning. The doorway* is   30, n
flanked by two large, unmistakably Egyptian and probably female caryatids, and
belongs to the extensive and varied works carried out for François I about 1540.*   n.62
It leads from the west side of the Jardin de Diane to a staircase and a passage towards the Cour du Cheval Blanc. No-one knows who designed it, but its style
and especially the heavy pediment seems more likely for Primaticcio than for
Rosso Fiorentino. Also Primaticcio was using Egyptian motifs, including incidentally sphinxes, in the decorative parts of his paintings in the Galerie d'Ulysse   31
at Fontainebleau (begun shortly after 1540). To explain the caryatids of the doorway it may be enough to refer to those of Tivoli drawn by Sangallo, to Bram-   19
ante's known visit or visits to Tivoli to draw the antiquities of the town* and   n.63
its environs, and to Primaticcio's task of taking casts of ancient sculpture to
France. In addition, Giulio Romano's *Triumph of Scipio* already referred to is
known to have been in the hands of François I by 1534.*   n.64

It may also from a different and perhaps more significant angle be useful to
an understanding of the doorway at Fontainebleau to remember Primaticcio's
adherence to the formal and spiritual tenets of Mannerism and ascribe the explanation of his choice of so odd, so unexpected, and so novel a motif to that.

32 *Engravings of caryatids by Ducerceau*

33 *Tomb of Diane de Poitiers, 1576*

Another artist who could possibly have transmitted this motif was Ducerceau, of whom twelve sheets of engravings with terms and caryatids, one of them of an Egyptian canephorus, are known. He had been in Rome and could have brought drawings home.*

It is just possible that there was, over and above all these, a more recondite and subtle reason. We have already seen that Isis had ever since Antiquity been identified with Diana of Ephesus. There is a book of *Imprese* or devices published in 1566 by H. Ruscelli in Venice, and this, on page 180, shows an impresa for Henri II of France, a crescent moon flanked by two Egyptian caryatids.*

Now the crescent moon is certainly an illusion to Henri's mistress Diane de Poitiers, and the caryatids therefore may well play on the suggested identity of Greek Diana and Egyptian Isis. However, Diane was no more than a lady at the court of François I. There is no evidence seriously to point to a liaison between the king and her. She fell in love with the future Henri II when she was thirty-four and he seventeen—that is in 1535 or 1536. So whether an allusion to her at François I's favourite palace about 1540 is probable or not must remain open. There is, however, one fascinating piece or corroborating evidence in favour of the equation Diane—Diana—Isis. In a series of (not surviving) pictures for Anet, Diane's country house, the temple of Isis appeared in the image of the Château of Anet.* And in her funerary monument completed in 1576 the sarcophagus rested on four sphinxes. It was drawn by Gaignières, and fragments of it are said to remain in the cellars of Versailles.*

34 *Impresa of Henri II, published in 1566*

We have now reached the middle of the sixteenth century, a moment in time marked by three important publications: the Tabula Bembi in 1559 by Eneo Vico (as mentioned above), Celio Calcagnini's *De Rebus Aegyptianis* in 1544, and Piero Valeriano's *Hieroglyphica* in 1566. Valeriano's is a mighty compendium of hieroglyphic lore. During the next two hundred years journeys were undertaken more and more frequently and thoroughly, reports were published which were less and less fanciful, research was carried out into Egyptian history and especially Egyptian script, and speculations into the mysteries of Egyptian wisdom went parallel. The hermetic studies seem to have found their centre early in the seventeenth century in the Order of the Rosy Cross or the

32
n.65

n.66

n.67

33
n.68

Rosicrucian Order. Alchemy was a partner in the murky business. The man to be mentioned in our context is Count Michael Maier, who was born somewhere in Holstein in 1568, became physician to the Emperor Rudolph II (who was addicted to magic of all kinds), later visited Amsterdam and London, published his *Arcana Arcanissima, Hoc est Hieroglyphica Aegyptio-Graeca* in 1614, and two books on the Rosicrucians a little later (*Silentium post Clamores, Themis Aurea*).* *37 n.69*

It is a far cry from these muddled imaginings to the clear and matter-of-fact representation of the pyramids in their landscape setting in G. Sandys's *Relation of a Journey, begun anno domini 1610,* London, 1615. Sandys calls them 'the barbarous monuments of prodigality and vain glory.'* He was not impressed by unsolved secrets. *35 n.70*

As for art and architecture of the late sixteenth and early seventeenth centuries not much needs reporting. Bits of Egyptian decoration are carried on by Mannerists in divers places: the title page of Dosio's *Relics of Rome* (1566), Ruscelli's *Imprese* mentioned above (also 1566) which contains Egyptian devices for others as well as Henri II* and a decorative little campanile from Ferdinand II's *Kunstkammer** at Ambras, now in the Vienna Museum. All this is work on a small scale. *34 n.71 n.72*

On a large scale the most important events to draw public attention to Egyptian history and hieroglyphic script were the erection of several obelisks in public squares in Rome. The beginning was Sixtus V's town planning scheme. The obelisk in front of St Peter's, to which reference has been made earlier, was erected by Domenico Fontana. It was a feat of engineering. The erection was done in fifty-two stages, and up to nine hundred workmen were engaged on it. The final moment was reached on 10 September 1586, in the presence of thousands of onlookers. The obelisk in front of S. Giovanni in Laterano followed in 1588, that in the Piazza del Popolo in 1589, that facing the apse of Sta Maria Maggiore also before 1614.* All three are referred to in Maier's *Arcana*. *n.73*

For the mid-seventeenth century three names deserve special mention, Peiresc, Greaves and Kircher. Claude-Nicolas Fabri de Peiresc, 'that illustrious and incomparable virtuoso' as John Evelyn called him,* was born in 1580. He lived most of his life at Aix, but visited Italy in 1599–1602, Paris in 1605 and England for a month in 1606. The years 1616 to 1623 he spent in Paris. He was a scholar brilliant in many fields and a friend of men of such varied attainments as Malherbe, Casaubon, Gassendi and Rubens. He was one of the first to use a telescope, one of the discoverers of the nebula of Orion, the first to see Mars and Venus in daylight, the designer of the first map of the moon, one of the discoverers of the chyliferous vessels in the human body and the possessor of a large collection of books and curiosities. He never published anything but carried on a vast correspondence with the whole of Europe.* From this we see that Egypt- *n.74 n.75*

35 *The pyramids from Sandys's 'Relation', 1615*

36 Titlepage of Pignoria's edition of the Tabula Bembi, 1669

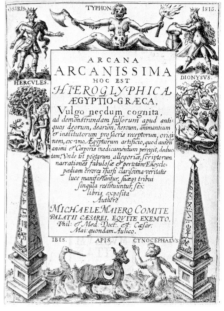

37 Titlepage of Maier's 'Arcana Arcanissima', 1614

ology was included in the wide range of his interests. He tried to solve the mystery of hieroglyphics by research into the Coptic language. A letter of his to
Camden* of 1618 deals with a figure of Isis which Camden possessed or knew of. Camden also wrote about this to the Dutch scholar Sweertius who asked for
the advice of Rubens, 'antiquarii et seculi nostri Apellis'.* Indeed somewhat later, in 1636, Rubens sent Peiresc the drawing of a mummy which may have
belonged to him.* In the case of Camden's figure, Peiresc consulted Lorenzo Pignoria, who in 1669 re-edited the Tabula Bembi, and Girolamo Aleandro who
was secretary to Cardinal Francesco Barberini. The Barberini seem to have been specially interested in Egyptian matters. The celebration arranged in 1634 by
Cardinal A. Barberini in honour of King Charles of Poland was given an Egyptian subject though not an Egyptian guise.* The designs for the occasion seem to
have been made by Andrea Sacchi.* In the Barberini Palace at Palestrina is a mosaic pavement from the temple of Praeneste which depicts Egyptian life and
which Poussin used for his *Flight to Egypt* painted in 1658 for Chantelou.*

n.76

n.77

n.78

36

n.79

n.80

n.81

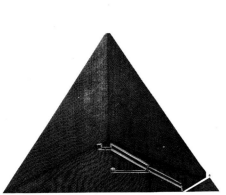

39 *The Pyramids, drawn by Stefano della Bella, probably in the 1640s*

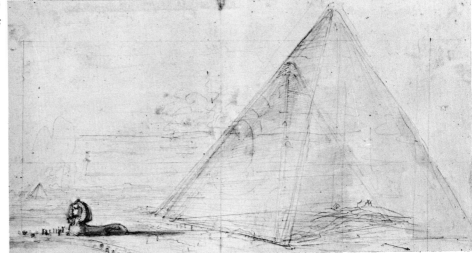

38 The Great Pyramid, from Greaves's 'Pyramidographia', 1646

In 1633 Peiresc was visited by a German Jesuit, aged thirty-one, Athanasius Kircher. Kircher was working on the Egyptian script and for this reason went to call on Peiresc. He had with him an obscure treatise in Arabic by one Barachias which he wanted to publish. Peiresc engaged him as his secretary—another was the Jew Solomon Azubius—and then made him go to Rome and try to get Cardinal Francesco Barberini's help. Kircher indeed went to Rome and remained there for the rest of his life. On thoroughly unsound foundations he succeeded in establishing himself as the recognized authority on Egyptian matters. He began by following Peiresc's promising idea of searching for Coptic relationships with Egyptian hieroglyphs, and got hold of a Coptic-Arabic glossary which Pietro della Valle had brought to Rome from Egypt. He published it as *Prodromus Coptus* in 1636. Pietro della Valle (1586–1652) had spent twelve years in the Orient, but published his *Viaggi* only thirty or forty years later in 1650. The journey, one of many which took place in the seventeenth century, is of artistic importance in so far as it seems possible that Stefano della Bella, the Italian engraver who lived in Rome from 1633 to 1639 and in Paris from 1639 onwards, made his remarkable pyramid landscape as a projected illustration to della Valle's book.   *39*

Stefano della Bella's landscape* however, which remained the most accurate representation for some time to come, was in all probability based on a better source of information than Pietro della Valle. It is known that Stefano was a friend of the physicist and orientalist Tito Livio Burattini, and Burattini had been in Egypt in 1637–40.* On his return to Europe he seems to have travelled in France and Germany before settling down in Poland. It was probably during those years that he met Stefano in Paris.*   *n.82* *n.83* *n.84*

Now Burattini spent his time in Egypt with an Englishman, John Greaves. Greaves (1602–52) was of all seventeenth-century travellers perhaps the most important. He was a fellow of Merton College, professor of geometry at Gresham College, London, and later of astronomy at Oxford. In 1648 he was for political reasons deposed from his chair at Oxford, the same chair to which Sir Christopher Wren was elected twelve years later. Greaves published his *Pyramidographia* in 1646. The book is the first scientific treatment of the pyramids. It is based on a thorough visit with Burattini to the interior of the Great Pyramid, and contains accurate measurements and a drawn section.   *38*

Athanasius Kircher was the very opposite of Greaves, inaccurate, fantastical, coolly successful. He lived in the Collegio Romano in Rome, made large collections (now partly in the Vatican, partly presumably somewhere at the College, where however they cannot be traced) and published sumptuous folios of bogus Egyptology: *Enigma Aegyptiana Restituta* (1643), *Oedipus Aegyptianus* (1652), *Obelisci Aegyptiani* (1666). He died in 1680.   *40*

40 Frontispiece to Kircher's 'Sphingis Mystagogae', 1676

41 The Pyramids, from Fischer von Erlach, 1721

42 The Great Sphinx, from Norden's 'Travels', 1757

The Museo Kircheriano was the first museum taking a more than casual interest in Egyptian material. Egyptian statues, statuettes, inscriptions, etc., existed of course in plenty of Italian, French and also English collections. Kircher mentions the Farnese and other Roman collections, the collection of the Duke of Tuscany, and of a merchant van Werle in Amsterdam. There is also the story of two statues which arrived at Marseilles in 1632. They got into the hands of Fouquet, Louis XIV's minister and owner of Vaux-le-Vicomte, then of Le Nôtre, Louis XIV's gardener, and then of Bernini de Valentiné, Controleur Général de la Maison du Roi.*   In England Sir Hans Sloane as well as Dr Mead owned mummies.*

n.85
n.86

The chief books between 1680 and Piranesi's *Cammini* are Montfaucon's, Norden's and Caylus's.*   Bernard de Montfaucon (1655–1741), a Benedictine, travelled in Italy in 1698–1701 and published his *Antiquité Expliquée* in ten volumes in 1719–24.*   It is the first comprehensive general archaeology, and it gives Egypt (which Montfaucon did not know personally) its due place. To him as to Sandys a hundred years before the Egyptians are amongst the barbaric fore-runners of Greek civilization, but he illustrates a pyramid landscape, mummies, sphinxes, gods and goddesses and so on.

n.87

n.88

Travellers of the same years who were much read and used are J. M. Wans-leben, Jean de Thevenot and Paul Lucas. For its illustrations rather than any archaeological value Johann Bernhard Fischer von Erlach, the great Austrian architect, must here also find mention. His *Historische Architektur* was completed in manuscript in 1712 and published in Vienna in 1721 and at Leipzig in 1725. An English translation came out in 1730. The short text accompanying the plate with the pyramid and the sphinx refers to Thevenot and Lucas, and explains the addition in the foreground of a Roman sphinx 'volveris pennis, pedibus fera, fronte puella', as Ausonius put it. On other plates are Egyptian vases which Fischer had seen. Two of them belonged to a nobleman in Naples and were drawn by Fischer in 1685, two had belonged to the Gonzaga collections at Mantua and were drawn by him from a drawing in the possession of Queen Christina of Sweden in Rome.*

41

n.89

Norden's *Travels in Egypt and Nubia* was the most comprehensive and in-formative travel book up to date. It came out in French in 1755 and in English in 1757, but F. L. Norden, a Dane from Glücksburg, had visited Egypt as early as 1737 and 1738 and addressed a letter on Egyptian antiquities to the Royal Society in 1741, the year in which he came to London. In the same year he became one of the founder members of a club which called itself the Egyptian Society.

42

William Stukeley of English pre-history fame* was another early member. Yet another founder member was Richard Pococke, who had explored at exactly the same moment as Norden. Their barges might have passed each other

n.90

one night on the Nile. Pococke is best known for his lively descriptions of tours through England, Scotland and Ireland. In 1741 he explored the Mer de Glace near Chamonix and thereby carved himself a niche in the history of Alpinism as well. His *Observations on Egypt* came out earlier than Norden's *Travels,* in 1743. Norden's and Pococke's books were the most widely used books on Egypt in their time. Norden's is superbly illustrated. With so much information and so   *42* many pictures about, it is no matter for surprise that the most common objects of Egyptian art, obelisks, sphinxes and pyramids were reproduced or translated freely in Europe in the eighteenth century. Sphinxes in gardens are so common   *43,44* and often look so frankly Rococo that one tends to forget their Egyptian ancestry. Obelisks are more common still and more obviously naturalized. Pyramids are rarer, though the border-line between obelisk and pyramid is not always easy to draw, especially since—this has already been said—the Roman monument to Cestius was universally known as a non-Egyptianly steep pyramid. However, Vanbrugh knew the difference; for in 1724 he mentions apropos Stowe both a '*Gulio* or Pyramid' in the middle of a pond (that is an obelisk) and 'The Pyramid at the end of one of the walks' which is to be 'a copy in miniature of the most famous one in Egypt and the only thing of this kind, I think, in   *n.91* England'.*

43 Sphinx at Chiswick House

It would indeed have been surprising if eighteenth-century England had not given hospitality to Egyptian forms in her picturesque gardens graced with the Roman and the Chinese, the Gothic and the Greek and occasionally even the Moorish. A rare French counter-example is the curious and boring novel *Sethos* written by Jean Terrasson in 1731 and translated at once (1732) into English. This is the story of a virtuous and courageous, wise and kindly Egyptian prince, and holds in its moral and form an intermediate position between Fénelon's *Télémaque* (1699) and Montesquieu's *Lettres Persanes* (1721). The moral is that of Fénelon and the age of reason, the form is Rococo in so far as the Rococo liked to clothe its enlightened or its sceptical messages in outlandish forms. Besides the *Lettres Persanes* there is Voltaire's *Zadig* to remind one of this and Horace Walpole's *Letter from Xotlo* (1757), and indeed, as was pointed out earlier, Piranesi's *Cammini.*

But there is another aspect to *Sethos*, and this takes us one decisive step beyond Piranesi and the attitude of the Rococo. Two whole books of the ten of which *Sethos* consists are given over to a description of the prince's initiation into the mysteries of Isis. Here there is a link with the suggestive obscurities of Michael Maier and the Rosicrucians. Egypt in *Sethos* appears not only as one of a number of curious countries, but as the seat of wisdom and of hermetic secrets. The novel, as far as our knowledge goes, is in this respect unique for its date.

If one wants to see more examples of this new attitude, one has to go to the crucial years about 1760, the years in which in all fields the Rococo ended in the dawn of the Classical and Romantic Movement, the years indeed of the *Nouvelle Héloise* as much as of the *Contrat Social*, of the *Antiquities of Athens* as much as of Goethe at Strassburg.

44 Sphinx at Veitshöchheim

In Egyptology the new spirit first makes itself heard in the *Recueil d'antiquités, égyptiennes, étrusques, grecques et romaines* by Anne-Claude-Philippe de Tubières, Comte de Caylus (1692–1765).* Caylus had travelled extensively in   *n.92* Italy, Greece and Asia Minor. His book began to appear in 1752. It contains the earliest appreciation of specific aesthetic qualities in Egyptian art.

This is now no longer merely considered an initial stage of what was going to be classic Greek art, but art in its own right. And this change of judgment was not due to any denial of the primitive character of Egyptian art, but to a growing respect for primitivity. Here the understanding of Egyptian and of Greek Doric run parallel.* The Egyptians are now *ce peuple sage et éclairé,* and   *n.93* their buildings are so solid and bare and massive that to an Egyptian Greek temple and other buildings 'devoient paroitre des châteaux de carte chargés de colisfichets.' These passages were published in 1759 and 1762. They were to find an enthusiastic echo in the designs of the younger generation of French architects

45, 46 Aquatints of imaginary tombs by Desprez, after 1777

almost at once. Their own dreams of gigantic ponderously symmetrical groups of buildings for vaguely public purposes were encouraged by the Academy and even more the Académie de France in Rome. A first published result is Peyre's *Livre d'architecture*, which came out in 1765. A typical example is the 'Temple Funéraire destiné à honorer les cendres des rois et des grands hommes, dédié à Monsieur de Voltaire.' This is by Jean-Louis Desprez (1743–1804) and was pre-miated by the Academy in 1766. Its centre is domed inside but crowned outside by a steep pyramid à la Cestius, and there are plenty of obelisks about, short as well as long and needle-like. Now Desprez went to Rome in 1777 and there, like the other young French architects of his generation, caught the Piranesi germ. The useless vastness of their Parisian academic programmes became imbued with Piranesi's sense of fantastically exaggerated contrasts in scale and also with Piranesi's enthusiasm for the primeval and colossal. The *Cammini* had been out for eight years when Desprez arrived. In the course of his stay he must have done

47 'Camera Sepolcrale Egiziana' by Tesi, 1762

45, 46 the four aquatints of tombs, of which two are here illustrated. In them, in spite of all their dependence on Piranesi, the Egyptian forms are, we suggest, presented with a totally new intention. What Blondel and Patte had called the 'formes carrées, pesantes' of the Egyptians and still mentioned in one breath with the **n.94** 'marmousets des Gots,'* are now beautiful because square and weighty. The heavily ashlared segmental arches lie low above the sombre tombs.

In order to appreciate to the full the visual novelty of these designs of Desprez, they may for a moment be compared with an etching by Mauro Tesi **47** called *Camera Sepolcrale Egiziana*, etc. The subject is more or less the same, but the spirit is utterly different. Tesi was born in 1730. He taught Count Algarotti design, and after Algarotti's death in 1764 sent a letter and some of his drawings, **n.95** including the Egyptian Tomb Chamber to the Earl of Chatham.* The Tomb is **n.96** mentioned in a letter of 1762,* that is before Piranesi's *Cammini*. Tesi lived in North Italy, not in Rome, and was a stage designer. So it is not likely that he knew the Caffè Inglese. Tesi's *Camera Sepolcrale* is theatrical, and it is certainly **n.97** Rococo in its picturesque disorder.*

The style which appears so powerfully in Desprez's tombs of the late seventies is that nowadays often called the style of the French Revolution, regardless of whether the architects working in this style were in fact for or against the **n.98** revolution. The most famous are Ledoux and Boullée.* Boullée's monumental **48** designs for a projected treatise on architecture in general belong largely to the eighties. Here we find the Egyptians praised for their 'idées très grandes' and the 'genre colossal' of their images. It is likely that, when Boullée wrote this, he was acquainted with a prize essay submitted to the Académie des Inscriptions et Belles Lettres in 1785 by a much younger architect and writer Antoine-Chrysostome Quatremère de Quincy (1755–1849). Quatremère de Quincy's was an analysis of

48 Design for a cenotaph by Boullée

Egyptian architecture and a comparison with that of Greece. He is on the side of the Greeks, as is to be expected, but—even if not for reasons of praise—he also emphasizes the excessive solidity of Egyptian work, its unremitting monotony, its preference for the colossal, and he adds, almost against his will, it seems, that one cannot help admiring these qualities in Egyptian buildings. The essay* was   n. 99 published only in 1803, but its contents were no doubt known beyond the Academy. Boullée never published his large and magnificent drawings.

Ledoux was luckier. He published his *Architecture* in 1804, and there the new   *49* message of Egypt is felt and expressed to the full. The pyramid was one of his favourite themes, because of its geometrical simplicity. He may even have had a chance of building a pyramid in a picturesque garden—if, that is, the pyramid   *50* of *c.* 1780 at Maupertuis is by him.*   n. 100

While in this group inspiration from Egypt is inspiration from a primeval civilization, Egypt as the source of hermetic mysteries appealed to another group within the growing Romantic movement. Here we have to look to the history of freemasonry and to the unexpected fact that Egyptian rites and embellishments do not seem to have entered freemasonry seriously before the 1780s. Traditions existed of course tracing back the craft and the skill of masonry proper to Egypt. The earliest English manuscript on the mason's craft tells of the origin of the craft 'in Egypte lande,' and the second earliest relates how the Israelites 'lernyd ye craft of masonry' in Egypt.* Craft guilds in the course of the   n. 101 sixteenth and seventeenth centuries developed into lodges of a membership called 'speculative,' that is philosophical, instead of vocational, and by 1717 the first English Grand Master was elected. But masonic documents of the following decades seem in no way to stress any special connection with Egyptian wisdom or Egyptian rites* in spite of the fact that the Rosicrucian Order, as we have   n. 102

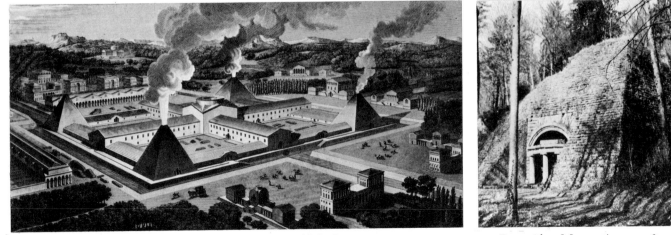

49 Design for the gun-foundry at Chaux by Ledoux, published 1804

50 Pyramid at Maupertius, c. 1780

seen, had quite marked Egyptian sympathies, and that in the course of the eighteenth century the Rosicrucian movement so often crossed the path of the growing movement of freemasonry.

The ingenious move to the pyramids for a suggestive ceremonial seems to have been made by masons in the third quarter of the century. We are chiefly concerned with two names, Carl Friedrich Köppen and the notorious Count Cagliostro. Köppen published in 1778 his *Crata Repoa, oder Einweihung der ägyptischen Priester* (i.e., initiation of the Egyptian priests). His lodge at Berlin was called the Afrikanische Bauherren and seems to have been founded as early as 1756. It came to an end in 1787. Cagliostro* received a life sentence in 1789. He had travelled in the Orient in the sixties, had become a mason in London in 1777 and had his lodge in Paris in the rue de la Soudière in the eighties. A private temple of Isis was attached to it, and Cagliostro was its grand master, second only to that mysterious character, the Grand-Cophta who never appeared but was always round the corner. *Der Grosskophta* became the title of a minor play by Goethe, inspired by the *cause célèbre* of the diamond necklace.

n.103

However much Cagliostro and his Egyptian Rites were a fraud, the Egyptian ritual in a very short time established itself in the lodges of the masons. The master of the lodge Zur wahren Eintracht at Vienna in 1781 was Ignatz von Born. He founded a Journal for Freemasons (*Journal für Freimaurer*) in 1784 and in the first volume of this published a long paper on the mysteries of the Egyptians.* In the same year Mozart had joined another masons' lodge in Vienna, after having been an apprentice in Born's lodge in 1783. Here clearly are the premisses of the *Magic Flute* with its text by Schikaneder, another mason, based partly on masons' ceremonial, partly on the initiation rites in Terrasson's *Sethos*.*

n.104

51

n.105

51 Titlepage of 'The Magic Flute', 1791

Now, as soon as later eighteenth-century Germany and primeval mysteries as well as primeval simplicity in art and architecture are considered, the connoisseur of the history of ideas will at once turn to Johann Gottfried Herder, the most universal spirit of *Sturm und Drang* and the inspirer of Goethe. And indeed, just as in the appreciation of folk poetry and of Shakespeare, Herder is the first to reveal to the full what Egypt might have to give the romantic age. Here is a strange passage to prove this claim, translated as best one can translate German *Sturm und Drang*. It comes from the *Älteste Urkunde des Menschengeschlechtes** and dates from 1774.

n.106

'According to legend, the first Egyptian temples, like the sacred heights and groves of all nations, were without images and statues. People say stones were worshipped because they were meant to represent statues, represent the earth; but I say they were not to represent anything but what they were: stones, memorials, the first monuments in the world. Hence people liked so much to combine everywhere square and round shapes and it became the well-known figure of Hermes: stone with a sphere on, that is, in the eyes of the Greeks, and the interpretation of the Egyptians, stone with a human head. From this derived the whole system behind the first steps in art. All this is still told wrongly in the histories of art. For what has this first raw, square, sphere-surmounted stone to do with a human statue as a work of art? In the shapes of the stones they wanted to connect the square and the sphere with the point, the One . . .

'When man turned into the open from the cave and added art, to create a building, a lasting building, what could be made by putting together stone and shape, but pyramid and obelisk? Square, sphere, and point connected in the simplest, most lasting manner—what else could it be?'*

n.107

This passage from Herder is the philosophical foundation of the early nineteenth century, severe, primeval Egyptian Revival, just as Piranesi's *Cammini* had been the foundation of the earlier playful and fantastical revival. The Renaissance had first introduced Egyptian motifs, Mannerism took them up with zest, the Rococo used them in one way, *Sturm und Drang,* the architects of the French Revolution, and the Romantics in another, while Egyptology ran parallel, reporting facts in a detached manner or with a bias this way or that.

Since this essay was written further research has brought to light more examples of Egyptian Revival from Denon to the middle of the nineteenth century. Rather than disturb the proportions of the essay by incorporating this new material I give it here as an appendix.

52 *Stoke Newington Cemetery, London, 1840*

53 *Plate from Pugin's 'Apology', 1843*

The directest descendants of Denon are the doorway of the Hôtel de Beauharnais in the rue de Lille in Paris, designed about 1805 by Kléber who was a general by occupation,* and the fountain in the rue de Sèvres of 1806 by   n.108
Beauvallet.* For Britain the examples mentioned in the text can be supple-   n.109
mented by the following: the design for a Court House on the Isle of Thanet by
James Elmes exhibited in the Royal Academy in 1805;* the Library at White-   n.110
knights near Reading of *c.* 1810 by S. P. Cockerell or of 1815 by J. B. Pep-
worth;* and a chimneypiece at Bayhambury in Herts of 1812.* The house   n.111,
No.144 Fore Street at Exeter is not dated, but is likely to be after 1823, the date of
Foulston's Library at Devonport.* In a book of 1806, T. S. Surr: *A Winter in*   n.113
London (II, cap. 7), we hear that it was then fashionable to decorate one's apartments with hieroglyphs—clearly another echo of Denon.* Flaxman devoted   n.114
one of his Academy lectures to Egyptian sculpture. Cemeteries came a little
later, when the need arose for areas larger than churchyards could provide. The
best-known is Stoke Newington, of 1840. Pugin in his *Apology for the Revival of*   52
Christian Architecture published in 1843 castigated the fashion by word and   53
illustration.

Examples assembled from other countries, mostly since this paper was
originally published, are mostly all of the twenties and later. For the United States
Professor Carrott* lists as *facile princeps* Benjamin Latrobe's design for the Library   n.115
of Congress in the Capitol of 1801. This has Egyptian motifs, but is not an Egyptian *ensemble*. The first building completely, if mildly, Egyptian is Strickland's
Mikveh Israel Synagogue at Philadelphia of 1822–5. More convincedly Egyptian
is T.U. Walter's Moyamensing Debtors' Prison at Philadelphia of 1832–5. Other
prisons followed, as the style seemed particularly suitable for displays of unassail-
able strength: the New Jersey State Prison at Trenton by Haviland in 1836 and
the most famous of all Egyptianizing buildings of America, the Tombs, the New
York City gaol, of the same year and by the same architect. However Davis,   55
always so eager for 'firsts', records that he had already done a neo-Egyptian
design for it.* Hamlin (p. 321) quotes a forty-page article on Egyptian architec-   n.116
ture published in 1829 in the *American Quarterly Review*. Of 1840 is the small rail-
way station at New Bedford, Mass., by Russell Warren (Hamlin p. 168), of 1836

54 the Pennsylvania Fire Insurance building in Philadelphia, and of 1837 Haviland's County Court House at Newark, N.J.

Another type of building for which Egyptian seemed especially suitable is cemetery gates—because eternity is evoked by the massive forms of Egyptian architecture. Professor Carrott gives the Mount Auburn Cemetery in Boston as the first. Its date is 1831. Then follow Mount Hope at Rochester of 1838 and Laurel Hill at Philadelphia of the same tear, and so on to the famous and familiar

56 Grove Street Cemetery Gates at New Haven, Conn., by Austin (1845–8).

For Germany it may be enough to refer to Haller von Hallerstein's design

n.117 for the Glyptothek at Munich dating from 1814* and Schinkel's stage designs

83,17 for the *Magic Flute* of 1815. For Austria the omniscient Professor Otto Kurz has drawn our attention to a chest of drawers in St Peter's Abbey at Salzburg, illustrated in the respective volume of the *Österreichische Kunsttopographie* (p. 107). It is signed by Johann Hoegl and dated 1828. The front represents a temple façade with five doors and is derived from Denon.

n.118 For Italy the late Carroll Meeks* has described a number of cases, the foremost being Canina's propylaea in the Borghese Gardens in Rome of the 1820s and a room in the celebrated Caffè Pedrocchi at Padua of *c.* 1830. Carroll Meeks also refers to the suspension bridge of 1832 over the Garigliano river at Minturno and to Barabino's original design for the chapel of the Staglieno cemetery near Genoa which was to have a Doric portico, a Pantheon body and a pyramid on top—a fine example of nineteenth century syncretism. Two designs for the entrance gates of the Villa Floridiana near Naples by Antonio Niccolini seem to date from 1816 or 1817 and are therefore earlier than any of Carroll Meeks's

n.119 examples.*

54 County Court House, Newark, New Jersey, 1837

55 Halls of Justice ('The Tombs'), New York, 1836–8

THE DEAD SHALL BE RAISED.

56 New Haven Cemetery, Connecticut, 1845–8

Notes

I The Counter-Reformation and Mannerism
pages 10–33

1 'L'Inghilterra e il Manierismo', *Bollettino del Centro Internazionale di Studi di Architettura Andrea Palladio*, IX, Vicenza 1967. Some xeroxed copies of the lecture in English are available for libraries.
2 E. Gothein: 'Staat und Gesellschaft des Zeitalters der Gegenreformation', in *Die Kultur der Gegenwart*, Leipzig 1908. He accepts the chronological divisions used in my essay but ignores them as soon as he turns to art, erroneously referring to a whole series of seventeenth-century phenomena under the heading of Counter-Reformation.
3. *Cf. Zeitschrift für bildende Kunst*, Leipzig 1919.
4 'Greco und der Manierismus', published in *Kunstgeschichte als Geistgeschichte*, Munich 1924.
5 The work of definition and categorization continued, as is shown by the writings of Troeltsch, Burdach, Strich and others.
6 *Cf.* Ludwig Pastor: *Geschichte der Päpste*, Book V, Freiburg im Breisgau 1901 etc.; English ed., *The History of the Popes*, London 1894 etc.
7 As for contemporary philosophy, Gothein says: 'By the middle of the sixteenth century the return to scholasticism was complete everywhere.' Panofsky (*Idea*, p. 50) emphasizes 'the acceptance of scholastic ways of thought' apropos the *Idea* of Federigo Zuccari.
8 In the very year in which Charles V gave up his empire and retired into the monastery of San Yuste.
9 He nevertheless took a keen scholarly interest in Antiquity. His achievements as director of the Vatican Library are well known; as was often the case, a reaction against the ideals of the Renaissance did not preclude an interest in archaeology. On the contrary, the Antique plays a very prominent role in the architectural treatise of the Mannerists, and, at precisely this time, a marked increase in the activities of collectors and editors of classical works is to be noted. However, Huelsen (*Römische Antikengärten*, Heidelberg 1917) draws attention to the fact that the collection of Ippolito Gonzaga, which was not started until after 1550, was formed 'primarily with a view to incorporation in architectural or garden designs' and not with reference to 'the antiquarian value of the monuments, the *erudizione*, which set

the tone of the Carpi collection in particular'. The Carpi collection dated from the 1530s and 1540s.
10 Report dated 23 October 1557.
11 The Casino is exactly contemporary with the last buildings of Michelangelo.
12 *Cf. Monumenta Ignat.*, Series I, nos 100, 103, 136, 257. Dvořák refers to this: *Geschichte der Italienischen Kunst*, Vol. II, Munich 1928, p. 85.
13 Austerity as well as a rationalistic practical sense are qualities shared by St Ignatius and his fellow student in Paris, Jean Calvin.
14 Weisbach ('Der Manierismus', in *Zeitschrift für bildende Kunst*, Leipzig 1919, p. 170) stresses this himself.
15 As when he refers to the Madonna as *la mamma*, smacks his lips with pleasure when consuming the Host, advises a visionary to spit out his visions to make them disappear, or boxes the ears of a passer-by whose peevish expression displeases him.
16 He wore knotted chains under his habit.
17 *Cf.* the important hearing at which Veronese appeared before the Inquisition, printed in Guhl and Rosenberg: *Künstlerbriefe*, Vol. II, p. 363; and in R. Friedenthal, *Letters of the Great Artists*, London 1963, pp. 113 ff.
18 *Die Entstehung der Barockkunst in Rom*, Vienna 1908, pp. 153 ff.
19 The paper then proceeded to run through Weisbach's categories of art of the Counter-Reformation and to prove that they are entirely or essentially categories not of sixteenth-century Mannerism but of seventeenth-century Baroque.
20 In his picture-book *Die Kunst des Barock*, Berlin 1924, he begins his sequence of illustrations with Caravaggio, Carracci and Bernini, and this would suggest that he had come to share the point of view which I put forward in this paper. However, the detailed introduction to the plates still maintains the parallel between Counter-Reformation and Baroque which I am trying to invalidate.
21 *Cf.* Weisbach: *Der Barock als Kunst der Gegenreformation*, Berlin 1921, p. 12.
22 Julius von Schlosser points out in his book *Die Kunstliteratur*, Vienna 1924, p. 282, that 'this period saw the first appearance of prudery and of its symbol, still a potent one in our own environment: the figleaf.' One can go further. With certain engravings by Marcantonio Raimondi after drawings by Giulio Romano, kept in the poison cupboards of print rooms, and with Aretino's *Ragionamenti*, pornography appears on the

scene. Aretino indeed wrote sonnets to go with the engravings. The subject of engravings and sonnets is the positions in copulation. As the sonnets, according to C. G. von Murr, date from 1524, the drawings are probably of *c.* 1520 or thereabouts. There is a tradition that Marcantonio was gaoled for doing the engravings. The details here summarized are repeated from miscellaneous papers kept at the British Museum with the engravings.
23 *Cf.* here the extremely valuable notes on the German sculpture of the same period in Bruhns: *Würzburger Bildhauer . . .*, Munich 1923, p. 223.
24 They belonged, almost without exception, to the first generation. The work of the second generation, that of the artists active during the period of greatest austerity, is virtually devoid of exhibited sensuality. This distinction applies e.g. to the differences between Parmigianino and Bedolo.
25 An instance is the comparison, proposed by Weisbach himself, between the austerity of Tasso and the sensual luxuriance of Marino.
26 Weisbach invalidates his own argument, when he says (*op. cit.*, p. 135) that in Lanfranco's *St Margaret* 'there is no reference to the transcendental'. How then can there be mysticism?
27 The star witness for the truth of my interpretation is once more Weisbach himself, who writes of Ribera (*op. cit.*, p. 125): 'This materialistic illusionism is almost entirely devoid of the spiritualistic mysticism which is so characteristic of El Greco and other Spanish artists.'
28 Gilio's *Trattato . . . de la emulatione che il Demonio a fatto a Dio ne l'adorazione . . .*, Venice 1563, which Weisbach naturally instances in support of his thesis, is in fact an isolated case.
29 *Cf.* for Germany Wackernagel, in F. Burger and A. E. Brinckmann: *Handbuch der Kunstwissenschaft*, Berlin 1915 etc., pp. 12–13.
30 When this paper was originally published, I wrote in a footnote: 'I can, in any case, do no more than this without anticipating a contribution by Wilhelm Pinder which is due to appear in this journal in the near future. My own paper is considerably indebted to the ideas which Pinder is to develop in his article; I myself participated in their elaboration in the course of a series of lectures and seminar papers. W. Friedländer's paper on the beginnings of the anti-classical style, on the other hand, which appeared in the second

issue of this year, did not come to my attention until my own work was completed. It was gratifying to find that, on fundamental issues such as the homogeneity and independence of Mannerism as a stylistic epoch and its initial date of *c.* 1520, Friedländer is in agreement with the conclusions set out here.' What has happened to the term Mannerism and its uses since, is outlined in the Foreword.

After the original version of this paper had been published, in 1928, the volume of the *Handbuch der Kunstwissenschaft* came out in which I discussed in about 100 pages the Italian painters of Mannerism. The volume had come out originally in instalments, beginning in 1925, if I remember rightly. A paper I wrote on Mannerism in Italian architecture was included in *The Mint*, II, 1936, and is going to be reprinted shortly in the United States.

II EARLY AND HIGH BAROQUE

pages 34–55

1 *Monatshefte für Kunstwissenschaft*, Leipzig 1922, pp. 241*ff.*
2 'Der entwicklungsgeschichtliche Pantheismus', in *Gesammelte Schriften*, Vol. II. Turning to our narrower field of enquiry, it was Herman Voss (*Die Malerei der Spätrenaissance in Rom und Florenz*, Berlin 1920, pp. 14ff.) who pointed most clearly to the necessity of recognizing 1600 as the historical watershed. Some of his analogies are drawn from the history of music.
3 Martin Luther: *Tischreden*, Vol. II, p. 419.
4 Laurentius Valla: *De Voluptate ac vero bono* . . . , Paris 1512, I, 13.
5 Ludwig von Pastor: *Geschichte der Päpste*, Book XII, Freiburg im Breisgau 1927.
6 Weisbach draws attention to this in his *Der Barock als Kunst der Gegenreformation*, Berlin 1921, p. 28, a study highly illuminative for the spirit of the Baroque.
7 *Geschichte der Päpste*, Book VII, chapter 3.
8 Ernst Bergmann: *Katechismus der Jesuitenmoral*, Leipzig 1913.
9 'I Gesuiti che dovrebbero essere come altre volte defensori della Santa Sede piu degli altri la pongono in compromesso' ('The Jesuits, who ought to be, as they formerly were, defenders of the Holy See, are now more actively compromising its position than anyone'). From a report sent by the Papal Nuncio Scotti, in April 1641, quoted by Leopold von Ranke: *Französische Geschichte* . . . , Tübingen 1852 etc., Vol. II; English ed. *Civil Wars and Monarchy in France* . . . , London 1852
10 Benedetto Croce: *Saggi sulla litteratura italiana del Seicento*, Bari 1921.
11 Looked at in another way, these constituted a method by which the Church might combat the new religions.
12 J. J. I. Döllinger and F. H. Reusch: *Geschichte der Moralstreitigkeiten in der römisch-katholischen Kirche*, Vol. I, Nördlingen 1889; Honigsheim: *Die Staats- und Soziallehren der französischen Jansenisten im 17. Jahrhundert*, Diss. Heidelberg 1914; Cornelius Jansenius:

Augustinus, Louvain 1640 etc., Vol. II, Book 5, chapter 3.
13 Carl Vossler: *Frankreichs Kultur im Spiegel seiner Sprachentwicklung*, 3rd ed. Heidelberg 1921, p. 354.
14 The Ursulines established themselves in France in 1596, the purely contemplative reformed Carmelites in 1604. In 1606 the community of Jeanne Lestonnec was founded in Bordeaux, in 1609 Mary Ward founded her Institute of Mary in Flanders, in 1612 the Ursulines transformed themselves into a regular order, in 1615 the Sisters of the Christian Doctrine was formed in Nancy. See Pastor, *loc. cit.*, and Max Heimbucher: *Die Orden und Kongregationen der katholischen Kirche*, Paderborn 1896, 3rd ed. Paderborn 1933–4.
15 *Cf.* Max Weber: 'Die protestantische Ethik und der Geist des Kapitalismus', in *Archiv für Sozialwissenschaft und Sozialpolitik*, XX, XXI, Heidelberg 1888 etc.; English ed., *The Protestant Ethic and the Spirit of Capitalism*, London 1930; and Ernst Troeltsch: 'Die Soziallehren der christlichen Kirchen', in *Gesammelte Schriften*, Tübingen 1912–25; English ed., *The Social Teaching of the Christian Churches*, London and New York 1931.
16 *Revue de métaphysique et de morale*, Paris 1896, p. 529.
17 *Cf.* above all Dilthey: 'Weltanschauung und Analyse des Menschen seit Renaissance und Reformation', in *Gesammelte Schriften*, Leipzig and Berlin 1923, Vol. II.
18 August Schmarsow: *Barock und Rokoko*, Leipzig 1897, p. 27.
19 An entertaining sidelight on this 'sense of superiority' is afforded by the appearance, about 1625, of the wig, introduced by Louis XIII, the expression of the general desire for expansion of the individual personality.
20 *Cinna*, Act V, Scene 3.
21 Bacon, *Novum Organum*, Book I, London 1620.
22 *Cf.* Dilthey: 'Das natürliche System der Geisteswissenschaften im 17. Jahrhundert', in *Gesammelte Schriften*, Berlin and Leipzig 1923, Vol. II.
23 The French Protestants who suffered forcible 'conversion' during Louis XIV's notorious *dragonnades* fell victim 'not to the zeal of the Catholic world in general but to the idea of a Gallican church and of the unity of France' (Ranke: *Französische Geschichte*, Tübingen 1852 etc., Vol. XIII, chapter 5); in other words they were persecuted in the name of the ideal of the state. The situation had been the same under Richelieu.
24 *Cf.* Pinder in Burger: *Handbuch der Kunstwissenschaft*, pp. 246–54.
25 It might be said that Corneille's line in *Horace* (Act II, Scene 3), '*Rome a choisi mon bras, je n'examine rien*', is in fact characteristic of the 'man of will' of both the Mannerist and Baroque periods, if one understands by 'Rome' in one case the Roman church, in the other the Roman state. The idea of absolute monarchy first took shape in the age of Mannerism in the Papal States.

26 ' . . . ed il Caravaggio disse che tanta manifattura gli era a fare un quadro buono di fiori come di figure . . .' ('Caravaggio said that it cost him as much labour to paint a picture of flowers as of figures'). Reported by Vincente Giustiniani, see G. G. Bottari and S. Ticozzi: *Raccolta di Lettere sulla Pittura*, Milan 1822–5, Vol. VI, pp. 247 sqq.
27 Carl Vossler: *Italienische Literaturgeschichte*, Sammlung Göschen, 4th ed.
28 *Saggi sulla litteratura italiana del Seicento*, Bari 1921.
29 There is a correspondence between the perspective *trompe-l'oeil* effects of Bernini and Borromini and the literary technique of Marinism: profuse imagery, the accumulation of decorative epithets, antitheses, plays on words. Marino's couplet: '*È del poeta il fin la maraviglia. Chi non sa far stupir vada alla striglia*' ('The poet's end is wonderment; a poet who knows not how to amaze deserves no reward but blows'), could equally well have been intended to refer to the painters, sculptors and architects of the Baroque.
30 In his *Saggi* . . . (see Note 10) Croce quotes the *Poesie sacre e morali* of B. Morando (1662), who complains as follows: '*Pare che oggidi non si trovino spiriti piu vivaci al comporre di quelli che dai sospiri degli amori profani e dal fiato delle trombe guerriere sogliono derivare*' ('It seems that there are today no spirits more lively in [literary] composition than those derived from the sighs of profane love or the breath of martial trumpets') Croce goes on to instance, among many other examples, three lyric poets, Giovanetti, Maria-Materdona and Brignole-Sale, who handled the dubious theme of *La Cortigiana frustata*, ('The Courtesan whipped'). Marino himself made the unabashed statement that '*Spesso l'orror va col diletto*' ('often horror accompanies delight').
31 Pietro da Cortona: *Trattato della Pittura e della Scultura*, Florence 1652.
32 Paul Fréart de Chantelou: *Journal du voyage en France du Cavalier Bernin* . . . , Paris 1930.
33 Rose: *Spätbarock*, Munich 1922.
34 Willy Andreas: 'Richelieu', in *Meister der Politik*, Vol. II, 1923.
35 All these quotations are from the second volume of Ranke's *Französische Geschichte* (see Note 9).
36 Gustave Lanson: *Corneille*, 3rd ed., Paris 1909; and Klemperer: 'Vom Cid zu Polyeucte', in *Neuere Sprachen*, Marburg 1920.
37 *Loc. cit.* (Note 36), and 'Zur französischen Klassik', in *Vom Geiste neuer Literaturforschung. Festschrift für Oskar Walzel*, ed. J. Wahle and V. Klemperer, Potsdam 1924.
38 Fréart de Chantelou, *op. cit.*
39 In Corneille's hands, even the Christian martyr Polyeucte becomes an activist. See Klemperer, *loc. cit.* (Note 36).
40 Carl Vossler: *op. cit.* (Note 13), pp. 355–6.
41 He can be seen putting this into practice in one of the letters (5 March 1712) of his German sister-in-law, the second Madame, Liselotte of the Palatinate, written after the death of Louis XIV's son and grandson, the Dauphin and the Duc de Bourgogne: '*Der*

König jammert mich von Hertzen: er zwingt sich um gute Mienen zu machen undt man sieht doch dass er innerlich leidt ('the king makes my heart bleed; he forces himself to look cheerful, and yet one can see that he is suffering within').

42 The volume of the *Handbuch der Kunstwissenschaft* to which reference was made at the end of the preceding essay (Note 30) has, as its second part, about 100 pages on Early and High Baroque in Italian painting.

III The Crisis of 1650 in Italian Painting
pages 56–76

1 A much broader treatment of the subject of this paper and of Italian painting between 1650 and 1750 altogether, can be found in my *Habilitationsschrift* in the Göttingen University Library. It was meant to be Part Three of my volume of the *Handbuch der Kunstwissenschaft* which is supposed to deal with Italian painting from the end of the Renaissance to the end of the Rococo. However, I was bound by my contract not to exceed a certain length of text, and so of Part Three only a summary was printed.

2 Since this was written much more literature has of course come out. The second edition of V. Golzio: *Seicento e Settecento*, Turin n.d. (1960), has a very full bibliography. More recent still is the second edition of R. Wittkower: *Art and Architecture in Italy, 1600–1750* (Pelican History of Art), Harmondsworth 1967. These two books save me more detailed bibliographical annotation.

3 *Cf.*, above all, Roberto Longhi, in an article in *La Voce*, V, Florence 1913. Here, in Longhi's characteristically succinct manner, Preti is described as 'the saviour of Neapolitan painting, and therefore, in the context of that period, the saviour of Italian painting'.

4 The documentary sources for the dating of the picture are all in V. Mariani: *Mattia Preti a Malta*, Rome 1928.

5 Brera No. 599 (illustration in Chimirri and Frangipane's biography, Milan 1914); Dresden No. 467 (Gallery Catalogue); Rome, Palazzo Corsini No. 1566 (catalogued as L. Spada); Rome, Palazzo Doria No. 400. The Genoa *Raising of Lazarus* was given to Caravaggio in the Catalogue of 1912.

6 The fresco, mentioned in contemporary documents published by V. Ruffo in *Bolletino d'arte*, X, Rome 1916, and in Longhi's review in *Arte*, XIX, 1916, p. 370, long remained unphotographed. I owed the opportunity to publish the first reproduction of it to the kindness of Federigo Hermanin.

7 Preti's frescoes in San Biagio, at Modena, had previously been reproduced only in a rare work by Bertoni and Crescimbeni, *Il patrimonio artistico della Congregazione della Carità*, Modena n.d. On external evidence one would be inclined to suppose the frescoes of San Biagio to stem from the master's early Emilian period; but the style of these mag-

nificently free, expansive and richly-coloured scenes is much closer to that of Valmontone than to that of Sant' Andrea della Valle, so that it would be hard to justify a dating before the mid-1650s.

8 Valerio Mariani: *Matteo Preti a Malta*, Rome 1928.

9 Monographs: E. Petraccone, Naples 1919; Posse, in Thieme-Becker's *Künstlerlexikon*; De Rinaldis, in the *Piccola Collezione d'Arte*, Florence 1922. No monograph has since been published.

10 It is probable that the type of Giordano's Banquets also dates back to these early years. Supporting evidence is provided by Preti's Banquets, painted in Naples, i.e. before 1661 —if one accepts the hypothesis that this theme, which became popular among Neapolitan artists so suddenly, was taken from Giordano by Preti and not the other way round. We gather from De Dominici, who is particularly well informed on the subject of Preti and the artistic cliques of the period, that for all Preti's natural dislike of Giordano's affectations he was influenced in spite of himself by the other artist's '*maniera vaga ed ideale*'.

11 Illustrated in *Art in America*, I.

12 *Cf.* Desjardins: *La Méthode des classiques français*, Paris 1904.

13 The most recent monograph is by N. Ivanhoff, Padua 1942.

14 *Cf* M. Labò, in *Biblioteca d'arte illustrata*, Rome 1928.

15 It will probably be necessary to add to the names of the two North Italian innovators, Maffei and Castello, that of a third artist of whose career too little is yet known for it to be possible to say whether his style was fully formed by the 1650s. This artist is Sebastiano Mazzoni, a Florentine, who lived from 1611 to 1678, and is known to have worked in Venice (*cf.* an article by Fiocco in *Dedalo*, X, Milan 1928/9). His principal works, in the church of San Benedetto, are of 1649 and recall both Maffei and Preti; as one of the first teachers of Sebastiano Ricci, Mazzoni holds a special position as an intermediary between the Late Baroque and the transitional art of the early eighteenth century.

16 *Cf.* H. Voss, *Malerei des Barock in Rom*, Berlin n.d., pp. 583–7, and for the ample literature of the 1650s Vincenzo Golzio's bibliography (see Note 2).

17 In addition, for some of the types it would be worth considering links with the Preti of Valmontone.

18 *Cf.* A. M. Cerrato in *Commentari*, Florence 1959.

19 *Cf.* Voss, *op. cit.* (Note 17), pp. 573–83; for recent literature Golzio's bibliography (see Note 2).

20 *Cf.* Voss, *op. cit.* (Note 17), pp. 592–603; Lorenzetti, in *Arte*, XVII, Rome 1914; Cantalamessa, in *Bolletino d'arte*, 2nd series, I, Rome 1921/2; A. Mezzetti, in *Rivista dell' Instituto Nazionale d'Archeologia e Storia dell' Arte*, Rome 1955.

21 *Spätbarock*, Munich 1922.

22 This is shown most convincingly by

Fraenger (*Die Bildanalysen des Roland Fréart de Chambray*, Heidelberg 1917) by means of a comparison between Poussin and Fréart. *Cf.* also Desjardins: *op. cit.* (see Note 12). It is French artistic theory, not French art, that offers the conclusive parallels with the renewal of Italian painting in the 1650s. I am thinking of the theories of Roger de Piles (born 1635) concerning the superiority of colour to drawing (1688, 1673) and the freedom of genius from teachable rules (1681). *Cf.* my *Academies of Art, past and present*, Cambridge 1941.

23 It would be equally instructive to examine Ranke's account of the character of the late seventeenth century within the framework of Italian history. He calls this 'an age of enjoyment', and says of the 1660s: 'The power of the Church was undergoing a transition from the boldness and decision of a monarchy to the calm deliberation and leisureliness of an aristocracy' (12th ed., p. 615). 'The tendencies of the restoration and the conquest were a thing of the past' (*ibid.*, p. 650).

24 *Cf.* the masterly account in Ranke's *Französische Geschichte*, Tübingen 1852 etc., Vol. I, pp. 189–96.

IV The Genesis of the Picturesque
pages 78–101

1 This paper owes much throughout to Christopher Hussey's classic *The Picturesque* published as early as 1927 and recently—at last—reprinted. A recent book of interest in the context of this and the following paper is D. Clifford, *A History of Garden Design*, London 1962.

2 On the word Sharawaggi and its connotations see below, pp. 102–7.

3 Quotations are from A. F. Sieveking's edition, London 1908, pp. 50–54.

4 Quotations are from Vol. II of the 1732 edition.

5 A passage not quoted in the original essay connects Addison also with Shaftesbury's contrast between the orderly planning of the house and the informality of the garden. It appears in *The Spectator* No. 415 on the 'Art of Architecture' and introduces a new and fruitful argument: 'A thing that we see in succession ought to have variety . . . those on the contrary that we see at one glance ought to have symmetry; thus, at one glance, we see the front of a building.'

6 Sources for these letters will be found in W. E. and W. J. Courthorpe (eds.), *The Works of Alexander Pope*, London 1871–89, Vols. VI, VIII and IX.

7 See G. Sherburn, *The Early Career of Alexander Pope*, Oxford 1934.

8 In this connection it is eminently important that Charles Coypel in his *Discours sur la Peinture* of 1732 (delivered at the Royal Academy of Art in Paris in 1726) defined the Picturesque as '*un choix piquant et singulier des effets de la nature*'. I found this quotation in Fiske Kimball's *The Creation of the Rococo*, Philadelphia 1943, p. 153.

9 To the sources here registered and discussed I should now add one to which Mr H. F. Clark has drawn attention, first in *The Architectural Review*, XCV, 1944, p. 125 *ff.* then in his book, *The English Landscape Garden*, London 1948. It is Richard Castell's *The Villas of the Ancients,* published in 1728 under the patronage of Lord Burlington himself. The book comes a little late in the context of my *Florilegium,* but one can assume that Pliny was already earlier used by Lord Burlington and perhaps by Pope as an authority to justify what they wanted to do anyway. Mr Clark's quotation about the *imitatio ruris* is very telling: 'Hills, rocks, cascades, rivulets, woods and buildings . . . thrown into such an agreeable disorder as to have pleased the eye from several views, like so many beautiful landskips'. Bridgeman also might have been given more prominence by me, if I had known what Mr Peter Willis has brought out in his Cambridge Ph.D. thesis of 1961. He proves there that Bridgeman deserves a little less credit than Walpole gives him, but some credit all the same. Dr Willis's summing-up is: 'He symbolized the break with the old and the beginning of the new, and if his part was no more than that of the herald of the landscape era it was no mean part to play.' Dr Willis is particularly interesting in his weighting of the evidence between Vanbrugh and Bridgeman, and his emphasis on the earliest occurrences of the ha-ha and of winding paths in French gardens and garden books before 1700. The title of Mr Willis's thesis is *Charles Bridgeman, Royal Gardener,* and there is hope that it will be converted into a book.

V A NOTE ON SHARAWAGGI
pages 102–107

1 Homer E. Woodbridge, *Sir William Temple, the Man and his Works,* 1940.
2 Y. Z. Chang, 'A Note on Sharawadgi', *Modern Language Notes,* 1930, p. 221.
3 'China and the English Literature of the seventeenth century', *Quarterly Bulletin of Chinese Bibliography,* English edition, N.S., I, No. 4, December 1940.
4 For more recent research on the Chinese derivation see R. C. Bald: 'Sir William Chambers and the Chinese Garden' in *Journal of the History of Ideas,* XI, 1950, p. 287; and Needham: *Science and Civilization in China,* Vol. II, pp. 359–363. We are indebted to Mr Basil Gray for these references.
5 'The Influence of Chinese Art in the West', in *The Spirit of China,* London 1942.
6 Not only did several of the published accounts of China have transcribed word lists added as, for example, Athanasius Kircher's *Atlas Chinensis,* Amsterdam 1667, there also were separately printed dictionaries. This transpires from Robert Hooke's paper quoted in note 7. Besides, a number of manuscript dictionaries were available in England. Two such from Sir Hans Sloane's collections are in the British Museum:

Vocabulario de la lengua mandarina (a Spanish-Chinese dictionary in alphabetical order, seventeenth century, Sloane 3419) and *Dictionarium Chinese, hoc est lingua Belgica juxta alphabeti ordinem, et Latini et Mandarinice quoque explicati Chinensum Charactares,* (seventeenth century, Sloane 2746). Others are in the Bodleian Library at Oxford, for instance one attached to Peter Mundy's account of his travels to China (MS. Rawl. A. 399). Moreover, amongst the manuscripts of Thomas Hyde (1636–1703), the great orientalist, and Bodley's Librarian from 1665 to 1701, there is one catalogued as *Parvum Vocabularium Sinico-Anglicum* and *Aliud Parvum Vocabularium Sinense* (Edward Bernard, *Catalogi Librorum Manuscriptorum Anglicae et Hiberniae in unum collecti Oxoniae MDCXCVII,* p. 286. *Librorum Manuscriptorum Bibliothecae Bodleianae Classis XIII. continet autem illa Codices Orientales XXIX. E. Bibliotheca Viri Clarissimi Thomas Hyde, Pecunia Universitatis Comperatos A.D. MDCXCII,* 1692), and amongst papers 'brought out of the study of the late Dr. Thomas Hyde of Oxford' (B.M. Sloane 853) are various word lists with Chinese characters, their transcriptions and translations. Besides, Anthony Wood tells us in *Athenae Oxonienses,* ed. Bliss, Vol. IV, 1820, p. 526, that amongst 'books by Dr. Hyde designed for the press, if he lives to finish them, he having already done something towards all of them' was a '*Curiosa Chinensia and Selanensia*' and '*Varia Chinensia . . . omnia excerpta ex Ora et Scriptis nativi Chinensis Shin Fo-burgh.*'
7 John Webb: *The Antiquity of China,* London 1678, which though quite crazy in its attempt to link the Chinese with the Jews and in asserting that China was the place where Noah's Ark landed, does show at least the fascination of matters Chinese. Mr Chen in an article 'John Webb, a forgotten page in the early history of Sinology in Europe' in *Chinese social and political Review,* XIX, No. 3, 1935, pp. 295–330, has dealt in detail with Webb's sinological endeavours. Robert Hooke read a paper to the Royal Society (*Philological Transacations,* XVI, No. 180, 1686) which was entirely devoted to the Chinese language, 'Some Observations and Conjectures concerning the Character and Language of the Chinese, Made by R.H., F.R.S.' What he has to say about his method seems worth quoting: 'By a Chinese Manuscript out of which I transcribed the Lord's Prayer in the year 1666 (when it was lost), I found that the pronuntiation had no Affinity with the strooks of the Character . . . Since that time I procured from China a Dictionary of the Court Language (as I found it written upon by the person that sent it me from thence). But this whole Book (which I found was Printed) consisted only of the Chinese Characters without any interpretation, or Pronuntiation, however by the help of the pictures of that, and a Chinese Almanack, I finally found out their Characters for numbers. . . .' (p. 66). 'I have not yet been able to procure sufficient helps to Inform

myself of the whole Art of Writing and Reading the Chinese Characters . . . the best help I had was the Perusal of Some Books Printed in Chinese with the Pronuntiation and Signification of the Character in Latin Letters. . . .' (p. 69).
8 Moreover, Temple's remarkable knowledge of Confucius indicates that he must have been familiar with the 1687 translation of the philosopher's works by Prosper Intorcetta, Christian Herdritch, Francis Rougemont and Philippe Couplet.
9 *Histoire de l'Expedition Chrestienne au Royaume de la Chine enterprise par les P.P. de la compagnie de Jesus . . . tirées des commentaires du Père Matthieu Riccius par le Père Nicole Trigault nouvellement traduicte en français,* Lyon 1616, p. 611.
10 *The History of the . . . Monarchy of China* by F. Alvarez Semedo, *now put into English,* London 1655, p. 112.
11 *China and France or Two Treatises. The One of The Present State of China from the observation of two Jesuits lately returned from that Country. Written and published by the French King's cosmographer (Father Grueber, S.J.) and now Englished,* London 1676, p. 74.
12 *An Embassy from the East India Company of the United Provinces to the Grand Tartar Cham, Emperour of China, delivered by their Excell'cies P. de Goyer and J. de Keyser . . . and ingeniously described by Mr. J. Nieuhoff. Englished by J. Ogilby,* London 1669. Second edition of Vol. I, 1673, identical with first edition to which belongs Vol. II, *Atlas Chinensis being a second part of a relation of remarkable passages in two embassies from the East-India Company of the United Provinces to the Vice-Roy Singlamong and General Taising Lipon and to Kouchi Emperor of China and East Tartary. Englished by J. Ogilby, etc.,* 1671.
13 Very much later G. de Magalhaens (*Nouvelle Relation de la Chine Composée en l'année 1668,* Paris 1668. *Englished by Ogilby,* 1688) also mentions in the precincts of the Fourth Palace or Lama Tien 'a Mountain made with hands like a Sugarloaf and environ'd with Rocks which were brought thither in former times from the Seaside, though far more remote with great labour and expense. These Rocks are for the most part full of holes and hollowness, occasioned by the continual dashing of the waves; the Chinese taking great delight to behold those unpolished works of nature. And they are so disposed as to counterfeit the high out-juttings and steep and rugged Precipices of Rocks; so that at a moderate distance the whole seems to represent some craggy wild Mountain, the first work of Nature.'
14 Also transcribed as Chin-fo-Cum and Tschin-fo-Tsung, according to H. Belevitch-Stankevitch: *Le Goût Chinois en France au temps de Louis XIV,* Paris 1906, p. 228, or Shen Fun-tsung, according to J. J. L. Duyvendak in 'An old Chinese Fragment in the Bodleian', in *Bodleian Library Record,* II, No. 28, 1949; we are indebted to Professor Beeston for having drawn our attention to the latter reference.

15 V. Pinot: *La Chine et la formation de l'esprit philosophique en France*, Paris 1932, brings a letter published in *Mercure Galant*, Sept. 1684, with a description of the Chinaman's visit at the Court of Versailles.

16 *The Life and Time of Anthony Wood Antiquary of Oxford, 1632–1695, described by himself, collected from his Diaries and other Papers* by A. Clark. Vol. III, 1894, p. 230: 'After his majesty was sate, he asked the vice-chancellor (standing by him) for certaine books. To which the vice-chancellor answered that Dr. Hyde the Library keeper could answer him more fully than he. Whereupon he was called from the other part of the library, where his study was and being come, he kneeled downe whereupon the King gave him his hand to kiss. Which being done his majesty said, "Well, Dr. Hyde, was the Chinese here?" to which he answered "Yes, if it may please your majesty; and I learned many things of him." Then said his majesty, "He was a little blinking fellow, was he not?" to which he answered "Yes," and added that "all the Chineses, Tartars, and all that part of the world was narrow-eyed".'

17 A. H. Rowbotham in *Missionary and Mandarin*, Berkeley and Los Angeles 1942, p. 279, suggests that Pepys refers to Kircher's volume. In addition Chinese pictures seem to be mentioned in Gregorius Sharpe's re-edition of some of Thomas Hyde's works (*Syntagma Dissertationum Quas Olim auctor doctissimus Thomas Hyde S.T.P. separation edidit A Gregorio Sharpe*, Oxford 1767, Vol. II, p. 521): 'Horti Chinensis descriptio quae sequitur quamvis sine nomine in adversariis appareat proculdulit data es ab codem viro Sinensi qui epistolas jamjam exscriptas ad Hydium misit: Explicatio videtur esse cujusdam Tabulae pictae e China allatae.' Sloane also owned some Chinese pictures, but again nothing is known as to when he acquired them (B.M. Sloane 5304, 5292–3, 5252, since transferred to the Department of Oriental Antiquities, now, under Chinese Woodcuts, B. 21–41.)

18 It seems to have been usual to question returned travellers; the Académie des Sciences in Paris prepared in 1685 a memoir (published by V. Pinot in *Documents inédits relatifs à la connaissance de la Chine en France*, Paris 1932, p. 7) of questions to be put to F. Couplet.

VI RICHARD PAYNE KNIGHT
pages 108–125

1 On Payne Knight's life, see the article in the *Dictionary of National Biography* and its bibliography.

2 *Cf.* Thieme-Becker's *Künstlerlexikon*.

3 This paper in its original form had as an appendix lengthy passages from the diary tentatively translated back into English by Brian Miller.

4 See A. T. Bolton: *The Works of Robert Adam*, London 1922.

5 See *The Complete Works of Sir John Vanbrugh*, Vol. IV, *The Letters*, ed. G. Webb,

London 1928; and Christopher Hussey in *English Homes*, ed. H. Avray Tipping, London 1928, Period IV, Vol. II.

6 See G. H. Lovegrove in *London Topographical Record*, IV, 1907.

7 Kindly conducted by the Headmaster of the Alexander Duckham Memorial Schools.

8 *The Letters*, p. 14, letter of 1707 about Kimbolton.

9 *Ibid.*, p. 163.

10 P. Simpson and C. F. Bell: *Designs by Inigo Jones*, Walpole Society, 1924, pls. 36 and 40; A Nicoll: *Stuart Masques*, London 1937, pp. 20, 145. Compare also the plate showing a performance by French actors at St Salvator in Munich in about 1658. It is illustrated in S. W. Holsboer: *L' Histoire de la mise en scène dans le théâtre français de 1600 à 1657*, Paris 1933, pl. XI.

11 J. Gregor: *Monumenta Scenica*, Vol. II, pls. VII, VIII; also C. Ricci: *La Scenografia italiana*, Milan 1930, pl. 37; and A. Hyatt Mayor, *The Bibiena Family*, New York 1945, pl. 38 (ascribed to Giuseppe).

12 On the history of the building of Strawberry Hill, see Wilmarth S. Lewis's exemplary paper in the *Metropolitan Museum Studies*, I, New York 1934.

13 Letter of 19 December 1753, to Bentley.

14 The owner of Downton Castle at the time when I wrote this paper, Mr C. A. Rouse-Boughton-Knight, kindly lent me the two pictures of Downton, and allowed me to reproduce them.

15 *An Analytical Enquiry into the Principles of Taste*, London 1805; quoted here from the third edition, 1806.

16 *Ibid.*, p. 218.

17 *Ibid.*, p. 225.

18 *Ibid.*, p. 222.

19 *Ibid.*, p. 157.

20 Letter of 22 March 1796.

21 Preface to *Alfred*, 1823.

22 *Symbolical Language*, ed. in *Specimens of Ancient Sculpture*, Vol. II, p. 20.

23 *Enquiry into the Principles of Taste*, p. 123.

24 *Worship of Priapus*.

25 *Ibid.*

26 *Reports from Committees*, I, 1816, Vol. III.

27 P. XXXIX.

28 XIV, January, 1816.

29 *The Judgement of Connoisseurs Upon the Works of Art*, 1916, p. 6.

30 On the first phase see above, pp. 78–101.

31 Quoted from E. W. Manwaring, *Italian Landscape in Eighteenth Century England*, 1925, p. 133.

32 *An Essay on . . . Pope*, Vol. II, ed. of 1806, p. 179.

33 *Letters*, September 10, 1763.

34 On Price see below, pp. 122–137.

35 *Farington Diary*, ed. Greig, Vol. I, p. 146.

36 On Repton see below, pp. 138–155.

37 *The Landscape*, I, 17–20.

38 *Essay on the Picturesque*, ed. 1810, I, p. 14.

39 *The Landscape*, II, 51–52.

40 *Ibid.*, II, 82–84.

41 *Ibid.*, II, 75–76.

42 *Ibid.*, I, 140–142.

43 *Ibid.*, I, 145–146.

44 *Essay*, I, 231.

45 *The Landscape*, I, 114.

46 *Ibid.*, II, 190.

47 *Ibid.*, II, 194.

48 *Ibid.*, II, 195.

49 *Ibid.*, I, 293.

50 See pp. 156–163.

51 *Sketches and Hints*, p. 101 of Loudon's edition.

52 *Ibid.*, p. 103.

53 *Ibid.*, p. 232.

54 *Three Essays on the Picturesque*, quoted from W. D. Templeman: *The Life and Work of William Gilpin*, Illinois Studies in Language and Literature, XXIV, Nos. 3–4, 1939. On Gilpin more recently: C. P. Barbier, *William Gilpin*, Oxford 1963.

55 *Letters*, 21 March, 1821.

56 *The Landscape*, I, 369.

57 *Ibid.*, III, 402.

58 *Ibid.*, III, note 243.

59 *Farington Diary*, ed. Greig, Vols. III, p. 252, and IV, p. 31.

60 He had said apropos Tatton Park that one way of showing the extent of a man's property could be to place coats-of-arms on inns, milestones, or such-like objects. Knight ridiculed this remark.

61 *The Landscape*, III, 334.

62 Not in 1808, as the *D.N.B.* says.

63 He also renewed his attacks on Repton, and Repton answered back.

64 *Analytical Enquiry*, p. 234.

65 *Ibid.*, p. 234.

66 *Ibid.*, p. 238.

67 *Ibid.*, p. 237.

68 *Ibid.*, p. 236.

69 *Ibid.*, p. 196.

70 *Ibid.*, p. 16.

71 *Ibid.*, pp. 145 and 148.

72 *Ibid.*, p. 154.

73 *Ibid.*, p. 69.

74 *Ibid.*, pp. 65, 67.

75 *Ibid.*, p. 151.

76 *Ibid.*, p. 145.

77 *Ibid.*, p. 9.

78 *Ibid.*, p. 88.

79 *Ibid.*, p. 202.

80 *Ibid.*, p. 186.

81 *Ibid.*, p. 70.

82 Very recently Dr Lang has re-formulated the significance of Payne Knight in a way which somewhat differs from my interpretation. The paper is published in *Concerning Architecture* (ed. Sir John Summerson), London 1968.

83 Knight's French biographer, M. Jean-Jacques Mayoux, is of the same opinion. He writes of Knight's 'esthétique d' idéologue qui porte la marque de la raideur des derniers représentants du XVIII siècle intellectualiste' (p. 120), calls him very aptly a *'rationaliste fantaisiste'* (p. 72), and ranges him with the last generation of the classicists rather than with the romantics (p. 119). The book (*Richard Payne Knight et le pittoresque*, Paris 1932) was not available to me until I had completed this article. Its chief use lies in its analysis of Knight's *Enquiry*.

84 *Analytical Enquiry*, p. 310.

85 *Ibid.*, p. 300.

86 *Ibid.*, p. 304.

87 *Ibid.*, p. 302. Incidentally, Samuel Palmer in his Shoreham days was as infuriated by these sentences as Haydon was by Knight's Elgin evidence. The first of the two passages quoted left him speechless. He only scribbled into the margins: 'He produced some compositions of real excellence!! Michelangelo produced some compositions of real excellence!!!' On the second passage he is more explicit: 'Those artists who are so base that they do not attempt grandeur of form and yet lyingly pretend to grand effect are now called modest; but those who, as William Blake, do attempt and achieve both, will, with time, by blind cunning and stupid wilfulness be set down impudent madmen: for our taste is Dutch; Rembrandt is our Da Vinci, and Rubens our Michelangelo! This is not an oversounding of the depth of our degradation' (A. H. Palmer: *The Life and Letters of Samuel Palmer*, London 1892, pp. 35 and 36). Geoffrey Grigson drew my attention to this passage.

88 *Farington Diary*, Vol. V, p. 14.

89 *Ibid.*, Vol. III, p. 99.

90 *Ibid.*, Vol. III, p. 91.

91 *Analytical Enquiry*, p. 103.

92 *Ibid.*, p. 149.

93 *The Landscape*, note to II, 105.

94 *Analytical Enquiry*, p. 304.

95 *Ibid.*, p. 110.

96 *Ibid.*, p. 109.

97 *Ibid.*, p. 109.

VII UVEDALE PRICE
pages 126–137

1 On the controversies see pp. 118–124.

2 See W. D. Templeman, *Illinois Studies in Language and Literature*, XXIV, 1939.

VIII HUMPHRY REPTON
pages 138–155

1 On Repton's quarrels with Payne Knight and Uvedale Price something has been reported on pp. 118–122. They do not concern the following quotations much.

2 On calling the Elizabethan style Gothic see the following essay, pp. 160–161.

3 A topical remark, as written in 1794.

IX 'GOOD KING JAMES'S GOTHIC'
pages 156–163

1 Only Mr Hussey says of Easton Neston that 'its plan is an adaptation of that which prevailed in England in Plantagenet and Tudor times,' *English Homes,* ed. H. Avray Tipping, London 1928, Period IV, Vol. II, p. 132.

2 See above pp. 110–111.

3 *English Homes*, Period IV, Vol. II.

4 Fig. LXI.

5 See e.g. M. Jourdain: *English Decorative*

Plasterwork of the Renaissance, London 1926.

6 It may be retorted that even if the ceiling is not Jacobean, it would be more plausible to attribute it to *c.* 1785, the time when other Neo-Jacobean work went on at Audley End —see later in this article, and Tipping *loc. cit.* (see Note 1), Period II, Vol. II, pp. 261, etc. But the pattern of the staircase ceiling is, it seems to me, incomparably bolder. I am glad to see that the official guidebook of the Ministry of Public Building and Works (HMSO 1958 and later) has accepted my dating and my attribution.

7 See above p. 111, Ills. 3 and 4.

8 See Mrs Esdaile: *Walpole Society,* XV, 1926–27.

9 *The Art of J. M. Rysbrack in Terracotta,* Spink & Son, 1932.

10 *Cf.* D. Stroud: *Capability Brown,* London 1950. Just in time for adding to this note comes a reminder from John Newman that at Cobham Hall in Kent considerable Jacobean alterations were made in 1770.

11 3 November 1754; ed. Cunningham, Vol. II, p. 401. On Belhouse see Royal Commission on Historic Monuments, volume *South East Essex*, 1923, p. 6; *An Eighteenth Century Correspondence,* ed. Lilian Dickins and Mary Stanton, London 1910, and *Country Life,* XLVII, p. 656, etc.

12 *See An Eighteenth Century Correspondence,* p. 334.

13 The Aubrey quotation comes from his *Chronologia Architectonica;* the Evelyn quotation I took from Mark Girouard: 'Elizabethan Retrospects', in *Concerning Architecture* (ed. Sir John Summerson), London 1968. In the same volume Howard M. Colvin has written on Aubrey's *Chronologia.*

14 Quoted from *Blickling Hall,* National Trust Guide Book, 4th edition, 1959, p. 18.

15 Quoted from *Country Life,* XXXII, p. 130. Professor Marcus Whiffen drew my attention to this passage.

16 Other instances in Walpole's letters of Elizabethan as part of Gothic: 25 July 1748: 'the bad taste that came between the charming venerable Gothic and pure architecture' —the bad taste being the seventeenth century including Wren as against Palladianism (II, 119); 4 August 1753: a 'sweet little chapel' of 1620 (II, 348).—On the other hand: Hardwick Hall 'not Gothic but of the betweenity, that intervened when Gothic declined and Palladian was creeping in' (III, 338; 1 September 1760). On this consciousness of a *betweenity, cf.* e.g. also Baron von Pöllnitz the adventurer and observant traveller's remark on the Palace of Heidelberg: 'Ce qui reste du palais est dans un goût d'Architecture, que j'aurois peine à définir: il est ni Gothique, ni Moderne' (*Mémoires,* 1734–37).

17 12 Aug. 1769; ed. Cunningham, Vol. V, p. 180, Yale edition, Vol. I, p. 189, etc.

18 *Sketches and Hints,* ed. Loudon, 1840, p. 53. The 'mixed style of Queen Elizabeth's Gothic' occurs again in Repton's *Designs for the Pavilion at Brighton* in 1808; ed. Loudon, p. 384.

19 First Series, Vol. III, First Series, Vol. II,

Second Series, Vol. II. Dr Girouard in the paper to which reference has already been made has drawn attention to them.

20 On p. xx Loudon calls him Selim and says that he lived in Wiltshire. Whoever he really was, Barry is credited by Loudon with revising front elevation and plan, *ibid.,* p. xix.

21 More on these in Dr Girouard's paper.

22 Neale's *Seats*, Second Series, Vol. V. In the same year Webster also built Underley Hall in Westmorland, a very successful piece of Elizabethanism.

X GOETHE AND ARCHITECTURE
pages 164–173

1 Weimar Edn., 1st series, Vol. 36, p. 202.

2 The Apollo even to Goethe still seemed to be superior to all other classical statues. (*Dichtung und Wahrheit*, Weimar Edn., 1st series, Vol. 28, p. 85).

3 *Collected Works,* ed. Suphan, Vol. V, p. 164.

4 *Ibidem,* Vol. IV, pp. 124 and 142.

5 These are words used by Herder, *ibidem,* Vol. V, p. 206.

6 27 April 1753.

7 4 March 1753.

8 12 June 1754.

9 An excellent edition of *Von deutscher Baukunst,* with commentary by E. Beutler, was published in Munich in 1943. Other recent German publications on the subject of this article are: K. Koetschau: 'Saggio su Goethe e l'architettura gotica', in *P. Clemen-Festschrift,* 1926; H. von Einem, new edition of *Italienische Reise,* ed. Christian Wegner, Hamburg 1954; Theodor Fischer, *Goethes Verhältnis zur Baukunst,* Munich 1948. Fischer, an early twentieth-century architect of some importance, gave this lecture in 1932. A translation of *Von deutscher Baukunst* by Geoffrey Grigson and myself was published in *The Architectural Review,* XCVIII, 1945, and it is from this that the present quotations are taken. For further and more recent literature see the introductory remark to this paper.

10 On Laugier there is now an excellent book: Wolfgang Herrmann, *Laugier and Eighteenth Century French Theory,* London 1962.

11 Weimar Edn., 1st series, Vol. 28, p. 84 *ff.*

12 *Aus Goethes Brieftasche—Dritte Wallfahrt zur Erwins Grabe.* Published as appendix to H. L. Wagner's translation of *Du Théâtre,* by L. S. Mercier.

13 Goethe himself wrote of Palladio: 'We must recognise merit where it is due: the English have long appreciated his qualities'. (27 September 1786).

14 Weimar Edn., 1st series, Vol. 30, p. 135.

15 *Italienische Reise,* 23 March 1787—Weimar Edn., 1st series, Vol. 31, p. 71.

16 Weimar Edn., 1st series, Vol. 31, p. 238.

17 19 September 1786—Weimar Edn., 1st series, Vol. 30, p. 77.

18 2 October 1786—Weimar Edn., 1st series, Vol. 30, p. 109.

19 30 December 1795—Weimar Edn., 1st series, Vol. 10, p. 360.

20 'Zur Theorie der bildenden Künste', 1788, Weimar Edn., 1st series, Vol. 47, p. 62.

21 Weimar Edn., 1st series, Vol. 47, p. 68.

22 What Goethe writes is this: 'We experience a pleasurable sensation when we move in a dance according to certain laws; it ought to be possible to induce a similar sensation by leading a person blindfold through a well-built house.' But this same insistence on direct aesthetic experience in art and architecture led Goethe, on the other hand, to establish *en passant* (in the same article, dating from 1795, from which the previous quotation was taken) a principle of architectural criticism, re-established by Schmarsow and his school from 1892 onwards, and which is still valid today: that is, that architecture is an art to appraise not only with our eyes, but also with our sense of moving through space. I have added a note on Schmarsow's ancestors and descendants in this conception of architecture to an address I gave at the Royal Institute of British Architects. (*Journal*, August 1967). (Weimar Edn., 1st series, Vol. 47, p. 68).

23 17 March 1817–Weimar Edn., 4th series, Vol. 28, p. 23.

24 Weimar Edn., 4th series, Vol. 21, p. 296.

25 The theory of the Saracen origin of Gothic architecture was already familiar to Sir Christopher Wren. ('What we now call the Gothic style in architecture . . . I think should more correctly be termed the Saracen style' ('Report on Westminster Abbey', 1713, printed in *Parentalia*, 1750, p. 297). He had it from John Evelyn, who puts it forward in the second edition of his translation of Roland Fréart's *Parallèle (Parallel between Ancient and Modern Architecture, originally written in French, by Roland Fréart, Sieur de Chambray)*. The reference is in the appendix on architects. The second edition is dedicated to Wren, and the dedication is dated 1697. Publication, however, took place only in 1707. On French Gothicism see now P. Frankl, *The Gothic, literary sources and interpretations*, Princeton, 1960; and in much greater detail and with a juster appreciation of what is significantly French in the French Gothic Revival: Robin Middleton's brilliant Ph.D. thesis and his 'The Abbé de Cordemoy and the Graeco-Gothic Ideal', in the *Journal of the Warburg and Courtauld Institutes*, XXV, 1962. Dr Middleton mentions that Florent Le Comte in 1699 also claimed that the Arabs invented Gothic. However, as with Wren, it is more likely that he got the suggestion from Evelyn verbally.

26 Weimar Edn., 1st series, Vol. 28, p. 99.

27 W. Freiherr von Biedermann, *Goethes Gespräche*, Vol. 3, 1889, n. 637, 8 August 1815, n. 28, *ib.*, n. 666, 3 October 1815.

28 *Ibidem*, n. 665, 2 October 1815.

29 *Kleine Schriften zur Kunst, Deutsche Literaturdenkmäle des 18 und 19 Jahrhunderts*, Heidelberg, 1886, pp. 106, 116 and 117.

30 *Conversations with Eckermann*, 2 Apr. 1829.

31 21 March 1830.

32 Weimar Edn., 1st series, vol. 48, p. 206. English translation by Philip Wayne.

33 *Conversations with Eckermann*, 21 October 1823. This idea was not new to him. Already in the letter, dated 1810, to Reinhart, quoted above, he called the Middle Ages 'a form of grub or larval state' (Weimar Edn., 4th series, Vol. 21, p. 296).

34 Weimar Edn., 1st series, Vol. 49, part II, p. 165.

35 *Ibidem*, p. 161.

36 *Conversations with Eckermann*, 11 March 1828.

37 Weimar Edn, 1st series, Vol. 49, part II, p. 161.

38 Published in two volumes in 1675 and 1683—that is to say, in Boileau's time. The quotation given here comes from the end of Chapter 16.

XI KARL FRIEDRICH SCHINKEL
pages 174–195

1 For French architecture from 1750 to 1815 see L. Hautecoeur: *Histoire de l'architecture classique en France*, Vols. IV and V, 1952 and 1953.

2 The standard work on Schinkel is still: *Aus Schinkels Nachlass*, edited by A. Freiherr von Wolzogen, 3 vol., 1862–63. A selection from this was edited by H. Mackowsky in 1932. A great many of Schinkel's designs were published in exquisite engravings in *Sammlung Architektonischer Entwürfe*, 1819–40. The best modern biography is by A. Grisebach, 1924. In 1939 the Academy of Architecture in Berlin decided the publication of a *corpus* of the whole *oeuvre* of Schinkel on the lines of the volumes of the Wren Society in this country. Eight volumes have so far come out (1942–62).

3 Quoted from Grisebach, p. 9.

4 On Gilly see Alste Oncken, Berlin 1935, an admirable monograph. Wolzogen, *op. cit.* (see Note 2), Vol. I, p. 173.

5 What we know about them nowadays we owe chiefly to the researches of Emil Kaufmann, first in Vienna and later in America. He published first an article in *Zeitschrift für bildende Kunst*, 1929–30, then *Von Ledoux bis Le Corbusier*, 1933, and later 'Three revolutionary Architects', in *Transactions of the American Philosophical Society*, New Series, XLII, Pt. 3, 1952, and *Architecture in the Age of Reason*, Cambridge, Mass., 1955. On Ledoux see also G. Levallet-Haug, 1934. On Boullée, see H. Rosenau, London 1953. The most recent treatment of architecture of the Ledoux to Schinkel age is a chapter in R. Rosenblum: *Transformations in late eighteenth century Art*, Princeton, 1967.

6 *L'Architecture considérée sous le rapport de l'art, des moeurs et de la législation*.

7 See below, pp. 204–9, especially pp. 208–9

8 Legrand, incidentally, was a pupil and son-in-law of the mysterious Clérisseau, the friend of both Robert Adam and Charles Cameron.

9 Lithographed by F. Frick and published in 1799.

10 Ill. Grisebach, p. 29; Oncken pls. 92, 93.

11 Wolzogen, Vol. I, 160, etc.

12 On the panorama see F. Whitley: *Artists and their Friends in England, 1700–1799*, 2 vol., London 1928 and *1800–1820*, 1928.

13 Ill. Grisebach, p. 39.

14 Ill. Grisebach, p. 55.

15 Wolzogen, Vol. III, p. 161.

16 Wolzogen, Vol. III, p. 153.

17 On the British Museum see my article in *The Architectural Review*, CXIII, 1953, pp. 179–182.

18 Recently an excellent and exhaustive paper has been published on the history of museum buildings from the beginning to about 1820, H. Seling: 'The Genesis of the Museum', in *The Architectural Review*, CXLI, 1967.

19 Ill. Grisebach, pp. 161–65 and 170–74.

20 They are familiar from Loudon's *Encyclopaedia* of 1833 (e.g., pp. 854, 857, 950). Early examples actually carried out are, for instance, at Edensor (1838).

21 By Persius the Heilandskirche at Sacrow, 1841, and the Friedenskirche at Potsdam, 1843. On Persius in English see R. and P. Fleetwood-Hesketh in *Architects' Journal*, LXVIII, 1928, pp. 77 etc. and 113 etc.

22 *Cf.* L. D. Ettlinger in *The Architectural Review*, XCVII, 1945.

23 Ill. Grisebach, p. 65.

24 Painting by Canaletto in the National Gallery.

25 Ill. Grisebach, p. 111, more in F. Stahl: *Schinkel*, Berlin 1912, pp. 49, 62, 63; L. and D. Joseph: *Geschichte der Baukunst des XIX Jahrhunderts*, p. 19.

26 Wolzogen, Vol. II, p. 208.

27 *Ibid.*, pp. 211*ff* and Vol. III, pp. 373*ff*.

28 Although he visited factories on the Continent too, potteries such as that of Herr Villeroi at Mettlach on the Saar, and the machine building works of Cockrill at Seraing in Belgium and Aron Manby at Charenton near Paris. Aron Manby moved to Charenton from Tipton near Birmingham and Cockrill of course was English too.

29 Ill. Stahl, p. 21.

30 See Vol. II of these Essays, p. 15.

XII THE DORIC REVIVAL
pages 196–211

1 Letter to Volkmann 27 March 1761.

2 Letter of 21 November 1761. We owe this quotation to John Fleming who communicated the unpublished letter to us on 2 February 1956. We thank him for his generosity.

3 Ed. Morgan, Cambridge, Mass., 1914.

4 See S. Lang, 'Sull' Origine della Disposizione a Scacchiera nelle Città Medioevali', in *Palladio*, Anno VIII, IV, 1955, p. 105.

5 *Cat. of Books Printed in the 15th C. now in the British Museum*, Pt. IV, 1916, p.124. The Reading Room copy carries a MS note to the effect that the date is still unknown.

6 Serlio also illustrates the 'Triumphal Arch'

of Verona, which has fluted Doric columns, without bases, attached to its upper storey.

7 Florence, Gab. dei Disegni, Arch. 477r. Reproduced in Bartoli, Vol. II, pl. CLXXXVI, fig. 321.

8 Guarini incidentally in his *Architettura Civile* of 1737 (p. 96) gives a fairly full list of Doric columns without a base: 'Le Base gli Antichi esclusono, come in Roma si vede nel Tempio della Pietà al Carcere Juliano descritto del Serlio lib 3. Così parimente si trova il secondo ordine dell' Anfiteatro di Pola, e l'Arco trionfale a Verona tiene eziandio le Colonne Doriche del terz' ordine senza base, così le prime del Teatro di Marcello a Roma; siccome nel Duomo di Siracusa si veggono grossissime colonne Doriche accanalate, ma senza base; nè Vitruvio ancorchè descriva minutamente molte basi, nullamente parla niente della Dorica'.

9 E. W. Bodnar, S.J., 'Cyriacus of Ancona and Athens', in *Collection Latomus*, XLIII, Brussels 1960, p. 35ff.

10 Vat. lat. 4424, fol. 28v; C. Huelsen, *Il Libro di Giuliano da Sangallo*, Leipzig 1910. The story of the manuscript tradition and the stay of Ciriaco in Athens has been fully told by E. W. Bodnar, *op. cit.*

11 See Huelsen, text vol., p. 43.

12 Huelsen, *op. cit.*, p. 42. Bodnar, *op. cit.*, p. 29 is more cautious, but also suggests that the Codex Manzoni is a copy of perhaps yet another set of excerpts for another friend.

13 Ed. H. Lemonnier, 1911 etc., e.g. Vol. II, p. 332 (July 1696: 'il est . . . plus à propos d'y mettre une base'), Vol. III, p. 128 (May 1701: 'la base attique qui est employée d'ordinaire dans cet ordre'), Vol. V, p. 295 (1741: 16 radii preferred to 18).

14 J. M. Paton, *Chapters on Mediaeval and Renaissance Visitors to Greek Lands*, Princeton 1951, contains no relevant material, but shows that many visitors to the Holy Land passed through Greece and visited the Parthenon. None of them had much to say, and they certainly did not worry about bases to columns.

15 *Voyage d'Italie, de Dalmatie, de Grèce et du Levant*, 1678, Vol. II, pp. 143, 188.

16 Francesco Fanelli's *Atene Attica*, c. 1690, has a description of the temples on the Acropolis in which the Parthenon appears as 'of the Doric order with forty-eight columns of $17\frac{1}{2}$ feet in circumference above the bases' and two very summary illustrations of the whole Acropolis. In J. Potter's *Archaeologia Graeca*, Oxford 1699, the Parthenon and the Theseion are also shown, but with bases to the columns!

17 A. Fraser Tytler of Woodhouselee: *Memoirs of the Life and Writings of the Hon. Henry Home of Kames*, Edinburgh 1814, 2nd ed., Vol. III, app. to Vol. II.

18 J. J. Winckelmann, 'Anmerkungen über die Baukunst der alten Tempel zu Girgenti in Sicilien', in *Sömtliche Werke*, Donaueschingen 1825, Vol. II.

19 'Anmerkungen über die Baukunst der Alten', in *Sömtliche Werke*.

20 The following story was told us by John Fleming in his letter of 2 February 1956 already referred to.

21 J. Dennistoun: *Memoirs of Strange and Lumisden*, London 1855, Vol. II, pp. 48–49.

22 *Suite de plans, coupes, profils . . . des trois temples antiques . . . dans la bourgade de Poesto.* On the Gazola-Soufflot case see the correspondence of the Abbé Barthélemy, another Parisian amateur, and also that of the Comte de Caylus. For more details on the re-discovery of Paestum, and also on the connection of Hubert Robert with Paestum, see S. Lang in the *Journal of the Warburg and Courtauld Institutes*, XIII, 1950. Robert and Fragonard had accompanied the Abbé de St Non to Naples in 1760 and drawn as much of antique architecture in the neighbourhood as they possibly could. Gazola had helped them with his advice just as he had helped Marigny, Cochin and Soufflot. The result of the studies of the St Non team came out in St Non's *Voyage Pittoresque* of 1781–86, i.e. at the same time as the final publication of the Gazola material by Paoli.

23 The attribution of the book to Berkenhout appears now to be unfounded.

24 Winckelmann's conception of Greek art was inspired by Shaftesbury. See S. Lang: 'Vanbrugh's Theory and Hawksmoor's Buildings', in *Journal of the Society of Architectural Historians*, XXIV, 1965, p. 140 ff.

25 However some writers of the fifteenth century explicitly gave preference to the Romans, e.g. Antonio Manetti who states in his *Life of Brunelleschi* (ed. Holtzinger, 1887, p. 23) that 'in Rome the masters [of architecture] flourished more marvellously than in Greece'.

26 The best account of the battle is to be found in two papers by Professor Wittkower and Miss L. Lawrence in the *Journal of the Warburg Institute*, II, 1938–39. *Cf.* also for much valuable material L. Hautecoeur: *Rome et la renaissance de l'antiquité à la fin du XVIIIe siècle*, Paris 1912.

27 Illustrated in D. Irwin: *English Neo-classical Art*, London 1966. On Hamilton in particular, see D. Irwin in *Art Bulletin*, XLIV, 1962.

28 'Historical Remarks on Ancient Architecture', in *Annual Register*, 1767, p. 144, and *The Grecian Orders of Architecture*, p. 46.

29 The first of these proposed lectures is in a finished state and deals with general principles of architecture. The second with which we are concerned here is also complete, but most of it is crossed out. In the third edition of his *Civil Architecture*, 1755, Chambers says that his remarks had been 'intended for the second edition of this work' but then suppressed (p. 26), and the second edition came out in 1768.

30 That in itself was not new. It was a view put forward, e.g., by Caylus and explicitly opposed by Winckelmann. A less familiar quotation is the following from *Nouveaux Mémoires ou Observations sur l'Italie par Deux Gentilshommes Suédois*, London 1764, supposed to be by P. J. Grosley. They mention the striking similarity of Paestum to extant buildings in Upper Egypt; 'It is easy to convince oneself that their construction preceded the birth of the arts even in Greece.' The Greeks only copied from them.

31 It is worth noting that in the appreciation of Greek literature and philosophy exactly the same battle was being fought in England at the same time. We have taken most of the following facts from M. L. Clarke: *Greek Studies in England, 1700–1830*, Cambridge 1945.

32 To be precise, the first appeared in 1765, the second in 1767.

33 Pythagoras: *Antient Metaphysics*, Vol. III, 1799; Orang Outang: *Of the Origin and Progress of Language*, Vol. I, 1773, p. 239.

34 See H. Grigson in *The Architectural Review*, CIV, 1948.

35 See the translation and comment by G. Grigson and N. Pevsner in *The Architectural Review*, XCVIII, 1945 and also the paper on Goethe and Architecture in the present volume, p. 165 ff.

36 In this connection it may also be worth recording that the same Riou who defended the Greeks so valiantly wrote in the very same *Annual Register* (1767) in defence of Gothic—although in a different context. He contrasts the 'monstrous taste of heavy architexture' prevalent in Norman times, what Wren called Anglo-Saxon, with Wren's 'Saracenic', i.e. the 'Modern Gothic . . . distinguished by the lightness of its works, the excessive boldness of its elaborations and of its sections, by the delicacy, profusion and extravagant fancy of its ornament.' The passage has not been noticed before, I think, in discussions of the Gothic Revival. Its source is probably Laugier who praises (*Essai*, p. 4, 1753) 'the boldness of design, delicacy of carving' and 'majesty and freedom of the Gothic style.' On Laugier see W. Hermann, *Laugier and Eighteenth Century French Theory*, London 1962. On Wren's Saracenic origin of the Gothic style see my paper on Goethe and Architecture, note 25.

37 Goethe in 1811, as we have seen in a previous paper, wrote the biography of the landscape painter Philipp Hackert, and Hackert had visited Sicily in 1777, accompanying Richard Payne Knight. A large painting of the temples of Agrigento by Hackert, dated 1778, has recently been published by Professor Krönig in 'Philipp Hackert und Russland', in *Wallraf-Richartz-Jahrbuch*, XXVIII, 1966, p. 318.

38 Named after the Temple of Apollo on Delos.

39 On Payne Knight see this volume pp. 108–125. The chimneypiece however was overlooked by us, and we owe information on it to Dr David Watkin whose outstandingly excellent doctoral thesis on Thomas Hope (Cambridge 1967) is yet unpublished but will, we hope, be published soon. He provides also a list of Greek Doric examples from Britain and also France and Germany, which is fuller than our list here following.

40 The drawings are in the British Museum. The temple front is illustrated in Donald R.

Stewart, 'James Essex', in *The Architectural Review*, CVIII, 1950, p. 320.

41 At the same time he designed a kennel for the Bishop of Derry ('Residence for a canine family') which also has Doric columns. On the Triumphal Bridge see D. Stroud in *The Architectural Review*, CXXI, 1957, pp. 261–2, where earlier triumphal bridges by Piranesi (1750) and Thomas Sandby (1760) are mentioned.

42 In any case there are drawings of Paestum which are undoubtedly by the elder Piranesi and which incidentally are more evocative of the grandeur of the Doric than the etchings.

43 The Dumont design is for a Monument to Painting, Sculpture and Architecture. It was presented by Dumont to the Accademia di S. Luca in Rome in 1746 and published in 1764 (in *Morceaux d'Architecture* and also in *Suite de projets détaillés de salles de spectacle*). The same plan appears again not essentially modified in one of Ledoux's Gates (ill. in M. Raval's book, Paris 1945, p. 66).

44 Unless, in publishing it, he had doctored it, as he is known to have done more than once. See W. Herrmann in *Art Bulletin*, XLII, 1960 and J. Langner in *Zeitschrift für Kunstgeschichte*, XXIII, 1960.

45 A. Boinet: *Les Eglises parisiennes*, Paris 1958, Vol. I, p. 325. We owe this and several more French references to R. Rosenblum: *Transformations in late eighteenth century Art*, Princeton 1967.

46 See M. Petzet: *Soufflots Sainte-Geneviève*, Berlin 1961, p. 122.

47 J. Stern: *A l'ombre de Sophie Arnould; François Joseph Belanger*, Paris 1930, Vol. I, 140: Sirén, *loc. cit.*, pl. 185; and Connolly and Zerbe, *loc. cit.* p. 158 etc.

48 A few more early French examples are the following: a portal in the Charité Convent in Paris by Antoine of *c.* 1779–80, illustrated by Hautecoeur, *Histoire de l'architecture classique en France*, Vol. IV, 1952, p. 23, an undated *tondo* by Hubert Robert in the museum of Amiens, now illustrated by Professor Rosenblum, *loc. cit.*, fig. 120, a design by Lequeu dated 1780 which is for the portal of an Augustinian church (ill. Petzet *loc. cit.* fig. 72), the Cork Monument, Méréville by R. Pajou, 1782 (Watkin), the remodelling of the chancel of St Médard in Paris by L.–F. Petit-Radel in 1784 (see Rosenblum *loc. cit.*, fig. 116), Ledoux's Barrière de Monceau, a rotunda and part of the series of monumental toll-houses on which Ledoux worked from 1784 to 1789, several works by Desprez which will be referred to in the text, Vaudoyer's design for a 'Maison d'un Cosmopolite', dated 1785 (E. Kaufmann: *Architecture in the Age of Reason*, Cambridge, Mass., 1955, p. 185 and fig. 192), Dufourny's *Ginnasio* in the Botanic Gardens at Palermo which was built in 1789–92 and appears in C. L. V. Meeks: *Italian Architecture, 1750–1914*, New Haven 1966, fig. 28, F. A. Vincent's *Zeuxis* exhibited in the Salon of 1789 and illustrated by Professor Rosenblum (fig. 19), and Detournelle's design for a prison (mentioned by Hautecoeur, *op. cit.*, Vol. V, p. 131) which combines crenellations with Doric columns. Professor Rosenblum also quotes from Delécluze's biography of David the telling fact that *Les Barbus*, the French primitivist group of young painters, admired in architecture only the Greek Doric of Sicily and Paestum (p. 436).

49 I. Grabar: *Istoria Russkago Isskustva*, 1910–15, Vol. III, p. 375 (in Russian), also Loukomski: *Charles Cameron*, London 1943, p. 66 and illustration on half-title.

50 Contributed by Dr Watkin.

51 See Dr Watkin's thesis referred to before.

52 We owe information on this to a letter from Dr Schenk von Schweinsberg. He also sent us the photograph illustrated and referred us to A. Klebe: *Gotha und die umliegende Gegend*, Gotha 1796.

53 See G. Wietek in *Festschrift für G. Grundmann*, 1962, p. 170.

54 H. Koch: *Sächsische Gartenkunst*, Berlin 1910, p. 376 *ff.*

55 Wietek, *loc. cit.* (see Note 46), p. 166.

56 The corresponding buildings and dates for Scandinavia and Russia are as follows. Scandinavia: Olof Templeman's Orangery at Uppsala *c.* 1780 (Professor Sirén kindly told me of this), Desprez's stage decoration for *Frigga c.* 1784–6 (Hautecoeur, *loc. cit.*, Vol. V, p. 83), the wooden Skärfva for Admiral Chapman, also in Sweden, and also of *c.* 1785 (O. Sirén: *China and the Gardens of Europe*, Stockholm 1950, p. 210 and pl. 186) and the south porch of Hämeenlinna (formerly Tavastehus) in Finland, again by Desprez and of 1798 (J. M. Richards: *A Guide to Finnish Architecture*, London 1966, fig. 41). For more examples see N. G. A. Wollin, *Desprez en Suède*, Malmö, 1939. Russia: Rotunda at Tsarskoe Selo, see text above; then lighthouses as Doric columns designed by Zakharov in 1792 (G. G. Grimm: *Zakharov*, 1940, figs. 1–4.)

57 A. Oncken: *Friedrich Gilly*, Berlin 1935, p. 48.

58 Shown at the Royal Academy winter exhibition of French eighteenth-century art in 1967–8 (no. 430). *Cf.* P.-G. Dreyfus, *Lépicié*, 1922.

59 See R. Crozet: 'David et l'architecture néo-classique', in *Gazette des Beaux-Arts*, 6th series, XLV, 1955. Professor Rosenblum stresses the fact so telling in the context of the present article that a preparatory drawing for the Horatii still has bases for the Tuscan columns (*ibid.*, fig. 139), and he also mentions the Hôpital Cochin of 1778–81 as a specially early example and the church of St Pierre et St Paul at Courbevoie of 1789 as a specially impressive example (fig. 137). But the earliest French examples belong to Ledoux. They occur at the Hôtel Montmorency in 1772, the grand entrance to the salt works at Arc et Senans in 1775, and then the Hôtel Thelusson in 1778–81. The squat Tuscan columns of the basement of the Chinese Pavilion at Cassan, L'Isle-Adam of *c.* 1780 are illustrated in O. Sirén: *China and the Gardens of Europe*, and in C. Connolly and J. Zerbe: *Les Pavillons* (London 1962), p. 125, and Dr Rosenau in her paper 'The Engravings of the Grands Prix of the French Academy of Architecture', in *Architectural History*, III, 1960, shows P. Bernard's design for a Royal Exchange which won a prize in 1782 and Fontaine's Cenotaph which received second prize in 1785. Dr Watkin in his thesis mentioned more than once before has more early examples. In England the earliest seems to be the Warwick Gaol as executed in 1779–82. Again Dr Watkin has a lengthy list. For Russia Igor Grabar shows the church at Tsarskoe Selo by Cameron of 1782–88; for Germany there seems to be nothing before 1790. Professor Rosenblum wisely places on one page an early Gilly drawing and a Weinbrenner drawing of 1795 as instances of the squattest of squat Tuscan columns (figs. 175 and 176).

XIII THE EGYPTIAN REVIVAL
pages 212–215

1 *The Works of James Barry*, 1809, Vol. I, p. 163.

2 See *A Companion to Mr Bullock's London Museum and Pantherion . . . now open for public inspection in the Egyptian Temple . . . in Piccadilly*, London 1812. Also H. Honour in *Country Life*, CXV, 1954, pp. 38 *ff.*

3 Robinson (1776–1858), who had been supervising assistant to Porden on the Moorish stables at Brighton, and later published two successful pattern books of Tudor houses and of cottages, is known for his work at Leamington. He built York Castle in Doric, Trelissick in Cornwall in Ionic, and the Swiss Cottage in Regent's Park in the chalet style.

4 Second Series, Vol. VIII, p. 153; according to information kindly communicated by Mr Stratton Davis, Papworth, the architect of Cheltenham, in 1827 provided Bullock with plans for a new town to be called Hygeia, which Bullock who had gone to America intended to build on land which he owned on the Ohio River in Kentucky. (See S. Giedion: *Space, Time and Architecture*, first edition, Cambridge, Mass., 1941, pp. 505 and 510.)

5 *Lectures on Architecture*, ed. A. T. Bolton, Sir John Soane's Museum Publications, No. 14, 1929. The lectures were delivered between 1809 and 1836.

6 On Denon see P. Lelièvre, Paris 1942.

7 In the *Recueil de décorations intérieures* of 1812. There are only two examples: a *secrétaire exécuté pour M.V. à Amsterdam*—the town where Thomas Hope came from—and a clock made for a gentleman in Spain. Two years earlier Soane's pupil, J. M. Gandy, in his *Rural Architect* had suggested and illustrated 'Lodges after the model of the Egyptian Entrances to their temples', and in 1809 publication had started of the *Description de l'Egypte*, a sumptuous affair in folio which at the time of its completion in 1829 had reached ten text volumes and fourteen volumes of plates.

8 See *Lectures*, pp. 20–21.

9 One case of direct American offspring must be recorded, the Bazaar and Casino of Mrs Frances Milton Trollope at Cincinnati opened at the end of the twenties, it seems. Mrs Trollope was a friend of the Bullocks (see Una Pope Hennessy: *Three English Women in America*, London 1929, p. 70). Alexander Jackson Davis incidentally claims in his diary to have 'introduced into the United States the Egyptian fashion, by exhibiting designs at the National Academy of Design in 1829'. (See R. H. Newton: *Town and Davis*, New York 1942, p. 61.)

10 In 1843 it was described in the *Penny Magazine*, p. 503. The details, we read there, were 'derived from the drawings and designs of Bonomi and David Roberts'. The younger Bonomi (1796–1878) was an architect and had been in Egypt in 1824–33 and again in 1842. David Roberts (1796–1864) is better known as a painter of architectural subjects. He published books on the Holy Land, Syria, Arabia, Egypt and Nubia in 1842 and in 1846–49. We owe the reference to the Marshall factory and to the literature on it to Mr C. Sharp. It was incidentally also illustrated in the *British Almanac* for 1844, pp. 241–2. On Messrs. Marshall's see now W. G. Rimmer: *Marshalls of Leeds*. Cambridge 1960.

11 On Thomas Hope see now Dr D. Watkin's excellent Ph.D. thesis, Cambridge 1967, to which reference has already been made in the preceding essay.

12 Illustrated in H. Clifford Smith, *Buckingham Palace*, London 1931, pl. 109.

13 Illustrated in A. Hoffmann, *Der Landschafts-Garten* (*Geschichte der Gartenkunst*, Vol. III), Hamburg 1963, p. 154.

13A We owe both these references to Dr David Watkins.

14 See John Harris in *The Architectural Review*, CXXII, 1957, p. 2. Mr Harris suggests the late fifties as the date, but on the strength of our findings this seems too early.

15 Quoted from E. Kaufmann: *Architecture in the Age of Reason*, Harvard 1955, p. 50.

16 Hautecoeur, *L'Architecture classique en France*, vol. IV, 1952, enumerates early dates, pp. 23*ff* and 504*ff*. There is no point in repeating all of them here. See also Hautecoeur vol. V, 1953, pp. 289*ff*.

17 It was shown at the Royal Academy Winter Exhibition of French eighteenth-century art, 1967–8 (no. 590). Also shown there were a painting with an Egyptian motif dated 1768 (no. 582, from the Bowes Museum, Barnard Castle) and a drawing of the late eighteenth century with Egyptian motifs (no. 189).

18 Hautecoeur, Vol. IV, p. 25.

19 N. G. A. Wollin, *Les Gravures originales de Desprez*, Malmö 1935, pl. 9–11.

20 N. G. A. Wollin: *Desprez en Italie*, Malmö 1935. Also in *Les Gravures originales de Desprez*, pl. 18–19.

21 See M. Gallet: *Demeures parisiennes; l'époque de Louis XVI*, Paris, n.d., p. 54. As M. Gallet kindly pointed out to Mr Harris

Clodion exhibited a relief from the chapel in the Salon of 1773 (no. 250), and a section through the chapel which was destroyed in the Revolution is in the Archives Nationales (ZIJ 1036). One of the two figures is almost a copy after one in Piranesi's *Cammini* (see below).

22 The last two items are quoted by Hautecoeur *op. cit.*, Vol. V, p. 33 and Vol. IV, p. 25.

23 *Frigga* 1787.

24 N. G. A. Wollin: *Desprez en Suède*, Malmö 1939.

25 Mme J.W.C.D.R.: *Altichiero*, Padua 1787. The authoress is Justine Wynne, Countess de Rosenberg. Count Rosenberg had been Austrian Ambassador in Venice. Before she married him, she had been one of Casanova's innumerable mistresses, and before that she was pursued by Andrea Memmo, a Venetian patrician who followed her as far as Paris. Memmo, apart from being the editor of that interesting architectural theorist, the Padre Lodoli, was one of the earliest Venetian freemasons, having been initiated by Casanova. The immediate cause of Casanova's arrest and confinement to the Piombi was this very initiation. Another early case of Egyptianism in Italy has recently been illustrated by Mario Praz. It is a table dated 1776 (M. Praz: *Illustrated History of Interior Decoration*, London 1966, p. 171). Of shortly before 1800 is a sketchbook by Valadier which, according to Dr Eva Brües (*Kunstchronik* XVIII, 1965, p. 315) contains 'Egyptianizing elements'. Incidentally, one odd early case occurs even in America. The great seal of the United States, dated 1776 and adopted in 1782, is unmistakably Egypticizing (see M. Frebault in *The Architectural Review*, CXXI, 1957, p. 152).

26 The Villa Altichiero had, apart from the Canope, a Chinese Pavilion and a *Bois de Young*.

27 The literature on Piranesi is too extensive to be quoted here. Hylton Thomas's book on Piranesi's drawings (London 1954) contains a bibliography. Reference must also be made to a correspondence in *The Times Literary Supplement* 26 June to 31 July 1953) apropos an article published on 13 February. The most recent Piranesi book is by H. Volkmann, 1965. We have not seen this. Hubert Robert's *Capriccio* must be an immediate reaction to the Caffè Greco.

28 Vol. III, p. LVIII.

29 Hautecoeur refers once or twice to Cornelius Pauw's *Recherches Philosophiques sur les Egyptiens et les Chinois*, 1773, a book read e.g. by Goethe. The idea must however be older; for Stukeley in 1743 asserted a common principle for Chinese script and Egyptian hieroglyphs (see W. R. Dawson, in *Studies presented to F.Ll. Griffith*, London 1932), and the same theory was put forward in a letter from P. Bouret to Leibniz, written in 1698 (See F. Merkel: *Leibniz und China*, Berlin 1952, p. 19).

30 In Migne's *Patrologia Latina*, Vol. 82, coll. 552 and 654.

31 For Sta Maria in Trastevere see *Architek-*

tonische Studien des Kais. Dtsch. Archaeol. Inst., Heft III, 1889, p. 77. For Viterbo, etc., see A. Venturi: *Storia dell'Arte Italiana*, Vol. III, Milan 1904, pp. 796*ff*.

32 It must be borne in mind that wingless sphinxes had been represented on Etruscan vases for example, and these might have been known. A. Chastel ('L' "Etruscan Revival" du XVe siècle', in *Revue Arch.*, 1959, I, p. 179, n.2) tells us that Fra Giovanni Nenni, the promoter of Etruscology, tried to establish the ancient role of Viterbo. Professor Chastel also quotes Stendhal (p. 165), who reports in his *Histoire de la Peinture en Italie*: 'On trouve dans la bibliothèque Riccardi à Florence un manuscrit qui porte la date 1282. L'auteur est Ristoro d'Arezzo. Il raconte que l'on venait de découvrir dans son pays une grande quantité de vases étrusques.'

33 *Voyageurs et écrivains français en Egypte*, Cairo 1932.

34 *Le Voyage d'outremer de Jean Thenaud*, etc., ed. C. Schefer, Paris 1884, pp. 53–54. Thenaud travelled in 1511.

35 Carré, Vol. I, p. 6, note ii.

36 See K. Giehlow: 'Die Hieroglyphenkunde des Humanismus', in *Jahrbuch der kunsthistorischen Sammlungen des Allerhöchsten Kaiserhauses*, XXXII, 1915, the classic on the subject. We have made much use of Giehlow's paper.

37 For the next paragraphs see, apart from Giehlow's paper, the book by L. Volkmann: *Bilderschriften der Renaissance*, Leipzig 1923.

38 Professor Glanville kindly drew our attention to F. Sbordone: *Hori Apollonis Hieroglyphica*, Naples 1940. We are very grateful to him for having looked through this essay in its original form before it went to press.

39 See J. Seznec: *Survival of the Pagan Gods*, Bollingen Series, Vol. 38, New York 1953, p. 100*ff*.; also Fritz Saxl: 'The Appartamento Borgia', in his *Lectures*, London 1957; and most recently E. H. Gombrich: 'Vom Wert der Kunstwissenschaft für die Symbolforschung', in *Probleme der Kunstwissenschaft*, II, Berlin 1966, p. 30*ff*.

40 Book VIII, chapters 2 and 4.

41 See Campana's *Vita* in Muratori, *Rev. Ital. Script*, new ed., III, 3, p. 60. We owe this item to Mrs N. Rubinstein.

42 *Cf.* J. R. Spencer, ed.: *Filarete's Treatise on Architecture*, New Haven and London 1965, pp. 152*ff*.

43 Professor E. Wind has tried to explain the pyramid here as an echo of Origen's idea of Noah's Ark as a pyramid—a mathematical-mystical fantasy already refuted in the twelfth century by Hugh of St Victor. See *Studies in Art and Literature for Bella de Costa Greene*, Princeton 1954, p. 419.

44 See E. Müntz: *Raphael*, Paris 1881, p. 590, from Fulvio's *Antiquitates Urbis*.

45 See E. Visconti: *Museo Pio-Clementino*, 1784, Vol. 2.

46 The *Villa Adriana* is mentioned for the first time in the Renaissance in Flavio Biondo's *Italia Illustrata*, 1450. See H. Winnefeld: 'Die Villa des Hadrian,' in *Jahrb, d. deutschen Archäol. Inst.*, 3 Ergänzungsheft,

Berlin 1895, specially pp. 2*ff.*

47 *Cf.* C. Huelsen, *Il Libro di Giuliano da Sangallo*, Leipzig 1910, text vol. p. XXVII. Giuliano also drew obelisks, some in the *Libro*, one with hieroglyphs in a drawing in the Bayonne Museum, and in his Sienese sketchbook.

48 F. Saxl, *Lectures*, 1957, Vol. I, pp. 174*ff.*

49 Before condemning Nanni one should bear in mind that representations of Etruscan sphinxes not too different from the Egyptian ones are now known to have existed (*cf.* Note 32 above).

50 E. H. Gombrich, in *Journal of the Warburg and Courtauld Institutes*, XIV, 1951, p. 120. More recently Professor Murray in 'Bramante milanese: the Paintings and Engravings', in *Arte Lombarda*, VII, 1962, has argued (p. 31) against this conception and suggested that the hieroglyphs planned for the Belvedere reveal a rather different intention, namely a kind of guessing game rather like an anagram, that is they were to be intelligible; he also mentions (p. 30) Bramante's fresco of *Heraclitus and Democritos* with a hieroglyphic frieze and in particular (p. 32) in Mantegna's *St James led to Execution* a panel with a hieroglyphic commentary on martyrdom: the vase stands for life, the circle for eternity, the palm for victory and the rudder for guidance.

51 Nicholas V, the first humanist on the Papal throne, intended to re-erect the obelisk of Old St Peter's in front of his new church to be rebuilt in the Renaissance style. The reason for this intention was that the obelisk was considered a witness of the martyrdom of St Peter. Paul II took this legacy over, and of Raphael it is known that he offered to transport an obelisk from the Mausoleum of Augustus to St Peter's for 90,000 ducats (see V. Golzio: *Raffaello*, Città del Vaticano 1936, p. 101, from the diary of the Venetian ambassador Marino Sanuto).

52 For the date of the discovery there is a *terminus ante quem*, since Bembo sent drawings of it to some friends before he left Rome in 1520 (Giehlow p. 111).

53 *Cf.* E. Mandowsky and C. Mitchell, *Pirro Ligorio*, London 1963, p. 140. We are greatly indebted to the Warburg Institute for making it possible for us to study the material of their *Census of Antique Works of Art known to Renaissance Artists*, which is being compiled in conjunction with the Institute of Fine Arts at New York University.

54 *Ibid.*, p. 32.

55 H. Egger: 'Entwürfe Baldassare Peruzzis für den Einzug Karls V in Rom. Eine Studie zur Frage über die Echtheit des Sienesischen Skizzenbuches', in *Jahrbuch der Kunsthist. Sammlungen des Allerhöchsten Kaiserhauses*, XXIII, 1902.

56 These lions were taken by Pope Sixtus V to the Fontana Felice, erected by him near the Baths of Diocletian 'per essere sua impresa' in 1586 (O. Marucchi, *Il Museo Egizio Vaticano*, Rome 1899, p. 136).

57 *Cf.* S. Schéle, *Cornelis Bos*, Stockholm 1965, p. 145. F. Hartt, *Giulio Romano*, New-

haven 1958, Vol. I, p. 22 has only a few lines on the dado of the Stanza and attributes its basic design to Giulio too.

58 *Cf. A Descriptive Catalogue of the Latin Manuscripts in the John Rylands Library at Manchester*, Manchester 1921. The date of the Missal is uncertain. Pompeo Colonna, whose name appears, is given the title 'Divus' which makes it probable that the manuscript was written after his death in 1532 (he was created cardinal in 1517, which would create the *terminus post quem*). We are indebted to Mr Hall and Dr Taylor of the John Rylands Library for pointing this out. Mlle A. H. M. Roullet, however, has suggested an even later date, arguing that the features deriving from the Tabula Bembi were taken from a publication rather than from the original, and that the hieroglyphs were too 'good' to be early in the century. We are deeply grateful to Mlle Roullet for much help and advice.

59 A. Lhotsky, 'Apis Colonna, Fabeln und Theorien über die Abkunft der Habsburger' in *Mitteilungen des Österreichischen Instituts für Geschichtsforschung*, LV, 1942, p. 187, quoting the Cron. Austr. (printed in Pez, *SS rer. Austr.*, 2, p. 841): 'Erant duo germani fratres cuisdem prepotentis Romani filii genere de Columpne Apis nomine', etc. We are indebted to Professor O. Kurz for drawing our attention to the Colonna Missal and to the above reference. *Cf.* also F. Mugnus, *Historia della Augustissima Famiglia Colonna*, Venice 1658, p. 29.

60 A type created by Sansovino at Sta Maria del Popolo about 1500 and imported into France by the Chabot Monument now in the Louvre.

61 Our attention was first drawn to its existence by Sir John Summerson.

62 *Cf.* also Schéle, *op. cit.*, p. 145.

63 See Vasari, ed. Milanesi, Vol. 4, p. 154.

64 Schéle, *op. cit.* has drawn attention to the very close relationship between an engraving of an Egyptian caryatid by Bos (pl. 27, no. 71) and the caryatids at Fontainebleau: both are female, both are terms—unlike the caryatids in the Stanze and their Egyptian prototypes from Tivoli. Bos's engraving appears to be undated, but he was in Paris probably prior to 1540, possibly even before 1537 (Schéle, p. 24). While there is no reason why Bos should transform the Egyptian male prototype into a woman (and there is no evidence as to his source), there *is* some justification for the sculptor at Fontainebleau to do so, assuming our contention (see below) that the Egyptian motif can be linked with Diane de Poitiers, to be correct.

65 There is an engraving by Ducerceau in the Metropolitan Museum which shows the same caryatid as Bos and is of much higher quality. In spite of that Schéle is of the opinion that Ducerceau copied Bos. Ducerceau probably returned from Italy about 1545. So he either copied the Fontainebleau doorway or the doorway must date from after *c.* 1545, or else all three—the doorway, Ducerceau's engraving, and Bos—must go back to an unknown prototype.

66 The Ruscelli caryatids almost certainly derive from an engraving by Cornelis Bos (Schéle, *op. cit.*, pl. 37 no. 123), dated 1546.

67 F. A. Yates: *The French Academies of the sixteenth century*, London 1947, p. 135.

68 J. d'Orliac: *The Moon Mistress*, London 1931, p. 312.

69 See J. B. Craven: *Count Michael Maier*, Kirkwall 1910. Mr C. H. Josten, of the Oxford Museum of the History of Science, drew our attention to the *Arcana*.

70 p. 127.

71 pp. 155, 401.

72 See illustration in J. von Schlosser: *Kunst-und Wunderkammern der Spätrenaissance*, Leipzig 1908, fig. 34.

73 Others came later. The obelisk now on the Pincio was found in the sixteenth century and taken to the Palazzo Barberini in 1633, that of Bernini's fountain in the Plazza Navona was erected in 1649, that by the Pantheon in 1711, and Pius VI put up three obelisks: 1787 (Quirinal), and 1789 (Trinità dei Monti and Montecitorio).

74 Letter of 10 January 1657.

75 See P. Humbert, Paris 1933, and G. Cahen-Salvador, Paris 1951, also F. W. Gravit in *The University of Michigan Contributions in Modern Philology*, No. 14, 1950, and *Bull. de la Société d'Archéol. Copte*, IV, 1938.

76 G. Camdeni . . . *Epistolae*, ed. T. Smith, London 1691, p. 212.

77 *Ibid.*, p. 224, Rubens's answer is printed in M. Rooses: *Correspondence de Rubens*, Vol. II, 1898, No. CLXII.

78 R. Lebegue: *Les Correspondants de Peiresc dans les anciens Pays Bas*, Brussels 1943, p. 49.

79 See R. Enking: *Der Apisaltar J. M. Dinglingers*, Glückstadt, Hamburg and New York 1939, p. 24, etc.

80 See the illustrations in V. Mascardi's *Festa fatta in Roma alli 25 di Febraio, MDCXXXIV*, Rome 1635, one of which is marked 'A.S. inventor' (*see* also Preface).

81 *See Lettres de Poussin*, ed. P. du Colombier, Paris 1929, p. 299. In his letter (25 November 1658) Poussin explains the Egyptian motif by referring to 'novelty and variety', but also by stressing that it would make it evident that the Virgin is in Egypt (see e.g. E. G. Holt, *A Documentary History of Art*, Vol. II, p. 156).

82 *See* A. Blunt: *The Drawings of G. B. Castiglione and Stefano della Bella in the Collection of H.M. the Queen at Windsor Castle*, London 1954, p. 30, catalogue No. 124. Mr Wilfrid Blunt has pointed out that the sphinx actually differs from both Sandys's and Valle's descriptions. The lion's body is however mentioned by Pliny.

83 A. Favaro in *Mem. del R. Ist. Veneto di Scienze, Lettere ed Arti*, XXV, 1896, p. 76. Here Burattini in a letter to Hevelius, the astronomer, calls Stefano his 'singularis amicus'.

84 Burattini also supplied Kircher with information. *See* Kircher's *Oedipus*, mentioned below, Vol. II, pt. 2, pp. 303, etc., and Vol. III, pp. 339–41.

85 *See* MS. entry in the British Museum copy of Kircher's *Oedipus*, 1654 (BM. 87, I, 7)

supposed to come from G. Brice's *Description de Paris.*

86 Letter of the Duchess of Portland, 1742, quoted in G. R. de Beer: *Sir Hans Sloane,* Oxford 1953, p. 117.

87 We say the chief books; there were of course many more. Blondel for instance in his *Cours* from which we have quoted before and which was the principal corpus of architectural theory in France in the later eighteenth century names as his sources for Egypt P. W. Dorigny's *L'Egypte ancienne* of 1762 and the measurements of the pyramids taken in 1693 by Jean-Matthieu de Chaselles.

88 English translation by D. Humphries, 1721–1725.

89 Book V, pl. 2 and 3. The most recent references are the Catalogue (by Hans Aurenhammer) of the Fischer von Erlach exhibition held in 1956–7 at Graz, Vienna and Salzburg, pp. 210 and 214, G. Kunoth: *Die Historische Architektur Fischers von Erlach,* Düsseldorf 1956, and H. Sedlmayr: *Johann Bernhard Fischer von Erlach,* Munich 1956.

90 *See* S. Piggott, Oxford 1950, pp. 144 and 154. Stukeley's Egyptian interest is referred to in note 13.

91 L. Whistler: *The Imagination of Vanburgh,* London 1954, p. 183.

92 *See* S. Rocheblave, 1889. The quotations below come from the *Recueil,* Vol. III, Avant-propos and Vol. V, p. 3.

93 On this *see* the preceeding essay.

94 *Cours,* Vol. IV, p. 245.

95 F. Viglione, in *Studi di Letteratura Italiana,* XIII, 1919, p. 67.

96 Count F. Algarotti: *Opere,* Venice 1791–4, Vol. X, pt. II, p. 244.

97 It might be worth investigating whether Egyptian theatrical sets may not have appeared in the mid-eighteenth century. P. Zucker: *Die Theaterdekoration des Klassizismus,* Berlin 1925; C. Ricci: *La Scenografia Italiana,* Milan 1930; G. Freedley: *Theatrical Design from the Baroque through Neo-Classicism,* 3 vols., New York 1940, and J. Scholz: *Baroque and Romantic Stage Design,* New York 1950, are silent.

98 E. Kaufmann, in *Transactions of the American Philosophical Society,* New Ser., Vol. 42, 1952; H. Rosenau, London 1953.

99 *De l'architecture égyptienne* . . . 1803, pp. 208, 219, also p. 83.

100 The pyramid cannot here be followed through the next few decades, when it was a hallmark of progressiveness, i.e. of faith in elementary geometry in architecture and in the primeval. After all, the Cestius Pyramid, as has already been said, was there for all to see. Hence e.g. Jardin's Sepulchral Chapel of 1748 (illustrated in John Harris's important

paper on Legeay, *Essays in the History of Architecture presented to Rudolf Wittkower,* London 1967, fig. 30) or the pyramid of the *Folie de Chartres,* i.e. the Parc Monceau, of 1773–8 (illustrated in O. Sirén: *China and the Gardens of Europe,* New York 1950, p. 125) or John Carter's Pyramidical Dairy of 1774–8 already mentioned. Further examples are Carl August Ehrensvärd's proposed monument to Gustavus II Adolphus for the square named after him in Stockholm (1782: see S. . A. Nilsson in *Konsthistorisk Tidskrift,* XXXIII, 1964, and more recently R. Rosenblum: *Transformations in late eighteenth century Art,* Princeton 1967), Wyatt's mausoleum in the grounds of Cobham in Kent, of 1783, with a pyramid on the top, Gilly's design of 1791 with four attached Doric porticos (A. Oncken: *Friedrich Gilly,* Berlin 1935, pl. 13), Bonomi's mausoleum in the grounds of Blickling in Norfolk, 45 by 45 feet and erected in 1793, Peter Josef Krahe's suggested monument to General Marceau, a pyramid surrounded in the Boullée way by poplars (1799, see H. Vogel 'Aegyptisierende Baukunst des Klassizismus', in *Zeitschrift für bildende Kunst,* LXII, 1928, p. 161), Selva's suggested monument to Napoleon (1813; see Elena Bessi: *Selva,* Padua 1936) and Weinbrenner's actually erected monument in the Market Place at Karlsruhe. This is as late as 1823–5, but Weinbrenner belonged to the group directly inspired by Gilly.

101 *See* D. Knoop and G. P. Jones: *The Mediaeval Mason,* Manchester 1933, and the many papers published by Professors Knoop and Jones, especially in the *Ars Quatuor Coronatorum.* The manuscripts referred to are Regius and Cooke, of the late fourteenth and early fifteenth centuries.

102 *See* A. E. Waite: *A New Encyclopaedia of Freemasonry,* 1921. Waite and other masonic writers are positive on this point. There are, however, occasional minor indications of a connection between freemasonry and the mysteries of Egypt in the mid-eighteenth century. An example is the mock procession held in London by the Scald Miserable Masons in 1742 to annoy the masons who at that time were holding real processions. In this mock procession there appeared 'the Sun Hieroglyphical to rule the Day, the Moon emblematical to rule the Night', *See* J. Nichols and G. Steevens: *The Genuine Works of William Hogarth,* 1810, Vol. II, p. 161.

103 H. d'Almeras, *Cagliostro,* Paris 1904.

104 An excerpt of this was put into his *Symbolische Weisheit der Aegypter,* Berlin 1793, by Karl Philipp Moritz, the author who died at the age of thirty-seven in 1795, whose psychological novel *Anton Reiser* Goethe admired so much, and who had in 1782

travelled in England. His entertaining report of the journey is familiar in English translations.

105 On the history of freemasonry in Germany and Austria, *cf.* F. Kneisner: *Geschichte der deutschen Freimaurerei,* Berlin 1912, also still J. G. Friedel: *Geschichte der Freimaurerei,* Leipzig 1861.

106 Ed. Suphan, Vol. VI, p. 416 *ff.*

107 Herder, *Älteste Urkundes des Menschengeschlechts* (1774): 'Nach der Sage waren auch die ersten Aegyptertempel, wis die heiligen Höhen und Haine aller Nationen, ohne Götterbilder und Statuen: Es heisst man verehrte Steine . . . "Sie sollten Statuen vorstellen, die Erde vorstellen"—und ich sage, sie sollen nichts vorstellen, als was sie waren, Steine, Denkmale, die ersten Denkmale der Welt. Daher verbanden sie so gern allwegen das Viereckte und Runde—und es ward die bekannte Hermesfigur: Stein, worauf eine Kugel lag, das ist, nach dem Auge der Griechen, und der Deutung der Agypter Stein, mit einem Menschenkopf, daraus dann das ganze System des ersten Kunstschrittes entstanden, was noch in allen Kunstgeschichten—falsch ist; denn was hat dieser erste rohe viereckte, kugelgedeckte Stein mit einer Menschlichen Statue als Kunst gemein? In der Figur der Steine suchten sie ferner das Viereck, und das Rund mit der Spitze, dem Eins zu verbinden. . . . Als man nun in freie Luft kam, und sich die Kunst zufügte; zum Gebäude, zu ewigem Gebäude, was konnte aus Stein und Figur anders werden, als Pyramide und Obelisk? Viereck, Runde und Spitze auf die simpelste, ewigste Art verbunden, was konnt anders werden?'

108 Hautecoeur, Vol. V, p. 287.

109 *See* M. L. Biver: *Le Paris de Napoléon,* Paris 1963, p. 75 and fig. 12.

110 H. M. Colvin: *Biogr. Dict.,* 1954, 139.

111 *See* David Watkin, *op. cit.*

112 *Country Life,* LVII, 1925, p. 130.

113 Still considerably later is the Masonic Lodge at Boston in Lincolnshire: 1860–3.

114 D. Irwin: *English Neo-Classical Art,* London 1966, 142.

115 Text p. 174, pl. 135. Professor Carrott built on the foundations laid in a paper in *The Magazine of Art* (XXXIII, 1940) by Professor Frank J. Roos Jr. and of course on Talbot Hamlin's *Greek Revival Architecture in America,* New York 1944.

116 See R. Hale Newton: *Town and Davis,* New York 1942, p. 176.

117 See H. Vogel (Note 100 above).

118 *Italian Architecture, 1750–1914,* New Haven 1966.

119 A. Venditti: *Architettura neoclassica a Napoli,* 1961, p. 264.

List of Illustrations

Sources of photographs are given in italics

Index

Numbers in italic indicate pages on which illustrations appear